Johnny

Johnny

The authorised biography of Johnny Mathis

TONY JASPER

W.H. ALLEN · LONDON
A Howard & Wyndham Company
1983

Copyright © 1983 by Tony Jasper

Typeset by Phoenix Photosetting, Chatham
Printed and bound in Great Britain by
Mackays of Chatham Ltd, Kent
for the Publishers, W.H. Allen & Co. Ltd,
44 Hill Street, London W1X 8LB

ISBN 0 491 03380 X

To

Ernest Marvin
John and Christine Blakey

Extra-special thanks to Dave Barnett, Derek Block, Keith Skues, Audrey Barber, Maria Niemela, Ray Haughn, Ralph Mathis, Jo Baker, Bob Kilby, Linda Richardson and many thanks to all the people who talked about Johnny with me.

And John himself.

Contents

Overture

Lennie Reynolds of the Black Abbots toured with Johnny. He remembers well one incident.

'I'd always smoked. Johnny didn't like the habit. We were on the golf course in South Africa. It was so hot the cigarette smoke lingered. He asked me why I smoked. I didn't have a reasonable answer so he took the cigarette from my lips! Then he asked me if I had any others and told me to turn out my pockets. He then asked me if I had anymore. I said, "My two hundred duty frees." He wanted them as well and got rid of them. Some time later he was in England and playing at the Palladium. I went to see him in his dressing room. When I went into the room he was arranging some roses which someone had sent. He threw the flowers into the air and came across and hugged me, and said, "You haven't touched cigarettes since?" I said, "No," and he said with a smile and pat of the hand, "OK!"'

Caroline Bates, then Wilkes, worked for CBS in the company's promotion department in London. She thought Johnny should be at the top of Britain's record charts. She became known around radio stations as 'here's Johnny Mathis again'. Her efforts were rewarded in 1976 as 'When A Child Is Born' topped the British singles chart.

'He's a fantastic guy. He's not part of nostalgia for he's so contemporary. As a person he is as down to earth as the next. We used to go out eating – Johnny, me, the record company people and others. He was dieting fanatically! You would find he would sample everyone else's food!'

In Manchester, during December 1982, Johnny's Northern fans with friends from elsewhere gathered at a special Christmas meal to discuss, hear and see (on film) their star. They were part of the British Mathis Connection, Johnny's fan club. They generated amazing enthusiasm and greeted with pleasure words from this writer that he was working on the first ever book on Johnny Mathis.

The fans, Caroline Bates, Lennie Reynolds are part of the Mathis story – the life adventure of a man who decided he would be a star and who became one even though the odds were against him.

Everyone loves Johnny but this story is not sycophantic. It tells, I trust, why he is regarded with such affection and how he has earned this admiration. His times have been permeated with much joy but there has been the sour and disjointed. But I've enjoyed being involved with the guy who with Nat King Cole has the dubious honour of being credited on the first two records I ever owned!

Tony Jasper

1

First Things

Johnny Mathis, the kid, had only vague dreams of greatness. He dreamed of wonderful things happening to other people, but not to himself!

He floated through his younger childhood years. He was busy, always busy, which made him an angel in the eyes of his mother.

He remembers a change in his outlook on life when he was about nine or ten years old. It was then that music gripped him, and it has kept hold of him ever since. The Mathis house resounded with music and some of the great names of jazz would visit.

'I fantasised about singing in the same manner, at the same venues. It was always the supper clubs, the small intimate places of which I heard speak. I thought one day I'm going to study music. I never felt for anything else – just music.'

Johnny was the fourth child of seven born to hardworking Methodist parents, Clement and Mildred Mathis. The family wasn't poor but there was little money to spare. His parents were domestic workers and often worked day and night. Both are now dead. Mildred died of cancer on December 30th, 1963 while Clement, who eventually ran the Mathis ranch twenty miles north of Santa Barbara, died in March, 1974.

Johnny was close to his parents. He loved them and the world closed in on him after each of their deaths. His successful career meant that he did not see enough of them.

11

He's always regretted it but life doesn't allow any of us, not even a superstar like Johnny Mathis, to have it both ways. But then the young Johnny had another choice to make, beyond that of whether he should leave home and take up residence with the Nogas, who had discovered him and became his managers. He was a high-jumper of some ability, indeed of Olympic standard. One morning he had to face a straight choice: athletics or singing. He chose singing and for the Nogas there was the battle to get Johnny jumping show-business hurdles.

Johnny was born on September 30, 1935. His family lived in a basement flat in the centre of San Francisco. There were five rooms, and the Mathis family of nine plus four relatives crowded themselves into the limited space. By the time Johnny was twelve the family had moved to a three-storey house in the Richmond area of the city, and, compared with their previous home, it was paradise. They were not living in poverty, they were just poor. There was money for basics but not luxuries, except at Christmas. Johnny's brother Ralph sums up their existence: 'Let's say we had a little.' It meant everyone grafted. And they were black Americans, which made things harder.

'My father had been a vaudeville singer and pianist back in the twenties. But when things became tough in that field and he had a wife and kids to look after, he had to look for work elsewhere. Mostly he did decorating or domestic jobs but he would turn his hand to anything.' Clement found work in Golden Gate City. Mum was mum, and Johnny often thought of her and film actress Irene Dunn in the same context!

'I've never met her. But every movie role Irene Dunn ever played is just the way my mother was. She was the nicest lady you ever wanted to meet. She worked hard and always looked wonderful. She looked just like a lady. And that was my mother. It's true.'

Johnny grew up singing at home, in school choirs, in church, and his singing ability was noted. The Mathis household was Methodist. Johnny remembers the Methodists of San Francisco as somewhat prim and proper. He attended their church but he also went to the Baptists'.

'They went on all day, so you could get along there later. I had a period of Christian experiences and I loved the singing and excitement. Later, when I was older, and by then a performer on stage, I had a huge thrill when I followed Mahalia Jackson into a studio. I heard all those gospel singers when I was a kid, like Clara Ward, Rosetta Tharpe, Marion Williams, Alex Bradford and others.'

But it was Johnny's singing which attracted the early interest of friends and some of the famous who called. His dad knew trumpet ace Dizzy Gillespie and singer Billy Eckstine and they too added their praise. The jazz legends were fascinated by this choirboy who had a jazzy feel to his voice and no one put down the thirteen-year-old because of his age; no one told him to wait around until he was into long trousers. Johnny, of course, had heard his father sing and once said Clement could have been another Nat King Cole if he hadn't had the responsibility and the task of bringing up a family. But Johnny did hear some of the most famous artists: Ella Fitzgerald, Nat King Cole and Lena Horne were three vocal influences.

'Ella has a quality that is mournful, a tear, on up tones or ballads, that is appealing. She has a fantastic control of her voice, too. Nat is the big man to me. He's got so much warmth. He's never farther away from you than your heart is. And Lena is the greatest entertainer I've ever seen, the greatest interpreter.'

Miles Davis, John Lewis and Stan Getz are other names Johnny recalls as artists who gave him infinite pleasure.

Johnny was a thirteen-year-old with promise, a boy who was a little too young to realise he might be the 'one in a million'. They – the family – were united in one thing: that young Johnny should have singing lessons. There was a certain degree of optimism, not to mention courage in sticking to this view, for, at thirteen, Johnny's voice hadn't yet broken. There was also the task of finding a teacher and even more awkward the question of how they could finance the project.

The name of a local voice coach, Connie Cox, came to mind, especially because she was known for her kindness and generosity to the less well-off. She genuinely loved talent, and lack of cash was no barrier if she believed in someone and had the necessary commitment from the prospective pupil. It was Clement who came up with her name and it was he who hauled Johnny over to her house. The meeting of the Mathis' and Connie made the lady aware of two things – the first was the unlikelihood of any monetary payment coming her way and the second, and ultimately more important realisation, was that this rather scrawny kid had a voice in a million.

'She taught me from there and then. She just got pleasure from being aware she could really help me,' Johnny says.

The journey there and back took anything up to two hours and involved both train and bus. John did his school homework on the way and occasionally thought he could have been playing basketball or practising track and field sports. Somehow he found time for the latter, though as a young teenager it wasn't too easy persuading his mates he actually enjoyed singing!

In the seven years that Connie Cox was his teacher, she never took a cent from him. But Johnny had his pride, and no one wants total charity. He repaid Connie by busying himself on each visit with odd jobs, and particularly with the garden.

For Johnny's parents the aim of these voice-training lessons was to give him the basic skills which might lead him into some kind of singing career. Certainly he worked hard.

'I sat quietly in a corner and listened. I observed every sound, every innuendo . . . I soaked in all the advice she gave to her other charges. Then, when her paying pupils had gone, she patiently spent time with me, gently imparting to me her wisdom and experience. I don't know how to say it, except that Connie was and is a real angel.'

Connie was in her late twenties, perhaps early thirties. Johnny the young teenager never really noticed. He was conscious merely of her enthusiasm. She impressed on him the importance of basics in singing.

'She got me to do tones properly and she said if I could then I would have no problems. I studied in an operatic manner, arias. I learnt tones loudly, softly, in-between.'

She was amazed at Johnny's ability, when so young, to sustain notes. And she taught him more than he had hitherto known of breathing techniques. The training proved invaluable and one of the most distinctive marks of Johnny as a vocalist became his ability to hold a note so long that it occasioned gasps from the audience, though Johnny says he was aware such a vocal mannerism could lose its freshness and become a cliché. It was a musical education. A great thing too, for Johnny, was Connie's musical catholicity. She loved the classics but she also enjoyed jazz and indeed to supplement her income she would take off at night and play the hammond organ in nightclubs.

Meantime Clement encouraged the rather shy teenager and cajoled him into singing at any public event he could find which took 'guest' artists, from churches, to schools and community musical programmes. He even took a piano to pieces and had it carried part by part into the Mathis' house because it wouldn't go through the doors or windows.

There was a father who was fully aware that his kid was something special.

Clement had an absolute determination to make Johnny aware of his talent and of his future career possibilities. Although he worked a long, hard day himself, the family says his energy seemed to be boundless. He was always 'up and about' and he always made time, somehow. He was aware that it wasn't all that easy for Johnny – while other kids played games, Johnny was practising or performing, and there were kids who ribbed Johnny and called him names because he seemed to be different.

Ralph Mathis says there were good and bad times, and moments when Johnny's own determination had to be propped up by his father. Ralph recalls how Johnny would get up and say, 'I've got vocal lessons. I must go,' and he would set off with purpose in his stride.

'Really, the whole family had music,' Ralph says. 'There was a lot of music around and we were all encouraged to sing and we did. Dad had touches of Nat Cole and he was a singer John really admired. I think Dad could have gotten places himself. I really think he could have been tremendous. He knew what good music was. Johnny, though, was his project. In a way I think he wanted Johnny to achieve what he could have if it wasn't for family commitments. Whenever we had friends he would get Johnny to sing for them, and John would be embarrassed. Dad would be there at the piano and Johnny would sing. He would say afterwards, ''Dad, why do you make me sing?'' Dad would say, ''It's your voice.''

'I reckon Dad has this insight – in our family there was a wealth of musical talent and my father was shrewd enough to look through all his cards and find an ace. That was Johnny. And all Dad's energies went on to Johnny. He was never too tired to further Johnny's hoped-for future. He spent money he didn't have to get John's clothes, which were necessary for his public performances.'

And Johnny, looking back, has always recognised this relentless belief which his father had in him; it was a love which would not let him go. It should be placed in the context of general possibilities for black people at this time. For many blacks there were few avenues into the 'better life', and music was one way. When someone was seen with a talent which might lead to a rosy future for themselves and for their family, then it was the case of all guns firing to get them there.

There was general family support for John. Ralph says it took them over. John was fighting not just for himself but for all of them.

'You have a little and then all of a sudden there seems to come a light and things start happening,' Ralph says. In this case it was Johnny who brought the 'extra' into a hard existence, who gave everyone the thought of something larger, who made them dream dreams.

Johnny praises his mother, as much as anyone. She was all for his singing, even if she lacked the expertise to offer real guidance.

'While Dad was out and taking me around Mum had to take care of the family, look after the clothing, cook, do the household chores. She was as important as my father; she was very supportive.'

There was the time when the family were living in Port Street, San Francisco. Johnny was off to an amateur show, and the family spent the evening huddled around a rather battered radio listening to a programme. Later in the evening they heard the sound of Johnny running into the house, and shouting out to his brothers and sisters, 'Help me'. He said he had a television set. They laughed. He persisted. Eventually they gave him some of their attention, took him seriously and to their delight realised he was not joking. He had won a television set at an amateur singing contest. It was a sign to everyone that there might really be a brighter future. In those days only the wealthy had television.

'Our family,' says Ralph, 'became pulled together from a bunch of people who existed into people who began to experience things. There were continual happenings. It was very exciting. We thought things we would not otherwise have thought. We had a brother who could be going places, though I should say we weren't thinking Johnny would be some world star. That was a dream, I mean being a big singer. We thought John would become a teacher. Well, we did dream, but then we thought we were fooling ourselves, our brother a celebrity!'

Johnny attended the George Washington High School. He became the first black student president in a school which had a third white, a third black, and a third Oriental children.

Johnny says: 'I was super-responsible and took on many extra activities like student government and athletics. It wasn't easy, either.

'Some of my brothers and sisters weren't as industrious as I, so I usually ended up doing a lot of the housework and studying under conditions like that. I think this early training helped me later in my career.'

He sang with the choir. Each Christmas they sang at major department stores and local people recall how the Christmas of 1952 saw Johnny's solo lead stop shoppers in their tracks. He became known as the 'kid who sings'.

Johnny's voice, now it was broken, still let him hit the very high notes. Connie's tuition gave him range, an ability to hold and phrase, and also the all-important vocal projection. The respect between pupil and teacher was mutual, for Connie felt she was involved with a young kid with a future, and Johnny became her protégé. And of course, during their time together, Johnny had grown from a gawky kid reaching for his teens into a young man.

But for all Connie's promptings, his father's constant pushing and general acclaim from friends and school, Johnny had another heart-tugging demand on his time and it came from the world of athletics. He excelled at George Washington and later at the San Francisco State College. At the former he was a hurdles champion and his good reach made him a very good basketball player. At SFSC he broke high-jump records. During 1954-5 he was within reach of the World high-jump record as he cleared the bar at 6'5½", back-aches or no back-aches! He spent his spare time – when important demands were not thrust his way – practising and beginning to feel he might become a physical education teacher, maybe a coach. Singing, as a career, was not his serious consideration, though he was aware he had a good deal of talent.

Oddly enough, it was a fellow athlete, a shot putter by the name of Johnny Bologna, who set him on the road toward a singing career. Bologna had a friend who ran a small club, and realising Johnny was in need of a part-time job while he was training during the summer of 1955, he brought Johnny to the notice of the owner. Johnny was offered a weekend singing spot for ten dollars a night. His Saturday-Sunday jaunt at the tavern led him to a further summer job at Anne Dee's 440 Club across the road. His singing ability attracted wide attention, even, as some would, say 'a commotion'.

A baritone saxophonist Virgil Gonzales, whose sextet was working at the Black Hawk at the time, was the next important influence that lead Johnny to a singing career. He persuaded Johnny, with some friends, to turn up at an informal jam session one Sunday afternoon in the late summer of 1955. Constant pushing and cajoling from his friends finally put Johnny on stage and in the audience was the Black Hawk's co-owner, Helen Noga. She couldn't believe what she heard; it was an unforgettable moment for her. He was singing the evergreen 'Tenderly', and he kept hitting the high notes time and time again. Helen wondered whether he would hit a high 'C' and decided not. But he did.

The lady had been enthusiastic before over young singers, but this one was different, and even Columbia Records' executive George Avakian was able to pick up the difference in her voice as she excitedly told him over the telephone: 'I've found a star.' And she had.

Avakian, contrary to the popular story that he rushed down to hear Johnny immediately, took his time.

He says: 'A recording executive does not need to be on vacation to try to avoid auditioning young singers recommended by friends. There is a permanent open season on members of our industry for this purpose, so a conditioned reflex is built up anyway, but it is a little firmer where holidays are involved.

'This explains why it was not until the ninth day of an attempted vacation in San Francisco in the late summer of 1955 that I gave in to the blandishments of my good friend Helen Noga, co-owner of the Black Hawk night club, and agreed to go listen to a nineteen-year-old local boy. "George," she said, "he's the best young singer you ever heard in your life." She was right.'

Meantime Helen Noga said that Johnny had so much potential she wanted to manage him herself – he was that promising. Johnny brought his family down to see her and discuss things a little. And at the back of his mind was his other interest in life, athletics, and that was a world in which success, if it came, would be immediate. The

Olympic selectors were getting interested in this lanky, slim high-jumper.

Helen Noga had a winning line which was quite simple: 'If I get Johnny a record contract, is it a deal?' The family said yes.

Later Johnny was to describe her as the greatest business woman he'd ever met. She was already on the way to becoming the most important person in his life after his mother and father.

Avakian came to see Johnny and was immediately impressed. 'Before Johnny finished his second song, I knew I was going to sign him. He had so much that I was not surprised to learn he was doubling weekends in an opera group production of Leonard Bernstein's "Trouble in Tahiti". Obviously he had more training than most pop singers; his extraordinary breath control and sweeping range indicated that. He could do as many different things as four very different singers might, and do them well. All he needed was experience and seasoning.'

Avakian cabled CBS: 'Have found phenomenal nineteen-year-old boy who could go all the way. Send contracts.' Avakian's gesture made history. His telegram line has adorned the pages of countless magazines and journals and has been recalled by endless interviewers. But the record executive was not in a hurry to push Johnny. It was another six months before he took action, and by this time Johnny had begun to wonder what was happening. He was now the star act at a new Bay area club, The Fallen Angel. At least, in terms of the places he was singing in, he was on the up, though he fondly recalls the times when he, with Connie accompanying, played breakfast clubs in the Oakland-Alameda area.

'People used to go out and get drunk and stay until eight or nine in the morning, then they'd have some breakfast and start all over again. We'd sing and joke and pass the hat. We played the suburban clubs because that's where the heavy drinkers were. San Franciscans were good drinkers, but got drunk too early.'

Eventually Avakian made his move. After wisely letting

Johnny develop his act and his self-confidence, Avakian journeyed to San Francisco from the East Coast early in January 1956 to see jazz legend Louis Armstrong and to hear more of Johnny. At this time Erroll Garner, the famed jazz pianist, was opening a season at the Black Hawk and the club was filled with important local people and the press. Helen Noga, with the opportunism and flair which was to make Johnny a star, came into the club and asked everyone to come with her to the Hungry I where Johnny had a spot. It amused the gathering and many of them went with her. Later in the evening Helen worked another magical trick – she asked Erroll if Johnny could sing a couple of songs after his first set finished, and her request was granted.

Avakian observed the growth of Johnny's repertoire and its diversity and noticed the new poise and control.

'Johnny had learned what to do with his hands, how to make and maintain close contact with his audience, and to programme his songs most effectively. Best of all, he had grown so much in quality that I had no doubt that the time had come to record.'

Avakian was determined these recordings should take place in New York, partly because he knew the music people well in that city.

'I visualised a series of intimate small-band sessions with a variety of arrangers, each given *carte blanche* as to instrumentation and treatment within the overall interpretation of each song, as taped as a guide by Johnny in San Francisco. Johnny's singing is thoroughly jazz-orientated, so naturally arrangers were chosen who had a thorough command of the jazz idiom, as well as the ability to write imaginatively for a pop vocalist.'

It was to Avakian's credit and to that of Helen Noga that they did not push Johnny into the easiest of available fields, making him an artist who would pick up the immediate trend of the time and become yet another hopeful trying to break through into an overcrowded field. Rock 'n' roll and the more commercial R&B reigned, and Johnny could easily have either covered existing hits or recorded similar material.

However, there was still the matter of Johnny's athletics.

The crunch came one day in March, 1955. Johnny received an invitation to go for trials which could make him one of the USA's team for the 1956 Olympics, to be held in Melbourne that summer. It was the same week he was due to record in New York! While he stayed on the West Coast he could put off any final decision on the matter of athletics versus singing. He could train during the day and sing at night. But now the time for hesitation was ended. There was no way he could do two things. He reasoned he could train somewhere in the New York area, but it was a new city to him and it was a very different environment from San Francisco. Again, he realised that recording schedules do not fit neatly into a regular time slot like a club booking.

'It was the toughest decision I'd ever had to make,' he says, from the vantage point of time. But even then he was fully aware of the serious and critical nature of his response. What he couldn't know was whether he would make the US Olympic team. He was uncertain whether he could postpone the recording session until the fall of 1956. There were pressures on him from all angles. In the end the safe career course won.

The family supported his decision. The athletics was very much a hit or miss and as Ralph says, 'He might have won a medal, maybe not, and if he did someone a little later would have jumped higher and he would be left with memories but not an on-going thing.' But the family's response came after hours and hours of discussion.

Brother Ralph says: 'It was a trying time, for it wasn't just the question of whether Johnny should have a manager. It also revolved on his leaving home, and of course going to live with the Nogas. Our parents were very conservative in some ways. I mean, they loved us and they wanted things for us, and especially John, but it's one thing to say and think this and another when the actual situation comes when one of your boys is going to leave. Dad was very religious and he prayed about it a lot and he talked, we all talked. Finally I think it was Mum who said, "go ahead Johnny." Johnny was elated. To him, the thought of New York was something else! It was the big city on the East Coast, thousands of miles away. You know, when he went off I didn't see him for five years. Five years! When he came back he was a star and the city here made it a Johnny Mathis Day! It was a bunch of crazies around that day – we all went wild. But of course having said this, you've got to remember there was the athletics decision which opened up the whole question again.'

As Johnny says, 'I sent the Olympic committee my regrets and headed for New York. I was unknown and I figured this record session gave me the chance I might not get again. It could lead to a life-long career, whereas even if I made the Olympics and did well, it would mean at most just a few years of fame.

'My parents agreed with me, but I wished a thousand times it was a decision I hadn't had to make.'

He still looks back and wonders! It's tough the way it so often happens in life that crisis points converge on each other, but at least Johnny knows that his singing career has paid off handsomely and in terms of his ultimate success the choice he made has proved a good one.

George Avakian and Helen Noga breathed a sigh of relief at Johnny's decision. And off to New York, in March 1956, he went.

When Johnny reached New York he found some aspects of the city were not as attractive as he had imagined.

San Francisco in the late 1950s was a small town by comparison. He was awed by the sights, mesmerised by the endless musical variety the city offered. Money was scarce, accommodation expensive. He stayed for a time at the Wellington Hotel and he was helped by the management who, on seeing his lack of funds, offered him what was virtually a small alcove for a very moderate sum. It had been occupied by maids and was very basic, but it had a bed and Johnny paid half the normal room rate.

Once he found his way around the city he used every ploy he knew to get into theatres and clubs.

'I think New York was, still is, the only place in the world where you could hear so many stars within walking distance. It varied from Dizzy Gillespie to Beverly Sills. If you like jazz, opera and ballet, if you planned things right, kept a careful watch on theatre or performing times, you could do one after the other. I made friends who got me in back-doors.'

As for Johnny's main purpose at being in New York, that of recording, it was another case of finding things rather different than he expected. CBS seemed a huge company, impersonal to the ultimate degree. People fell into a particular slot and that was that. 'It's like my first album, which some people saw as a jazz release. It took the pop people a year to realise I was around.'

Johnny's only recording experience had been in making some demonstration tapes, including a few with Connie Cox. He was used to working with good musicians though the sight of people like John Lewis of the Modern Jazz Quartet in his session band made him feel distinctly nervous.

'I was determined to make a good record. George and I were of the same mind. He wanted songs that would show off my voice and it would all happen in the manner of jazz musicians, very improvisational. And you have to remember these were times before all the sophisticated recording equipment arrived and you could play at various takes and select the one where you hit the note the way you wanted.'

The session players were kind, but showed no favours and they soon respected the young kid from San Francisco. Johnny himself lapped up the comradeship which grew between them all, and was later, for this reason, to believe that modern studio techniques detracted from that ensemble feel. He certainly felt this way when he had to record with orchestras. He felt most of the people who played in them were uninterested in the actual project. It was purely a way of earning a living.

Avakian thought his signing of Johnny had been the right decision. The record executive has commented:

'Bringing Johnny to New York for his recordings worked out better than expected. No one would hire him "cold" except Ralph Watkins of Basin Street, who took him for a week and simply to accommodate Bert Block of the Joe Glaser office and myself. That Sunday night, Max Gordon of the Blue Angel auditioned Johnny at his club and promptly signed him for a series of engagements; after four weeks at the Angel, Max moved him downtown to his other club, the Village Vanguard, where the more intimate atmosphere proved even more suited to Johnny's style.'

The Vanguard was famous – it was the kind of place which hired only long-established stars. Johnny was unknown and that he should be there created an image and made his name familiar to all the New York club clientele.

CBS backed up Avakian's judgement by agreeing to something very unusual for a young, untried artist – Johnny's first release was to be a complete LP. It was titled after Johnny. Avakian had five arrangers on the LP. He said: 'All are keenly interested in contemporary serious music, and have done a certain amount of what might be called experimental writing. Under the circumstances, it is not surprising that these arrangements contain many elements seldom encountered in pop vocal accompaniments; however, even Bob Prince's shifting time signatures in the instrumental section of "Star Eyes" are within reach of the average listener. As I hoped for, each arranger's individuality comes through, so that there is a change of pace in this set which is perhaps unique in vocal albums.'

He noted the variety of songs and duly complimented Johnny on the dexterity with which he made full use of his vocal range. He felt there was an awareness of modern jazz which was especially to be seen in Johnny's improvisational flights in all tempos and moods. The LP's moderate success caused CBS to release a single, 'Wonderful Wonderful', which reached the stores in November 1956. Initial reaction from the consumer was cautious but between January and March of 1957 it snowballed into a major-selling disc. It started to roll first in Boston and San Francisco, and was then picked up across the nation until it merited attention from *Billboard* in its national sales and radio chart reckoning. Johnny began to pick up the major media shows. There was the *Ed Sullivan Show* in June 1957, and he obtained a part in the film *Lizzie*, in which he sang two songs – although the producer had only scheduled one – until he heard Johnny sing. The songs, 'It's Not For Me To Say' and 'Warm And Tender', later became hit numbers. Almost from the start Johnny began collecting flattering reviews in major journals of the time. *Time* wrote of Johnny as early as September, 1956:

> As a singer his virtues are many, for he can warble a lyrical tune with husky tenderness and a fine sense of phrasing, light into a torchy tune with a dramatic sense of rhythm, or blend neatly with his cool jazz background, all with equal ease. In each style he has a distinctive little trick of rushing words here and there in a manner that once would have been called corny, but according to today's taste is passable.

He was described by *Variety* as a promising newcomer when they reviewed one of his appearances at the Angel in New York. *Billboard* said Avakian had discovered a unique and versatile song stylist and they thought record retailers should be willing to stock his recorded material for they were sure sales would result.

Early New York club bookings proved invaluable initially, but whereas club managements were prepared to let a newcomer of considerable promise perform, they were not so keen once he ceased being new. They headlined the greats and provided an appetiser with the unknown. Johnny had became an artist who was moving up the rating rungs, and until he became famous he had to find work elsewhere. He performed up and down the East Coast, in cities like Boston, and he began to do bookings on the college and University circuit, at the instigation of Helen Noga.

Helen had got the idea from her dealings with Dave Brubeck. Brubeck, along with Paul Desmond, had been given floor space at Helen's Black Hawk Club in San Francisco. 'His (Brubeck's) music was very cerebral, it appealed to college bands. He went out, and it gave him a considerable living. Helen thought it would be good for me. So there I was week in and week out in college halls, gymnasiums and wherever there was room. The kids came to hear me, the guy with a couple of single hits. As soon as you sang them they knew who you were.'

Johnny found no end of college promoters who suggested how he might soup up his act.

'I told them the voice was the important thing. I don't know if they knew what I meant. I said the voice is all; I said songs are important. I didn't want to be a performer; I just wanted to sing. I understand theatrics, if we were talking about the voice, not personality. In these gymnasiums I learnt a lot about perfecting vocal technique, microphone skills, I could utilise distance from the microphone skilfully. I'd get a natural sound.'

The West Coast seemed far away. So did home. When he left his parents in San Francisco Johnny told them he would be back in three days. The days became three years and eventually he bought a house on the East Coast. He also bought a house for his parents in San Francisco.

By 1960 Johnny had become a major star. The money rolled in and some press portraits gave the idea it was Johnny's main motivation. Helen Noga had built up Johnny's pay packet from £75 to £12,000 a week by the end of 1960. By then she said he was owner of three apartment buildings in New York and three publishing businesses. She commented: 'But he has no idea of what he's worth.'

Apparently he had neither car nor furniture and on the West Coast he had continued living with the Noga family which included their daughter Beverly, then a teenager. Johnny once said he had no friends but Helen and daughter.

'I've got to think of him as my own child,' Helen once said. She kept Johnny busy in the late fifties and through

1960. The LPs and singles poured and there were magazine articles of all kinds. He was hardly still for a moment.
He was wanted everywhere and the price increased
accordingly.

Picturegoer writer Godfrey Morgan zeroed in on this
when he wrote his feature for the popular American journal in June, 1959.

'"Hurry or we'll be late!" says his manager. Those five
urgent words – they rule the life of recording star
Johnny Mathis. Whatever he does, wherever he goes,
he's ruled by a rigid timetable that makes it virtually
impossible for him to have any personal life.'

There was no time for romance and when the girls did
appear it was for the purposes of promotion, for it seemed
good to those around him that he should be seen with
desirable young ladies of naturally good character. Morgan
wrote:

'His manager is always at hand to urge him on . . . on to
Miami, Chicago, Pittsburgh, Philadelphia, Syracuse,
New York, Salisbury Beach in Massachusetts – there's
just no stopping the dizzy whirl.
    The effect on the fellow is a feeling of loneliness, a
sensing that he's missing out on an awful lot of fun in
life. Even his public appearances lack lift. What about
vacations?'

Johnny's reply was this:

'Most of the spare time I do get is spent with my manager, planning next year's schedules. Now is the time
for me to think about work. Later, maybe, I can settle
down and have some fun with my money.'

Morgan had a cryptic message and the journal put it in
block capitals: HURRY JOHNNY MATHIS – OR IT MAY BE TOO
LATE.

It was good emotional stuff and to a point it made sense. The basic weakness lay in its assumption that a star's life can be regulated in the way of an ordinary person who has a regular income, fixed hours, an awareness of Monday to Friday with days off following, plus an annual holiday. But show-business doesn't work that way. When you are hot you need ultimate commitment because you must work like mad to stay there. The eventual aim is the mysterious plateau of fame where whenever you appear, fans will come. You need only to release records and they will sell, and you can please yourself when you appear in public and when you record. That existence belongs with the superstar. Johnny was big by the end of the fifties but he had to work for it – all the time. And he was not a superstar yet.

Johnny knew he was still fairly raw and had only partially distilled his abundant talent. He knew he was still both consciously and subconsciously developing his own style, and in spite of his LP and single success, he needed to mature and grow as an artist. And ballads rather than rock and roll interested him most. He had a real feeling for the former and it was an idiom which constantly threw up new and beautiful material. One song he particularly praised during this period was Sid Shaw's 'Will I Find My Love Today'. Johnny said, 'It's a beautiful tune, the words and the music have great feeling. That's the kind of thing I love to sing.'

Those who observed him said there was an intensity and an exuberance in his music and singing which quickly communicated itself to those who were around him. He was very intense and restless, with an insistent desire to jump time and become the mature performer there and then when he was just three years into his career.

'In show business, there's always the possibility that you'll drop as fast as you went up. What I wanted for myself was a level of consistency. I mean, I wanted to sing well, like Nat King Cole or Frank Sinatra. I wanted to sing everything and make it worthwhile.'

He spent many an afternoon in a small apartment in

New York's West Side, owned by Dede Emerson. He had Emerson play as many as forty or fifty songs a time. As soon as one song had been played Johnny would already be thrusting the next forward. It was as if he couldn't wait too long. He had to know the kind of material which was available – the songs which would help make him great. And in those early days he had already made the statement: 'I'm not a performer. I'm basically a singer. I just sing.' It had to be repeated many times and he still says it against the ever-present criticism that he doesn't do enough on stage.

But most of this criticism comes from people who do not always appreciate the sheer beauty of a human voice and who are more concerned with show-biz 'flash' and 'glam' and who cannot see beyond the theatricals. It comes from those who want to be entertained rather than elevated spiritually. But not all of the early audiences misunderstood his intent, nor did the reviewers. Nick Flocos in the *Pittsburgh Sunday Telegraph* for June 24, 1959 commented on Johnny's set at the Lenny Litman's Copa Club. 'Here is a non-rock entertainer who relies on a marvellous voice and lots of mystery, originality and heart.'

And even the lack of a frenzied rock 'n' roll style didn't prevent Johnny, on this occasion, from being mobbed and losing part of his tuxedo collar as fans fought police to get near him. *Variety*, in reviewing his residency at the Sands Hotel, said he performed like a veteran and singled out a number of things: 'He's relaxed, and has warm humility. He has a keen lyric consciousness so that every word he sings, no matter if he's whispering or belting, can be understood.'

Johnny found his translation from club singer into national hero within a few years somewhat of a problem. In 1959 he said: 'All of a sudden you become famous. It takes a lot of getting used to that. For one thing you have to learn how to talk with people. I've found that most people want to hear what you really think. So I've been very frank. But I also avoid knocking anybody. Many times, I'll be asked what I think of such and such a singer.

If I don't like him I plead innocent. I just don't listen to somebody I don't like, so how can I discuss him?'

It was of course energetic intelligent Helen Noga who kept Johnny together as a person during these formative years. She was everything to him, from manager to substitute mother. Her time and energy was his and really he wasn't on his own until 1964, following the sad affair which saw both locked in court action, and parting, the event almost coinciding with the death of his mother. Helen had brought Johnny into a totally new environment – the cut and thrust of show-biz and the fickleness of public adulation.

And what also kept Johnny on the rails during these early formative days of his career was his total humility. He could not see why he was a star and why people should see him in that light. And he also had a belief in luck; not that it was everything, merely useful. And by the end of the decade he had formulated some thoughts on his future. He decided against a close association with jazz. He admits he had had a strong desire to be an artist in that musical idiom but at the same time he was discouraged by the lack of real financial return.

He says he was rather pragmatic. 'I made a jazz album first, then decided to make a pop single. I decided to go with the one that clicked. The pop side clicked and I went that way.'

He was also concerned he should have more time for himself. He saw the ideal as spending twenty weeks in a year working. It seemed a vain hope, when considered against the demand which was continually building up for his services.

His enthusiasm for night club work had waned while film and television seemed more interesting. Stage acting had always attracted him, but he had no training as an actor, though film producer Hal Wallis had said he might be wanted as a personality. Musical comedy was an attraction. He even considered the future and thought that he might by 1980 be a record company adviser, no longer with any desire to be a performer. He was fascinated by what he called 'executive responsibility'.

But all depended on his stage notices and, more important, the record sales, and outside of individual promotion there was little he could do about that. It was here that another positive facet of Helen Noga's character came into play. She was a woman in a man's world and it wasn't easy. She received from Bob Moering, Columbia's veteran West Coast promotion man, quite a verbal accolade when he said she had established a great rapport with promotion men all over the country.

'She was hard and told me, "It's a man's world and if a woman is to be successful, she has to act like a man." But I found her warm underneath and concerned with all of us promotion men. She was fair and just and honest.'

And promoting a singer of ballads was not easy. It continued to be just as hard in 1959 as it had been in 1956, for the rock 'n' roll craze which came out of the mid-fifties didn't go away, but Johnny was sanguine about the whole affair and was pleasantly positive.

'I was a very young singer singing meaningful songs for the young with a taste I had learned from Nat Cole, but the kids could identify more with me than Nat. At the time I was as relative to Elvis as he was to me. When kids tired of Elvis, they wanted to hear me. Elvis and I worked as a sounding board for one another.'

And by the end of the decade there had grown an insistent demand for Johnny from across the waters – Britain. Music lovers there had heard of this new American great. They wanted to see him, hear him, and generally satisfy their curiosity. It was obviously the next major step in his life, but the demand went unheeded during 1960. For some while British music journals (and in Britain there is, of course, a weekly national music press, as well as continual national radio service) had been reporting rumours of his imminent arrival. The universal cry was one of 'what's stopping you, Johnny?'

2

The British Love Affair

JOHNNY ADMITTED IN 1959 it was getting harder for him to remain on top. He was as aware as anyone else that the career of a popular artist is often brief.

Yet not everyone shared his doubt. There were those who believed rock 'n' roll had found a level and ballads were regaining the popularity they had enjoyed in the early fifties. Such an analysis led to the conclusion that Johnny had no reason to fear: an artist of his class and calibre would always be in demand. And he was the rare artist who could sell LPs just as well as singles. The British magazine *Hit Parade* thought the really outstanding LP artists in the world of the late fifties could be counted on the fingers of one hand. Naturally they named Frank Sinatra and they included Britain's own Mantovani; America had Mitch Miller – and Johnny Mathis.

Those with most to fear from Johnny's slight pessimism were his British fans, for they had yet to welcome Johnny in Britain, in spite of the fact that Johnny had had almost three years of musical triumph in the US. Should his career fold, then they would never have seen their star perform.

They – and the general showbusiness press of the time – asked the simple question – when will Johnny come to Britain? They inquired many times and were only partially consoled by being told Johnny had expressed a wish to visit Britain at the earliest moment.

Certainly, with some Scottish blood in him, the

33

American superstar had every reason to think fondly of the 'old country' and he was aware of his fairly large following in Britain. He had seen British record charts and these by 1959 had given him three appearances, with 'Teacher Teacher', 'A Certain Smile' (which had been the most successful in reaching Number Four) and 'Winter Wonderland'. And since 1957 his LPs had been issued in the UK. The popular music journals had given oceans of coverage to his American successes.

The reasons for his non-appearance in Britain were to be expected. It was said he had a full cabaret season at major US centres. He had numerous recording commitments. There were plans for him to become an actor with the possibility of a serious venture into films. Helen Noga was quoted as saying that Hollywood movies were Johnny's next objective and that as filming took time, it didn't allow a tour-date itinerary to be formulated too far ahead and certainly not one as complicated to arrange as a trip to another country. So Johnny didn't come and he hadn't ventured across the Atlantic by the time the first year of the new decade had drawn to a close. Perhaps a visit in 1960 would have halted a sudden downward lurch in his British record sales. Johnny worried over this, but he was in the midst of a hectic US schedule.

Johnny was still magic for Stateside record buyers and club-goers, and indeed in 1960 he broke new ground by beginning a tour of a one-man show at the legendary Greek Theatre, in Los Angeles. His albums 'Faithfully' and 'Johnny's Mood' walked tall in the US charts. Johnny Noga said Johnny was working constantly. His artist thought the continual activity was a grind but was content to say: 'But when there's an audience out front who've paid good money to hear you, a fellow can't complain. Sure I like show business, but at the same time I'm bound to admit that's a hard business.'

But a visit to Britain could not be put off forever. It was finally arranged by promoter Vic Lewis. Lewis was new in the promoting game and had behind him a pretty illustrious career as a band leader with popularity on both sides of the Atlantic. He cast an eye around the British concert scene and soon concluded Mathis was the 'big' name yet to travel the seas. He soon learnt that the response from America, for one reason or another, had been in the negative to whomever tried their luck at arranging a Johnny Mathis concert tour of Britain.

Undaunted, Lewis flew from Britain to Los Angeles and proceeded toward Helen Noga's residence in Beverly Hills.

'I rang the bell. No maid answered. It was Helen Noga.

'"What do you want?" she said, and expressed she wasn't too keen on the English. I told her I would like Johnny over in England. "Why England?" was her comment. I told her he was an international star but only on record and not in person. "You've only got 500-seaters," was her comment and then, "You've only got six-piece bands." I told her I was a band leader and added a few other things. I suggested she telephoned Jerry Perenchio at MCA, this was before the company was broken up.'

Lewis told her he could get the well-respected Ted Heath Band to back Johnny and strived to impress her.

His persuasion had results. Helen Noga telephoned Jerry, who vouched for what Vic Lewis had said and reiterated that Britain did, contrary to her belief, have some large halls – places like the Royal Festival Hall and the Royal Albert Hall which could take a few thousands or more. Negotiations began. Johnny finally arrived in Britain in 1961 and was termed by the New Record Mirror '£1 A MINUTE MATHIS' for his concert take-away was £1500 a day. However, Helen Noga denied that Johnny was money mad. 'Money and Johnny Mathis get on well together. He doesn't bother about it,' she was quoted as saying.

The press were unconvinced, and they remarked how carefully she had invested his money in apartment buildings and publishing businesses. Mrs Noga responded that Johnny didn't know or care anything about them. However, she insisted he cared about the music. His musical director Allyn Ferguson stressed to the British journalists how Johnny had studied voice control and intonation and was much more than a ballad singer – the man could swing. But the money and the wealth attracted journalists the most. The facts came thick and thin. John Noga talked of their Beverly Hills home with tennis courts, swimming pool, basketball court. Johnny said he bought fifty suits a year from Ronnie Poston, a Beverly Hills tailor, and they cost from £90 to £230 each. Stage suits were cleaned and pressed after every show, a process which prolonged their life-span.

John Noga told of turning down fifty film offers which had been for around £25,000 a film. 'That might keep Johnny three months in the studios. He earns around £10,000 a week as a live performer, so it's been no deal. We want £70,000 a film – plus a cut in the profits. I think there'll be something soon on those terms.' Noga said Johnny earned £8,000 for the title song of the film *A Certain Smile*. For a day's work!

To British journalists on £500 a year it seemed a land of fantasy and perhaps the good-intentioned American entourage were oblivious that the endless recital of money and wealth acquisition was not sweet music to their listeners and would be written-up by some writers in a slightly sneering fashion. But most sensed the genuineness of the American party who after all had yet to learn the innate and often hypocritical attitude of British people toward wealth and success – that you keep quiet about it.

The great man arrived on July 9th. The weather was fair though it hardly resembled the sunny brilliance of Los Angeles. And the fans were there in force – a fact which must have delighted Johnny's British record label, Fontana, especially in view of an early disaster which made some executives rather queasy. Fontana had contacted the Johnny Mathis Fan Club and secretary Raymond Ewles and said they would run coaches from the Bayswater Road in London out to Heathrow for fans. Ewles dutifully sent out the information and asked for a fan response. It was disappointing. When the day arrived and the several coaches waited patiently a mere nine people made use of the service, two guys and seven girls.

But at the airport hundreds saw their revered star wave and once he was through customs he surprised and delighted everyone by appearing and signing numerous autographs. Johnny arrived five days before the first concert (at the New Victoria, London, on the 14th) with the express purpose of recording some television spots and particularly an hour-long show for Granada. And he wanted time of his own. Pat Pretty of the Vic Lewis office said Johnny wanted to combine his tour with a holiday in Britain.

In fact Johnny had spent some days secretly in Britain some months previously, so the country was not entirely new territory but he still felt a newcomer. He told *Hit Parade*:

> 'Stop any American man-in-the-street and ask him where he'd like to spend his next holiday, and like as not, he'll reply: "Europe – especially Britain." Apart from seeing the country and visiting all the places of historic interest, it'll give me an opportunity to get to know some of the grand people who have helped me on the way to success in your country.'

And what Johnny saw he pronounced good. Ever since he has combined concert tours with holidays and on numerous occasions he's visited Britain without fans being aware of his presence. And if fans have made it a British love-affair between themselves and the velvet-voiced singing star so, too, has Johnny in his way with Britain and its people.

Mathis fans who attended the first 'live' concert still remember the excitement of the evening and speak of an electric atmosphere. There was the inevitable tension largely arising from the equally imaginary mishaps. There were those who were convinced that he would have a cold and not come and some even postulated the horror of a fire emergency and the theatre being cleared.

When he did appear on stage the initial reaction of fans resembled the worst excesses of a teeny-bopper affair, with shrieks, yelps, tears and other manifestations of hysteria, but it soon became a 'listening' house. There were some who thought the orchestra was far too loud and indeed one person hollered the notion for one and all to hear. Johnny was backed by the excellent Ted Heath Orchestra but at this juncture Heath was not conducting. Mathis fans still, though, remember the shout of, 'Can't we have a quiet orchestra please!' It was fair comment, for the orchestra was in danger of drowning Johnny. The man himself stood, sat, and did little else, but loud band or no his voice commanded the proceedings. It was like listening to an LP, hardly any difference save of course the fact he was there, to be seen, and the atmosphere was something in itself.

He came with a reputation for being exceptionally slick, polished and highly professional; someone who tried to make every performance the best of his career. Those elements were present but there was also an obvious sincerity, a desire to do well, and a vulnerability which, apart from a degree of nervousness in gesture and early vocal notes, was most evidenced in the few words he said. There would be ten or fifteen minutes of vocal artistry and then a rather shy, diffident but friendly 'howdy'.

He seemed slim, even small (though, of course, he is not really a small man). He wore a midnight blue dinner suit with four white buttons close together and he opened his set standing in front of Ted Heath's string-augmented orchestra with Johnny's own MD – Allyn Ferguson – conducting.

The first number was 'Ring The Bell'. Later he sang 'When My Sugar Walks Down the Street', 'Stairway to Paradise', 'There Goes My Heart', an exquisite 'I've Grown Accustomed To Her Face', 'Love Look Away', the hit song 'Wonderful Wonderful' and 'Wild Is The Wind'. And of course there was his renowned singing of 'Maria' from *West Side Story* plus a string of known singles like 'Chances Are', 'It's Not For Me To Say', 'Misty' and 'My Love For You'.

The press raved. One writer, Andy Grey, wrote in the *New Musical Express*:

'His listeners knew they were witnessing another of the few great performers left in the world. His superb artistry gave him a supreme confidence. He opened his mouth wide and out of it came a deluge of tuneful notes, versatile in their range, exciting in their construction. He also imparted every ounce of meaning to his lyrics.'

Melody Maker shouted the headline. 'HE ESTABLISHES AN UNSHAKEABLE GRIP' above even larger type below which said, 'MATHIS WOWS HIS FIRST-NIGHT AUDIENCE'.

Backstage, after the concert itself Mathis, clad only in briefs, and obviously cooling off, imparted his pleasure at the audience's reaction to *Melody Maker* reporter Tony Brown, who wondered whether he always came across so big. Mathis smiled enigmatically and said: 'We get by'. Soon the overjoyed Mathis was telling everyone he must come back. He hadn't realised he was so popular this side of the Atlantic. 'The people are wonderful. Tactful and well-mannered. The audiences everywhere have been attentive and responsive. Quite a lot of my material was new to them but they showed their appreciation.'

The stage was truly set for this continuing love affair of Mathis and Britain, although the first show had not been without a backstage rumpus. Promoter Vic Lewis said things had gone well, particularly in view of some fears.

'Helen had come down and heard the band and loved them. I was the blue-eyed boy. She went off to the hotel and came back on the first evening about half-past five. Outside the Odeon Theatre there were hundreds and hundreds of people all trying to get in. She stormed towards me and said, "I want you," and let fly a torrent of abuse. She asked me why I hadn't put a string of sold-out notices across the front of the Odeon, Hammersmith. Well, in those days it was a cinema for most of the time and the management would not have appreciated their film billings and promotional posters being covered up. Well, there was quite a row. I was upset by the whole affair, especially because it ruined the joy of reading some great reviews. I suppose she made amends by treating me to a sumptuous meal the next time I was in America.'

In 1961 the Granada TV show marked his television debut in the UK. It gave Johnny the chance of renewing his friendship with French puppeteer, Andre Tahon, who was one of the guests on the show. Tahon had toured with Johnny the autumn and winter of 1960 through the States, Canada and the Philippines.

Johnny's Granada show was quite a lavish affair and he even had dancing on his bill of fare. It was great, though Johnny recalls to this day a microphone cover-up! His dance routines meant the use of a small radio-mike with the aerial tightly strapped around his waist. The microphone nestled innocently in a special pocket in his shirt. It meant few knew how he managed both dancing and singing at the same time. He recalls the total amazement when he even turned a complete somersault.

So he went home happy. A number of misapprehensions had been removed, one of which had revolved around fear that British musicianship might be of a poor standard.

Johnny saw little of Britain, the country. Vic Lewis drove him from gig to gig in his Mark 10 Jag, through what was in those days a jungle of poor, over-used roads which often were the scenes of sprawling massed static traffic. The motorways had yet to arrive. Johnny spent much of his time in the back of a car, in a hotel room or on stage.

He came back in 1962 for what proved a successful musical tour, but he left behind a veritable furore.

Johnny's second tour was originally proposed for early 1962 and so would be a quick and important follow-up to the success of the previous summer. Alas for the singer and his fans a back injury led to the cancellation of the projected schedule. It was rearranged for November with dates running through from Saturday the 24th at the Finsbury Park Astoria, London to the finale at the Gaumont,

Hammersmith on December 2nd. Two days later he would record a special show for BBC TV. Once again the Ted Heath band was chosen to accompany Johnny.

Heath commented: 'Last year's tour was successful from every viewpoint. Mathis' orchestrations are first-class and my band with Johnny was a happy mixture – we seem to appeal to the same people. His sophisticated approach to music is very professional and he is a thorough artist. I feel sure this new tour will be every bit as enjoyable as Johnny's first trip here.' This trip would be shorter and would concentrate on the major provincial centres.

The tour's announcement coincided with reports of Johnny starring in an open-air concert in New Jersey which drew a crowd of 134,000 – it was a story to further interest in his British visit. And long before the event the publicity machine stirred into action, as the magazine world chorused 'Welcome back Johnny Mathis' – 'Mathis Glad to Be Back' and a headline which simply said, 'Mathis Here'.

'I don't want to sing the same old stuff,' was Johnny's message to British fans and he recalls how he looked forward much more to this second visit than the first. But he remembers everything seemed 'small, small, small. I think what most blew my mind were the sandwiches. You felt the wind could blow them away! I think over the years I've come to like the delicacy of an English cucumber sandwich!

'When I came and came I began to appreciate more and more English culture. My musicians – if it's their first visit – say they're disappointed in Britain, I say to them "wait and you'll find it charming".

'Somehow I thought British people were cold and lacking in humour. It's one of those things you kinda pick up without knowing from where really. I found out something quite different – that they're warm at heart.'

Johnny was to acquire a passion for British-made cashmere sweaters which he ordered in bulk. Twenty years later the love of cashmere hasn't died as his British promoter and representative Derek Block knows well.

'Johnny sees something he likes, the style or whatever. Later he asks me to get him this or that sweater. I ring

Harrods and ask them whether they still have so and so. They say yes. The man asks me which colour. I ask him how many colours there are. He says ten. So I say, send one of each.'

Johnny remembers early impressions: 'Europe, I like. I love travelling anyway, but that part of the world – well, it's interesting. The way of life over there I found fascinating and there's all that tradition. And I thought to myself: well, it's good to get about to other places and meet the people who buy my records. I didn't know what to expect that first time. I knew my records sold a lot in Britain but to what sort of people? That, I didn't know. It's an education to find this out! I had heard of the Ted Heath music. I had heard the band's records and I said to myself: "Yes, sir!" When Ted and his band rehearsed with me I knew I'd done the right thing. I mean, I did worry over the musical backing and it was the first time I would not have my musicians backing me and really that worried me.'

By November, 1962, Johnny had a new British record company – at least in name. The mighty US company Columbia had set up business in Britain under the title of CBS, since British-owned EMI owned the name Columbia for one of their major labels. Previously CBS has licensed its material to Philips who had issued Johnny on Fontana.

For his visit they issued his seventeenth LP, 'Rapture', described as 'made up of twelve beautiful ballads delivered with the warmth, sincerity and sheer vocal artistry that audiences all over the world have come to associate with Johnny Mathis.'

Johnny flew into London at dawn, a day later than he had intended, on the Wednesday prior to the tour's opening night.

'We put the flight back a day because I had things to do back home. I had to record my latest record "Gina" in Spanish and Italian.'

He arrived in sporting attire and perhaps had forgotten that Britain was hardly a West Coast sun paradise, least of all in November. He sported a windbreaker, light tan slacks and light shoes.

'Good to be back,' he said to the waiting hordes of press and fans. 'I mean it. When I came over last year, I was surprised that my records sold as well as they do. I'm looking forward to having Ted Heath with me again.'

One of the first things Johnny did after he arrived was to check that he had a ringside seat to see Shirley Bassey at London's Talk of the Town. He also acquainted himself with a steady build-up of media bookings, from interviews to radio and television. He learnt CBS was issuing as his tour single, 'Small World' coupled with 'Everything's Coming Up Roses'. The top side was in a slow ballad form while the flip was a fast production. Both numbers came from the musical 'Gypsy'. It was only four weeks previously that CBS had issued the haunting ballad 'Gina' which was by November firmly ensconced in the US Top Ten. It seemed on the surface one of those strange things record companies perpetuate on the great buying public from time to time, a sudden change of mind which in the end rather leaves one bewildered. The tour was virtually a sell-out.

The increased sales over his earlier tour were partly because this time the seaside resorts were out and the larger provincial city venues favoured. Ted Heath had something to say about the visit.

'When Johnny was here last time he brought all his arrangements with him. He also brought his own MD. If he hadn't, we couldn't have got through rehearsals in the limited amount of time we had. This time he's doing the same. He brings in at least forty arrangements and we rehearse each one of them. I've found it necessary to increase my string section for his visits, but apart from this there is no adaptation to be done.'

Heath thought the orchestrations were excellent and Mathis was a fine musician. 'He has the habit of switching his programme each night. That's why we routine forty numbers. He only sings about twelve, but no one wants to be caught out when he suddenly changes his mind during performance.

'All this is terrific experience for the boys, for they really enjoy working with an artist like this. And he *is* an artist. His timing is perfect, and what is almost as important is he is one of us – he gets on extremely well with the band.'

To many, including the all-important music paper editor of the time, Andy Gray of the *New Musical Express*, Johnny looked much taller and more confident when he opened his second tour at Finsbury Park Astoria. He thought Johnny lacked Sinatra's personality but he felt that Johnny had a greater vocal range.

'He is a perfectionist, equally versed in up-wingers, tender ballads, or big-voiced inspirationals, all of which he gave us in his varied repertoire.'

On this second UK visit Johnny seemed to be more at ease, he moved around a lot more on stage and only on two occasions was there a slight lapse into uncertainty. The first came when a girl fan threw him a box of chocolates and Johnny, rather embarrassed, who had been engrossed in his set and was hardly thinking of whether they were plain or milk chocolates or assorted varieties, forgot the lines of the current US big hit 'Gina'!

By the tour's end Johnny was really hitting the heights. At the Gaumont, Hammersmith hundreds were turned away without tickets but some who came were allowed to stand at the back of the auditorium. The set was seventy-five minutes long and Mathis appeared in an expensive, smartly-tailored dark mohair suit with red handkerchief. Not unexpectedly there was tremendous applause when he bounced on stage and even more when he opened his set with 'Got A Lot Of Livin' To Do' and launched into a programme which varied from the up-tempo swinger to tender ballad. John, though, was hardly talkative on stage, with five numbers and a medley of hits passing on their way before he said a few words.

But words were not in short supply when Johnny made his appearance on the BBC TV top-rated show *Juke Box Jury*. The programme's format was simple. There was a panel each week of three or four people from the record and entertainment business. The chairman was David Jacobs. Over the years few guests on the programme said very much which could be seen as controversial, but the usually quiet and restrained Johnny proved a major exception to the rather established blandness.

His comments caused an uproar.

On Anne Shelton: 'This woman can't be serious. She must be singing with her tongue in her cheek.' The lady was of course one of Britain's most revered artists. On US artists Chubby Checker and Bobby Rydell there was merely a wide-eyed, silent expression of sarcasm from John. On another British hero of the time, Tommy Steele: 'he should learn how to sing.'

Melody Maker said: 'Who was this Judge Jeffreys of Pop? Johnny Mathis – the invited guest on *Juke Box Jury* who flayed his hosts with a blast of criticism that is still echoing around Britain.'

Johnny's attorney Morton H. Farber was hauled into the arena to bring some peace into an affair which became a topic for discussion far beyond the pop community. 'Johnny wanted to be frank, honest and outspoken. He was provocative but he likes being that way, and many people admire him for it.'

Inevitably a flood of angry mail poured into the press offices with some people saying Johnny was embarrassing, offensive and conceited.

And sadly, though again not unexpectedly, there were those who turned it all into a mini Anglo-American confrontation with the British line that here once more was the American 'we're the greatest' syndrome, but fortunately such a sentiment was short-lived. The programme's compere David Jacobs told *Melody Maker*:

'We hire people for their opinions and Johnny gave his. I respect him for them. But I must say I can't agree with him about Anne and Tommy. If he thinks Anne has an offensive voice, then he must have a very strange sense of quality. Tommy Steele is a man who relies on a great deal of talent. Singing is only part of it.'

Arthur Askey, the famed British comedian, said: 'I thought Mr

Mathis a very offensive gentleman. I could have turned to him and said: "What are you – a coroner?" He was certainly probing very deep. I think if I had been an alien in a strange country I would have guarded my tongue and not been quite so vicious.'

The event lingered long in people's minds and indeed as late as September, 1974 *Melody Maker* ran a heading DIPLOMATIC MATHIS and remarked:

'Time was when the honey-sweet voice of American Johnny Mathis turned a little sour and he told some home truths about British singers on the now defunct BBC-TV programme, *Juke Box Jury* . . . But that was all of eleven years ago. And it was a diplomatic Mathis who talked to *MM* as he was about to embark on his latest tour. Some viewers couldn't take kindly to a visiting fireman pouring cold water on the recorded efforts of top British stars.'

And in 1962 there were some DJs who said they would no longer play Johnny's records, others who said they would not buy his records. It rather soured memories of a highly successful second British tour but it was really a ridiculous storm in a teacup which, once given press attention, had welled up and acquired an importance far beyond what it deserved. After all, in the immediate context, Johnny was merely expressing an opinion or two and many would not disagree with his sentiments which were based on a cursory hearing of a few brief minutes of an artist's record. It might be argued that such comment as was made should not be forthcoming from such a flimsy acquaintanceship with someone's music. Such a criticism has validity but it ought not to be levelled against Johnny. After all he was asked to comment on what he heard and not what he might hear and see elsewhere. The remark has more point when levelled against the show's concept, for it was the programme which set up the rules of the game – a brief listening to part of a record and then comment. And Johnny should not be penalised for outspokenness and honesty when his opinion was requested, after all it was hardly his fault that many of the programme's guests over the years had contributed nothing more than mediocre blandness, which made his views seem more outspoken. Nor was he familiar with the curious British habit which prevails in some places that you never speak you mind in public, just mouth platitudes. The verbal knifing is saved for behind the scenes.

As it was, Tommy Steele had not had a chart hit since August of 1961, and then with 'Writing On The Wall'. His most recent Top Ten record was 'What A Mouth' in the summer of 1960. He was, of course, becoming one of the most talented British actor-singers. Anne Shelton's 'Tell Me Again In The Morning' also never charted. Obviously the 'moaners' at Johnny's remarks did not exactly rush out into the shops the following Monday, to buy the criticised records and so – at least in success terms – prove John wrong.

Whatever the pros and cons of the event it did mean, in ruthless publicity terms, that Johnny became a household name in Britain.

Oddly enough though, Johnny's popularity in Britain was not translated into success in the singles charts of the time. By the time what was to be his last hit of the 1960s, 'What Will Mary Say', reached a lowly 49 on April 4th 1963, he had had nine hits with a mere three making the Top Twenty. These were 'A Certain Smile', in 1958, 'Someone', a number six a year later, and 'Misty', which charted to twelve in 1960. He was not listed in the British Top Fifty again until 1975 with 'I'm Stone In Love With You' his career underwent a rejuvenation.

In one sense it was not surprising that his singles sales were weak and that the 45s were released as much to gain airplay and help LP sales as to become hits. Britain from 1963 onwards was to say farewell to traditional class singers and the balladeers as the Beatles arrived and an endless succession of new groups sprang from major cities like Liverpool, Manchester, the Birmingham area, Newcastle, London and Bristol. For once American artists were edged out of the way here, and, of course, also in the States.

Johnny became predominantly an LP artist and, of course, a much sought-after television act. He continued as one of the world's biggest live concert draws.

In 1966 Johnny had his dancers and singers with him as he played London's Talk Of The Town for a month and then moved across the street to the Prince Of Wales for another month. A year later he was once more booked into a three week engagement at the Talk Of The Town. It was the first time he played there as a solo performer.

Ray Haughn recalls how they stayed in one of the old residences of W. S. Gilbert at 24, The Boltons, and he remembers particularly the wonderful housekeeper at the Boltons house, Camille Hole.

'Although she knew little of Johnny Mathis at the time she was hired for the job and she became a big fan. Her meals were the greatest thing that could happen to our bunch of Americans. The house itself was so charming that the time seemed to pass very quickly.'

The engagement at the Talk Of The Town finished on October 28th and early on the 30th the Mathis contingent loaded their luggage into a van and left London for South-ampton to fulfil what was one of Johnny's most unusual career bookings. He, Ray and team boarded the *Queen Mary* for her last voyage to Long Beach, California, where she would remain as a tourist exhibit. Johnny would per-form during the voyage, at least this was the intention.

Their journey to Southampton took place on a rather overcast day and the drive seemed very long with inter-minable traffic delays. When they finally arrived they were ushered to their cabins. John was assigned to his stateroom #1 on the Main Deck. Manager Ray was sent to #40 on the same Main Deck. This meant John was in the prow of the ship and Ray was roughly mid-ship.

'This really had little bearing until after we sailed out of the Channel and right into a fierce storm that battered us for three or four days. After John's first night of being tos-sed almost out of his bunk and then lifted and slammed back by the mountainous seas, he asked me how I fared. I told him I had a little trouble, but nothing like what he was describing. So the second and third nights, I had John bunking with me in my stateroom. The storm continued, but at least John was getting the rest he needed to perform his first show.'

However even before the ship had sailed Ray had found himself in rather delicate negotiations concerning Johnny's performance.

'I had spent most of the day before we sailed with the Musicians' Union in London, begging them to permit our "string section" to be merged with the Meyer Davis Band from New York for our ship orchestra. The Union wanted nothing to do with such a merger. They said it was inconceivable that an agreement could be reached. I continued to do my pleading; and finally with the consent of each of the individual violin, viola and cello players, the Union agreed to let them go with us on the voyage. They would play the four shows involving John: the first was to be when we were three days out and the second was to be the first day out of Lisbon. In order to entertain the ship's complement, that really meant two shows on each evening. The storm seemed to gather momentum – John's valet was almost washed overboard on the second morning. He had gotten up early and decided to walk out on to the prow of the ship. The area was closed off to passengers but he climbed over the fence and trod to the rail near the enormous anchor winches. Luckily he was an ex-pugilist, since all at once a gigantic wave flung itself over the prow of the *Queen Mary* and only through his physical strength was he able to grasp the rail and cling to the ship. The officer on deck noticed what happened and sent some crew members to get him and bring him to sick bay and into dry clothing.'

Ray says he still remembers vividly the incident and even today, when he visits the *Queen Mary* in Long Beach, he can recall the fury of that storm.

He recollects the first show Johnny performed – the musicians had rehearsed that afternoon but two of them, string players, were too ill to continue. By showtime, two more had been confined to their cabins. However John and his conductor Dick Bellis sailed on – as it were – regardless.

'The show started. I had climbed up a ladder to the projection room about twenty feet up the back wall of the main lounge. Two sailors were operating the spotlights and it was a difficult time. The ship was rolling and swaying so much that my directions to keep the light on John were hard to execute. I tried my hand at steadying the lights. The salon was only about two-thirds filled, since those who planned this event couldn't get away from their cabins. The show was great and the second performance was equally well received by those who were able to come. I think in all my years I have never seen circumstances equal to those that John endured during his first shipboard cruise that evening. After Lisbon the seas flattened and it was like a serene lake when we did our last show prior to arriving in Las Palmas in the Canary Islands.'

In 1968 Johnny was in Britain for two Charity Shows which had been organised by Vic Lewis. One was at the Royal Festival Hall, London and the other was in Coventry. Allyn Ferguson, who had been Johnny's musical director on his first visit to Britain, had been brought over at the last minute to help with the two shows. He was aided by Jerry Grollnek, who had been one of the earlier lighting managers. The Mathis entourage came through London in January of 1969, to record for television.

The next time John, Ray and their team came to Britain it had almost nothing to do with Vic Lewis. Derek Smith, the talent booker of the Batley Variety Club in Yorkshire (now called The Frontier) had telephoned Ray directly and asked if an engagement could be arranged for his club.

Ray comments: 'Derek Smith was a big Johnny Mathis fan and had been having great success at his nitery with such artists as Shirley Bassey, Neil Sedaka, and many more. Derek felt that it had been too long since the fans in the UK had been able to see Johnny, and made an offer to bring Johnny to his club in late February, 1971.

Haughn talked with the CBS International office in New

York City, had discussions with Bunny Freidus who immediately went to work to see what she could do to arrange other promotional activities; not only in the UK but in France and perhaps Spain. A short tour was finally assembled. There would be one week of shows at Batley Variety Club and it would be followed by a charity event at the Palladium arranged through Vic Lewis. The planning was not good. It meant they had to finish the one Saturday night show at Batley; pack up and catch the train from Leeds to King's Cross, arriving in the early morning hours. They would check in at the hotel, have some lunch and attend the afternoon rehearsal for the two shows on Sunday Night at the Palladium. They managed some rest on the Sunday night and then did the Vera Lynn television show and the Dickie Henderson show. Next on the agenda was a train journey to Manchester for the eventual appearance by Johnny on two charity shows in the city.

Ray brought with him for this trip his public relations agent Joan Bullard and together with Roy Rogosin the music director, McGiveney the lighting man and a new valet, Les Fink, the party left Britain for television work in France and Spain.

The next date set for a British visit was August 1972 because John had been invited to entertain in Munich by the Olympic Committee on September 2nd. But for the new decade, Johnny badly needed a major British uplift. The man who would provide it was Derek Block, a British promoter who was in charge of a growing empire.

He believed in the Mathis magic, liked Johnny as a person and enjoyed his music. He knew LP sales had kept a consistent level through the sixties after those first years of enormous promise when Johnny had arrived in Britain. But it was true to say that John's career had fallen into a comfortable rut.

As Ray says of the post 1972 era: 'At last John was able to be seen and enjoyed by the UK! It was at this time that CBS and Derek Block formed an alliance from the standpoint of Rojon Productions. It's sometimes difficult to not think of the combination as one entity. This was the time when Thom Bell's "Stone In Love With You" was being recorded and CBS records' Caroline Wilkes (now Mrs Simon Bates) was planning many promotional ventures in London and environs together with Derek Block and his staff.'

Derek Block comments: 'His live work in the UK was limited to a couple of cabaret weeks at Batley or Wakefield and a couple of Sunday shows at the London Palladium. When I took over Johnny's dates I decided to book him five or six concerts around the country, but there just wasn't the level of interest, particularly in Scotland. I was amazed because I thought that he was a superstar.' Block's efforts of 1973 were redoubled when he planned a visit from Johnny for 1974. It ran from October 2 to 17 and was just twelve months on from the previous nationwide tour which had begun on September 2 at the Palladium, London and ended at the same venue a fortnight later. Johnny's national travels had been preceded by a fortnight at the Batley Variety Club.

The publicity machine geared itself up to re-establish with the British people Johnny's greatness in the world of contemporary music.

'Today, Johnny Mathis has not only fulfilled, but surpassed all expectations. His achievements as a recording artist are remarkable. During his fourteen year association with CBS records, he has made a long series of albums – all bestsellers – of which eight received Gold Records, signifying sales in excess of one million dollars. His biggest album is, in fact, one of the bestselling albums of all time: "Johnny's Greatest Hits" earned him a special *Billboard* award for being the only artist to have one album remain in the American charts for over four hundred consecutive weeks. Moreover, all of Johnny Mathis' recordings have reached over the half million dollar sales mark. Pretty impressive data for a soft-spoken young man who, as a prime exponent of the understatement, commented, "I think I can say my style has done pretty well for me through the years."'

Block, who fires words with the speed of a machine gun, says: 'I started working closely with CBS on Johnny's UK career, to the extent that I was more than just his British concert promoter. I also worked as a team with his American manager, Ray Haughn. The second time around Johnny played before 12,000 fans in Scotland and sold out the Glasgow Appollo twice.'

By 1981 Block could say with confidence: 'Generally he visits the UK every eighteen months but he has so many fans that they need only come to see him once every six years or third tour to make it pay.

'To me, he is as fresh a client as UB40 or Siouxsie & the Banshees, although he is a lot more serious about what he does than a lot of young kids who come into the business.'

His untiring efforts to re-establish Johnny on the plateau he had known in the early sixties were helped by several events outside of his control. Briefly now – greater detail later – in 1975 Johnny became a major pop hit across the world due to his collaboration with famed soul man, Thom Bell, which gave Johnny a real black American audience. This was a major pop happening, moving him across the musical boundaries, and he had a Top Ten hit with 'I'm Stone In Love With You', a number which three years earlier had given the Stylistics similar good fortune in the UK and US markets. And in 1976 Johnny topped the British charts with the plaintive, rather moving 'When A Child Is Born'. At the end of the seventies Johnny's association with producer Jack Gold and song partnership with Deniece Williams produced disco hits 'Too Much Too Little Too Late' and 'You're All I Need To Get By' while, solo, Johnny charted with another disco-ish cut, 'Gone Gone Gone'. And there were two number one LPs. All this record buzz was complemented by Block's promotional talents and by the early eighties Johnny had assumed superstar status once more with major LP successes and television shows drawing enormous audiences for the BBC. The pick of the LP triumphs lay with the TV-promoted 'The Mathis Collection'. Britain was once more his in a major way and another album 'Celebration' – featuring new takes of twenty songs from his twenty-five years up to 1982, with a spoken introduction from Johnny

– sold heavily and reminded people of his length of career
and his appeal in Britain. In America 1981 was Mathis'
twenty-fifth year, his Silver Anniversary, but for Britain
this event lay in 1983, twenty-five years onward from his
very first single hit, with concerts across the nation which
were all a sell-out by mid-November of 1982, some three
months ahead of his arrival.

Johnny himself says of his British love affair: 'It's always
a wonderful feeling I get when I'm going back to Britain.
It's been a great place for me because I seem to get on so
well with the audiences. Every time I go I just hope I stay
healthy!'.

3

Hard Times

HE DIDN'T STAY healthy.

Johnny returned home to America in 1962, happy and contented. His second trip across the Atlantic had established him as a major star outside the protection of his homeland. But major battles lay ahead, and he had only an inkling of them as 1963 dawned.

Soon a major promoter would say: 'He was high when he came, he was high when he went on. He was drugged to his eye-balls. Talk about pills. Yet he never gave a bad performance.' His revered and much-loved mother would die from cancer. And he would have a bitter quarrel, and court wrangle, with his discoverer and manager, Helen Noga.

The remainder of the sixties – after he had so ably taken Britain as another successful musical territory for himself – would be turbulent times which would threaten him as a person, seeming likely to destroy his career, and bury him as a musical star. Yet with all the odds stacked against him, he survived. Mathis' tenacity, the self-belief which took him out of near poverty, the inner strength and courage and belief in his own destiny as one amongst the greats of music, all came together, and in the end he won.

Johnny played the Las Vegas Riviera. He became known for the wild parties he held in his dressing room. A security head warned him about his behaviour. Another person is reported as saying: 'Maybe they're on drugs. They act crazy.'

The press reported a lounge brawl at the same club. Johnny was accused of insulting a waitress. The woman's husband laid into Johnny and flattened him. Later, Johnny hurriedly left the club and a replacement artist had to be found.

His current manager, Ray Haughn, who, though he only began to work for Johnny in 1964, already knew him at this time, says Johnny never indulged in any so-called vices until certain people who were around him suggested he tried this and that. At first it was innocent enough, although hardly the fare of someone who once took pride in his body and rated physical fitness high in his list of priorities.

He was told alcohol would be good for him and would relax him before he took the stage. So he drank. He was told cigarettes were good for him because they would calm the nerves. So he smoked. When Haughn began managing Johnny, he found an artist who took three hours to clear his throat before he could perform. His earlier and indeed unique breath control began deserting Johnny as the sixties moved remorselessly onwards.

It was the same with pills – only here it seemed innocent enough. He – along with other celebrities – became involved with a doctor called Max Jacobson.

'He started giving me injections – vitamin injections – and it was terrific. I felt wonderful.'

What Johnny didn't know, and what many other stars were unaware of, was that the vitamins were laced with amphetamines.

Jacobson attended to Johnny's needs for five years. Doc even taught Johnny – along with his other patients – how to inject himself, just in case he wasn't around.

The Doc was known amongst the trendy as Dr Feelgood, and his ministrations were gratefully received by many.

'We were a network of Dr Max's children. He would come backstage and while he was there, would fix everybody up and make everybody feel good.'

But all this was before the so-called drug culture became

popular and people realised the power and effect of drugs. At this time, speed was seen in the same light as someone having a few drinks too many.

'Sure I looked and acted peculiar, but Helen and the others figured I was under a doctor's care and that he knew what he was doing.'

Eventually, Johnny became dependent on these pills. When he had them he was on cloud nine and the world, the stage, the audience, were his. Without them he was down, oppressed, trampled upon by every slight sign of aggression from any person, quarter, audience. 'When I wasn't performing, I would not take the injections and therefore I'd have a reaction – withdrawal symptoms.'

He ended up in hospital. It was a far cry from the young man who had slain audiences so early in his career, and impressed people with his boundless energy as he radiated the wholesomeness of a young athlete's body in peak condition. He was only twenty-nine in 1964 and yet he was ageing fast.

They thought Johnny had epilepsy; a doctor said so. His behaviour pattern when experiencing withdrawal was very much akin to an epileptic fit. No one in the medical world knew they were dealing with a national figure who had a drug problem. And even Johnny himself didn't know. It was bizarre, but that's the way it was.

Johnny was put on Dilantin – for life. The months passed and there was still medical uncertainty. And then a third physician looked more closely into the situation. He learnt of the pills and had them analysed, and the truth was out. Johnny was not epileptic. He was an amphetamine-packed slave. He had been taking four deximils three times a day without fail, every day.

'Believe me, I didn't know that taking the pills was wrong. I took them for the physical strength of being able to sing the demanding songs I liked. They did help me on many occasions, just to get the strength to sing. They did, however, hamper me vocally. There was no concerted effort to put feeling into a song. I imagine for two to three years my performances were really hit and miss.'

But why hadn't he mentioned the pills when he was taken into medical care?

'I took tests in hospital and the doctors kept asking if I took any medication. The pills weren't medication, so I never bothered to mention them.'

And because he had 'fits', epilepsy seemed a reasonable deduction.

His manager, Helen Noga, knew. She kept quiet his activities from the world, but kept after him to stop.

'I always had money to buy more, and at that time you could almost buy them over the counter.' And there was the doctor. When the truth came out it meant a major re-evaluation of his total attitude to himself and to his body. And there was his career. His total withdrawal had its obvious penalty. If Johnny had known the dispiriting effect of not taking pills after performances, he was to experience it to a greater degree when they were totally absent from his day-to-day routine.

'To sing without this stimulation; to learn to get up in the morning without taking some false sense of security, all this took time. Especially when you have to work. I'm just fortunate that I was strong enough physically and mentally to stop when I did.'

The family knew something was wrong. Brother Ralph – who had been with the US armed services and had some medical experience – was soon aware that it was no case of epilepsy. Johnny, of course, had a busy schedule and was seeing little of the family; however, something went dreadfully amiss on the day which American families, like many families all over the world, most enjoy – Christmas Day, when the family gathers to share a meal and to express their love for each other. It was the time to unwrap the presents and in a large family like the Mathis' this took a while, and with so many children it was a rather noisy affair. And Johnny was home, the brother who had done well.

It was Christmas morning. Festivities were under way. Laughter echoed round the large house.

And then it happened. The laughter was silenced. The

scene was suddenly reminiscent of a family which has suffered a bereavement. Johnny had got up and he had walked into the centre of a room and had begun to open a present, somewhat slowly and tortuously to be sure, but this was regarded by the onlookers as part of that familiar Yuletide ritual where someone takes time to open a present, and having done so, explodes the built-up suspense and curiosity with joyful whoops of delight. So it seemed. But not quite.

'He began walking round in circles. It was kinda strange. We all stopped what we were doing. He looked up toward the ceiling and then he fell to the ground. Convulsive,' Ralph remembers.

There was silence. Some screams followed. The kids remained transfixed. It was beyond their limited experience.

Ralph rushed across to Johnny and he had the presence of mind to lay Johnny carefully down straight, to put his finger in his mouth and control his tongue to prevent him choking, while the spasms subsided.

Johnny fell into a deep sleep. It was a late reaction from a recent pill-taking session. He hadn't rested or slept for a while, and had scurried home from the East Coast on a plane which had landed that morning or perhaps the night before. No one can quite remember. Only the actual event of Christmas morning claims reliable memory from the Mathis family.

It was the last thing on earth anyone wished to see, let alone on Christmas Day with the family gathered around. Some members had had an inkling that not all was well with Johnny; even his parents were aware of this.

'But you know how parents are. Sometimes they think things but they don't want to believe it and even all the evidence in the world will not change things. But this made them real worried.'

Yet no one really thought it was that bad.

At first they – like Johnny and some of the people around him – toyed with the idea that epilepsy might be the cause of his behaviour, and that Christmas morning lent support to this theory. Some were persuaded – as had been others – that an apparent 'fit' and other symptoms suggested this.

'We never had this kind of thing in the family before – this problem. It became apparent to some of us at least that it was true – brother John was dependent on pills. It was really pretty hard to do anything about it.'

So some of them worked on persuading Johnny to give up. Brother Ralph says they were also aware of the contributory strains of Johnny's life, and particularly his career arrangement with Helen Noga. It seemed Johnny wanted a clean break from his involvement with the lady who had founded his career.

And while he was searching his soul for personal sense, and at the same time was attempting to stay at the top in the music world, there was another deadly blow coming his way. He was told his mother had little time to live. She had terminal cancer, but she did not die quickly. She lingered. Johnny and the family visited her regularly in hospital.

A day or so after one visit he was with his brother, Ralph, in Los Angeles when the news came through that she had died. The two of them rushed back and began making the necessary arrangements for her burial.

'To lose a loved one is hard, very hard. You know the doctors say they've done all they can, you don't want anything sudden, and yet it seems the best thing, but in Mum's case it wasn't that quick.

'Johnny took it hard. He didn't show too much. He's a private person really. He keeps his emotions to himself.'

It hastened a major decision of his career. He left the Noga residence, found a motel and stayed there for six days. They say he left with just a pair of tennis shoes, jeans and a shirt. He needed time to himself, and there were many things to think about. His decision was that he should make a complete break with Helen's management. But life is never that simple – not when you're an artist with financial and business matters of some complexity. It was all suddenly far, far from the evening when hope dawned for them both in a San Francisco club.

'I stood there listening to this boy singing "Tenderly" for a few minutes, and then I turned to my husband and I said, "This is it!" We walked in and sat down to get a look at him now. He was about nineteen, I figured, but he looked like a little baby standing there, his eyes closed, his hands at his sides. You know he still keeps his eyes closed a lot when he sings . . . but anyway that first night we heard Johnny sing we rushed over to him after the show and asked him who was managing him. He said nobody was. I asked him to bring his parents to see me the next day.'

So spoke Helen Noga. However, in 1964 an almost ten-year association was on the rocks. The details were laid out in the cold formulations of the legal system. The document was twenty-eight pages long and it was filed in 1964 at the Los Angeles Superior Court by Johnny, naming the Nogas, eight other companies and twenty unidentified persons. The suit charged – among other things – that while his income in three-and-a-half years exceeded $975,000, various 'appropriations' under the guise of commissions and otherwise, 'left him with a net increase of only $25,000.'

Johnny wanted to get away and be his own man. He had been very much directed, and brother Ralph says he was 'very much dominated and imprisoned' and had been under a 'lot of stress'. The Nogas brought a counter-action. They said their stewardship had meant $1.6 million for Johnny.

Johnny told the magazine *Ebony*, many years later:

'A lawsuit tends to connote unhappiness and hatred and everything, when in essence that was not the case with Helen and myself. We came to a point in our relationship where I was bored and tired of living with someone else. I was a man now; when she found me I was a boy. I had also decided that I wanted a choice in matters that pertained to my career and personal life. I didn't have a choice when I was with Helen.'

He said he rarely disagreed with whatever the Nogas
said because he disliked public rows.

'I don't like bickering; I never have. I like quiet, subtle, sophisticated types of people. Helen was not very
quiet and not very subtle. But she was a wonderful
woman who did everything for me in the beginning.
She is the reason there is a Johnny Mathis today. I
would never have had the fortitude to do the things she
had to do for me.
'It was not a matter of how much money does she get,
and how much do I get. It was a matter of how much
was she entitled to and how much would I give her,
because it was my money. I had worked for it and she
had merely invested it in what she thought was appropriate.'

He said he was satisfied with the private arrangement
which was reached; 'I'm sure she was to a certain extent.
And she still gets payments, a certain percentage of contracts made when she was there, which is only fair.'
On another occasion Johnny said:

'Helen made me feel that I could compete with other
popular singers. I never felt secure about my singing. I
felt that I sang well, but a lot of people do. And I felt I
had no special attraction. In fact, I felt I had a lot of
negative points. I wasn't forceful; I wasn't glamorous. I
wasn't all those things that one is supposed to be to be
successful . . . But Helen made me feel something so
that I could continue . . . It didn't matter what you did
one night – if you sang well – it's whether you could do
it the next night, and the next night . . . You have to
make sure you outlast, outsing, outdo them forever,
and she instilled that in me from a very early age. . .
'She had all these incredible goals and she would say
them to me. Every day of my life that I was with Helen,
I could be sure to hear two or three of the same things I
heard every day. And she treated me like her own son

. . . But, of course, she was impossible to live with. When I became a little older . . . I had to have a life of my own. She even found my house for me . . . because it was close to hers. She didn't want for me to get far even though I was going to move out.'

So they parted. Johnny was scared to death. His shelter had gone. 'She had done everything for me. It's like I didn't even know how much money I made, you know, or whether I could afford certain things. So when I left Helen, I said, "Well, okay, who's going to run my life?"'

A former co-worker of Helen Noga's, Don Riber, was a good contact. Riber brought attorney Ed Blau into Johnny's life and they, with Ray Haughn (later Johnny's full-time manager) began to plan Mathis' new life. Almost.

Johnny began learning the business side of his musical success; for instance, where monies had been invested and how to record the revenue which consequently came in at appointed moments.

But there was still the problem of those pills. Johnny's father had been appointed Vice-President of the Rojon company which Johnny had formed to administer his empire. Clement persuaded John to let Ralph work with him, with the intent of keeping an eye on John's activities and more so the people who hung around and sold to him.

Johnny finally kicked the drug habit in 1969 after some eight to nine years. Ralph worked for him some fourteen to fifteen months.

'If I found drugs, I threw them away. There were always people hanging around. I didn't like them. To me, they hadn't Johnny's best interests in mind, just theirs.

'I guess the whole thing wasn't surprising. It goes on in the pop world, but it doesn't have to. It went this way. We would go off for the concert. And we would return to wherever at about one-thirty or two in the morning. But we wouldn't go to bed. When we got back there would be people in John's place – they'd gotten keys. There would be these parties. No sleep. Maybe one or two hours, no more. And then next morning there would be interviews, then stage or something checks. And he'd be on stage again.'

It went on and on with incalculable damage being caused to John's formerly excellent physical condition.

Ralph travelled with Johnny and tried to get rid of these pills. He had a room in Johnny's house for a while, and he even kept a gun because he never knew who might call – they were strangers to him, and not always pleasant.

'People would come to the door at night. I kept sending them away, but it worried me. I kept changing the locks, getting the house more secure. As far as I was concerned, people were taking advantage of Johnny. They were doing things which were harming him.

'You know, we'd get calls on the phone. It was one of these people. I'd say he wasn't around. Johnny would say to me "Who was that?" I'd say it was no one.

'Then of course, Johnny would meet the guy and then he knew he had called. He would be angry.'

Ralph was a buffer, ready and willing to get knocked and pushed around and to suffer and still come back for more. For a while things got better. Ralph was ready to leave, but before he did he went through the house searching for those pills in order to get rid of them.

'I could see why Johnny was tempted. These were trying times for him. Pills were things which could boost him, get him in the mood for the stage, but slowly they were eating him up.'

Manager Ray Haughn says there was one key experience which proved the turning point in John's rehabilitation from drug taking and other debilitating practices.

He remembers he arrived at the Rojon office, on Sunset Boulevard, at about 8.30 a.m. and shortly before nine John arrived looking very distressed. He could barely talk through his extremely swollen tongue and his head was drawn back by a tightening of the muscles in the nape of his neck.

'Our lighting man, Jerry Grollnek, came into the office

as I was telephoning a medical specialist, and we hurried John into his open convertible and headed for the hospital. By the time we arrived the doctor had left to go to his own offices in Beverly Hills, since he felt adverse publicity might emanate from treating John in the hospital. We immediately turned the car around and headed for Beverly Hills.

'Robert Feder, MD, was awaiting our arrival. Through my description of John's condition, he was able to determine what drug would cause such an extreme condition.'

Ralph was at John's home and he received a call from Ray, who told him of John's dilemma and asked him to look in the pockets of the Levi's John had been wearing to see if there was another of the pills John had been taking there. There was.

Ray says: 'The pills had been prescribed for one of the Mathis brothers', Michael, who had been visiting John's house. The medication was a very strong tranquilliser that had an allergic effect on John. The problem was that John had talked his brother into giving him two of the capsules, thinking that if they made his brother feel good, they would do the same thing for him.'

The eventual outcome was a happy one. The doctor gave Johnny the vital antidote and Ray and Ralph both see the incident as 'the last straw which broke the camel's back' – it really made Johnny think about himself and the consequences which could have ensued from his latest pill adventure. It was the critical incident which led to Johnny abandoning drugs.

Manager Ray Haughn says this final incident happened around eighteen months after John had taken the first step to solve his problem in February of 1967.

He also recalls how John broke another habit. John was booked at the Latin Casino in Cherry Hill, New Jersey. The weather was miserably cold and snowy. John performed two shows each evening and after the second show he would leave the stage during the orchestral musical bows and go directly to his car which was waiting outside the stage door.

He remembers one particular evening. 'About half-way into our one week engagement, a fan was standing in wait as John and I came out of the stage door. Without meaning any harm, she delayed him long enough to get an autograph; however, the temperature must have been well below freezing and blustery cold winds were swirling snow all around. I tried to pull the cashmere scarf around John's neck, but the chill had its effect. The next morning John could not utter a sound . . . he had a bad case of laryngitis! I had been through this situation with John during February of 1965 and knew exactly what should be done. The first thing to go was his cigarettes. At this point in his life he had picked up the habit of smoking about three packs of very strong English cigarettes per day. And, of course, a doctor was summoned. John was not permitted to use his voice at all, and we communicated by sign language.'

Medical treatment worked a reasonable wonder and John made the decision to do the two shows that evening. At showtime, albeit a little hoarse, the voice was back and the four thousand fans that had already booked for the two shows that night were not disappointed.

After the show Ray had a quiet, firm word with Johnny and advised him that now he had been off cigarettes for one full day he might try and give his throat some more relief by extending his non-smoking at least one more day. He did.

'And from that day he never again took up a pack of cigarettes seriously,' says Ray, and adds that the effect on members of the orchestra was 'phenomenal'.

'They heard John singing with greater control and resonance than they could remember. So to further insure that he would not go back to his old habit, I asked the individual musicians to convey their assessment of his vocal prowess to him directly. It was that reassurance and John's will power that put behind him one of the most damaging habits he had at that time.'

There were, of course, other significant events in the sixties after the second British visit had taken place. The most important was Johnny's shift to Mercury Records after spending so much time growing and expanding with Columbia from the moment he flew into New York to record the very first album.

The change in record company was partially prompted by an offer of more money, and on May 15th, 1963, Helen Noga and Irving Green, the Mercury president, put their signatures to a contract. The deal was seen by the music business press as interesting. Helen Noga set up for Johnny a firm called Global Records. Johnny would record for Global and the masters he made would be leased to Mercury. It carried a considerable guarantee and the first recording sessions were planned for July when the Columbia contract ceased.

In Britain it meant that Johnny moved from Fontana to the EMI/HMV label. The first disc issued this way was a single, 'Your Teenage Dreams', coupled with 'Come Back'. An LP of Christmas songs entitled 'Sound of Christmas' was scheduled to follow. At the time it was said there were seventy-five people on Johnny's personal payroll and he was seen by *Record Mail* as one of the hardest working performers in the business. A spokesman for EMI, then a British company with a world reputation, commented:

'We are particularly pleased to welcome to our labels such a great artiste as Johnny Mathis, and we look forward to a long and happy association with him.'

EMI said his recording manager in the UK would be Norman Newell, and his marketing manager Rex Oldfield.

There were many who saw the move as a mistake. It never seemed a happy affair, although of course the relationship was doubtless affected by the other events which had encroached upon Johnny's time during this period. It produced little which became generally popular, although many fans of his music believe it was a profitable period and certainly his recording with Norman Newell proved a welcome move. But the arrangement floundered and eventually John returned to Columbia, where he has stayed, and it was under their wing that he was to achieve two major come-backs in the seventies.

'I thought one record company was like another. Mercury paid me a ton of money to sign with them. It sure was different. I missed my old friends at Columbia, and the differences in recording and marketing approaches,' Johnny said.

There were, of course, natural events and situations caused by other people over which Johnny had no possible control. Towards the end of the decade he had several narrow escapes from death.

In 1968 he was on tour, using Indianapolis as a base from which he would make one- or two-day concert expeditions. There was an evening when Johnny was due at Bloomington, Illinois. The crew had gone ahead with the equipment by road. The weather was foul, with heavy rain and then snow and Johnny was airborne. Conditions put the nearest airport out of operation, yet the next nearest was fifty miles away. If the plane landed there, Johnny would then have to face at least an hour, maybe more, of driving, arriving long after the concert audience had gone home. It was decided that a landing would be attempted. The plane – a small charter affair – descended to around thirty to forty feet from the ground. There was still nothing visible, but the pilot decided he would land and was just about to touch down when the control tower loomed up ahead. The plane went up, hurriedly, as if engaged in sudden combat manoeuvres with an enemy plane. Eventually they landed on the grass which separated the two airport strips. Not unexpectedly, they skidded to a halt. Everyone got off and decided a big stiff drink was in order.

Another occasion was in South America in the San Paulo area. Johnny, Ralph and the others were in a small plane which was coming in to land. It was almost ready for touch-down when it soared upwards and down below they saw another plane which was busily taking off in the direction from which they had come.

'We had a basketful of close calls,' says Ralph. But it was symptomatic of Johnny's life in the sixties. The next decade was much better – very much so.

The survivor Johnny marched on. But not by luck – far from it, for he analysed himself and realised he had sung not for people, friends, even his manager Helen Noga before they split – he just wanted to please his mother. When his mother died on December 31st, 1963, it was the beginning of the realisation that he didn't have to be the shining symbol Helen wanted him to be.

'I had wanted to give my mother something none of the other women in the neighbourhood had – a famous son – and I did. Helen had lived each day of the week for my success. She was like a mother to me. My own mother took great offence at Helen usurping her role. Funny, they had absolutely nothing in common – complete opposite ends of the spectrum . . . except they both loved me.'

It was what Johnny told American black women in the magazine *Essence*. Who knows how the readers reacted?

As for him? It took him years to come to terms with this – it was the case of assuming responsibility for himself.

'It didn't seem possible at first. Then it was. I was taking care of Johnny Mathis.' And it made for a great future.

4

All Becomes Well

THE SEVENTIES WAS a decade which saw Johnny revitalised, but in so saying it should be borne in mind that the sixties, for all their downers, were not a total write-off. The decade had its quota of good concerts, singles and LPs. And beyond the vinyl and stage attractions, some basic facts about the real Johnny Mathis had become apparent – here was a guy with a strong constitution, and a bull-like tenacity to come through whatever might befall him; a strong inner core and an eventually overwhelming desire to claim the musical greatness which he had always believed would be his.

The seventies was a decade which saw Johnny snug and warm once more with Columbia Records. It was a period of record experimentation with a number of producers who were imaginative and inspired the genuine creativity in Johnny. He became as relevant to the general run of record buyers in the latter half of the decade as he had been in the late fifties. During the late fifties and early sixties he had survived the challenge of rock 'n' roll and maintained the place of the ballad. In the period from 1975 onwards, Johnny maintained his musical place despite the American concentration on the basic rock music of the Fleetwood Macs and the Eagles, the pop of the Bee Gees or Peter Frampton, while in Britain he rode high even when punk was at its rebellious peak and some rock stars were sniffing cocaine at the cost of wallet and nose.

Johnny's record sale revival gave him more time to

himself and much of it was spent playing golf. He had no drug dependency problems.

His business affairs were now directed by Ray Haughn, and there were no problems from this quarter, as the business base was now functioning smoothly. His touring arrangements were immaculate and timed so that Johnny could balance the demands of public with the stresses and strains on his body, for – to use the well-worn cliché – he was getting no younger and was forty in 1975.

As brother Ralph has calmly put it:

'This was a period when he got things into focus. Like anyone, he had had the problem of being a star. In the seventies he got his head together as Johnny Mathis the music star, and John Mathis, the guy we all love. He is a very precious human being.'

Fortunate, though, is the person for whom all goes well. There was one major dark period during this decade. It was the death of his father on March 9th, 1974, in Santa Barbara, almost eleven years from the time when his mother left behind a grieving and much upset son.

His father had always been a powerful influence in his life – that was obvious. His influence had increased once he was aware of John's drug dependency and he had been much more involved with the business side once John and Helen Noga had split. By 1971 he was beginning to be less involved with the day-to-day running of Johnny's business. Ray Haughn and Ed Blau coped with it admirably. Clement lived on a ranch Johnny had bought in Santa Ynez in the Santa Barbara region. His rôle lay in advising Johnny rather than running the company. He travelled a fair amount, and in practical terms he was semi-retired. He watched from the wings, and was proud to see his son become the kind of person he respected. He noted the human side of Johnny coming through increasingly, and observed the changing pattern of his career. He read with pleasure the article, already made mention of, in *Essence*. During the course of the excellent feature by Alan Ebert, Johnny said:

'I really am a very happy man. I have a good life, a fine

life. It took me years, thanks to being raised in that great swatch of Methodist thinking that said to just *be*, to do nothing, was to do the devil's will. To putter with the car if I like: and I like to golf when I choose: and I frequently choose. To cook or chase sunbeams when I wish. I have no monumental problems. No great aspirations. I'm not a great singer and I'm never going to be one of the greats, but I'm accepted.'

It was a modest Johnny, for 'greatness' had hovered around him almost from the word go, at least once the whisperings of disappointment over the sales of the first LP had died from the corridors of CBS, and 'Wonderful Wonderful' had become a smash hit single. Clement had seen it happen; he had watched Johnny from the time when, as a toddler, he had first mouthed something which people kindly said was singing, to the time when, as a young teenager, Johnny was appearing in the clubs and his father would sit outside waiting rather than let Johnny feel he was being peered at. Johnny was the kid in whom he invested his energy and hard-earned money, and over whom he spent hours in prayer, asking whether Johnny should go and live with the Nogas. He had seen Johnny go to New York, and then the family had seen nothing of him for several years, relying instead on the occasional letter or telephone call, and the records to remind them of his presence. He had stood by his son when pills threatened him physically, and he had been overjoyed at seeing Johnny win through and survive into a new decade with all its attendant possibilities. He was, though, denied by his death the chance of seeing Johnny's total rejuvenation which had its real flowering in the second half of the decade.

Johnny's father was a great man, for the family and for his fourth child. Love and genuine respect for him comes from his sons and daughters, in-laws, nephews and nieces. His influence was enormous. He was sensitive. He was intelligent. He was shrewd. Johnny says:

'I always sang for my father. I needed his approval. He was very dear to me.'

His father's death created a void in Johnny's life, but he was, after all, of an age to know that things must continue however hard it seems. And he had a family. He was not alone. At first, familiar places and locations reminded him of so many precious things, but then it's the same for anyone who has lost someone they really loved. He had to reach beyond and, by drawing on inner reserves, plough onwards. At least he soon had a renewal of his record success when he recorded with Thom Bell in 1975.

He celebrated his fifteenth year in the music world in 1971. Fifteen doesn't seem an exciting number, but it was made into something special by a major supplement in the world's trade record journal *Billboard*. The supplement contained the usual bout of advertisements congratulating Johnny on his longevity, and there was feature material covering the most important times in his life.

In 1972 he found himself a worthy subject for the Walk of Fame. This is located in the district of the City of Los Angeles called Hollywood. The Hollywood Walk of Fame has achieved international fame as a major tourist mecca. It was started in 1961 and it honours the past and present stars who have enabled Hollywood to see itself as the entertainment capital of the world.

The Walk of Fame comprises sidewalks which line both sides of Hollywood Boulevard for a distance of some blocks, and the sidewalks of Vine Street for three blocks. These famous sidewalks are made up of 2,519 bronze stars embedded in a pink and charcoal terrazzo. Each star measures around thirty-four inches across, from point to point. The name of each star is written in bronze letters embedded in the pink marble, within the boundaries of their bronze star, and then beneath the name is the accompanying bronze emblem, designating the category: a television set for a television star, a film camera for a film (or as the Americans say, motion picture) star, and for the recording star there is a record disc with a record-player arm across it.

Johnny was elected to receive a Walk of Fame star on June 1 at 10.00 a.m.

The morning was drenched in that exquisite Californian sun. Traffic was mild along the Boulevard; there were just a few cars in Vine Street. Johnny's star was veiled with a wood-frame 'star' that was totally covered with rich green velvet, and was secured to two gold-braid ropes.

The crowd began assembling a considerable time before ten. There was an interesting mix of friends, fans, people from Columbia Records, Rojon, officials from Hollywood's Chamber of Commerce, and photographers and reporters.

Ralph Mathis was there; he was looking very smart and natty in a dark green suit, and even got mistaken for Johnny by some over-eager fans, which amused him and passed the time of day. And then Johnny arrived, in the company of his father, Clem. He looked pleased with life and so he should have – it's not everybody who receives this kind of star! Clem kept beaming. This was another landmark in his life, with all the hard work of yesteryear paying off handsomely. Clement kept looking at Johnny and imparting to one and all the smile proud parents are wont to wear on their faces.

Johnny came bedecked in a light-weight summer blazer with a tartan pattern of red and green on white, pale yellow short-sleeve turtle-neck light-weight sweater, immaculate white trousers and white shoes. Clem wore a navy blue summer suit, white shirt and blue-on-white print tie.

Next to arrive was Johnny's manager, Ray Haughn, who sported an impeccably tailored dark brown suit. Joan Bullard, Johnny's public relations lady, accompanied him. Johnny took his place in front of the star, along with the gentlemen from the Chamber of Commerce. The ceremoney began. Johnny was presented with a wood plaque in the form of a shield by a young boy from the Hollywood YMCA. It recognised Johnny's continued financial assistance to this organisation. This was followed by a presentation from the Chamber of Commerce – a large, and rather impressive official certificate-plaque of the City of Los Angeles to commemorate this occasion.

And onwards the ceremony rolled towards the main point of the gathering and Johnny's presence – the unveiling of the star. Along with two men from the Commerce department, Johnny took hold of the golden ropes and lifted the velvet covering off the sidewalk. The bronze of the star and his name, the record disc, gleamed brightly in the sun. There was appreciative applause from the assembled on-lookers. Johnny wore a satisfied smile on his face as he gazed at the star and then at the onlookers. Various spoken congratulations came from those near enough to gain his hearing, and the photographer assembled various people in the poses he desired.

Johnny's US fan club lady, Maria Niemela, remarked:

'Johnny did not seem to tire as he stood there signing his name to an endless stream of pieces of paper, photos and album covers. And it seemed to be a timeless scene . . . all of its aspects were perfect. Johnny Mathis, the corner of Sunset and Vine, in front of Wallich's Music City, loving fans abounding, California sunshine on our shoulders! Eventually Johnny began to ease slowly away from the crowd, still signing a few remaining autographs while he took little sideways steps. Joan led the way, and people reluctantly parted to make a path for Johnny. He chanced to walk beside me . . . and quite unexpectedly our eyes met. I received this quick but friendly gesture from him . . . "Hi, Maria. How are the kids?" Before I could answer, a dozen fans got in front of me . . . it doesn't pay to be short! There was a last glimpse of him as he walked across Sunset . . . and then Vine . . . and he disappeared through the doors of the Tower. . . Many of us stayed to linger . . . and to have a good look, to admire and photograph the star now that the area was clear. It had been a unique and memorable event . . . it had been a day of pride and reflection for Johnny, for his family, for everyone who loves him and is concerned with his career. And although that day is but a lovely and indelible memory . . . we have the ever-present knowledge that Johnny's Walk of Fame star will remain on that exclusive spot of Los Angeles for a tangible always. Now and in the future, any of us may visit

this medallion that adorns that very special sidewalk . . .
that proclaims the fame and greatness of our beloved and
very favourite recording star . . . *Johnny Mathis*.'

As mentioned in Chapter Two, Johnny was in Britain in
1973. Top selling tabloid *The Sun* headlined it as – MISTY
MR MATHIS JUST SPINS ON AND ON.

By now Johnny was well back into the recording groove,
and by the end of 1973 all of sixteen new Mathis LP
releases had been issued in the States. And in 1973 he had
made his first foray into the *Billboard* charts since 1969
when 'I'm Coming Home' hit the Top One Hundred, as
did 'Life Is A Song Worth Singing'. His 1969 hit 'A Time
For Us', had been his first single to chart since 1965. It was
the beginning of a vinyl rejuvenation, augmented in 1973
when he worked with renowned black soul producer-
arranger-writer Thom Bell.

'I'm Coming Home' paved the way for the black community to start appreciating their son. *Jet* magazine, at the
beginning of 1974, put him on their cover. And inside,
their feature writer, William Earl Berry, put the new
Mathis facts before his readers with striking clarity:

'There are two ways to find out how popular and successful a recording artist is.
One: check his/her record sales.
Two: check the box office receipts after a performance.
Any recording star who claims success without making
it in one of these areas is just talking – he/she is not selling. Johnny Mathis IS selling. And Johnny Mathis has
been selling for a long time.'

Berry's proof lay in Johnny's Hollywood Hills home, his
properties, investments, even if Johnny told him: 'I don't
speculate on the stock market, I never have enjoyed it.'

Berry said LP 56 had brought Johnny into black consciousness in a way which had been lacking for some
time. The LP had the same title as the hit single – 'I'm
Coming Home'. And it was the LP 'that is sparking a
Mathis craze within Black America. Radio stations, record

shops, soul record charts . . . the message is clear enough, Mathis is breaking out all over.'

It was Johnny's collaboration with Bell and songwriter Linda Creed which had caused the pleasing furore. The two had already experienced similar career revivals with The Stylistics (who became huge sellers in Britain) and The Spinners (known as The Detroit Spinners in the UK because of the Liverpool folkish group having prior claim to the name Spinners), a dance-orientated New York City group.

Berry agreed that Johnny had not changed his style, that he had always possessed a sense of 'soul'; it was more a case of Johnny vocalising off a backing of earthy bass, fingerpopping drums, swaying strings and horns that characterised Bell's sound under the Philadelphia record company umbrella.

'I'd always been a fan of his,' Johnny says, 'and I recorded one of his songs, "Betcha By Golly Wow", on one of my albums.' He says it was Columbia record chief of the time, Clive Davis, who first thought of his working with Bell. At the outset he had played Johnny some of Bell's music, and with Johnny's interest aroused, he dropped the word that Bell would like to record with him.

'It was just a mutual admiration thing,' Johnny adds.

Davis, talking of Johnny, says: 'The final test of art has always been measured by time, and in the case of the singing of Johnny Mathis, time has proven its excellence. Johnny has remained one of the most popular entertainers in contemporary music for one reason, and this is because he is truly an original. No matter what he chooses to sing, once he gives it the Mathis interpretation it belongs to him.'

One reason for the immediate empathy of John and Thom Bell was the feeling of the Mathis camp that Bell had done his homework. He had studied Johnny's vocal technique, his record product, and was genuinely keen on recording Johnny. This enthusiasm extended itself to lyric writer Linda Creed. She was a fan of Johnny's and so, with her commitment and Bell's sensitivity mixed with

Johnny's own affection for the two of them, the scene was set for some fine recordings. Ray Haughn says the scene was set for 'romance' even if the studio was hardly conducive! 'It was in an old part of Philadelphia, there was no air-conditioning. I remember a distinct pleasure at realising that here was a producer who had taken great care. The whole beauty of the man was in his elaborate preparations, and I mean he had pre-conceived what we were going to do six or eight weeks before it happened.'

And Clive Davis knew from the outset things would work out well.

The magazines were saying Johnny was more relaxed and busy trying to project a contemporary image with the ever-present cashmere sweater being replaced by an open-necked shirt.

An American paper cried THEY'RE STILL MISTY OVER MATHIS, and the man himself says: 'A lot of people think Johnny Mathis walks in front of clouds singing "Misty" – I'm forced to sing certain songs otherwise people feel deprived.' But in the end it didn't matter so much what people wanted and what the magazines said – the important thing for Johnny the artist in 1973, and into the following year, was that publications thought their readers were interested in hearing about him, however profound or trite the copy.

He was in Australia touring in 1974, and the screaming headline was – MATHIS MANIA!

He couldn't wish for anything better, and he found further welcome in Britain as once more he toured, busily recovering his lost British audience. It was the beginning of the era when promoter Derek Block began establishing Johnny Mathis as a major concert force on the British music scene. And accompanying Block's determination came the valuable support of television, as the BBC revived its interest in Johnny which had led previously to major TV shows in 1962, 1966 and 1967. In 1974 the BBC presented the Johnny Mathis Show as filmed at the Apollo Centre, Glasgow. Before the decade had ended, there were to be another three major BBC productions, while

Johnny made several appearances promoting his singles on the highly rated national pop show *Top Of The Pops*. He was to tour in 1976, 1977 and 1978.

Oddly enough, Johnny made no real impression with either of his American hit singles of 1973 in Britain. It was not until 1975 that the Bell-Creed partnership sparked off for him a sudden, rather unexpected UK smash hit. Johnny's version of 'I'm Stone In Love With You' came into the charts near the end of January 1975, and stayed in the charts for three months, reaching Number Ten. It was his first British chart single entry of the decade. Better was to come – in 1976 Johnny topped the British charts with 'When A Child Is Born'. One British paper – perhaps forgetting Johnny's hit of 1975 – said 'FORGOTTEN' MATHIS HITS THE POP JACKPOT. 'When A Child Is Born' was a melody which had been composed by an Italian, Crio Dammaco. Total world sales for Johnny climbed to around six million, and so put Johnny and the song into the category reserved for Belafonte and 'Mary's Boy Child', and Crosby's evergreen version of Irvin Berlin's 'White Christmas'. A disc jockey of some standing in Britain, Alan Freeman, said 'What Mathis has done has put some reality into Christmas and made people feel religious all over again.'

It certainly fitted well with Johnny's love of Christmas which stretched back to those childhood times in the Mathis family household. He once told the American journal *Black Stars* what Christmas meant to him. 'Christmas to me means being surrounded by and giving love.'

Suddenly, he was a household name. His record came on the airwaves with incessant regularity, and his face adorned the pop journals. It was back to the British popularity of the early sixties. It was welcomed!

It easily became his biggest Christmas season success – there was surprisingly little reaction to other Yuletide numbers like 'Christmas In The City Of Angels', released in America in 1979, and then 'The Lord's Prayer' with Gladys Knight in 1981, on which 'When a Child is Born' was the B-side, but soon became the main title. The success of 1976 was not repeated. On the latter occasion, American audiences were treated to the song on the syndicated Johnny Mathis Christmas Hour with Diahann Carroll, Henry Mancini and the International Children's Choir.

The singles success paved the way for an even more impressive onslaught by Johnny on British ears. CBS released an album entitled 'The Mathis Collection' in 1977, which initially caused some confusion with the cheap label 'The Johnny Mathis Collection' on Hallmark, which had come out the previous year.

'The Mathis Collection', some forty songs, received extensive TV and general media attention. It comprised many of Johnny's great recordings from the seventies. It soared up the LP charts, and to everyone's great delight, it took the Number One spot. And while 'The Mathis Collection' was faring so well, Volume 2 of 'The Johnny Mathis Collection' was finding its way into the shops! In 1977, CBS also issued Johnny's song 'Sweet Surrender' and in the following year the high-selling American collection, 'You Light Up My Life'. From this period onwards, a whole mass of repackaging began, and the same tracks appeared to be cropping up, albeit in different running order, on numerous albums – too many, it seemed, for fans. The number one, 'The Mathis Collection', paved the way for Derek Block's major thrust to persuade the British public to see Johnny in concert, preferably for him as promoter, in a concert hall, but also on television and, of course, to buy Johnny's records.

Johnny made two very successful UK tours in 1977 and 1978. Some reviews he collected must have made him feel he could walk on the moon.

'An outstanding performance'; 'Everybody's troubles disappeared as the inimitable Mathis tones echoed around the Colston Hall'; '"It's a beautiful evening" sang Johnny Mathis, and for seventy minutes or so he was probably right'; 'An immaculate man with a superb voice'; 'As a performer he is a miracle of economy, mesmerising with a flash from the dark eyes or a lift of the never-ending lips.

For me it is an evening which turns popular music into profound art'; 'In live performance you really get the benefit of the tremendous range of his voice. Mathis is a perfectionist and the standard of his performance made that perfectly evident'.

While he was in Britain in 1978, he appeared at two special charity concerts for the United World Colleges which went under the name of Supernight. The Duchess of Kent and the Prince of Wales both attended, and compering was the lustrous Farrah Fawcett-Majors, who shimmered her way to the microphone to introduce the shows. She was dubbed by Lord Mountbatten Miss Fawcett-Colonels.

It was Johnny who stole the headlines, none more so than the one in the up-market *Daily Telegraph*, which had – MATHIS STUNNING IN 'SUPERNIGHT' FINALE.

He made the audience gasp by holding one note, on 'Little Boy Lost', for a seeming eternity, stunned them with a dramatic rendering of 'Maria' from *West Side Story*, and departed with an extremely dramatic 'If We Only Have Love'. Only the duet with Deniece Williams caused some disappointment.

And his concert tour attracted the same kind of notice. It was a re-run of 1977, which was in turn a re-run of 1976. This time around there were comments like:

'Nobody delivers a smoochy song like Johnny Mathis. His voice is a natural wonder that will always be popular.'

'A Mathis performance is something for silent appreciation rather than an evening of excitement or hysteria. And to that extent, he has done a major service for contemporary show business.'

'By getting rid of the worst behavioural traits of modern "pop" audiences, he has made it possible for quality to defeat screaming sound.'

'He remembered his past with a glorious version of "Misty", that anthem of fifties besitter-land, and went on to unlikelier stuff like "99 Miles From LA" and Michel Legrand's intriguing "Pieces Of Dreams". He turned in a majestic version of the Commodores' "Three Times A Lady", making the song his own.'

That Johnny had come back into the national consciousness was shown by the major selling tabloid, *The Sun*, giving virtually a whole page to a feature by its writer Nina Myskow. She thought he looked splendid for forty-three, noted the beard he had turned up with for this British visit and heard he had grown it for a lark.

Johnny told her: 'Sometimes I just feel sorry for myself. I go off into a corner. Or I just sit up in bed by myself at night, play a little music, and think, oh God, everybody in the whole world is having a better time than me. I'll feel that I'm just doing the same old thing all the time. That my life is a total bore, and there's no excitement in it at all.'

While Britain took Johnny once more under her wing, he still had some headway to make up in the States. The Bell-Creed affair was, after all, a birth belonging to 1973, and by the last half of 1977 something was very much needed if the new momentum of the seventies was not to wind down. But Johnny's American musical life in 1976 was not without incident. There was, for instance, the Welcome Home Johnny received at Lost Angeles International Airport, the second in ten years. It's the airport he uses each time he comes home from a tour, and is, it seems, as familiar to him as an old friend – sometimes leaving it and just as often returning to it. The airport is twelve miles' drive from Johnny's home in Hollywood Hills. He usually makes the journey in a chauffeur-driven limousine. Maria Niemela, the International Fan Club President, who has seen many a departure and landing, remarks – with, one suspects, a little humour in her voice – that he has acquired a rapid stride in his walk. He scuttles down the passageways of the airport buildings and out on to the sidewalk – where the door to the limousine waits, opened and ready for his arrival. And off he goes into the sunset – or wherever. Johnny has a strong urge to be home once it's within his sights. Airport welcomes have been kept to a minimum.

However, in May – the time when his LP 'I Only Have Eyes For You' was released in America – the International Fan Club ran a contest in connection with the release.

Participants had to identify how many times Johnny vocalised the word 'I' on the new LP. The draw was announced for Monday, June 21st, at the Los Angeles International Airport. All were invited.

The day dawned the way it inevitably does in California – sunny. Inside the windowed hall several members of Johnny's staff were waiting. They included public relations gentleman Skip Heinicke, executive secretary Maxine Sibley, Lew Gilbert and Robert Scott. Fans were gathered in an assortment of groups. Their nervousness showed as 12.45, the arrival time, approached. The flight landed and passengers disembarked and they, like those who had come to meet them and general onlookers, tended to form their own groups as they wondered what was happening.

The fans first sightings were of the group, Gil Heigers, Randy Barber, Jim Ganduglia and conductor James Barnett. And then came the man himself, equipped with faded blue Levi jeans, royal blue and white striped T-shirt and white sneakers. His eyes were covered with mauve-tinted glasses which – for those who were not familiar with his appearance – partly hid his identity from curious bystanders. He carried a cassette player inside its shoulder-strapped leather case, and a shoulder-strapped luggage bag.

The fans swarmed forward; handshakes, gifts and flowers were their offerings. Photos were taken. He made his way towards the area set aside for the contest 'ceremony' and with one hand and arm clutching the flowers he had been given, he plunged the other into the box which held the names of contest entrants. The winners' names were called out and duly recorded. The main event was over. Autograph-time followed before he eventually bid goodbye to his huffing and panting army of followers, as he slid into his limousine and purred away into the afternoon. Maria rated his staff an undisputed 'ten out of ten' for organising Airport '76.

In 1977 he had American bookings as well as dates in Britain which included three concerts at the prestigious

London Palladium, known to some as the 'home of the stars'.

In 1977 he became the first US performer to give multi-racial concerts in South Africa.

Yet, in spite of all this activity, many felt a career-booster was needed. The seeds of a new career growth were sown as the year drew to a close.

During the first half of December 1977, Johnny toured Mexico and on his return discussed plans with producer Jack Gold, which were enacted at the beginning of 1978. A whole month was devoted to recording with Gold at A & M Studios in Los Angeles his next LP, 'You Light Up My Life'. A single of the LP's title song had been a tremendous hit for Debby Boone, daughter of Pat, and was seen by many as a religious offering. Two of the numbers were recorded with CBS artiste Deniece Williams: 'Too Much, Too Little, Too Late'; and 'Emotion'.

A seemingly endless North American performance schedule found Johnny in Florida and the Pacific North-west, through to the end of January 1978. Early the next month, 'Too Much, Too Little, Too Late' started to make significant advances on progressive black and R & B radio stations, and Johnny was being rediscovered once more, and this time by legions of teenagers who dug this guy with a voice quite unlike any other they had heard.

Markets which had never proved strong for Johnny since his earliest years in show business opened up to him once more. The media in America went mad – and therein was the key to the question why the record eventually gave Johnny and Deniece a chart-topper and a Top Ten placing in Britain. In the States, Johnny had TV appear-ances on the *Tonight Show*; NBC's *Darling I Love You*, their *Valentine's Day Special*, and the *Mike Douglas Show*, and he toured triumphantly through Mississippi, Louisiana, and the Lone Star state; San Antonio, Austin, Fort Worth, Dal-las and Houston. 'You Light Up My Life' was issued on March 3, and the next day Johnny and Deniece were in Los Angeles, appearing together on television for the first time as they videotaped *Soul Train*. A week later, the duo were again singing nationwide on television, where they performed the hit 'Thank You, Rock 'n' Roll', the special based on the premiere of the film *American Hot Wax*. Seven weeks later, Johnny was off to Europe for three weeks. The tour included two weeks at the Olympia Theatre in Paris with Jane Oliver. One-night concerts in Antwerp and Amsterdam followed. His visit climaxed in Britain, when he appeared on Supernight, a World Colleges fund benefit command performance which was attended by a member of the British Royal Family, Prince Charles. Deniece Williams flew across the Atlantic for the occasion to sing a duet on-stage with Johnny. They also appeared on *Top Of The Pops* and the BBC TV *Val Doonican Show*. Johnny was to appear on Val's show for the second time in 1980.

He spent the remainder of April back in the studios with Jack Gold, and once more with Deniece on sessions which would yield their LP 'That's What Friends Are For'.

May 1st saw Johnny opening a three-week season in the Mid-West, which included a week at Cleveland's Front Row Theatre. While he was getting ready to set off for the Mid-West, it was announced that the LP 'You Light Up My Life' had gone gold, and twenty-four hours later there was gold certification from the RIAA for the single 'Too Much, Too Little, Too Late'. To achieve two US million-plus sellers was pretty good for a guy who had been twenty-two years on the music scene.

Summer saw some slackening in Johnny's busy schedule. The main event was a week in June at Harrah's in Lake Tahoe, and in July there were dates at Buffalo's Melody Fair, the Westbury Music Fair and Connecticut's Oakdale Music Fair. In July, Johnny and Deniece saw their LP 'That's What Friends Are For' pass the million sale mark.

Johnny busied himself with television, including *Dinah!*, *The Merv Griffin Show*, and on the syndicated movie premiere special, *Weekend of Foul Play*. In mid-September he had another week at Harrah's before visiting Britain once more and taking in an eight-week tour in which he visited fourteen cities and included Dublin and Jersey in his itinerary. The concerts were a sell-out. Derek Block's efforts in previous years had paid off. While in Britain, Johnny also recorded a special interview for the nation's top-rated chat programme, the *Michael Parkinson Show*.

Back home he spent October and November with Jack Gold putting the finishing touches to yet another LP, 'The Best Days Of My Life', which he had begun recording during the late summer and early autumn. It was issued in 1979.

It seemed an ideal title for the year Mathis had just had, a year in which Johnny experienced one big success after another. It was an amazing twelve months. His adrenalin flowed with the kind of electric charge which had characterised the first dizzy days of success when he was a mere youngster. But now he was in his forty-fourth year, yet the buzz was the same. And who was to say he didn't deserve it – he had worked hard enough.

At the end of the year he could reflect on the hysteria he had created yet again in the record and showbiz worlds. He was once more hot property, and even the kids liked him.

He could survey the endless magazines and journals which had penned articles about him, or about him and Deniece. Some of them had given the two a front page, among them the US magazine *Soul*. Johnny and Deniece were pictured lightly cuddling each other and wearing the happiest of smiles. The headline read – DENIECE AND JOHNNY RUSH THE ALBUM THE PUBLIC DEMANDED.

Judith Spiegelman's article explored the whys and wherefores of Johnny's recent career where hits had become few. He told her:

'The music business is so eclectic and so constantly changing that in order to be heard on radio you have to fit the programming style to get one of those "Top Forty" slots. It got kind of frustrating for us because I don't think our records were loud enough.

'You turn the dial and all you really stop on are the big, powerful stations with the big sound. We simply weren't sounding "big" and we weren't getting played on those stations.'

She asked how his record with Deniece broke this seemingly impenetrable barrier. He said the record was good but believed the potent factor lay in the voice quality. The two gelled.

'I sorta give a beautiful cushion and she penetrates like a thunderbolt, bringing up all the nuances and just making it happen. We're like race horses when it comes to doing things; we work very quickly together and things get popping real fast.'

Obviously the two had a mutual musical admiration for each other. As Johnny said:

'When I sing with Deniece it's a very natural thing. I don't really sing any different than I ever sang in my life. I do sing a few notes that she chooses for me that she thinks are better notes. I ask her, I plead with her, "Give me some notes, I'm tired of singing this note and this note." And she gives me notes. . . "Sing this, sing this" – and it's fun and inspiring and interesting. But we're not in competition; we're in harmony and that's the most important thing, I think, to anyone who goes into any project . . . you can't just throw two people, just because they're talented, together. You have to have the whole thing.'

Judith Spiegelman told her readers of the impression she gained from watching the duo recording:

'Suddenly this was no ordinary excellent Mathis album; it had something special – Niecy. And Niecy brought something special to both the recording studio and their performances together. The sing facing each other, in performance and in the studio, and the electricity heard in the recording is visible, animating the usually staid Mathis and eliciting from him the most uninhibited deliveries of his career.'

There was one rather controversial affair which sprang from Deniece's hit with Johnny, when Johnny appeared on the Johnny Carson *Tonight* show. It seemed that Deniece had walked off the stage just before she and Johnny were to have appeared.

Apparently, she was informed that only Johnny would be talking with Johnny Carson, and Deniece took umbrage at this, also objecting to the fact that there was no dressing room for her, and it was suggested that she should use the basement where several members of the band were rehearsing.

'I wanted to walk out of that door exactly the way I walked in. And that's what I did,' she said.

According to *Tonight's* producer, Freddie De Cordova, she had been booked on the understanding that, as with most newcomers, she would not appear on the panel with Carson. He said Deniece had been booked as a singer and nothing more. He explained there was a limited number of dressing rooms, and for good measure pointed out some very famous all-time greats of show-business had changed in the basement.

'We made a professional mistake because it was planned that Mathis would talk about her and the record. We feel it was a silly decision on her management's part for her not to appear.'

Johnny went ahead and acted as if he were scheduled for a solo booking on the show. But at least Deniece, or 'Niecy' as the magazines call her, had the final satisfaction of knowing that her record with Johnny was a worldwide smash and that it had hastened her own growth into international recognition. Whatever the rights and wrongs of the *Tonight* situation, the outcome did not affect the coverage she was picking up from relevant musical journals.

'I would really like to feel my music is universal – it's not just R & B, not just pop – and with something like this record with Johnny, there are going to be a lot of people who never knew my music who will hopefully now tune into it,' she said. 'I'm really all for experimenting and this [her recording with Johnny of 'Too Much, Too Little, Too Late'] has been a beautifully successful experiment! It's definitely opened doors for me because, although the first single I had, "Free", crossed to a lot of pop stations, it didn't go quite as far as we all thought it might.'

Deniece had, of course, been touring with huge success with Earth Wind & Fire through the States, and as well as future work with Johnny, she had planned her own LP under the production of ace man Maurice White.

Jack Gold was obviously ecstatic with the whole affair. He had first dealings with Johnny around the mid-seventies. He was current head of A & R at Columbia. They had recorded several LPs together, including 'Romeo and Juliet'; 'A Christmas Album'; 'Raindrops'; 'Close To You' and 'Love Story'.

In 1976 Gold had described Johnny as an enormously talented person who had given a great deal of thought to the vocal process. Gold felt it was a voice which could do most things, and he mused on how sometimes in the studio a track would seem perfectly acceptable and Johnny would suddenly say they should try once more. Usually the ensuing result was a perfect take which sometimes made it seem as though he had been kidding all the way through and that, really, he could have done it the first time.

Gold – at this period in 1976 – felt that Johnny was best when he was recording a 'sensitive-type song', but he underwent a change of opinion in 1978. Gone was the sophisticated, night-club singer for older people, and in its place came the contemporary charting artist. Gold felt great joy at seeing Johnny do so well and reemerge as a potent musical force once more.

'He's the best singer of pop songs in the whole world, and he's singing better than at any time in his life. He's gone way beyond what I can teach him.

'I felt that if Johnny and Deniece sold a million records, the first 250,000 would be hers because she got them to listen, and the other three-fourths would be his because they were so shocked that he could do it.

'People were astonished and pleased by Johnny's emergence as a black participant. . . The first time I heard the single on the radio, a black DJ said, "Well, I guess we know what side of the fence he's standing on with this song." There's a lot of black awareness in Johnny.

'I'd been looking for a black singer to work with Johnny for one and a half years. . .' Gold added that Columbia's vice-president, Don Ellis, had at first suggested Minnie Ripperton, but the various details could not be finalised for one reason or another.

Gold was rather worried at what might come next. He said in 1978 he was scared to death – 'what do we do now?' was his question, with the comment 'Johnny can't go back and be what he was, but do we leave that behind forever?'

'You Light Up My Life' gave Johnny his first Top Ten US album since 1966. In the UK it took over a million pounds and there, as in America, it heralded a new popular phase for the artist.

For Gold his involvement in giving Johnny a hit album and his first Number One pop and soul recording after twenty-one years of striving was a momentous happening. He suffers from Parkinson's disease, a neurological disorder of which the chief symptom is involuntary shaking. Writer Paul Green reports how Johnny was asked by someone in the office how he managed to work with Jack in view of his continual bouncing around. It seems Johnny threw the guy an LP and told him to go and listen and see if he couldn't figure it out.

Gold was especially moved by the reply and told Green how he once had good weeks and bad weeks, but that in 1978 he ran the gamut each day for some twenty minutes as nothing much functioned.

In Green's final quote from Jack Gold, the producer describes his disease as one where progress could not be expected, and having said that, he added:

'That's why given the talent and application Johnny's got, rather than do ordinary things I only want to do great things, and make great records with him for another year, or two or three. No one knows how long anybody lasts.'

It was a brave statement deserving of applause.

1979 saw Johnny break an established three-year tour sequence of visiting Britain, but at least he had quality LP products to keep his name very much to the fore. February saw the British release of 'The Best Days Of My Life'. The title track was Gold's first new composition in years. Side two featured Johnny and Jane Oliver singing 'The Last Time I Felt Like This', the Berhman-Hamlisch theme of the Universal movie *Same Time Next Year*, based on the Broadway show. It was an association more familiar to Americans than to the British. Johnny had sung with Jane a number of times, and she had been support to him far back in 1977 when he played The New Greek Theatre, Griffith Park, Los Angeles, for the eighth time since his first concert there in 1960.

Oliver was a Brooklyn-born artist with an intense and dramatic approach which led to comparisons with Barbra Streisand, Edith Piaf and Judy Garland – if nothing else, the association with such names more than suggested her quality.

On this particular occasion, her set lasted thirty minutes and it was remarked that she was too gifted a performer to be placed in anyone's shadow, that she possessed both vitality and a compelling sense of artistic challenge.

The LP also contained pop songs familiar to American ears like Pattie Austrin's 'We're In Love' and 'The Bottom Line' from Lambert and Potter. Of the brand new material, one was welcomed by British disco fans especially – this was L. Russell Brown's, 'Gone, Gone, Gone'.

CBS brought it out as a single. It spent ten weeks in the British charts, and reached Number Fifteen. In America it meant nothing in chart terms. It is difficult to explain why Britain should have gone with the record and the States not. Record people will say it's just another example of the vagaries and indeterminate nature of public taste. In both countries Mathis' LPs continued selling well after their release. The Americans had bought 'You Light Up My Life' in huge quantities, and it slowly gathered momentum across the Atlantic. It had been described by reviewers as a super-tuneful package which featured yet again the talent, technique and excitement of Johnny Mathis. One journal had asked the question 'Why is Johnny Mathis among the most popular balladeers in the world?' And answered it quite simply: 'His magnificently mellow voice and heart-felt delivery always brings out the best in a song. And Johnny's one of our most contemporary vocalists, with the ability to take any musical style from rock to country and give it that Mathis appeal.'

Johnny ended the seventies by participating in the Hollywood Christmas Parade, an event which had begun as far back as 1928. The event promotes the entertainment industry and sets the mood for the Christmas season. Maria Niemela calls it 'Yuletide Glamour'. In the 1930s, the parade included the stars of the film industry, the likes of Jimmy Stewart, Bob Hope, Claudette Colbert, Bette Davis, Mary Pickford and John Wayne. It gradually became the largest celebrity-participant parade in the States. In international television rankings, only the Pasadena Rose Parade hauls in more viewers.

The evening of November 25, 1979, saw a million spectators in the streets of Hollywood as two hours of floats, marching bands, equestrian groups and an estimated one hundred stars of film, television and radio, slowly wound their way round the three-mile route.

Johnny – not a newcomer to participating in the Parade – travelled on a four-tiered float that represented the Los Angeles radio station KMPC. Station DJs accompanied. Maria recalls Johnny was wearing a dark green sweater with soft white-and-red-pattern stripe across the chest and upper arms, dark trousers, and a white collared shirt. Local TV station KTLA used Johnny's US Christmas release, 'Christmas In The City Of Angels', to introduce their coverage of the affair. And to Mathis fans present, it was a 'spine-tingling sensation to hear his beautiful voice singing about Christmas in Los Angeles, just as the two giant Christmas trees at the beginning of the Parade routes were lit and the grand red and white street-width banner announcing the 1979 Hollywood Christmas Parade came into view.'

During the Parade, television station KTTV had its announcer Bill Welsh stroll around the floats and interview various celebrities. Johnny told him his new single was a personal Christmas greeting to *everybody*.

There was another special Mathis tinge to the last Christmas of the decade. Johnny's picture was displayed at two locations, on Sunset Boulevard and in Hollywood Boulevard, where, as part of an old tradition which was revived in this year, lampposts along the parade route were decorated with tinselled wreaths and a picture of a celebrity who was taking part in the festivities.

Maria also tells of The People's Gallery, a California firm which furnishes the shopping malls of Northern and Southern California. These preparations include Mall Graphics, posters which adorn the inside and outside of the shopping centres. Johnny has been the only entertainment personality to have had a poster of himself suitably displayed over a ten-year period.

Maria told her members: 'Johnny's Christmas single . . . the Hollywood Christmas Parade . . . the lampposts along Sunset Boulevard and Hollywood Boulevard, the Mall Graphics at the shopping centres . . . this is Mathis land.'

So all became well for Johnny in the seventies – the upsets of the sixties were forgotten, and in looking forward to the eighties, he had thoughts of a Silver Anniversary.

5

Continuing Quite Happily

'JOHNNY STAY BEAUTIFUL' was a message from one advertiser in the *Billboard* magazine supplement of 1971 when Johnny celebrated his fifteenth year in show business. By 1981, when Johnny had his Silver Anniversary, it seemed very true.

His friends and associates gathered for a very special commemoration dinner, and there were other celebrations, in addition to a busy media schedule, as everyone wanted to be with, or meet, a guy who was running strong twenty-five years in the music business. The music industry made its own award by giving Johnny the 1981 *Spirit Of Life*. Hundreds of Johnny's admirers from the music world gathered for the occasion.

For British fans, there was the joy of organising a dinner on September 30th, and knowing that Johnny was in the country, on tour, and would be the guest of honour. But this was 1981. 1980 had its busy schedule of TV, media and concert performances for Johnny.

In American terms, one of his television bookings was yet another appearance on the top-rated Johnny Carson *Tonight* show. Originally intended for April 28, it didn't happen until December 16. Carson was on hand with a conservative grey suit, suitably brightened by a red tie. Johnny wore his familiar dark blue blazer with insignia on the front pocket, white trousers, shirt and shoes. The tie was dark blue with a thin white diagonal stripe. The set was suitably adorned to give it Christmas appeal – large red poinsettia plants, and an enormous 'pannelled-window' wall which gave the impression that the guests, compere and audience looked out onto a peaceful country snow scene. Johnny sang his 1976 chart topper, 'When A Child Is Born'. He sang other songs, and they talked of the impending Silver Anniversary, with Johnny saying how he had come to New York in 1956, a rather frightened kid.

'To be celebrating twenty-five years of just having a job is kind of outstanding!'

Carson, quick as ever with the follow-up, added:

'You've got a little more than a job,' eliciting from Johnny a noticeable chuckle.

Carson's final words were: 'I've said this before. Every time you are on the show you seem to sing better and better, with age!' It was a remark which Johnny appreciated.

Johnny's other appearance with Carson was at the time and date scheduled, August 27. On this show, Johnny was joined in a singing duet by Paulette McWilliams. They sang the LP title track, 'Different Kinda Different'. On this occasion, Johnny was nursing a cold, but added, 'I have to work anyway!'

He also made a major TV programme in Britain in 1980. His UK tour had begun on April 27 at Eastbourne as part of a long, 29-day schedule with forty-eight dates and nineteen different venues. During the visit he was pencilled in for the popular BBC TV *Val Doonican Show* for Saturday, April 16. He arrived, knowing his 'Tears And Laughter' album had reached Number One in the British charts, and with all its success it had been designated as 'LP of the week' on BBC Radio Two. It was Johnny's luck to find real British weather on the evening. It was cold and wet, but at least he arrived in warmth, though some fans who decided to arrive a couple of hours before the doors were opened were hardly in a similar state. They huddled together in the portals of the BBC's Shepherds Bush empire.

Obviously, it was Val Doonican's show, whatever the strong contingent of Johnny's supporters might have felt! Eventually it was time for the man, who was introduced as the person who, like good wine, kept getting better and better. It was the moment for wild cheering and clapping as the strains of 'Wonderful Wondeful' were heard. And there he was, in white shoes, white crew-necked T-shirt over which he was wearing a navy blue zip-up jacket.

'Wonderful Wonderful' was followed by 'Three Times A Lady'. Doonican, at the song's completion, walked towards him and, for all intents and purposes, appeared ready to shake his hand in warm appreciation. Instead he gestured as if he was teeing off on the golf course. It produced a big smile from Johnny, and then they did shake hands. The two of them sang 'Laughter In The Rain' together. After prolonged applause. Johnny's fans realised that that was it from their hero. The show went on, a little empty now.

There were concerts in the States and Britain. One of the US shows was in Miami, where the local paper, *The Miami Hurricane*, declared that Johnny used his stunning voice as a framework for emotional outpourings, and added, 'He fully conveyed his mastery of music. His interpretations are honest – worlds away from the emotionally stunted readings of some of his peers. The most telling moment of the evening was his rendering of ''Betcha By Golly Wow''. Granted, the title is laughable and the words are simplistic. But the resources of this song are limited on the surface. Mathis brought out the genuine sentiment of the words, and elevated the folkish quality of the music. He showed the real value of a song goes beyond the special gifts inherent in the words and music – the interpretation is the key.'

The only negative reaction from the paper's entertainment writer, Helen Alpert, came from Johnny's inclusion of the songs 'Ease On Down The Road' and 'I Will Survive'.

'There was no need to incorporate rock. Would Horowitz or Rubinstein leave Chopin for 12-tone or atonal music? Hardly. By the same reasoning, the MOR ballads of Mathis are a distinctive musical style and form an outstanding musical evening of their own right. Tunes by the likes of Dietz and Schwartz, Jerome Kern and Jimmy McHugh would have added variety and paid homage to the art of popular song.'

Johnny's version of the Gloria Gaynor hit 'I Will Survive' has annoyed other reviewers, one of them the well-known US music commentator, Ira Mayer. However, Johnny's close fans regard it as a highlight of his more recent performances.

A major British concert of the year took place at the Royal Albert Hall, London. *Stage And Television Today* reviewed the concert by first setting up the case for the ideal musical presentation: 'The essence of music in performance is creation through interpretation and in the popular music field there is no better example than Johnny Mathis. With little to offer in the way of showmanship, he succeeds time and time again in holding audiences simply by the way he shapes and moulds a song, bringing out any depth in the lyrics and subtly forcing the melody upon our consciousness, partly by the skill of his phrasing, partly by the extraordinary quality of that distinctive voice.'

It was further proof of Johnny Mathis' undiminished vocal powers. And the durability of his vocal appeal was made apparent in his twenty-fifth year in the business. In one sense, it was 'business as usual'.

There was a week's engagement at the Performing Arts Centre in Milwaukee, Wisconsin. At the beginning of 1981 there was plenty to occupy people's minds, including TV tapings, newspaper and magazine interviews, music rehearsals, photographic sessions, wardrobe selections and the task of finalising the year's tour details, which, apart from Britain, took in Australia.

He appeared at the outset of 1981 on a number of American TV shows, including one of America's newer television talk-shows – *The John Davidson Show*. When Johnny – looking smart in his three-piece dark grey suit, white shirt, dark grey stripes on light grey background tie and black shoes – bounced on stage and fell into the massive white sofa on the stage-set, it was to Davidson's words: 'Don't you love the way he walks out. "Well, it's just me, guys." Only twenty-five years of making great entertainment.' A great white '25' shone on the backdrop and Johnny – accompanied by his own group of musicians – sang a hits medley of 'It's Not For Me To Say', 'When Sunny Gets Blue' and 'Chances Are'. As Johnny finished his greatest hits set, Davidson joined him, pushing a little wheeled table towards the singer. It held an enormous round all-chocolate cake, decorated with a white '25' and with twenty-five white candles on top, and white musical staves and notes along the sides. Davidson placed an affectionate arm round Johnny – who was looking pleasantly surprised – and exclaimed: 'Twenty-five biggies! Congratulations! Happy Anniversary! Twenty-five more! There's only one Johnny Mathis!'

Johnny was summoned to the task of blowing out the candles which he did, and quickly. All twenty-five were expunged in one hearty breath – which says something for his lungs!

And there was the honouring of Johnny at the Grand Ballroom, of the Beverly Hilton Hotel on January 9. Johnny expressed his pleasure at the effort but felt it was some time yet before he would be ready for a big retirement blow-out.

It was a night of nights for people who had travelled the years with him. A detailed description is given in a later chapter 'Performance'.

It was during this period that Johnny told journalists of his involvement with top production team Bernard Edwards and Nile Rodgers, who had been partly responsible for a string of hits which had emanated from artists Sister Sledge, Diana Ross and their own group, Chic. The Edwards-Rodgers team had become known for the rather punchy, up-beat, discofied nature of their recordings. It was an association which Johnny enthused over.

'I think they'll write some wonderfully romantic songs for me, but they'll bring them in for me very soon.'

So he said in January, and an eventual recording schedule was settled and enacted.

The tapes from this association have only seen the light of day in the offices of recording companies and Rojon. The feeling is distinctly cold. The management is convinced neither producer knew anything about Johnny's music or style. And there is the story which manager Ray Haughn tells, of how the producers went away from CBS one fair day with a stack of Johnny's albums but without sufficient time to digest and hopefully appreciate. Both Johnny and Ray were appalled at the standard of lyrics and the monotonous repetition of musical notes which allowed for little if any vocal ability.

'My jaw dropped when I saw the material; the longest note was a quarter. I couldn't believe it. I think there was just one piece which could be termed a Johnny song. I think if the album was released in the States, it would have killed off Johnny; there might be more response in the UK. At least I feel a release there would not do the same amount of damage!

'And at the time when they were beginning to record Johnny, the two producers were involved with three or four other artists. I don't know why certain people had gotten it into their heads this would be a good project, though it might have seemed that way at first, before things developed.'

The result was unsatisfactory and ultimately disappointing for fans who were more than curious at this interesting mix of the production duo and Johnny. Later there was much criticism of an LP they had recorded with Debbie Harry of Blondie. Certainly the two producers and writers had previously inaugurated an exciting time in popular music.

For British fans, 1981 began with the various sections of The Mathis Connection (the official Johnny Mathis fan club), planning their festivities. In the case of the Newcastle branch, there was a special day at a hotel in (ironically) Manchester on Sunday, April 5. Other than food, the Connection promised raffles with prizes of some new, large colour posters of Johnny, UK Tour '80 jackets, copies of the latest compilation from America entitled 'The Best

Of Johnny Mathis 1975-1980', and a number of singles featuring Johnny's partnership with Gladys Knight – the single 'When A Child Is Born', coupled with 'The Lord's Prayer'.

There were celebrations elsewhere during the year, but even the best of parties and occasions can pale when compared with the chance of a front-row seat in a concert. Some British fans took to the skies, clearly unable to wait until he walked the theatre stages of England. These members of the British Johnny Mathis Connection, flying loud and clear their JMC and Union Jack badges, eventually sat, watched and made themselves highly emotional as they caught Johnny's concerts at the Greek Theatre in Los Angeles. Marie Wilson – one of those who made the trip – said their enthusiasm at the concerts and love for Johnny absolutely amazed the Americans present. It was described as a 'wonderful wonderful' occasion. Johnny seemed deeply touched by the warmth of the British contingent who, after all, were to take their flight back home and prepare for his visit. As a bonus, some members had been allowed to attend Johnny's rehearsal.

Some 182 British fans in all made the trip, which in entirety lasted fourteen days. Members – apart from attending five nights at the Greek Theatre – had a sight-seeing tour of Johnny's former home and school in San Francisco. Each member paid around £700 for the flight, hotel and tour fees. They set off from Heathrow with a surprise announcement coming over the plane's intercom from the chief steward:

'And your pilot today will be . . . Johnny Mathis!' Every flight they took there was a variation on the message: 'A special welcome aboard for the British Johnny Mathis Fans.'

Doubtless some of the 182 were present at The Mathis Connection birthday party on Wednesday, September 30, which was held at the Piccadilly Hotel, London, from 11.00 a.m. onwards. Guests were welcomed by the British society's President, Jo Baker. The occasion was graced by three hours of Johnny, and he dutifully posed for many photographs, read an amusing poem in praise of the Connection, and gratefully received a beautiful silver salver and a huge birthday card. The card contained all the names of Connection members who had made a contribution towards the gift. Naturally there was a huge birthday cake with appropriate candles, and in the form which had been witnessed at birthday occasions in America, he blew them out at one go. True fans were not surprised at this when they remembered the facts they knew well – his breath control and ability to hold a note for a considerable time. He sang two songs for the party gathering.

As he was preparing himself for departure, President Jo Baker called him back and informed Johnny that, as 1981 was the Year of the Disabled in Britain, they had decided to donate the money to the Stoke Mandeville Appeal, the appeal for the famous hospital for the handicapped, and there was a special gentleman who would receive the cheque. The President had given clues enough for the gathering to emit a considerable buzz, and for once shift its mind from the Star. To everyone's delight, Britain's most famous and popular DJ, television personality Jimmy Savile, OBE, walked in to a tremendous ovation. Briefly he outlined to Johnny Stoke Mandeville's point and purpose and the reason for the various appeals, and then accepted the cheque with obvious pleasure, thanking the Connection members. Johnny left soon afterwards and the assembled guests turned their minds to the affairs of the stomach and consumed a well-planned buffet lunch.

The large gift for Stoke Mandeville was as good as any proof that fan clubs – at least those of some artists – are not obsessively concerned with their star to the detriment of all else.

And British Johnny Mathis Connection members made another major effort for the less fortunate in 1981. Scottish members of the Connection approached the West of Scotland Wheelchair Basketball Team, who played under the auspices of the Scottish Paraplegic Association, and offered their services in raising funds. The Association said their biggest problem was in the field of transportation. They possessed an ageing transit van which was poorly equipped, and players without the support of their lower limbs suffered considerably from being thrown about as the van careered on sometimes less than perfect road surfaces.

The usual methods of fund raising were employed, which in British terms at least means sales of clothing and other articles donated by various people, the sale of freshly-made produce, cheese and wine parties, sponsored slims, sweet making and general collecting of money.

Eventually they had the chance of buying a disused Wimpey workers' bus. It was a dirty orange colour outside, part of the bodywork seemed fast unhinging itself from the main structure, the green seats were tattered, and dirt seemed the main occupant. The positive factor lay in some pretty sound mechanics.

The Connection members where soon busy cleaning and refurbishing. Scrubbing and polishing was the order of the day. But the basic problem was the fitting of a wheelchair lift. Obviously this was the most important item, since without such a device it was of little use to the paraplegic team. A discussion with the original makers gave momentary doubts as to its feasibility. However, the Connection members ploughed ahead. They decided they would risk cutting a huge hole in the rear of the coach. This was done. The coach did not disintegrate. A wheelchair lift was moved into position and the fitting process began, though at first little came from their efforts. Work was halted by members travelling to California for the purpose of seeing Johnny in concert, and while they were away the bus was left with the Strathclyde Passenger Transport Executive at their Larkfield Garage. They had agreed they would see the bus was painted, and it would be their contribution towards the International Year of the Disabled. The members set off across the Atlantic and took with them an artist's sketch of the project which could be shown to the Mathis management. The hope of members was a launching ceremony by Johnny.

Members arrived back in Scotland on August 3, 1981, and suffered a set-back and severe stifling of the ebullient state in which they had returned from a marvellous holiday – the bus was as they had left it. There had been a strike at the garage which – mysteriously it might seem – even affected the free giving of time to a worthy cause. Members were aghast. There were five weeks left before Johnny's visit. However, Larkfield Garage turned up trumps after all, and within a few weeks they had a gleaming red, white and blue vehicle with Johnny's twenty-fifth Anniversary Logo on the back and a Mathis Connection badge on the rear sides. The sides of the bus sported, in unmistakable lettering – 'West Of Scotland Wheelchair Basketball Team Donated By The Scottish Members Of The Mathis Connection'. The garage was back in popularity! It left two weeks for final interior decoration. Several raffles had raised £1,000 for this purpose. Two coats of lino paint was administered to a cleaned floor surface, the reupholstered seats were fitted, slightly less in number than the original so as to allow more freedom of movement, and the passage of wheelchairs, a bed was fitted for any player who might fall ill on a long journey, fitted curtains attached to the windows, and the chromework gleamed. Members were inspired and recharged by the news that Johnny, having seen the bus pictures, had agreed to forsake a day's holiday, and he would travel up to Scotland on Friday, 11th September.

He arrived at the Bellahouston Sports Centre at 12.45 p.m. Scottish Television and BBC cameras were present, and Yvonne Littlewood brought a film crew up from London with the purpose of including the event in a documentary she was making to celebrate Johnny's twenty-five years in music.

A friend of the Connection, Laurie Miles, flew up from London with his video camera to record the event for the members.

Johnny met leaders of the Scottish Connection, and then he was introduced to the Basketball Team and their coach, Robert Campbell. He appeared highly amused by some of the comments from the team, which Glasgow member May Toet says comprised lines like: 'Sorry, didn't catch the name, Johnny WHO?', 'We've got a spare wheel-chair here if you're feeling tired,' and 'Give us a song, Frank.' The formal presentation followed, keys, insurance and MOT. Johnny was presented with three photographs of the bus refurbished and another which showed the bus in its previous state. He posed with members of the Basket-ball Team, then inspected the coach, signed some photos, gave autographs, and suddenly it was two in the afternoon and time for him to go.

It was an impressive display from the star and from the fan club, and though it always sounds a trifle over-used as an expression – that day, the world seemed a better place.

In America Johnny was given the music business' the *Spirit of Life* Award, 'in recognition of his outstanding contributions to the Industry and professional achievements which have brought twenty-five years of joy and enrichment to the lives of countless millions throughout the world.' Hundreds attended the event. The Governor of California, Edmund G. Brown Jr, was present and made Johnny 'the first honorary member of the Governor's Council on Wellness and Physical Fitness'. The Lieutenant Governor, Mike Curb, read a letter from President Ronald Reagan, which congratulated Johnny on his twenty-fifth year as a record artist. There was even a special song from lyricist Sammy Cahn which he sang to the tune of 'There's No Business Like Show Business', changing the words to 'There's No Johnny Like This Johnny'. Tom Bradley, Mayor of Los Angeles, announced the week from July 6 to 11 would be Johnny Mathis week. Amongst other verbal outpourings, there was the statement that Johnny was 'one of the Music Industry's most prized possessions'.

To accompany the celebrations in the US, Columbia issued a sensually romatic song, 'Nothing Between Us But Love', with 'Deep Purple' on the flip side. The new LP – a double package – was aptly entitled 'The First 25 Years/The Silver Anniversary Album'. The songs were classics. The packaging was of the kind it should be.

During July most of the nation had a chance of seeing Johnny's *Portrait of a Legend*, which featured television clips from the previous three decades, and included the historic 1957 appearance on the *Ed Sullivan Show* and his BBC 1978 TV concert at the Royal Albert Hall. During August, he spent weeks at the Oakdale Musical Theatre, Wallingford, Connecticut, and the Blossom Music Center, Cleveland, Akron, Ohio. September 9 to October 3 saw him in Britain, making the birthday party among other things. He toured Australia and New Zealand from November 20 to December 13.

His first Australian concert took place on November 21 in Adelaide, and even though bookings only opened two weeks before the concert, there were 'house full' notices. Australian fan Joyce Griffiths felt Johnny looked very fit but thought he looked slightly plumper than the gentleman she remembered; however, she concluded that he looked better for it. The high spot was his version of 'Memory'. Johnny calls the country 'the end of the earth', and there were those who recalled his performance of two years earlier, which was far from his best. To their pleasure, he remembered the night and promised something rather better this time. His apology was seen by Alex Kennedy as 'charming as it was disarming' and the apology, and easy banter, set the mood of the evening. Kennedy felt the Adelaide audience was saying 'come back, Johnny, all is forgiven'.

And these fans who flocked to see the twenty-fifth Anniversary Johnny, what was their make up? *Superstar*, the British magazine of The Johnny Mathis Connection, printed research carried out by the President of the Johnny Mathis International Fan Club. From her 18,000 members, Maria Niemela used a computer and came up with the information that 73% of the members were under forty years of age, which, apart from anything else, suggested Johnny had considerable years of fan following ahead of him!

Ages 1–14:4.2%	Ages 20–24: 9.3%	Ages 30–34:19.9%
Ages 15–19:4.8%	Ages 25–29:17.9%	Ages 35–39:17.2%

Ages 40–44:12.0%   Ages 50–54:4.0%   Ages 55–92:3.2%
Ages 45–49: 7.5%

Beyond statistics, of course, is the more basic fact – for them there is one guy – Johnny Mathis.

The year 1982 showed no sign of the feeling abating. In Britain, as soon as Derek Block advertised the British concerts for 1983, his office phone lines were quickly taken up. A short strike at the London *Standard* saw main advertising in the national *Daily Mail*. All hell broke loose in Derek Block's office the first morning. I should know. I was there. Anyone who thought pop excitement was purely in the record charts of the moment would have found their theory rather disproved on that morning. You would have thought someone had announced this would be a 'farewell tour', and not the third visit in four years. But for others elsewhere, 1982 had also opened this way. Johnny was performing in Canada in January, with the usual plaudits coming his way. There was a slight incident in Vancouver on January 22nd. A rather over-zealous lady had sent him dozens of love notes and registered letters, and had informed him she would be sitting in the front row and demanded an audience after the show. Apparently she had a proposition for him, and it was coming sweetened with the offer of a cheque for $50,000 and a Lear jet. It was not taken up. Sweeter was the sound of a solid 27-piece orchestra, including a 10-piece string section, at the Opera House, Seattle, in January, where he played a two-date visit on January 25 and 26.

'Friends In Love' became his new American LP, and it included a duet with Dionne Warwick entitled 'I Got You Where I Want You'. The LP's title track – also a duet with Dionne – became the single and was released on Arista (Dionne's label), although in Britain it was CBS which issued the single.

NKR Productions began placing around the States a five-hour radio special on Johnny, entitled *Johnny Mathis – The First Twenty-five Years*. It was built around an interview Johnny had had with Wink Martindale, who will be remembered by many as the man who charted with 'Deck of Cards' in the fifties. The programme tape carried other interviews and vocal appearances from a host of music stars.

A lengthy American tour ensued between March 20 and September 25, and the Johnny Mathis show played on. The eighties-style Johnny showed no signs of faltering, and while he played the States, his favoured country across the waters was busy, with some of her JM fans planning their welcome for the hero's return in 1983. And if Johnny had no British visit planned for 1982, then at least they could be busy with their various Connection meetings. In Manchester, 170 people had gathered at the Portland Hotel in the city centre, and in December there was another gathering in the centre of Birmingham. Down in Exeter, Devon, though more precisely Clyst St. Mary, The Mathis Connection President, Jo Baker, was busily getting herself and the fan club services into smart order for the expected rush in April and May of 1983. At the very least she knew one headache would spread her way – fans without tickets and fans with tickets which were not in the front rows. But sadly, hall capacity is not endless, and not everyone can make the first ten rows.

Ah – the problems!

But even more important, what of Johnny as a performer? Johnny as the recording artist? Johnny as John, the man whose presence and voice has commanded attention from so many for so long? Read on!

6

Performance

'HEY,' SOMEONE SAID to Johnny one day, 'why do you make so many facial grimaces?'

And Johnny has admitted that his mouth is too big and his lips sprawl. But the critical voices have continued. And in the early days it deeply wounded the young, sensitive artiste who had been thrown into major fame after a minimum of time waiting in the wings.

But enough is enough, even for the most patient and tolerant of persons, and one day Johnny snapped back. His reply brought blushes to the faces of the critics. Johnny told of his home background; how his family, with relatively little money, had utilised the free dental clinics. These are rarely on a par with British free medical care. Johnny had problems with his teeth and the cavities were not filled. Instead, teeth were pulled out, particularly on one side, giving him a twisted mouth.

In brighter moments, he says 'I've got a deformity and I can't help it.'

But then there were other mannerisms which could eventually be conquered with the confidence of success, and expert coaching.

There was a time when Johnny said he closed his eyes, clenched his fist and sang as fast as he could to get it over with. His shyness is not to be doubted, but Johnny seems to be rather hard on himself. He's never been undisciplined or amateurish, a quick turn before someone else came with the real goods. Undoubtedly, though, performance has never been easy for him. He is fond of saying he is a singer and his aim is to sing songs, and that by and large it is not his province to cavort around in an attempt to sell himself. Yet his vulnerability endears him to audiences. Those sometimes taut, awkward gestures speak of his total concentration on voice and music. His voice is soft and comes with slight vibrato; it has been termed 'smoky' in texture, and it soars easily into falsetto territory. The critics say that he has the poet's understanding of some ethereal things, that his song interpretations, precise and magnetically enchanting, are part of his always-evident craftsmanship. There is talk of stylistic constancy, acceptable risk, an instantly identifiable voice. They say he chooses good songs, picks good people around him, and absorbs what's new selectively. In his time he's sung almost, if not all, kinds of modern music – soft rock, jazz, soul, country, gospel, rhythm-and-blues, show music, pop, disco, ballad and whatever else is left! But, no, he has not sung punk.

Johnny in performance comes with the minimum of fuss. He appears, looking slim, ever-youthful, smart and dashing in dress. He has a simple request to an audience: 'Sit back and relax.' He tells them what he has come to do: 'I'll sing for you.'

That's his *raison d'etre*, whether in Japan, Australia, back home in the States, on tour in Britain or in Europe. Wherever he is, there's usually just Johnny on stage – Johnny and microphone – and as writer John Coldstream of Britain's *Daily Telegraph* once expressed it, 'He commands total respect for his communion with the microphone – of which he is an unrivalled master – and his musicians.' He wrote this during Johnny's stay at London's Dominion Theatre, in October 1981, and earlier remarked: 'So if Johnny Mathis is in the mood for a pre-emptive strike against his lustrous CBS stable-mate [referring to Barbra Streisand who was reportedly in town and registering a treatment of Andrew Lloyd-Webber's feline *chef d'oeuvre*, 'Memory'], he might load a coach with the excellent orchestra which is evidently *enjoying its sojourn* with him this week; tuck under his arm the sheet music he has as an *aide-memoire* when performing this fascinating addition to a repertoire now twenty-five years strong; tape the song and sit back with the smile of, well, the cat who snaffled the cream, while it becomes the inevitable palpable hit.'

But then Johnny's eventual vinyl release of 'Memory' was pushed on to disc as a B-side, lest, so it is said, it might offend the lady or cause embarrassment to British CBS. Rumour is, of course, rumour.

In 1981, Britain's leading theatre-show journal *Stage* also picked up on Johnny and 'microphone', with editor Peter Hepple, who has claimed that Johnny is the best singer of romantic ballads in the world, saying: 'He does have another singular quality, that of a mystery that somehow adds to his appeal. Few singers can say so little between numbers, and fewer still command such rapt attention while they are singing. He has the trick of making notes hang in the air, so that we eagerly anticipate the next, and this may be due to his marvellous microphone technique. With Mathis, the microphone is almost part of the man, and we are seldom aware of its presence, so sensitively does he use it.'

Yvonne Littlewood, the famous and revered British light entertainment producer for BBC TV, is another who recognises Johnny's microphone technique. 'Absolutely brilliant, a lesson for anyone in sheer technique. The way he utilises the microphone is sheer chemistry as much as, say, his chemistry with the conductor. Johnny's microphone ability is as important as anything else in his act, but then everything in his act is of the highest standard. And he never gives the same performance.'

Few artists have lasted so long as he has, particularly in an international context. He more often than not appears without the support of high-flying chart singles, and so goes against the rather overdone dependence of promoters and venue bookers on presenting artists who have achieved so-called 'hit' records. But, as his manager says, there's never been a time when he has not sold records.

Every one of his American LPs has exceeded 250,000 sales. There have not been lean periods, although there may have been times when the newspaper column inches have diminished. Johnny feels his audience enjoy the same kind of songs he does, although on some occasions he has expressed a wish that radio programmers would be more adventurous in their choice of tracks rather than relying on the familiar territory of numbers like 'Misty' and 'A Certain Smile'.

'Some years ago I excluded all my old songs. A year later I put them back in.' He did so on the basis of demand and after observing other major acts, but qualified any presentation of popular recorded numbers by adding that there was no way in which he saw himself merely mouthing a studio performance. 'On a record, you're hearing what I felt eight months ago, and at this point in my life, you're hearing how I feel now. There is no way recordings can reflect what I feel in my heart.'

There was a time when recording had an adverse effect on Johnny the peformer.

'Mitch Miller told me about the difference between cutting a record and singing live. I was trying to make a record as I would sing to impress someone in person. Mitch got me out of that mould. But I do feel one of the main reasons I sounded so sterile in person for so long was the fact I was constantly recording. I've made so many records and was always thinking "record, record, record. . ." rather than thinking of the performing aspect.

'I don't think I'll ever fall back into that old trap, therefore there are so many things to look forward to. Especially the exciting new material that's available and the abundance I have to work with. Then, too, I can rework a lot of things and make sense out of them now, instead of just grinding them out like I used to.'

Johnny said this is 1971, and a decade later he feels the same way.

Of course, being a performer who has stradled four decades could have its problems. He might find himself –

even unconsciously – clinging to a particular era which had been good to him. Yet he has not so far stuck his head in that particular noose.

Yvonne Littlewood – who has produced British television programmes of his at varying times between 1962 and 1982 – has observed his programming over this considerable length of time.

'He's always contemporary. He is always hearing new songs and he chooses his book selectively. And it hasn't been easy for someone who does not write his own songs. We're in the era of the singer-songwriter and songwriters are not flush; it's hard to find people who write for others rather than songs they would like to sing.

'One of his finest moments of adapting to new material and in a sense making it his own was in 1977 with Stevie Wonder's song, "If It's Magic". He used simple harp accompaniment. Thelma Owen, the harpist, provided it. He was so thrilled with her that he's had her do it ever since, and even flown her to America. To him it was marvellous music and sound. And it was.

'I think in the television programmes he's done for the BBC he's often taken risks and done things he's not performed on stage. He rarely uses back-up singers. I mean, on record, he did with his big hit record "When A Child Is Born", but with us he's used the Mike Sammes Singers. We did "Come Sunday" by Duke Ellington, with harp and the singers. Beautiful.'

And, as she says, he has an enormous catalogue of material, a repertoire which is wide and varied and quite unequalled in the current quality market. He has spurned cheap material, even when it offers chart prospects.

Television, of course, is a different medium from stage, and Yvonne Littlewood, remembering 1967, believes even Johnny, with the limited movement of his early years, came across strongly.

'Yes, he's shy and he's shy on stage. I think part of my job as a producer is to get on friendly terms with someone. Time is very limited. We've not got two years, maybe we have a day and a bit.

'I've got to put him at ease. And remember the cameras and TV can be as far or as close as you want. It's a difficult medium. To get the right ambience is not easy; 6,000 in the Royal Albert Hall is one thing. We can get 400 in the BBC Theatre, that's different from 6,000, 4,000 and even 1,000. It's the question of ensuring, capturing the atmosphere. Well, there he is with this microphone skill, not a casual pick-up of a mike, with rapport with his sound man.

'You've got to show the essential artist. You can make or ruin someone within half-a-minute.'

She's pleased that he has made so many programmes with the BBC and there's been a special, trusting relationship. Obviously he – and his management – have been happy with the way he's been presented essentially as he is. There have not been kicking girls, knock-about comedians, jugglers or a pop group with a record to sell to clutter things up. He's also been spared the regular 'pick-me-up' which must occur on commercial channels where a song must follow the preceding advert which has already set a pace and feel, although too much perhaps can be made out of this point.

'I think – and 1962 is a long time ago, it amazes me really – he has matured as a performer and in performance over the years. He's always been tolerant, the nicest, always understanding in the studio and not dropped his high standards. Of course, he's had the best musicians, people who can work fast. Third-rate people are out. He didn't mind doing things again, if it came to it.

'He's got better. That marvellous voice – well, it's operatic – obviously he's more relaxed now. He can be singing when he's seventy. His performances have an unmistakable identity of their own. It's like his records. When I was first given him to produce, I ensured I went to hear him up and down the country, and studied his voice technique. I played all his records. You can drop the needle in the middle of any track and you know it's Mathis. I would have thought that in 1962!'

It's a view held by Johnny's one-time British agent, Vic

Lewis, who rates Johnny's vocal work on a par with the latter's hero, Nat King Cole.

'The voice – the greatest. He's a perfectionist. I can't praise it enough. I took him on spec years ago. When I persuaded Helen Noga she should bring John to Britain, it was really on the back of his recordings. I met him at her house. I think he appreciated he was wanted in Britain. He was a very shy boy.

'The risk was rewarding! There is no greater tribute – in some ways – than the fact of John filling halls twenty-five years after he first began his climb to the top. He's a super man and *the voice*! His performance has improved. In 1961 when I first presented him, he just stood there and sang. As I had been a band-leader and played with the best in the world, I knew the kind of musicians he needed around him.'

Lewis believes the eighties still hold some challenges for Johnny. He would like to see Johnny recording with a fully symphony orchestra, not necessarily singing classical music, but the in-between repertoire. He instances Barbra Streisand. She made an album of semi-classical material more for her own satisfaction than to set the cash tills ringing.

'Johnny can afford financially the self-satisfaction album. I know there's been controversy over these recordings but the nearest he has got to this must be the Mercury Recordings after he left Columbia. I think my favourite Johnny Mathis in record performance is found on the two albums he recorded with Nelson Riddle. In the eighties he's singing in a much lower register and it's a beautiful sound.'

To Vic Lewis, there is great pleasure to be gained from a Mathis performance; from the music, of course, but also from just observing his breath control and savouring his own individual quirk of hanging those notes out. He instances how you can be part of a silent audience of 3,000 people as they follow him through a song like 'Maria', and wait for the final high note! Johnny himself has observed he has thoughts on the finale of that song, and occasionally has doubts whether he will get up that high!

Lewis would have Mathis fans note the undeniable fact that singing in such a fashion carries inbuilt problems. 'It's a tremendous strain on the voice to use it night after night, and worse when an artist – like John – gives it his all. You inevitably get sore throats. When Johnny's been over there have been times when the doc has been summoned. Actually singers, whenever they feel low or have some other ailment, always blame the throat first.'

Johnny himself has known some of the cost. He talks less of sore throats than a mental torment which can eventually affect the whole attitude of mind and body:

'Mounting internal depression accompanied by building external success. I went through it not because of my music, but because of my unhappy private life. I didn't have any friends. My demanding work schedule made friendships impossible. I cared how the public felt about me. I took pills for physical strength to be able to sing the demanding songs I liked.'

The 'pill' phase and other attendant problems of the mid-sixties have been described elsewhere; the matter is resurrected here because it also relates to the subject of this chapter – performance. It is a symptom of the stress and strain which must accompany any public exhibition of person, voice and self.

Nowadays, those closest to Johnny say he is far more relaxed, at peace with himself. Someone like agent Vic Lewis would say golf is one of Johnny's 'soul' medicines (though recently, Johnny has become an addict of racquet ball).

Roy Rogosin, Johnny's musical director since 1969, and previous to this assistant music chief at Universal Studios, says Johnny has now blended his personal life with his professional life so that he doesn't jeopardize either.

But it's Derek Block, and his counterparts in other countries, who ensure the immediate peace of mind an artist like Johnny needs. He ensures dressing rooms and theatres are right. When a venue has a rather dull set of artists' rooms, Block makes sure they're refurbished. He makes the rooms seem lived in. 'I don't want rooms with no mirrors, no lights, chipboard and all that stuff. There are no problems. People are genuinely glad to put on John. Now he has done so many tours, I've ironed out the wrinkles.'

The right theatre surroundings enable Johnny to relax, at least when he's not undergoing what, to some people of similar age, would be excruciating exercises. In 1981 you could catch the 46-year-old limbering up in a major way. Before and/or between houses he would be skipping up and down the corridors and having two long sessions of gymnastics. Prior to his famous BBC TV shows at the Albert Hall, he refrained from talking. Block approached him during the day and said, 'OK Johnny?' Mathis covered his lips and pointed to his throat. He didn't talk for two days, though John must have been glad he spoke when he eventually made the move! It's his dedication as a professional, and it goes back to his early discipline.

Another way of aiding and relaxing Johnny the performer is ensuring he and the group stay at the right places. They may spend time at a hotel, country house, castle, just about anywhere, usually somewhere in the countryside. When the itinerary allows it – and it's generally planned that it does – John and the group stay at a central base from where they can be transported to gigs for quite a wide radius.

When they're in Britain, Derek Block arranges for a chef to be on permanent stand-by. 'If it's a hotel, I ring up and say we'll pay his wages. Too many places cannot serve meals at different times of day, and there's nothing worse than, say, coming back from golf mid-afternoon and finding no food, or worse still after a concert, and all they can do is cheese sandwiches. That's useless. I want John and the band to feel they don't have to worry about things. It's important, believe you me.'

Transport is the same – on tap. John has the choice of coach with video and all mod-cons; limo; sports car; train or air, and he has the option on the morning.

It's all appreciated, though. Block says he's had a few warnings of the kind which say 'you're going over the top, Derek, we'll be in Milwaukee next month, then what!'

Rogosin says Johnny's instincts are so sound that he is

able to make each performance seem as if it had never been done before.

'We have a relationship where, during a performance, he may change a tempo or hold a note without telling me about it. I stay with him all the time, but on the other hand, he always encourages me to do my own thing.

'He is always understanding of situations. If it's very bad, he is capable of tuning out. Johnny is an absolute professional.'

The musical director emphasizes the preparation involved. 'The curtain doesn't go up for him at show time, but many hours before, early in the afternoon. He concentrates all day on the evening's performance. Both of us become very quiet and introspective. There is very little communication. Whatever there is becomes very formal. He is very committed mentally and emotionally. He's very nervous until somewhere into the show. Then, there's a point, I never know when it's going to be, when there's a communication.

He talks of the moment when Johnny might turn and wink; during a bow he can whisper 'the orchestra's great' or the converse!

Not unexpectedly, praise for Johnny Mathis the performer comes from long-time friend and attorney, Ed Blau.

'He has become the consummate performer through his intelligence, astuteness and discipline.'

Johnny's manager, Ray Haughn, agrees with this assessment, and like Blau feels John is becoming a legend. Ruth Robinson, in a special Silver Anniversary supplement of *The Hollywood Reporter*, January 9, 1981, talked of his longevity and remarked how Johnny admired Bing Crosby and appreciates Perry Como, two performers who have had careers long past sixty-five, with Como still performing easily and well.

'He attributes their longevity to the fact they were careful and considerate with their ability to sing. So is he.'

For well known artiste and writer, Rod McKuen, Johnny almost personifies American music. 'I have known Johnny from the beginning, and in all of my own years of travelling and working, wherever the city or country, I can never remember walking into a single home, whatever the circumstances, and not finding a Mathis record in the smallest, most eclectic or haphazard collection. In twenty-five years musical tastes have zig-zagged, gone tumbling and fused one form to another, until it is impossible any more to discern what is really "American music". Throughout that time the single, steady, unshaking voice of popular music, whatever the style or dictate, has been Johnny Mathis. He is our Ambassador. Congratulations, America!'

Ambassador Johnny has been the 'voice' to adorn many first nights or special occasions. His 'pride' of performance occasions include an invitation to the White House when Richard Nixon was President, on the occasion of the visit of the President of Liberia. There was his visit to South Africa and a breaking down of racially segregated audiences. And he came to Britain and set sail on the last voyage of the historic *Queen Mary*, which departed from Southampton on October 31 and arrived at Long Beach, California, thirty-nine days later.

It's an invidious task to ask Johnny Mathis, his management, or his followers, to name favourite performing locations. There have been so many concerts, and many of those who have travelled with him over the years barely recall the early concert moments. But outside of the more obvious territories like Britain and the United States, he has a great affection for Brazil, with the visit to that country still recalled as a great moment.

Many fans obviously found the Silver Anniversary celebration outstanding. It is in sharp contrast to the memory of Johnny making one of his major early appearances at the Coconut Grove, part of the famous Ambassador Hotel, Los Angeles. The hotel had opened in 1921, and on that occasion the management had invited 3,000 guests from all over America. It was called 'a city within a city', with its location on the famous Wilshire Boulevard. Set in twenty-three acres of lush lawns, exotic gardens and splashing fountains, the hotel soon hosted some of the city's major social events and grandest celebrations, with the Academy Awards often being broadcast from its rooms. Much of the hotel's activity centred on the Coconut Grove, which was considered the most important nightclub, the swankiest supper club, the top night spot of Los Angeles. Guy Lombardo, Eddie Duchin, Paul Whiteman, Rudy Vallee, Ozzie Nelson, Ted Lewis and Phil Harris – great American dance bands – had worked there over the years. Dance contests played their part in shaping the Grove's history, with the famous participants including Loretta Young, Mary Pickford, Gloria Swanson, Barbara Stanwyck, Joan Bennett and Dolores Del Rio. Celebrated singers have included Bing Crosby, Frank Sinatra, Frankie Laine, Nat King Cole, Lena Horne, Dinah Shore, Sammy Davis Jr, Gordon Macrae, Tony Martin, Harry Belafonte and the very young Johnny Mathis. And for Johnny to follow such a list of luminaries was a sure sign in itself that he was going places.

He was engaged to sing at the Coconut Grove for three weeks in 1959. Johnny may have had a short career up to this point, but such was his growing reputation that he set new records for the Grove – his success was such that it resulted in the largest reservations demand in the history of the night club. It was even more impressive considering that he had appeared only eleven months earlier at the Crescendo, Los Angeles. Celebrities poured into the theatre which, on this occasion, had an atmosphere straight out of Arabian Nights. Potted palm trees, archways whose shape was stolen from a mosque and great plumes were everywhere. Warm and sensual colours were utilised, and mural paintings of exotic birds, monkeys and similar creatures adorned the walls. The stage was engulfed in pale blue mist and shaped in a semicircle that curved to meet little square tables all around. At the centre of each table was a muted red candle-light lamp, and there was seating for four.

Johnny was preceded each evening by a clever dance group, The Mattison Trio. He himself was accompanied by Freddy Martin and his Orchestra, and his own four-piece combo. His first number was 'Tomorrow Mountain'. He sang 'Cockeyed Optimist', from the musical *South Pacific*, and the ballad 'My Funny Valentine'; from *My Fair Lady* he took 'I Could Have Danced All Night', and Maria Niemela says: 'He nearly growled the statements contained in the lyric – goose bumps developed to accompany my chille spine.'

He also sang 'Goody Goody' and 'Day In Day Out'. There was 'There Goes My Heart', 'Let's Do It', 'The Lady Is A Tramp', and much more.

For the occasion he wore a black tuxedo and bow-tie. His hair was smoothed to the sides of his head, with strands of curls that swept high over the top of his head and came forward to almost touch his forehead.

Maria comments: 'His dark and innocent eyes looked especially enormous in relation to his narrow face. His mouth was wide, with full lips that parted to release high notes as well as low notes with the least amount of exertion.'

At the end of each show, Johnny would take his final bows and would then come down from the stage by way of some little steps to his right. He would weave his way through the tables and quickly move up the wide steps that led to a second tier of the room . . . and finally nearly to the main entrance of the showroom and out through an obscure door.

Maria Niemela says: 'What a thrilling time it was that January of 1959! It doesn't seem like half a lifetime ago . . . still only the years have passed, the memories are still vivid. At that point in my then single status life I concluded dramatically that the pursuit of happiness is always in order. And I proceeded to give myself the pleasure of attending five shows of Johnny's Coconut Grove debut engagement. It was an unheard of extravagance . . . but truly not one ever to regret. Now, in 1980, I sometimes chance to drive along Wilshire Boulevard and perhaps see the stately Ambassador Hotel, and instantly the projector in my head turns on and the scenes of Johnny in the Coconut Grove are leisurely portrayed on the screen of my mind. Thank goodness for the wonders of the human brain! And thank goodness for a life that has provided us with a beautiful and gifted human being to know and love and admire and enjoy . . . Johnny Mathis.'

Someone like Maria can talk of Johnny's Las Vegas debut at the Sands Hotel, in July of 1958, and of his visit soon after to Australia in the autumn. Early souvenir programmes include a photo of young Johnny in Australia, holding a cute and cuddly koala bear in his arms! At the Sands Hotel a beautiful oil painting of Johnny hung in the elegant casino – where there was a gallery of portraits with the stars who regularly appeared at the famous Copa Room. Among the luminaries were Frank Sinatra, Lena Horne, Judy Garland, Ella Fitzgerald, Sammy Davis and Nat King Cole. In those times, Johnny performed songs like 'Let's Do It', 'Wild Is The Wind', 'Day In Day Out', 'There Goes My Heart' and, of course, a hit like 'It's Not For Me To Say'.

And if Maria remembers his Coconut Grove booking with affection, she has the same attitude to a more recent Las Vegas affair in 1980.

They say there is no other city on earth quite like Las Vegas, the Monte Carlo of North America, which lies around 290 miles to the north east of Los Angeles but is easily reached by the super highway from LA to Vegas, which is smooth and straight, a four and a half hour drive through a rather bleak landscape of hills dotted with stunted juniper and pinon trees, and great sweeps of pungent sagebrush covered desert.

As Maria says, Las Vegas is home to the largest and most lavish of the world's spectacular resort hotels. It has three parts: the Strip, the Downtown Casino District and the City itself. The Strip is a glittering belt of dazzling marquees at night which almost makes nonsense of any division between night and day. The hotels are luxurious and those who come possess wealth. Tourism and gambling dominate Las Vegas, and there are the many famous nightspots like Caesar's Palace, the Hilton, Frontier, Riviera, Desert Inn, Aladdin, Sands (where Johnny appeared in 1958), Dunes, Stardust and MGM Grand.

In 1980, Johnny appeared at the MGM Grand Hotel, the Strip's newest, which claims itself as the world's largest resort hotel. It's an enormous $120 million, 2,100-room complex with two major showrooms, six restaurants, a film theatre, lounges, convention rooms, swimming, tennis, health clubs, a shopping arcade and (equally as large as the arcade) the casino. January 17th to 23rd was the Johnny Mathis season in the lavish Celebrity Room. He appeared in the 1700-seat room twice each evening, for a dinner show at eight and the late show at midnight.

Maria describes the Celebrity Room and Johnny's entrance: 'The silver curtain of the Celebrity Room lifted punctually for each performance to reveal a blue-hazed stage and the ladies and gentlemen of the orchestra, under the musical direction of Victor Vandacore. The overture was comprised of enduring Mathis songs that set the mood and prepared the audience for Johnny's arrival on stage. The familiar ''Wonderful Wonderful'' began, and soon Johnny could be heard from the wings. . . *"Sometimes we walk hand in hand"*. Suddenly he was there before his audience, beaming and smiling wondrously, looking splendid and slim and very handsome in his black tuxedo. The Las Vegas crowd greeted him with applause, Johnny went into his next number, ''I Believe In Love''. He sang with style and bounce and charm – and he perked up at the atmosphere to a peak of delighted expectation.'

And so he continued in the usual, familiar and much appreciated personal mood, which is free from distractions but benefits from clever lighting and a good overall presentation.

When he eventually came to 'Last Dance' (in the second half of his set, with the division featuring Jeannine Burnier) the showroom was covered with sparkling, dancing lights from a revolving, mirrored ball. It was an all-stops-out finish for Johnny.

Maria summarises the occasion by saying: 'The Celebrity Room had been filled with persons that were in Las Vegas to attend the gargantuan Home Builders Convention. A substantial percentage of these people had never before seen Johnny Mathis on stage. Conversations drifted throughout the showroom as it emptied . . . most of them expressing surprise and awe at how very great Johnny had been! It was a most gratifying and exciting thought to conclude that he had probably made thousands of new fans during his MGM Grand Hotel engagement. All over America, people would soon be returning to their homes, and when they reminisced about their trips to Las Vegas, they would remember that they had seen Johnny Mathis at the MGM Showroom . . . that singer that they had been hearing about for the past twenty-three years or so. Yes, and he'd sung those songs that they were acquainted with – "Misty" and "Chances Are" . . . and what a terrific job he'd done with the disco songs too! Perhaps they had lost their money in Las Vegas, but they would never lose the lovely memories of that time spent with the greatest singer of popular music that anybody will ever hear in any place.'

Of course there have been thousands of reviews and column mentions of concerts which have taken place. Dr R. W. Harris is one of many who has hugely enjoyed Johnny's visits to Australia. He recalls Johnny in Sydney, the cosmopolitan capital of the state of New South Wales. He played the Regent Theatre, once an old-time ornate interior movie theatre, but now set up for live shows.

Johnny appeared wearing an impeccable black dinner suit with a waistcoat, white shirt, black bow tie and patent black shoes. He sang his hits. He performed a Michel Legrand medley of four songs – 'What Are You Doing The Rest Of Your Life', 'I Was Born In Love With You', 'Summer Me, Winter Me' and 'Pieces Of Dreams'. During one performance Johnny adjusted his microphone, but it came to pieces, so after a muttered 'damn', he and Gil (his guitarist) reassembled it. Johnny then sang two songs from *Wiz*, 'Over The Rainbow' and the swinging 'Ease On Down The Road'.

Wynne Rollitt of Wythenshawe, Manchester, England, is one who recalls a very human incident at Johnny's second Manchester concert during his British 1980 tour:

'The performance was running late; a little girl walked shyly up to the stage with some flowers. John bent down, took hold of her hand and smiled, saying, "Hello, what is your name?" She told him; he then said, "the flowers are lovely, thank you, but should you still be up at this hour?" She smiled, hesitated for a minute and then went back to her seat. Then an attractive blonde lady walked up to the stage to give John her flowers, and he grinned at her and said, "Oh, you can stay up!"'

It would, of course, be untrue to say Johnny has always received wide acclaim for his performances, although the poor reviews are very few and far between. There was a lukewarm description of his concert in 1966 at London's Talk Of The Town from one music paper, the *New Musical Express*:

'He's opened on Monday, but was a disappointment to this writer. Admittedly, he got a big ovation from friends and fans, but his 70-minute act never got going. It was bogged down by so many slow numbers it got dreary . . . much better to have Mathis singing varied tunes on his own for thirty minutes instead of the slow, disjointed act we got (his set also featured Our Young Generation, who sang on their own).'

And *Evening Argus* writer, Tim Curran, after introducing Johnny in his review as 'an old-fashioned entertainer' and saying he gives 'a thoroughly professional show', remarked:

'He has the strange habit of singing a lot about lerv. There's unspoken lerv, wonderful lerv, and even lerv that would last until the bluebell lost its perfume. Perhaps he's been singing songs about it for so long he's bored with the word. Even in his tribute to Nat King Cole they tried to tell him was too yerng to be in lerv.'

But poor reviews, put-downs and send-ups are rare. For those who have travelled with Johnny through the years, he still – miraculously – retains the old magic. It was a theme well captured by Alan Niester in *The Globe And Mail*, Toronto, during Johnny's visit to Canada in June of 1982.

'There's a scene in the current hit movie *Diner* which is set in 1959, in which two of the film's central characters are discussing the relative merits of crooners Frank Sinatra and Johnny Mathis. The debate ranges back and forth until the first guy says: "Yeah, but when you wanna make out, whose records do you put on?" The second guy concedes. It's Mathis, and the debate is over.

'Now, twenty-three real-life years later, Johnny Mathis is still the kind of singer best suited to "making out" to. Last night, in the opening of an eight-night stint at the O'Keefe Centre, Mathis proved he was still the ballad singer's ballad singer.

'Not only does Mathis still sound as rich and full as he did when "Chances Are" first burned up the charts, he even looks pretty much the same . . . he still makes them sound fresh as ever.'

Ray Haughn says: 'Johnny's performances have always been praised. I really cannot remember a bad one. I mean there have been adverse comments on particular songs from time to time and always a reviewer is guided by popular taste as much as anyone is.

'I think the nearest to a put-down was a piece on one occasion in a Los Angeles paper. The girl who came along had intended to spend the evening reporting a folk-rock concert. At the last minute her duties were switched to accomodate a more senior person.

'She slammed the whole set though unfortunately for her some of her copy suggested she did not stay for some of the set. At the beginning I had given out a list of songs Johnny would sing. But he has the habit of changing things and he did so on this evening. He didn't sing some of the numbers which were printed.

'And there was the occasion in Adelaide, but the reason for the short set which brought later criticism was quite out of his control. There were two house and due to the late starting of the first because of operational difficulties the second house overan time and he had to finish. It wasn't Johnny's fault.'

Johnny captures both male and female with his

performance and many attend his concerts many times over. His visits become unique.

Yvonne Littlewood of BBC TV remarks how she met a real fan in the person of one of Britain's best known sportsmen, former Scotland goal-keeper Bob Wilson. She was attending a small informal dinner party for Johnny in London.

'Bob approached me and learnt I was producing a BBC TV show on Johnny and that I had worked with him before, ten years ago. He then proceeded to recount, shot after shot, all the numbers, and the presentation of the show.'

Yvonne calls this the 'real fan, the enthusiast'. And there are thousands and thousands of them to one degree or another, some famous and others not so.

Even manager Ray Haughn calls himself an 'enthusiast'! He was a fan from the first time he heard Johnny sing and he retains the same attitude.

'People somehow expect you maybe to be a little cool, especially after so many years of association with John. But I'm not. I've travelled with John for more years than I care to remember. I've been in studios, on TV sets, radio stations, and my admiration for him as an artist has remained undiminished.

'On stage he's a guy who is entirely different, a whole new personality. He never cheats his audience. I catch a bit of every show he does, sometimes a great deal more. Usually, though, there are many things to bother myself with, there may be a television crew or producer I must talk with and they've come to get their impressions.

'But when I can, it's the whole thing. Johnny is never less than good but when he's very good I always make the point of saying so. You have to do it there and then, that evening. If you say it the next morning there's a suspicion of an ulterior motive!'

The fact is this – Johnny Mathis is one of the all-time great popular music vocalists and performers. As the famous jazz singer Joe Williams once said, 'I'm grateful for this man.'

7

Records and Recording

It took six whole days to record and list from A to Z the song titles which Johnny has recorded on his British and American LPs, such has been his phenomenal output. It would be invidious and indeed impossible to provide a commentary on each and every LP let alone to accord this treatment to singles, demo and professional items and the re-packaged affairs which have accompanied the main output. Pop history tells of a guy who began recording in 1956. Plenty of people began recording in that year and some, like Johnny, made hit records. Virtually all of these have faded and rely on re-issues to resurrect their once-proud but short career. But Johnny Mathis? They haven't been able to stop him recording. It almost seems at times as if he lived in the studios and the guy on the road was a poser who busily mimed his recordings.

When Johnny had a singles hit the general pop fans and instant pop journalists thought he must be a pop star and they treated him accordingly. And when his singles didn't chart in the dizzy heights of the Top One Hundred they forgot all about him as they turned their attention toward the next supposed star. Unknown to them and yet well recognised by thousands and thousands across the world was in fact that this occasional pop single hero was in reality a quality artist. He sold LPs; each and every one has sold over 250,000 with the cumulative result of putting him into second place in the list of American all-time best selling artists.

The radio stations in the States – and Britain was substantially no different once her record industry flourished – played singles. In 1957 it suited the youthful Johnny to ride in the heights of the singles charts. But he was too good for the vagaries of a fluctuating youthful taste which likes to turn away from today's heroes and seek new ones for tomorrow. Different sections of the media did their best to fit the young Mathis into a conventional mould, but he and manager Helen Noga were unimpressed with the thought of bubble-gum and high-school hop music. Johnny for one thing was hardly the archetypal teen hero, although there were girls and guys who found him romantic. He was no great mover on stage. The reason for his longevity lies in the quality of his music, his vocal skill and sheer technique. Quality is occasionally seen to be rewarded in the pop world and from time to time Johnny had a hit single. He did equal Elvis in 1957 by having two records in the US charts of that year. The normal process was simple. A new artist has a hit and their next record sounds almost the same as the first, and joins the initial hit within weeks in the Top Ten. And then the artist fades. Johnny charted with 'Wonderful, Wonderful'. There was a time gap, no immediate similar-sounding follow-up and then he came up with 'It's Not For Me To Say', which joined 'Wonderful, Wonderful' in the charts. It was obvious that this guy was different from most of the rest.

America heard other singles like 'Chances Are', 'Twelfth Of Never', 'Teacher Teacher' and 'Come To Me'. They seemed to be relatively uncomplicated affairs! The backing was uncluttered, the voice was prominant, and the melody was obvious. They hardly stretched the artistry which he possessed. Indeed Johnny, reflecting on those early times, says: 'I had two categories in mind. There was what I called my serious singing and it came on the LPs. To get the market for those albums there was the other category, more frivolous, lacking the real content for a lasting career. But it was innocent enough, it wasn't bad, it was just bubble-gum, teeny-bopper and oh, there were

Above: An early publicity shot of Johnny.

Below: Johnny at home with his three brothers, three sisters, his niece and his parents, 1958.

Above: Johnny with 'Our Young Generation', the team of dancers who travelled with him and appeared at both Talk of the Town and The Prince of Wales in the early sixties.

Below: Johnny entertaining seven Mexican starlets after showing them around Hollywood.

The many faces of Johnny Mathis the golfer, at the Bob Hope British Classic in 1981. *(Courtesy The Mathis Connection)*.

Right: Johnny has always been a keen sportsman and he's as fit today as when he was an Olympic class athlete. *(David Vance).*

Below: As well as being a great high-jumper, Johnny's handy with a tennis racket.

Above: Johnny's sporting links are still strong – he is pictured here with Glenn Hoddle, rising soccer star.

Below: Johnny with his ex-manager, Helen Noga (far right), her husband John, daughter Beverly and friend.

Above: With attorney Ed Blau.

Below: With Ray Haughn, the manager who has done so much to help Johnny shape his career.

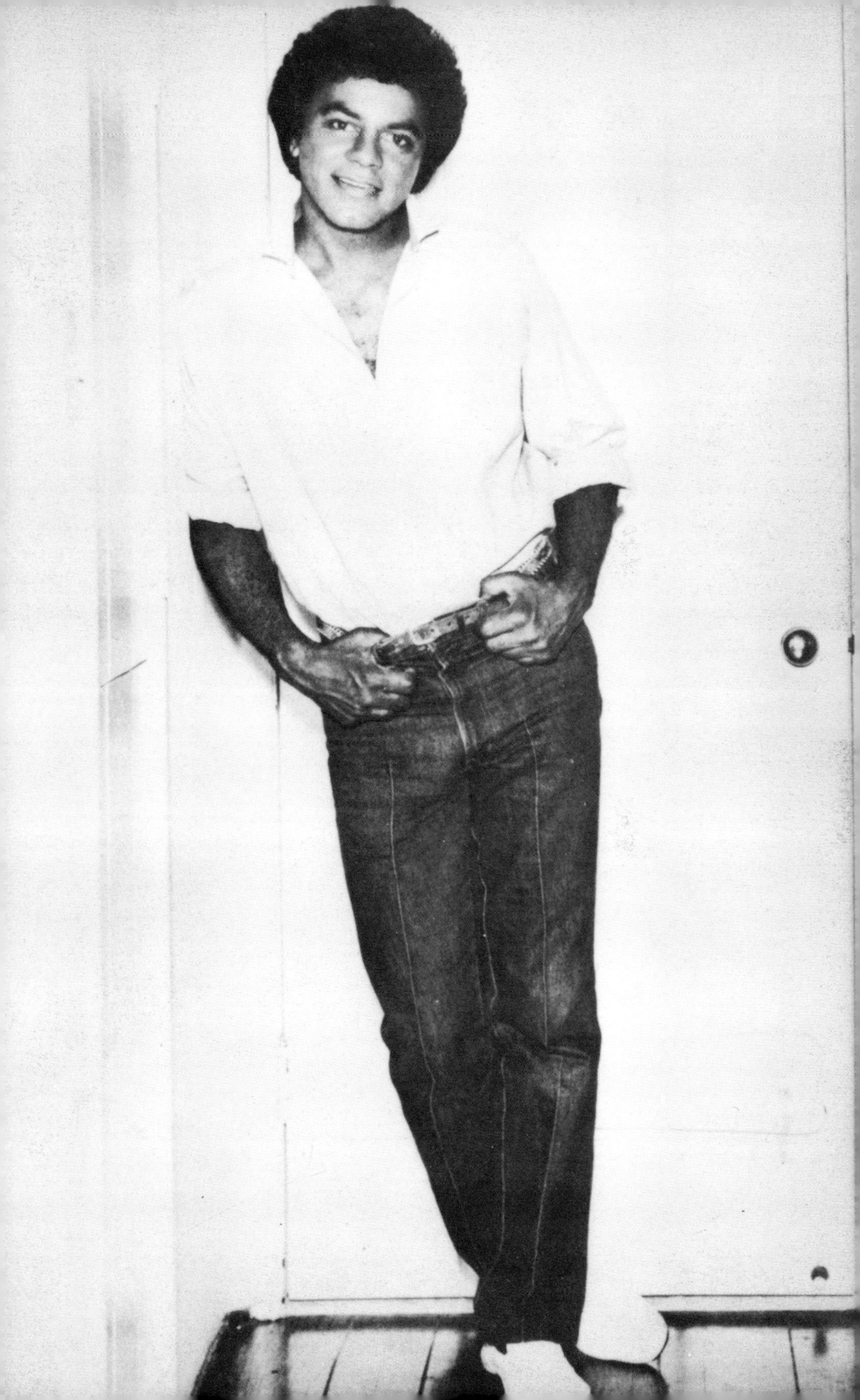

Left and Below: John loves London – and has been a regular visitor throughout his career.

Right: With Groucho Marx and Jackie Gleason; three great names in showbusiness.

Above: John with members of the British Mathis Connection fan club who travelled to Los Angeles to see him appearing at The Greek in 1981. *(Syndication International).*

Left: John tries on an Australian hat on his recent tour there. *(Courtesy The Mathis Connection).*

Johnny live on stage. (*Syndication International, Universal Pictorial Press, David Redfern*)

On 30 September 1981 The
Mathis Connection held a
birthday party for Johnny to
celebrate his twenty-five years
in the business. Johnny cuts his
cake *(left)* and sings with
guitarist Gil Evans *(below)*.
*(Courtesy The Mathis
Connection)*

Each of the fan club members presented John with cards and gifts and he had his photograph taken with each and every one of them! *(Courtesy The Mathis Connection).*

Classic Johnny. (*David Vance*)

a lot of songs in that vein. I did those singles and the company was pleased and so I could sing more substantial material. Those early single hits saw me with what I can only call a naked sound. The voice was everything.'

But a first is a first and Johnny remembers with affection the debut LP he made with George Avakian. 'It was pyrotechnical. It didn't do very well at all, and in fact it's relegated to the collector's item status, which means it didn't sell. It was a beginning.'

In the early years of his career show music still reigned on Broadway and among 'the awful lot of songs' he sang and recorded there were numerous numbers taken from musicals.

'I wanted to do all kinds of music, anything. I didn't have labels. When a great song would be around I wanted to do it. I had this wonderful respect in my early days – I still have it – for songs, style of songs. Cole Porter, Rodgers and Hart and everyone else! Which is why in the end I didn't jump up and down when I performed. I said songs are the important thing. The rest is nonsense. I still feel that. I understood the theatrics of conveying a song, not the personality.'

His recording of show songs also came out of his first enthusiastic response to the East Coast scene, as he gobbled up what New York had to give in the way of entertainment. In more practical, financial and business terms Johnny was part of the CBS empire and the company owned publishing rights to many scores. Their artists were expected to record songs in which the company had an interest. The American public assumed that the 'quality' artist who was not tied to a particular musical form would record the great songs of the day and they saw nothing amiss when in the same company's roster a number of artists recorded the same number. It was the way of things in those days and only the demise of songwriting and the paucity of hit shows has affected the situation radically.

In the late fifties Johnny was interested in record charts not so much for any acclaim but rather for the way in which a hit could send his name and voice into countless households. Certainly he prefers the old days, in this context, to the present. He feels that the endless research and eventual marketing which is the norm today gives the record – the song – the general appearance of being a 'product' and in a sense it bears little difference in sales terms to a tin of baked beans or a packet of cornflakes. He feels songs can be recorded or even written simply for their 'hit' potential rather than because someone has sat down and thought out what is a good or bad song. Manufactured hit records have produced or at least contributed to the closed system operated by many American radio stations where the same handful of numbers can be heard day in and day out. There is a great lack of what Johnny calls 'difference' and material which you feel has so much worth that it will last.

The early success in the US charts of 1957 to 1959 – whatever Johnny thought of the actual material – yielded for him eighteen credits in the *Billboard* listings. In Britain the first Mathis singles meant little other than an awakening interest from those who were, if nothing else, concerned about the demise of the ballad singer and the total emphasis being extended in some cities toward the rock 'n' rollers.

Britain ignored the early high flying American singles although the reviews were fine. 'Wonderful Wonderful' was backed with 'When Sunny Gets Blue' and one reviewer said, 'This coloured singer has a voice and style that are compelling and different'. Some thought the flip side, an off-beat ballad, might prove stronger.

'The Twelfth Of Never' was backed with 'Chances Are' and again the feeling was that Johnny deserved high sales. The top side was found to possess an outstanding lyric and the tune was seen as romantic but avoiding the whimsical.

Later Philips flipped the record over and gave the slow romantic ballad its turn at attracting attention. Conniff's melodious backing was praised.

In the tradition of the day – particularly to maintain

momentum in an artist's career and to fill the coffers – the early singles were gathered together on an EP in 1958. British fans could buy 'Wonderful, Wonderful', 'Chances Are', 'When Sunny Gets Blue' and 'It's Not For Me To Say'. The voice was described as 'fabulous' – it was a word Charlie Gracie rather liked as well!

Johnny's ninth US hit single gave him his British chart debut as 'Teacher Teacher' just inched its way into the Top Thirty.

It was the song 'A Certain Smile' from the film of the same name which consolidated Johnny's growing popularity in the States and ensured that he was here to stay. It was high in the charts while Johnny's 'Greatest Hits' topped the LP listing. His 'Swing Softly' LP was Top Ten. His 'Warm' and 'Goodnight Dear Lord' LPs hovered around the higher positions.

In Britain 'A Certain Smile' became a juke-box smash and with the film opening in London's West End on September 18, 1958, the signs were good. After all, in the film the title song was sung, cued and repeated orchestrally fourteen times.

In Britain's *Record And Show Mirror*, an uncredited writer wondered whether Johnny was too good for the British public. Fortunately the public went out and bought 'A Certain Smile'.

'A Certain Smile' had a top placing of nineteen in the States but in the UK it had major hit smash status with a top placing of four. Johnny had three other hits in the old country during this period with 'Winter Wonderland', 'Someone' and 'The Best Of Everything'. All three made the Top Thirty.

It was Mitch Miller (later of Yellow Rose Of Texas fame) who chose Johnny's material.

'He had a good idea of what would sell and be good for Johnny Mathis. I was a sort of a toy with him. There was no one else selling ballads and he took great pride in the fact that all our very soft-singing, pretty ballads were selling as well as rock 'n' roll. In that sense it was a mutual admiration society!'

Miller is graphically described as 'The Beard' by American chronicler Arnold Shaw: 'Snapping bullwhips . . . honking wild geese . . . barking dogs . . . braying French horns . . . bearded Mitch Miller brought sound gimmickry and excitement into the pop record scene'.

Miller was the US producer who found hits, who apparently rarely went for lunch but kept in his office the basic food in the American survival kit – a refrigerator – and who nibbled cheese and health foods yet smoked thick cigars throughout the day.

When he turned a song down, all you got was a negative swivel of the head. If you caught his eye, the lids fluttered sympathetically. When he liked a song, he became voluble on how it could be improved. His comments were generally sensitive. Since it spelled the difference between getting a song recorded or not, his suggestions prevailed.

Shaw says Miller was one of the few A and R men who opened his door to songwriters. Under his wing in the early to middle sixties came Frankie Laine from Mercury (where Miller himself had once found employment), Tony Bennett, Guy Mitchell, Rosemary Clooney, Jo Stafford, Mindy Carson, Johnny Ray, the Four Lads, Vic Damone, and, of course, Johnny. He was also to enjoy his own success when his sing-a-long albums caught the public's fancy. Apparently Miller was classically minded as well as possessing a marvellous sense of public taste. Shaw records that Miller was a solo oboist who played with symphony orchestras. It was this combination of popular and classical which drew him toward Johnny once the jazz section at CBS had more or less passed, and the popular division had noticed that the company had signed a guy who could sing jazz but had a commercial voice.

Shaw recalls in his excellent book how in the spring of 1957 Mitch Miller had telephoned with enough urgency in his voice to suggest that he had something important lying on his turntable. Shaw ran from his office in the RCA building to Columbia Records at 709 Seventh Avenue. He thought Miller had a new record from the Four Lads for his ears.

'What I heard in Miller's office was not a group, as I had hoped, but a strange new voice. It was young with chesty tenor tones and heady high notes almost falsetto in character. It had no sex or real warmth but it had lift and a sensuous feeling of exhilaration. And when the singer got to the arching, terminal phrase, "oh . . . so . . . won-der-ful my love," the tender and mature love of which he sang became a palpable reality.'

Miller, though, offered Johnny more solid material than some of the early hit songs which Johnny regarded as emphemeral (though over the years he's had to sing those hits separately or as part of a medley to please fans). He offered Johnny the catalogue of hit musicals like *Flower Drum Song, Gypsy, West Side Story* and the most famous of them all, *My Fair Lady*.

Johnny found his songs arranged and sometimes produced by a variety of well known names in the fifties. Many of these people became hit artists in their own right, and among them was Ray Conniff.

'Ray did the first two or three songs I had as hit records in America, well so many. Then he decided, and rightfully, that he should be a hit artist in his own right.

'There was Percy Faith who did my first few albums and then he decided he was going to do his own things. He was a very dear friend and I was very sad when he died in the mid-seventies.

'There was Ray Ellis. He produced 'Someone', 'The Best Of Everything', so many songs with him I just love. To me he's one of the best arrangers. I would like to do more with him.'

Conniff produced his own specialised LP sound and achieved individuality with the way in which he used the chorus as a section of the orchestra, employing the voices for colouring rather than lyrics, and placing them against various other sections in different combinations in order to achieve some unusual effects. Among his bestselling efforts around the time he was involved with Johnny were 'S'Wonderful, S'Marvellous, S'awful Nice', 'Concert In

Rhythm' and 'Broadway In Rhythm' with the latter including selections from *Oklahoma, The King And I, My Fair Lady* and *South Pacific*.

Percy Faith was known for his lush string arrangements and he was perhaps the predominant influence on England's major selling session-band orchestra led by Mantovanni.

Faith achieved major popular acclaim with his 'A Theme From A Summer Place' which in addition to its association with the film and the novel reached Number Two in the British charts of 1960.

It was a sign of how highly the young Johnny was regarded that he attracted the top names in recording at that time.

But were his records made with single releases in mind?

'I wasn't concerned either way. When I went to the studio I knew what I was recording and what it was for. Today, it's different. Now you record and they release what they see fit.'

Johnny became the first artist in record history to have his hits neatly parcelled together into one unit and titled 'Johnny's Greatest Hits'. It was at a period toward the end of the fifties when various commitments had made it hard for him to record further new LP material.

'Mitch Miller got the bright idea of putting my hits together and calling them something! At the last minute he called it 'Johnny's Greatest Hits' and started the avalanche of everyone having their own 'greatest hits'. It still goes on, even if someone has just got ''one'' hit these days!'

It sold half-a-million copies and it was the record which stayed in the American charts for 490 weeks.

And evident in those hits was a facet of the period which would seem strange to the youthful singers of the eighties – the process of recording in front of an orchestra.

'You had this boomy sound effect,' Johnny says. 'They didn't amplify each individual instrument as they do now. Things would have sounded more up-front if they had been done these days. I mean they just put three or four microphones in the studio and played loudly or softly or what have you. It sounded interesting.

'It was all done quickly. You did things there and then. It was just the beginning of the process where afterwards you could start to fiddle around. I remember hearing Patti Page and Les Paul and Mary Ford doing some incredible things with voice-overs and putting three or four voices on. It was fascinating to me but very foreign. I've never had too much understanding of recording studios other than going in and working as fast and frantically as I could.'

The hurry was quite simple. Johnny had so many dates and engagements lined up that trying to fit lengthy recording sessions into his diary schedule became an awkward and complicated process.

And in common with many other highly successful artists – Britain's Cliff Richard for instance – there were too many things going on for him really to take in every jot and tittle of what was happening. It was many years from his birth as a recording artist to the time when he set days specifically aside for recording.

By the end of the fifties American fans could find ten LPs of Johnny's in their record stores. And even then they would not have heard the complete Mathis output. Not everything he recorded was released.

Among the ten was a religious LP and a Christmas selection. His 'Goodnight Dear Lord' was catholic in its religious taste. There was the Jewish 'Eli Eli' and 'Kol Nidre'. Roman Catholics would appreciate 'The Rosary' and those of more protestant evangelical standing revel in 'Swing Low Sweet Chariot'. Some found it all rather sugary with sweet strings in super abundance. He gave 'Swing Low' a jazzy feel which had at least one reviewer comparing his vocals with Smokey Robinson. 'Merry Christmas' had the familiar 'The First Noel, 'What Child Is This', 'It Came Upon The Midnight Clear' and, among the rest, 'Silent Night, Holy Night'. The opening track 'Winter Wonderland' flowed and the British bought it as a single and put it into the singles chart. The flip was 'Sleigh Ride', the LP's third track on side one. Certainly the latter two cuts seemed to be the best and have lived on. Later in

Britain a Christmas LP appeared through the good auspices of Marks & Spencer, the chain store group. It disappeared almost as soon as it appeared on the shelves and remains now a valued collector's item.

Johnny says: 'There have been many recordings I made which have never been out on the market. Sometimes I know they were terrible songs and the performance awful but at other times I thought they were smashing records, but Columbia chose not to release them. Sometimes they wait too long and musical preferences change too fast and they wait a few months and things have come and gone.'

And even at the end of the fifties Johnny felt some material he was asked to record was a little mundane, if not downright simple-minded, but most of the time he felt the right choices had been made for him. Then, and a little later, he would rebel once in a while but he takes it all as part of life.

He wasn't too perturbed at being asked to record other people's songs which had become associated with that particular artist. He felt that a song was a song and it could be set into a different musical rhythm. In the final reckoning what mattered was whether or not a good record had been made.

He told Keith Skues on a Radio Hallam special assembled by the radio presenter: 'I'm not and was not worried provided what came out in the end was good to my ears. Many people have said why don't you do a song this way or that way and sometimes I take their advice, many times I've done songs in a strange way. Sometimes I've done ballads as an up-tempo.'

A later example is 'I Only Have Eyes For You', a ballad but, as he says, it 'certainly ain't by the end of my recording!'

As he became more experienced and successful so he took more responsibility. 'I got increasingly involved in a song's production. The song is chosen mostly because I can sing it so it's very important to me to give my opinion on how a song should be treated. I don't always because sometimes it's obvious. I've had very fine arrangers, bright and intelligent who wouldn't steer me wrong! The thing I get involved in most is instrumentation, key changes and whether there should be one or not. Beginnings and endings, they're very important.'

At the end of the fifties he charted with 'Misty' (it entered the British charts in January 1960), a song which has become synonymous with his career. It was an Erroll Garner composition. He had come into contact with Garner several times. His promotional 'push' by Helen Noga in a San Francisco club has already been described. There was another occasion at a CBS Records convention in Colorado. All the main acts in the company's catalogue were present. Few, though, of the other artists and few of the company's staff had heard Johnny except for Avakian. Garner's manager Martha Glaser recalls how Johnny sang a song from his first LP but those present felt it wasn't really him. Later an ad-lib session developed and there came the moment Johnny has never forgotten. Each of the singers present took the floor with his own accompaniment.

'Johnny had no one, so Garner offered to back him. Johnny just sang out of his mind. The next day when Johnny came down to breakfast he said, "My God, he pushed me over my head, I've never sung like that in my life." But Columbia sure took notice from that moment on. It was so exciting. He just tore it up and made his mark. I'll always remember that young, nervous boy who went out and knocked all those established heavies down.'

The occasion meant Garner and Johnny became friends and remained so.

Miss Glaser says their friendship was cemented by Johnny's recording of 'Misty'. 'Johnny has one of the very few throats that handle what Erroll writes. He has a real instrument.'

His recording of 'Misty' came by accident. He was in the studios recording material for his 1959 LP 'Heavenly' when Garner happened to be around. The famous jazz pianist had a song called 'Misty' which he played Johnny. The latter flipped. The obvious thing was done – the song was recorded.

The song had been recorded by Garner himself. Numerous other versions existed. One version prominent in Johnny's mind was by Quincy Jones and Sarah Vaughan. He told Ray Moore of BBC's Radio Two that he learned the song by listening to her recording. He recalled how Garner had befriended him many years back.

'I told him when I was thirteen that if I ever made a record that it would be one of his songs. And I was able to do it. I think the song did give me a little more clout with musicians. I think most singers are conscious of whether musicians like them or not. You know there are two sets of animals, singer and musician. Occasionally you get the two together and I've always wanted that. I hope with that song I had gotten it.'

Britain's *Record And Show Mirror* reviewer David Gell loved it! 'One of those rare records that is so lovely it just can't help but be so popular it ends up in the bestsellers. Glen Osser's introduction and backing for "Misty" are smooth, romantic, refreshing. And Mr Mathis is, of course, unique. The delightful melody comes over beautifully in this excellent interpretation.

'A brilliant touch is the manner in which Johnny returns following the last instrumental passage. Strings present the melody then an oboe picks it up and on an excitingly high note Johnny comes in on top of the woodwind so gently and effectively it isn't until he changes the note you realise it's Mr Mathis and not an instrument.'

'Misty' took the LP place originally alloted to a number from the musical *Flower Drum Song*, though which song it was remains forgotten by Johnny and others involved in the recording sessions.

During the first years of the sixties Johnny's singles continued charting in the States, most briefly. From March 1960 to June 1962 there were eight hits of rather lowly position. With the autumn release of 'Gina' and 'What Will Mary Say' in January of 1963 Johnny had a sudden elevation back into national popularity, it was the last major pop kick, with only Mary's follow-up, 'Every Step Of The Way', which reached thirty, able to keep any kind of general radio pop programming coming his way. 'Gina' made number six while 'What Will Mary Say' reached number nine. Once 'Every Step Of The Way' had disappeared from the *Billboard* Hot 200 at the end of March there was no other record to make even the Top Fifty until the sudden dramatic claiming of the number one spot with 'Too Much, Too Little, Too Late' in 1978. In Britain there was an equivalant silence as far as singles were concerned. 'What Will Mary Say' had a one week's chart outing at forty-nine and then there was utter silence in the Top Fifty until 'I'm Stone In Love With You' reminded kids of the guy who was once termed by American writer H. Kandy Rodhe as the 'king of necking music', which had less to do with actual physical drive than with Johnny being able 'to say those tender things we were too shy or inexperienced to think of. . .'

It wasn't the end of everything which really mattered, for Johnny carried his fans into quality musical pastures. It meant he was saved from the hysteria of the early years which saw him hunted by shrieking squealing school sorority groups. They said he gave them goose pimples.

Both Top Ten singles made their appearance on Johnny's 'Newest Hits' LP in 1963. It was the last LP for many years which could feature records which had charted in the Hot One Hundred, whatever their position and eventual staying power. The same year saw the release of 'Johnny', 'Romantically', 'I'll Search My Heart'. It was certainly a busy period of recording for Johnny and was somehow fitted in amongst the tours which now took him overseas. Don Costa arranged the material for 'Romantically'. He was known at the time for his work with *Never On Sunday*. The Christmas record fare was an odd mix: 'A Marshmallow World' was placed next to the 'Hallelujah Chorus'; giving a sharp contrast between schmaltz and majesty, but then religious people do it all the time in their worship so perhaps it surprised no one in the more evangelical of religious territories.

In 1964 there was a retrospective, 'The Great Years', which included perennial favourites and seemed to be a variation of the greatest hits idea, although it can always be argued that new fans arrive daily, weekly and monthly and there's a need to recall for them where the artist began. It was an American double-record set.

The same year saw previously released show material given a new cardboard dress under titles of 'Ballads Of Broadway' and 'Rhythms Of Broadway'. The reason for the bout of re-issues was that Johnny's Columbia contract was expiring. He was signed for Mercury, though he and management would own and lease the tapes. His first record for the new label was 'Wonderful World Of Make-Believe'. It seemed an apt name with tracks bearing titles like 'I'm Always Chasing Rainbows', 'Alice In Wonderland', 'When You Wish Upon A Star', 'Dream Dream Dream', 'House Of Flowers' and 'Beyond The Blue Horizon'.

Apart from Columbia re-issues Johnny would not appear under the great company's auspices until 1968 and 'Up, Up And Away'. In Britain he found himself on the HMV label, part of the giant EMI complex. Some describe his Mercury period as the wasted years. A commercial reading of the situation could suggest this, but there are many who judge the Mercury material to contain much of his finest vocal work even if it did not have the popular appeal of the preceding years.

During the Mercury period Johnny was in Britain for the purposes of recording with Norman Newell, one of the country's most respected producers of quality material. Keith Skues was one of those at the recording sessions and so was able to ask Johnny relevant questions when he interviewed him for a major special on Radio Hallam in 1976.

Johnny told him he didn't find British musicians less informal than Americans. He found it very much a case of being able to get what you want, for he found the British musician was of equal calibre with his fellow across the Atlantic. Mathis singled out particularly the outstanding nature of British string players during his 1965 recording work and to many they were the world's finest. He suggested one difference might be found in basic preparation, since British sessions seemed to be more worked out, though he felt it should be stressed how American writers know their musicians. He found the atmosphere different and refreshing and thought the 1965 British sessions were amongst his best.

'That particular album with Norman was certainly one. I think you couldn't say the songs were ditties which anyone can sing, where you don't have to try. I like a little more of a challenge, something which everyone can't do – we did material which was much more adventurous.'

The LP, released in 1965, was entitled 'Away From Home', an appropriate credit. On his show Skues played the powerful 'This Is Love' which on the second side precedes another number with surging effect, 'Arrivederci Roma' which, among others, had been well recorded in past days by Vic Damone. Other tracks included 'The Skye Boat Song', 'Danny Boy' and 'Autumn Leaves', numbers well-known to British listeners.

It was certainly a welcome high note. It ranks alongside an earlier LP, 'Live It Up', one of the two splendid affairs Johnny made with Nelson Riddle. Released in 1962, 'Live It Up' revealed a Mathis who swung at a mighty pace and made some familiar standards sound as if they had just been born. He hit his notes with an unprecedented accuracy and led many to hope and pray that he and Riddle would forge a partnership which could rival the superb Sinatra-Riddle era, Alas, it was not forthcoming, more's the pity.

The first Columbia LP of Johnny's second period with the record giant certainly had the apt title 'Up Up And Away', a number given popularity by the Fifth Dimension and the Johnny Mann Singers. 'Misty Roses' was one of the album's highspots. His version of the big Aretha Franklin smash 'I Say A Little Prayer' appeared on another 1968 Columbia-CBS album 'Love Is Blue'. It contained songs which were proving popular and would do so for others many years hence. There was the moving Beatle number, 'Here, There And Everywhere', Glen Campbell's

'By The Time I Get To Phoenix', 'Moon River' a la Henry Mancini, the British chart-topper for Elton John and Kiki Dee, 'Don't Go Breaking My Heart', the popular US number from the Association, 'Never My Love' and, amongst others, a fine rendering of Avalon's 'Venus'.

His 'Those Were The Days' released in 1968 continued a run of LP material which centred on big selling songs of the time. He surprised many with a pacey fiery version of 'Light My Fire', a song which gained massive success for the writers, The Doors, and chart fame for Jose Feliciano. He sang 'This Guy's In Love With You' from the Herb Alpert and Dionne Warwick catalogue and two others, numbers which can be described as two of his all-time low recordings. These are 'The 59th Street Bridge Song (Feelin' Groovy)' and 'Little Green Apples'. The first was by Simon and Garfunkel and given chart reckoning by Harpers Bizarre, an American male vocal group who had this and 'Anything Goes' as their only British success.

'Little Green Apples' had been expertly sung by Roger Miller, whose other hits included 'King Of The Road', 'Engine Engine No. 9', 'Kansas City Star' and the rather excruciating, though most popular, 'England Swings'.

Johnny told Skues: 'I hate my recording of "The 59th Street Bridge Song". It was a case of not knowing what you want and being confused in the studio. I said after hearing the number, "Oh, gawd no, me making records like this?" I listened to the playbacks and I just said get it out and then it might be forgotten, hopefully. It was a case of there not being enough time and the demands of those who want material released, maybe I shouldn't analyse it so! Some things you do, you would like buried! And "Little Green Apples" is also forgettable. I just say NO! Hear Roger's version.'

More popular fare came with 'Love Themes From Romeo And Juliet' in 1969 with some of the hit songs of the time. There was 'Aquarius' coupled, of course, with 'Let The Sunshine In', 'I'll Never Fall In Love Again', 'The Windmills Of Your Mind' and 'Yesterday When I Was Young' among its tracks.

The year 1969 also had Johnny singing the 'Music Of Bert Kaempfert' and closing the decade with another Christmas LP 'Give Me Your Love For Christmas' which contained a few songs he had previously recorded, such as 'The Little Drummer Boy', which had proved popular back in the late fifties with a number of artists. Again, as with other religious-styled LPs of Johnny's, there was a mix of the sacred (especially here 'The Lord's Prayer') and what some would call the quasi-religious, songs which have a religious festive air without suggesting in their lyric any particular religious base. These include the popular American song 'Have Yourself A Merry Little Christmas', 'Jingle Bell Rock' and 'Santa Claus Is Comin' To Town'. Johnny's first LP of the seventies, 'Raindrops Keeping Falling On My Head', included such songs as 'Everybody's Talkin'', the number from *Midnight Cowboy* and which Nilsson made popular, the epic of Simon and Garfunkel's, 'Bridge Over Troubled Water', the film song 'A Man And A Woman' and the George Harrison beauty entitled 'Something'. The Beatles recorded it in Britain and Shirley Bassey made an exquisite fighting take. Rock people loved the version by Joe Cocker. Johnny made it warm and mellow, for nights with roaring log fires, the right wine and relaxing company. The LP also contained 'Alfie', a big hit on British territory for Cilla Black but given popularity in the States by Cher and Dionne Warwick. Johnny coped well. The songs popped up again on the 1971 LP 'Johnny Mathis Sings The Music Of Bacharach and Kaempfert'. The tracks were familiar to any fan of Johnny's but at least collected together under the credits of two extremely popular songwriters of the time they assumed a greater significance. Johnny's 'This Guy's In Love' stole the show and was as attractive as it had been three years previously on 'Those Were The Days', although Johnny has said it's not one of his most memorable recordings. The song was utilised as title of a compilation issued on the American Harmony label in 1973.

The new decade also heralded another spate of re-packaging as CBS in Britain issued 'Johnny Mathis

Greatest Hits Volume 3' in 1971, and a year later, not without too much exercise of the mind, there came 'All-Time Greatest Hits'.

Both countries issued 'Johnny Mathis In Person' which included 'Wild Is The Wind' and 'When Sunny Gets Blue', two songs which for many fans represent Johnny at his best and which do not find themselves on the two-record sampler 'The Great Years'. 'Johnny Mathis In Person', of course, provided concert takes rather than studio versions.

For British singers, songwriters and music lovers there was much pleasure when in 1972 Johnny took a song by Gilbert O'Sullivan, 'Alone Again (Naturally)' and included it on the LP 'Song Sung Blue' (the UK title was 'Make It Easy On Yourself'). It had been the Irish singer's fifth British hit, had reached Number Three in the charts and had stayed in the Top Fifty for three months after initially being listed on March 4th. It was part of a 14-hit run which ended as suddenly and abruptly as his career began in 1975 with another catchy, slightly tongue-twisting song 'I Don't Love You But I Think I Like You'.

It became a regular in Johnny's nightclub act, a song which he says 'brought tears to my eyes; it's so sad, so touching. I get great satisfaction out of singing the song on so many occasions. In 1974, of course, it had its own poignancy for me when my father died and so both of my parents were dead.'

The album 'Song Sung Blue' again had more popular songs of the day, like 'Make It Easy On yourself', 'Lean On Me', 'How Can I Be So Sure' and 'He Ain't Heavy, He's My Brother'.

Another exquisite from 1972 was 'The First Time (I Saw Your Face)' the title track of the LP, a British song by writer Ewan McColl and given chart popularity by a gorgeous black singer, fairly new to the scene, called Roberta Flack. This writer had first heard her in 1969 at the Washington DC Church of St Stephen of the Incarnation and caught her first LP which had appeared late summer of 1969 on Atlantic. There was also an immaculate reading of 'Betcha, By Golly, Wow'.

1973 saw release of 'Me And Mrs Jones'. The title song is not one of Johnny's favourites.

'It's not much of one, is it? I haven't a clue who Mrs Jones was,' were his reactions to being asked by broadcaster Keith Skues for his opinion.

'Anytime you have to take a song or take words and over, say, a period of three bars make up your own melody it really isn't much of a song. But then I sing the songs they want me to sing'.

Some of the other songs on the LP were pretty good, particularly the Michel Legrand song 'I Was Born In Love With You'.

But the 1973 LP produced by Thom Bell, 'I'm Coming Home', was a corker. It was Johnny's black music rejuvination. It produced a major UK hit two years later, 'I'm Stone In Love With You'. American radio stations and juke-boxes picked up the title track. Johnny felt it was one of the best things he'd ever done.

'Tommy was and is a genius as far as I'm concerned.' Oddly enough, in-spite of fine reviews, the black music market pick-up and the turntable plays, it didn't sell in the expected quantities. Johnny believes part of the reason for this came from internal problems which afflicted Columbia at this time. It included the departure of Clive Davis, who was regarded by many as the best music boss in the business, whatever may or may not have been other negatives in his total make-up. And of course it was Davis who made the record deal with Tommy Bell to produce Johnny.

'The album got caught in the middle of all this nonsense and didn't really sell. But I was happy with the musical outcome. I love projects like that one. It was the opportunity for me to gain a couple of new friends in Tommy Bell and lyricist Linda Creed.'

While Johnny thought that much of the LP 'Me And Mrs Jones' had a great deal of inconsequential material, and 'I'm Coming Home' was a goodie, there was another LP which rather got lost but which has grown in popularity over the years. This was 'Killing Me Softly With Her

Song'. Don McLean's 'And I Love Her So' was included, so also Stevie Wonder's 'You Are The Sunshine Of My Life'. Most praise from Johnny comes for the introspective 'Arianne', which was part written by a friend Marty Charnon.

But it's 'Me And Mrs Jones' which keeps drawing Johnny's comments.

'In this business you have to grit your teeth a lot and smile and look cheerful when you don't want to be! It's part of the business.'

It was obvious why 'Me And Mrs Jones' had been chosen as the LP's title. It was a song which had been a major hit both sides of the Atlantic in 1973 for Billy Paul. Hence it was familiar and its title would provide an indentifiable focus point for the record buyer. Both Johnny and Billy Paul were signed to Columbia.

The next year, 1974, saw a surfeit of re-issued material, with only 'The Heart Of A Woman' LP including fresh recordings. Again, there was well-known material, among which was Johnny's version of the much played Roberta Flack hit of the year, 'Feel Like Makin' Love'.

The LP 'When Will I See You Again' was released a year later. The song had been a massive hit in Britain for three girls with infectious charm, The Three Degrees. Also included were Sedaka's 'Laughter In The Rain', the Manilow favourite 'Mandy' and 'Let Me Be The One'.

Morris Albert's 'Feelings' hit provided the title focus of Johnny's other 1975 release. Albert's record reached Number Four in Britain and during its 32-week US charting climbed to sixth position. There was another Sedaka gem included, 'Solitaire'.

The David Cassidy hit 'I Write The Songs', also of course a major smash in the States for Barry Manilow, provided the opening cut on an LP titled after Art Garfunkel's big single, 'I Only Have Eyes For You'. The two numbers provided scope for Johnny's superb voice on this 1976 release. There was a haunting version of '(Do You Know Where You're Going To) Theme From Mahogany' which had been a spectacular seller for Diana Ross and an equally skin-penetrating take of Sondheim's, 'Send In The Clowns', a song which was a massive UK chart success for Judy Collins across the Atlantic. Right at the end of the LP was 'When A Child Is Born' – the song which was to transform Johnny once more into a major selling artist in Britain and lead the way toward two Number One LPs, and, of course, become a Number One single itself.

'We just included the song on the album,' Johnny comments. 'I heard it in Britain as an instrumental with a lot of humming. I had the hunch I could sing it well, never dreaming the British public would take it as a Christmas song, and, of course, it became my biggest single over there.'

1977 produced a bout of re-issues and a couple of new albums. In America there was 'Hold Me, Thrill Me, Kiss Me' which was titled 'Sweet Surrender' in the UK. Once more Johnny sang some of the best hit material around and at this and every stage in tracing Johnny's recording activities throughout the seventies there comes the same insistent question: why didn't he have these songs first? He sang Leo Sayer's powerful UK chart-topper 'When I Need You', the plaintive 'We're All Alone' from Rita Coolidge, Barbra Streisand's 'Evergreen', and 'Don't Give Up On Us', a number one in Britain by David Soul, one-half of the Starsky and Hutch TV cop series of the time.

And then came 1978. The splendours of Johnny's recording feat have been described in the earlier chapter covering that period of his career since all other happenings grew out of it and it created a flood of media activity focused on Johnny. The boy was back. It was the LP 'You Light Up My Life' (a US chart-topper for Debby Boone and a mere two-week Top Fifty damp squib in Britain) which displayed the two duets with Deniece Williams; 'Emotion' and 'Too Much, Too Little, Too Late'. It also had a splendid rendering of the Gibb Brothers smash hit 'How Deep Is Your Love'.

'I think the Bee Gees, the Gibb Brothers, have attracted me for their melodies. They've written some great songs and I've often thought their records were intricately produced and really fascinating. I love their music. I really do. I heard one of their songs years ago. I heard Vera Lynn sing it. I loved it so much. It was called "The Morning Of My Life" and I've used it in my concerts. And there's also this song "How Deep Is Your Love". Delightful.'

The song of course came from the massive hit film of the time, *Saturday Night Fever*. The musical *The Wiz* provided Johnny with 'If You Believe' but all paled in the face of 'Too Much, Too Little, Too Late'. The LP – the singles – made Johnny hot selling property and as Ray Haughn says the back catalogue became re-activated.

In Britain the momentum had not been lost since 1975. LPs and singles had been supplemented by general airplay of sessions Johnny had especially made for the BBC with much thanks from the Mathis camp going to Derek Mills. The BBC does not have enough needle-time allowance (after negotiations with the various unions and societies) for its broadcasting hours and so it records 'live sessions' with musicians. Apart from anything else these sessions (not available on commercial disc) made various BBC producers aware of how good Johnny was in the studio and of his ability to cope with all situations. CBS has sold Johnny's music under the category of nostalgia. The advert for 'I Only Have Eyes For You' said quite simply: 'Today, it's Nostalgia, And no one captures it better than Mathis.'

It was a sales point which helped 'The Mathis Collection' but it was also very true that by 1978 Johnny's music was as fresh as ever.

'That's What Friends Are For' provided a fine follow-up to 'You Light Up My Life'. It brought Johnny and Deniece together for a complete LP. The only surprising thing was the lack of single hits in both Britain and America save 'You're All I Need To Get By' which had a brief run.

Hit singles or not, the LPs continued but at the dawn of the eighties Johnny's staunch fans must have wondered whether there was to be anything other than a series of LPs which contained previously released material.

Admittedly, there must have been pleasure for his fans at seeing 'Tears And Laughter' as the British Number One, as it galloped there on the vanguard of another mighty television campaign, but less pleasure at other British re-packaging affairs which included '99 Miles From LA', 'Evergreens', 'Johnny Mathis Sings Christmas Songs', 'Night And Day', and 'Celebration', (accorded special accolade by virtue of its tying in with Johnny's silver anniversary).

In America 'The Best Of Johnny Mathis 1975 – 1980' was released. The new material began with 'Different Kinda Different' in 1980 which was re-titled in Britain 'All For You'. The seventies policy of including proven hit material was continued. There was the Billy Preston-Syreeta hit 'With You I'm Born Again', the Gloria Gaynor smash 'I Will Survive' (which of course was utilised by Johnny in his stage set and had been much requested by fans) and of particular interest on the record, a duet with Paulette McWilliams. 1981 – the silver anniversary year – was bereft of new material.

In 1982 Johnny sang with Dionne Warwick though she was hardly a new face or voice to Johnny. The two had been friends for years. Dionne dueted on 'Got You Where I Want You' and the title track 'Friends In Love'. For Dionne 1982 was a very special year, for after being ignored, unjustly, for most of her career by British record buyers she found herself riding high there and in the States with a Bee Gees composition entitled 'Heart-breaker'.

Johnny's fans waited for more record material.

8

John's Life

When he was asked: 'You've never married?' Johnny Mathis replied, 'If everyone got married there would be no one who could marry.'

It was an amusing answer to the question which is constantly asked of any male music star who just happens to be single.

The other wearisome versions of this inevitable question come in the form, 'What kind of person would you marry?' 'What are the qualities about a woman you most like?' 'Have you ever been in love?'

Through the years permutations on the question have been asked and answered politely. Journalists given the task of filling their thousand-word features on this subject have speculated, and, at the very least, suggested Johnny would be a worthwhile capture. The same scribes and the media in general never think of asking the married star whether he has a good relationship with his wife, if the marriage is holding, and similar questions, though perhaps the way society is progressing and with innumerable break-ups which are taking place we can envisage the journalist's question of the future as 'Do you have your eye on anyone's wife?' 'Will you be settling for a married woman?'

Johnny Mathis has always calmly avoided the gossip columns and has never courted the searing headline for the purpose of furthering his career. He has never sunk to the depths of inventing imaginary love affairs to

150

keep his name filling newspaper and magazine column inches.

Yes, in the early days there were articles which talked of Johnny and girls or Johnny and love and carried headlines like 'The Kind of Girl I'll Marry'.

It was the British music weekly, the *New Musical Express*, and its 1959 annual which coined the forementioned headline. In the feature Johnny said: 'The first thing that attracts me to a girl is her manner of speech – whether it is direct, indirect, indifferent or idiotic. These are the things that enchant or disenchant me.'

He thought looks unimportant and remarked: 'After you get to know a girl and talk to her for a while, her looks seem to get better or worse merely by what she says.'

The girl he would marry, he said, would be a 'nice girl' and interestingly he added: 'It won't be important to me whether she is in the entertainment business or not. Because in the business I'm involved with people who, deep down in their hearts, really dislike show business. They're not comfortable in it. They don't really like it at all, but they work in it.'

Johnny's reaction to show business will be described more fully later, suffice it to say here that it's interesting to note that he brought 'marriage' and 'show business' into direct correlation so early in his press interviews. And this view still holds good.

Johnny makes no secret of the fact that he likes his own company. 'You can't accomplish things if you're around people a lot. I'm not a lonely person but I like to be alone. I happen to enjoy the company of people I feel comfortable around. Usually people in athletics I suppose! We talk about the same things, have the same interests. It's not something I consciously do. I suppose I'm drawn toward people who are physically active all the time. I'm in this business where your whole life is put before the public. There are some things which embarrass you. My private life is something very dear to me. If, and when, I get married it will be the most sacred and personal thing which has happened to me. Because I'm not married does not mean I'm dead.' The latter suggestion amuses him hugely.

So Johnny has claimed his loves and non-loves as his private territory, however interested the weeklies and monthlies may be.

He will say, though, that his career has come first. He points out that his constant travel and recording and performing schedules make if difficult to establish lasting relationships and the hectic nature of his professional career would perhaps place an unbearable onus upon any one woman.

'Maybe I'll marry one day. But as a performer I have to uproot myself so often, it doesn't seem right to ask someone to share my life. I'm sure I would have been married and divorced two or three times and that doesn't appeal to me, really. So many of my friends have been through that. It doesn't make them happy, it just confuses things.

'But I'm not lonely, I can shut the door on the outside world and be content with my own company. I'm lucky to have good friends, mostly they're married, so that I'm Uncle John a hundred times over.'

To all intents and purposes his life has revolved around his family, his house, a love for cooking and, in a more extrovert vein, golf.

The first three of those four things fall into the 'private' category. They belong to his personal world. He does not list as important the glamour of showbiz, its parties, premieres and so forth.

He is a shy person. He is more forthcoming these days than in earlier times yet still retiring; all of which is obvious from his stage performance where the accent is always on his voice, his songs, and the arrangements with a minimum of chatter.

'My concert days were agony. I would wake up frightened. And it would build during the day and never leave, even when working in front of an audience. It was totally debilitating, similar to what I felt in school athletics.'

The eighties still see Johnny with very little to say on stage and capable of being embarrassed by an over-eager female fan who eludes the security men and launches herself at him on stage.

He tells of how Barbra Streisand invited him to play tennis one day and he was so nervous about their meeting that he rang her secretary and said he could not come as he had sprained his ankle!

He has been interviewed hundreds of times for press, radio and television and yet his nervousness is still apparent. Any lengthy interview is fascinating to study. At first Johnny is a cautious man and the sentences are short and the answers have been heard before by Mathis fans. Slowly, if he takes to the interviewer, he opens out and becomes more forthcoming, he reveals a quick sense of humour and by the end the conversation is taking place between two friends. He is rarely rude to an interviewer; sometimes he is impatient and it would be surprising if he was not when so often an interview is seen by the host not as a special occasion with an important musical personality but as merely another item amongst hundreds in their programme or paper that week. Equally awkward is the interviewer who has done little research and merely asks the time-honoured questions.

There is a very early story of John's bashfulness. He was appearing at the Sands Hotel in Las Vegas in 1960. His act was over and he had changed out of his stage clothes and thought he might wander around the casino and observe his previously attentive audience now intent on playing the gambling tables.

Occasionally someone would look up and recognise him and he would respond with a nervous smile and move on quickly.

He was waylaid by a well-meaning couple who somewhat loudly exclaimed: 'Hi, Johnny. Where are you going?' It completely bowled over the youthful Johnny. There was a half-smile, a contorted wave and he was heard murmuring beneath his breath: 'Why don't they leave me alone? I don't even know them. Why do they become so familiar?'

Johnny recalls how on one occasion a mother asked him

to jump into the hotel pool with her daughter so she could take a picture of them. 'Are you mad?' he asked her.

Obviously the passage of time has enabled him to deal with these and similar situations with greater ease and without carrying for days afterwards a certain sense that there might have been a better way to handle the incident, and a regret that he might have hurt the feelings of people who were his fans.

One way, in earlier days, he used to deal with this tension between Johnny the music star and Johnny the person was the sudden disappearance act. He has just left his entourage and gone off on his own for days. It was both an assertion of his independence (in the early sixties from Helen Noga) and a desire for privacy, a reaction against the inevitable feeling which must come to any public figure that their whole life is of interest to someone.

The first time Johnny disappeared was a week before he was due in London to begin his 1961 tour. Helen Noga, who had booked into her suite in a Mayfair hotel some days previously, told journalists: 'We think he came through here. And then I got a letter from Rome saying, "I'm not lonesome." But we've called every possible place in Rome and there's no trace of him. Say, maybe he went to Spain.'

Her puzzlement grew. Later Helen said: 'You know when he left Los Angeles for Europe he took nothing but the cotton pants and shirt he was wearing and a briefcase.'

Johnny turned up, as he did again after skipping off to Europe once his 1962 tour was completed. It was the way he did things, and why not – it was his life. But his family have always been a major supportive base. None of Johnny's brothers and sisters have gone full-time into showbusiness – though two of his brothers are semi-pro singer-guitarists. Apart from a married sister who has lived in New York, all the others live in California.

'We are what we have always been – a very close family. We often have parties and we sing together, it's just like old times save for the fact that my mother and father are no longer alive.' All his brothers and sisters have always been close to him, partly because he was the fourth out of seven.

'There's great warmth between us all, no competition, we share in each other's successes. They all have the same genes I have, except I started and was rather serious about it [singing] at an early age. And they had their priorities and raised their families. And I'm very proud of what they've done. And they, I'm sure, feel the same way about me. I think there's always someone who meets them and says: "Oh, aren't you. . . ?" and I'm sure they get sick of that.'

'I'd guess Elizabeth is the sister I've been closest to; she's two years older than me. We'd talk a lot together when we were kids, all the time, about everything; me about the girls, Elizabeth about the boys, everything.'

He remembers the various escapades they got up to when their enthusiasms rather outran common sense. 'We used to get the urge to make brownies once in a while, and we'd make so many that even our family couldn't eat them all!'

At the last count Johnny had fifty nephews and nieces. In spite of his own heavy work schedules and being out of the States for months on end he says he takes an interest in each and every one.

'We are brothers and sisters and we know each other inside out and backwards. We are realistic. They don't care how many hit records I've had. I'm still John.'

He has two homes in California and one of them is the venue for the family get-together at Christmas.

'I usually say Christmas Day shouldn't start until a reasonable hour – say six-thirty or seven in the morning – but it's still dark when you hear the patter of tiny footsteps and all the little Mathises are crowding around outside my bedroom door, calling, "It's Christmas day, Uncle John."'

He says he's never spent a Christmas outside a family context, though he would love to see a White Christmas.

'As kids in San Francisco we all dreamed of seeing snow and once it was so cold that someone swore they saw a snowflake and the story made the papers – but home is what Christmas is all about.'

His memories of Christmas go back to the time when mum

and dad were alive and the whole Mathis family was together.

'The seven of us, of course, started to get excited the minute it was December.' And they would scour the department stores for cheap goods, ones they could afford, for presents.

'I remember one Christmas. I was nine. I'd saved up hard, you know, lots of pennies, and when December came I had a dollar – it seemed a lot then! I spent ages thinking what I might buy mum. I walked around the shopping areas and looked at the windows. Then I saw what I wanted to buy her. It was a flower shop I had stopped by and there was a lovely snake plant in the window. It was so beautiful, green and shiny! I just had to buy it. I was so excited I couldn't even wait for Christmas. I rushed off home and gave it to my mother right there and then.'

Strangely, a similar scene was enacted some years later when younger brother Mike, aged nine, came running into the family home three days before Christmas with his special present for mum – it was a snake plant! It seems he said almost identical words to his mother as Johnny had once uttered: 'I've got to give it to you now or else somebody else might have bought it!'

They'd also spend hours decorating the house and once Christmas was over they'd ensure everything utilised one year would be perfect for the next. 'As for the tree – well, we would steal that from out of the woods. It was more a bush really – we couldn't drag a full-grown tree down the streets!' He appreciates how his parents strove hard to make Christmas that bit different from the remainder of the year and saved hard to buy special food. 'Mum would cook us a really extravagant meal. It was wonderful.'

These days – with money no problem – Johnny has the pleasure of buying the kind of presents for his nephews which he yearned to have when younger but which, of course, his family could not afford. He begins listing presents for his fifty nephews and nieces as early as October! It's on Thanksgiving Day the family makes the decision whether Christmas will involve a total get-together.

Johnny's brother, Ralph, was a singer for many years and, in fact, made a couple of recordings, but things didn't really happen for him although he toured for a short while. He was more of a rock 'n' roller than brother John, much more a 'black' singer. For a while he toured with Johnny and was involved in the business side, but when he decided to get married he left Johnny's entourage.

He has a charming wife, Irene, and his voice is filled with enthusiasm when he talks about his kids. He has two step-children, Darin and Deniece, whom he has raised since they were five and four. Darin is a coastguard and lives away from home while Deneice is 'sure good-looking!' He has two more boys, Alex now aged eleven and Brendan, ten. Ralph says they are a wonderful bunch to have around.

For a time Ralph accompanied Johnny on some of his trips around the world, particularly during 1969–70.

Brother Michael is involved with music, busily writing songs though success hasn't come his way as yet and his musical efforts have been contained on a local level.

Johnny's closeness to his family has been intensified because of his feeling that he missed out on many things with his parents. Apart from the obvious fact that mum and dad had to work to maintain the family, and which meant they were sometimes working every day and seemingly every night, and so seeing little of the children, there was the fact that early on he left his immediate background to live with the Nogas. For seven years Helen Noga was a sub-stitute mother. He was taken out of a proud and intimate large scale family setting where nothing came easy, to the calm and affluence of a couple who lived in Beverly Hills.

Obviously the Nogas cared for him and without them his career would never have happened. But it did bring him into a different environment and certainly one where almost everyone was white. He mixed with a different set and circle of people. His time and energy was devoted to developing his singing, which rather prevented free and easy access to his family.

He always remained on good terms with his parents after he left home but when his mother died on December 30,

1963, he says he felt badly and felt he had missed out with his parents. Yet it was an inevitable process if he was to develop his career at a time when it was far from easy for a black artist to make inroads into the general record and showbiz world. The two worlds did not mix. His father died on March 9th, 1974. It was another blow, but at least he has his large family which provides him with personal security. And there is his house – a source of pride and joy, in itself hardly surprising when every aspect of it reflects its opulence, taste, magnificence and luxury.

The house was built in the early 1930s by Howard Hughes as a Hollywood hideaway for the platinum blonde bombshell, Jean Harlow. Although Johnny has made many changes, the cellar entrance to an underground tunnel which connected the millionaire recluse with the film actress remains. Johnny uses the tunnel for his prized wine collection.

Johnny – with the aid and the creative flair of interior designer Steven Chase – has made the place his own. Hughes – if he were to return – might not recognise his old haunt. Walls have been removed, there is a translucent roof over the swimming pool and an extra guest room, and, of course, the whole house has been redecorated and refitted.

A closed-circuit TV system scans the house and grounds, with a monitor in every room, even in the Roman bath and sauna. There are mirrors in abundance including a pink mirror over the main bed which Johnny – with a smile – says allows you to watch yourself sleeping.

The house boasts comfortable chairs and sofas, tables and cupboards, and art objects, some of which Johnny has collected during his world travels. A painting of Johnny dominates the reception area. His love for billiards finds expression in a handsome billiard table, but even the tasteful and expensive decor, including leopard-covered chairs, cannot compete with two other major elements. The first is the splendid view which the house commands from atop the Hollywood Hills, while his elegant den contains a swimming pool – dramatically unexpected – from which other rooms lead off. Johnny has told many, many magazines the reason for this – it's simply his desire to be able to jump out of bed, swim across the pool and grab some breakfast on the other side!

The kitchen is compact and has recently been renovated so that it not only provides the necessary equipment for Johnny to pursue his love of cooking, but gives space for guests.

He says he learnt cooking not merely from messing around in the kitchen with older sister, Elizabeth, but also from his mother.

'Mother started me off. She was in domestic service. I learned a great deal from her. I suppose I'm much more adventurous, but I've travelled the world and I pick up recipes wherever I go.'

One of his more unusual discoveries of a recipe occurred when he travelled on the *Queen Mary's* last voyage. She was in port in the Canary Islands, and the ship's master chef taught him the secret of true banana flambé.

'I don't know whether it sounds conceited but I think I'm a better than average cook and I think it would be hard to find someone who has a knowledge of the dish variety I can serve. I whip them up my way! It was all a case of fun when I began. I learnt simple Southern dishes, you know, chili and fried chicken.'

For his first cooking experiments he used the family as guinea-pigs and they raised no particular protest.

'To me the time I spend in the kitchen isn't a mere automatic routine of finding something to eat. It's an act of inventing, creating, expressing myself in a highly enjoyable way. It's also the key to survival when I'm travelling. I had a special metal box built to carry frying pans, pots, utensils, all the cooking equipment I'd need, plus spices and seasonings.'

A threat to his well-being, he believes, is the constant procession of hotel meals – 'it's a kind of slow death' – and he says when he stays at an hotel he doesn't care if the food in the dining room is lousy because the restaurant will probably be closed by the time he and his entourage have returned from the concert venue anyway! He admits he's not too sure he would bother with that type of restaurant even if it were open, but sometimes he's forced to put up with poor food on his travels. He often buys his own food – it's the case of shopping in disguise! It seems to work.

Some of his culinary skills have been learnt from his long-time housekeeper, Marsha. 'She's taught me a great deal about Eastern cooking. She's even showed me how the Japanese use chrysanthemum leaves in skkiyaki, and she's a wonder when it comes to using herbs and cooking vegetables.

'A few years ago I had the old kitchens ripped out and ultra-modern ones put in. I have micro-wave cookers and can do a roast in twenty minutes. I suppose I change my mind about favourite dishes. Mexican food featured strong at one time. I always remember what my father once told me: "Don't experiment on your friends. Try out anything new on yourself!"'

British fans, it seems, have a fond belief that he cannot fend for himself. 'I don't know what it is about British fans, but they are always giving me food. There's one woman who turns up at the stage door every night with something for me: a layer cake, apple pie, rum balls. I have never found out her name, but I just love her apple pie.' He says a British tour means a weight increase of between seven and eight pounds.

Promoter Derek Block says Mathis is the kind of person you love to work for. He's stood in the wings of a concert hall more times than he dare think. Acts have come off and passed him by as their heavies have moved in and escorted them to their dressing room or roadies have raced forward with towels and glasses of water.

'Johnny Mathis comes off and he says "thank-you" to me, the promoter. It's his show. But he appreciates and acknowledges what other people have done for him. Everyone else puts their talent first. Whatever you do, he's totally appreciative.'

Block tells instances of the well-known Mathis generosity. When his single 'When A Child Is Born' became his first Number One single anywhere in the world he rang London and asked what he might give the many people who had helped him gain this chart position. The usual things were mentioned as gifts, as for instance a hamper from Fortnum and Mason, London's very famous food shop in Piccadilly. But no, it seemed a good idea to give music people something musical, in part anyway. So everyone was given a portable radio, cassette and TV machine. The sales staff at CBS had the same unit without the TV. Block says there must have been 170 to 200 gifts. 'I reckon he spent twenty grand. He had a plate made up which thanked people for their efforts over "When A Child Is Born" and it was screwed into each gift. Obbie at CBS [Maurice Oberstein, Managing Director and head of CBS in Britain] told me that in all his years, and he's known them all from Abba to Clash, you name them, he's never seen an artist thank people so well. You know this is in a business where everyone normally thinks everyone is living off them!'

Block says he's one of the few artists you can really form a friendship with. 'I see him on tours. We're friends. Then again I go to New York and I hear him at Radio City. Afterwards we'll go for a meal somewhere. But he will not talk business. I've been on holiday with him. I've had some profound conversations with him over the years. He can switch off the business, the star side, and if people crowd around chattering to him as the star he moves away. He's quite a private person.'

Golf has been a strong feature of his life-style. The popular story of his introduction to the great sport is that while he was performing at Las Vegas, with little desire to gamble, he had a great deal of spare time. One of the dancers in the show was a first-class golfer and talked Johnny into trying the sport.

British agent Vic Lewis disputes this and says he was the real instigator of Johnny's long-lasting affair with golf. 'We were holidaying in Grenada and had got there by way of Trinidad, a rather tiring process. Anyway we rested on the beach, or at least Johnny did, but after a couple of hours he got bored and the sun was rather hot and his forehead suffered a little from the heat. I asked him whether he played golf. Anyway, I found out there was a beautiful golf course nearby. So off we went. He loved it. I mean he is so athletic and he has what people in sport call a "good ball sense". I don't know, I suppose we did twenty or thirty rounds. In a matter of a few days he was coming along fine. The next time he came over he told my promoter – since I was Johnny's agent – that he must book him at places where there was a golf course nearby.'

Johnny was indeed to the manner born as far as golf was concerned, although, Vic Lewis' praise aside, it took him some time to really learn the game.

'I had some really hopeless scores. Golf is a very humbling game.'

After a year his handicap was eighteen which he didn't consider too bad at the time. 'But those first days! Not long after starting I did a course in Los Angeles in 83! A few months later I was sure I was getting to grips with the game – I went back to the same course determined on a dramatic improvement. I took 86!'

In 1981 Johnny's handicap was 9. British courses please him. 'Our fairways back home are like greens. In Britain they are tough.' He now travels and arranges to stay near a first-rate golf course whenever possible. He has been a regular supporter of the star golf course circuit for many years. These include the Glen Campbell Open, the Bing Crosby and Bob Hope Desert Classic. He was selected to be one of the amateurs representing the United States in the first Annual United States versus United Kingdom Pro-Amateur played in Scotland. Johnny was partnered with Tom Weiskopf.

And golf has proved a major relaxation with its general ethos proving in tune with his character. 'I call it a marvellous therapy.' When home he plays a daily round and along with some tennis (he's been coached by star names of past days, Tony Trabert and Pancho Gonzales) snooker and swimming. Golf does bring him into the public eye –

his appearances in the Pro-Am Golf Tournaments pull in enormous crowds wherever they are staged. But since he is a good player he has nothing to fear, unlike some whose clowning exploits on the golf course are well known. But some players, like ex-President Gerald Ford, take it all in their stride, and not without some humour.

Johnny is religious. As we have seen, his parents were Methodists and he was reared on the lusty rhythmic hymns of Methodism and the liveliness of the music which came out of the American Sankey-Moody evangelistic era of the late nineteenth century, a music which has continued to be popular. Johnny sang as a kid in the Methodist church and his father was very philosophical by nature and often spoke in a religious vein. The young Johnny listened, often enraptured by his father's flow of words. Clement was someone who – if he had someone to listen – could talk for hours. He was never too busy to talk about life.

These days Johnny is a Roman Catholic, he was converted into its tradition in 1962 – at a time when it seemed likely he would appear in a film role as a Peruvian saint in St Martin De Porres.

He is very aware of an inner conscience and says: 'God is that voice you are or what you're doing. We all hear that voice that speaks to us in the strangest situations and places and tells you how sincere you are. That's why I find some of these people who are trying to sell religion on such a mass basis so comical. You must have God within you constantly. And you have to know this is the God that rules and makes you do what you do.'

The question of colour is one which Johnny veers away from. He has always felt accepted from early days and he soon almost forgot he was black since he was appealing to white audiences, moving in a white world, and given the star treatment. A great deal of his life has been spent in the company of white people and at various times during his life he has been aware that some black people have resented a basically white entourage around him. People have said, 'What no black faces around?' But then he hasn't himself consciously thought in racial terms, although of course he hasn't been responsible for the hiring of personnel. When choice has been exercised it has been in terms of who is right for the particular situation and he has not been guided by colour as the pre-eminent reason for the choice made.

It hasn't been for him the question of getting somewhere as a black person. He has got there as a person and instrumental in this has been hard work, sheer graft and a conviction that he was destined for big things. However, Johnny did donate funds from performances in Chicago and New York in 1963 to be divided equally between the NAACP and the Southern Christian Leadership Conference.

Also his managers Helen and John Noga had discussions with the Reverend Martin Luther King, Jr, president of the Southern Christian Leadership Conference and they conveyed Johnny's willingness to perform in fund-raising shows under the group's sponsorship in Atlanta, Georgia. Johnny's appearance on August 5, 1963, at the Civic Centre in Birmingham, Alabama was the first integrated show before the first integrated audience. It was called 'A Salute To Freedom 1963' with sponsorship and benefit for the NAACP, The Southern Leadership Christian Conference, CORE, the Urban League, Negro Labor Council and the Student Non-Violent Coordinating Committee.

Johnny has said little about discrimination, or about racism though he was quite obviously aware in his early days that his audiences had few black people. With the growth of a black middle-class in America the audiences have been less sharply defined.

He was brought up to sing what some would call white man's music. He sang Broadway songs rather than black music as typified in the soulful, exciting R and B which so energised white British groups like The Rolling Stones, and The Beatles in their early days.

It was a cultural inevitability rather than a deliberate racial spurning of his own colour group. It was the same for any black artist of the time trying to succeed in that particular musical sphere, but there were some who were a lot more conscious of their black roots even if they did sing for their supper in white man's clubs.

'The public doesn't think of me as being a particular colour. I don't think much about prejudice, and I will not let ignorance affect my life. Being black happened at birth.'

Yet he was delighted with the turn in his career which occurred in the mid-seventies. When his records were produced by the famous black musician, Thom Bell, suddenly black audiences became much more aware of Johnny. To many it was a case of Johnny coming home! The feeling was even more intensified when Johnny recorded with Deniece Williams, a partnership from which came a world smash hit 'Too Much, Too Little, Too Late', and later when he recorded with Dionne Warwick and starred with Natalie Cole.

The last ten years have seen regular features on Johnny in journals like *Jet, Ebony, and Soul*. It would though be incorrect to surmise from this that he was ignored by the black magazines before the Bell records or that his records were not bought by black people. He was given newspaper and magazine space and he had a black following but it was insignificant compared with the following he began to acquire after he worked with Bell. There were plenty of black and white people who would agree that he deserved the accolade of being called The Greatest Romantic Singer Of Our Time, the description given in a tour programme of the 1974.

The nearest Johnny has come to directly involving himself in racial questions lies in his visit to South Africa in 1977. He was one of several prominent American blacks who were allowed in at this time and who played to racially integrated audiences. He had a schedule of thirty-two performances in twenty-one days with three out of four shows mixed, an all-time high in liberalism, according to some sources in South Africa. And although some people might disagree, impressario Ronnie Quibell argued it was better for a star to come and appear before some multiracial audiences than not to come at all. Johnny closed his concerts with 'When A Child Is Born' and made it quite clear that the key line in the song is one which says colour of skin, black, white or yellow, is irrelevant.

'They got the message!' Johnny says with a beaming smile. Just before Johnny's visit Arthur Ashe, the tennis supremo, had also visited South Africa and had donated money to build a first-class tennis club in Soweto, a segregated city of a million blacks or more near to Johannesburg. However there were later reports that a bureaucratic mix up has partly contributed toward Johnny being allowed in to the country, for he had been given a visa that specifically granted him the unlimited right of appearing before multiracial audiences. Some say the authorities thought he was a much lighter shade of colour while there were those who thought he was white. Later he told Los Angeles writer Keith Dunstan: 'We made our bookings two years in advance and we weren't conscious of anything political. South Africa was just another place at the end of the world to me and I wanted to see the wild animals. I guess I was an innocent.

'Six months beforehand all the racial problems came up, and I had to make up my mind whether to go or not.

'But the promoter said if we would come he was positive I would not sing to segregated audiences.

'This was a big breakthrough. I didn't realise it at the time, no international artist had ever performed for integrated audiences. To an American it was like going back to the slavery days.

'But we went there with no antagonism. The only hostility came from a black reporter who asked, "Why are you doing this?"

'He was a little drunk at the time.' And manager Ray Haughn recalls one other protest which came from a group of blacks who felt it would have been better to do the concerts on the regular basis of white shows and black shows. 'Their argument was that when the same concerts are presented to black audiences the price of the ticket is cut roughly by two thirds. This meant the twenty Rand ticket could be purchased for an all black showing for about seven Rand. Now that we had fully integrated shows the blacks were compelled to sit in the cheaper seats in the far reaches of the last rows. John did not go to South Africa to try and solve political problems. He only wanted to sing and thank his fans for supporting him through their record purchases for the preceding twenty years.'

John says, 'The tour was incredible, huge audiences. If it wasn't the greatest reception I have received in my career it was close to it. Phenomenal!'

General politics have never been of much interest to Johnny. He says simply: 'I've not been involved in politics since I left school. I was the liaison officer between students and faculty. Actually the political scene is more showbiz than showbiz! Things have to get accomplished but there has to be a better way.'

He remains remarkably fit as he heads for his fiftieth year and it is hard to credit that he has nearly reached his half-century. He's almost as taut and fit as when a teenager. He likes to keep his weight at 155 pounds – he's 5'11" tall. He exercises a minimum forty-five minutes a day and he realises that it is psychologically good – apart from any other reason – to look and feel in fine fettle. He doesn't look his age at all.

'I think it's a state of mind really. It doesn't matter how you look but it does matter how you look! I've just a few suits these days and I gotta get into them!'

Physical fitness isn't his only way of surviving. He is careful about his daily routine. 'It's an extremely low key restful routine but highly disciplined. It keeps my energy high. It allows me to go out on the road for three or four weeks at a crack – even longer when overseas. I don't allow myself to get exhausted. This doesn't mean that I'm the smartest fellow on the block. It took me fifteen years to learn how to travel sensibly.'

He says the worst danger is being tired, since audiences demand freshness and without a strict schedule it would be so easy to fall into an ultimately tiring routine which would drain energy and reduce effectiveness. The eventual outcome would be a deterioration in his popularity, at first slow and almost imperceptible, but then gathering momentum. It's also a reason why he avoids the showbiz glamour scene. It saps energy. As he says, there have been many promising entertainers who have come and gone, not because they are musically no good or make bad records. Their demise has come from an inability to govern personal affairs, and ensure they have a firm career foundation.

Early in his career he existed on little sleep. Johnny Noga said in 1960: 'Johnny rarely goes to bed until the sun has risen. He's what you might call a "groggy night-owl" – which is the only thing a professional night club entertainer can be.'

Johnny said: 'A little better than four hours a day is my sleep.' And he got his sleep, such as it was, in the late morning and early afternoon.

In the eighties Johnny is a late morning riser unless, as frequently happens, he is in bed by 10.30 p.m. He believes he can be singing well at sixty-five and over: 'I don't want to be on a farm raising cows [he owns some cattle ranches], I want something to do!' And to Johnny, singing is in the end the only thing which claims him.

As a person he is universally respected. On occasions he can be angry but generally he is accommodating and relaxed, and he is regarded as a warm person by those who work close to him. To friends he is 'John' – 'Johnny' is his name but it's seen as his stage and record name. John is John, the man. But then, he became famous as Johnny, but John is the name he likes from friends.

And it's his friends who are most aware of the changes in his appearance and attitudes over the years. Fans tend to see an artist standing still, usually at the period they first discovered and had this love affair with a singer.

Maria Niemela a housewife from La Mirada is the director of Johnny's American fan club and has observed him for many years. 'I first heard him twenty-six and a half years ago! I just heard him on the radio like everybody else did. I just thought he had a really beautiful voice. The first song I ever heard was "It's Not For Me To Say".'

She sees Johnny as totally unaffected by his celebrity status. 'He's got a lot of humility. He doesn't think he is too great to go to a fan club party. Besides all that, he's a really nice person.'

The watershed year for Johnny, according to Maria, was 1969. Previously he had been very thin, his hair slicked down the sides of his head. However, he gained a little weight and took on a new appearance. The hair was longer and fluffy. 'This was the period when he began looking as he is now. His whole body fuller, he stopped smoking and I suppose this was a reason for his gain in weight, the face was very angular, the eyes looked bigger. I think a lot of people call it the year of the "big change" and really, everyone approved.'

She also, like his friends, knows that Johnny gives generous sums of money to a variety of causes. Over the years he had taken part in countless commercials for charity. It's part and parcel of his desire not to lose complete touch with the street atmosphere in which he grew up. In Los Angeles there is an exercise room named after him at the YMCA, and he is a donor to the Los Angeles Health Clinic for Gay People and the Gay Community Centres. The YMCA in Hollywood became termed The Johnny Mathis Youth Centre in 1982. He is active in charity work for cancer relief.

His health has remained good, fortunately. There have been the odd moments of sickness. His British tour of 1962 was held up because he strained his back and he was three to four months off work. Twelve years later he arrived in England seated in a bath chair. The event occasioning this rather unusual entry for a star through the customs occurred on March 7. He was at the Schubert Theatre, Los Angeles during the first week of March and on the last day he did some dancing with the troupe who were part of the show, three guys and two girls. He did some rather deep knee bends and felt a sharp twinge, but assumed it was nothing more than a strained muscle or a pinched nerve. It wasn't until later that he learnt that he had broken a bone in his leg. Ray Haughn says: 'The assumption at the time was that he had torn a ligament. So immediately, the choreographer was massaging the back of his leg vigorously. The pain intensified. It was curtain time for the second half of the show. What do we do? I looked in John's eyes, he really was suffering! It really was his decision, but no one was going to encourage him to go on! He asked for his coat, and asked if we would carry him on stage. We got a stool and then lifted him into position in front of the orchestra. It was one of the real show business bravery acts that are rarely publicised. He sang to at least six standing ovations; ninety per cent of the audience never even suspecting that there was anything wrong at all! The curtain fell, and we rushed John to his car and to his home, still thinking it was a torn ligament that would respond to massage, heat and rest in bed.

'I came by the house a few mintues after he arrived and gave him some aspirin to make him relax. Then the next morning we went to a medical specialist in Century City who discovered the fracture. The splintered ends of the bones were what they had been massaging. The bones were set and John was placed in a cast.'

He refused to cancel his British visit and the only way it was possible for him to move around was in an invalid chair. It certainly gave his British fans an unusual picture though the man himself looked remarkably pleased with the whole affair when he arrived at Heathrow. And his enthusiasm for a career now with its past over a quarter-century away remains undimmed.

'On average I'm away performing about six months of the year. But at home I may work harder than when away! I'm busy recording, rehearsing new songs and so on.'

Manager Ray Haughn says: 'Even when we're away he's learning – he's got this flair for learning languages. If we're in South America any length of time, he's soon getting his Spanish or Portuguese together and chatting to the locals.' Manager Ray said Johnny loves the company of musicians. 'We usually take a few key men with us. If we're somewhere for a season, Johnny is liable to book into a big luxury hotel and then get fed up after a few days and move into a smaller one where the musicians are staying.'

'My feelings are that Johnny can do anything. He can do Glen Campbell or even get into the things Johnny Cash can do. It's always been one hundred per cent commitment from Johnny. What has changed is his personal life and attitude. John is in control of his career and now has a rewarding life. He's on his own. Now he owns a ranch and can sing at any time.

'He doesn't fear the past: he faces it without embarrassment. He conveys in music what he really feels and he's accepted for what he is. There are certain things John has wanted to do and he's fulfilled them. For those who have great vocal equipment, and John certainly does, it's not a matter of their career slumping off. It's just a matter that it peaks at certain times. You can't plan it that way, but that's just how it seems to go.'

Brother Ralph says he finds himself in the strange position of being a brother and yet a fan. 'Sometimes I wish people would say to me, "Hey, Ralph, how are you?" and not "Hey Ralph, how's Johnny?" but I guess it's the way it has to be. Johnny was really the ideal brother years back. He always had a concern for others, he had a toughness but it didn't result in, say, fighting other kids, rather it was his non-involvement, for he could have flattened them, he was strong enough. He always tried to do the best with what he had. He was sensitive and he wasn't arrogant. He was determined he would go places.

'I mean, he was a very special person and when you say that it always sounds wet because people say, "Well, you're his brother and all that," but, I mean, he is special, see where he has gotten.

'I grew up with him but I think there are things about him I don't know, I mean maybe that's the special bit? I've known him all my life but there is something I can't put my finger on.'

171

The arresting time for Ralph is watching Johnny on stage and being part of a huge audience which goes wild once his brother walks out and greets them. He feels, on occasions, he should stand up and say, 'Hey, that's my brother,' and yet, for all the family association, Ralph somehow senses there are two different people wrapped up in Johnny.

'I find it a fascinating experience really – the guy on stage was the guy you had breakfast with, did things with and yet the performance is about something else. I can't really put my finger on it. I guess it's like two mirrors reflecting, reality and the person in the mirror. I feel proud of John.'

Ray Haughn would agree. As John's his long-standing manager he can justifiably claim to know him better than anyone. He has been the guiding hand in every facet of John's career for nineteen years. Britain's *Music And Video Week* well summed up the Haughn-Mathis relationship under the caption heading 'Ray Haughn: his manager and pal' when they discussed Ray's management role in their 25th Anniversary Supplement tribute to Johnny in 1981.

The Haughn-Mathis partnership must be one of the strongest and most enduring in popular music. It has brought untold musical riches to millions across the world. John and Ray have created one of showbusiness's greatest happenings.

The two have never actually signed a management contract! 'Ours is a very different working relationship to that of many artists and managers, and it has always been very good.

'To be honest, if something isn't good enough for Johnny, or for me, then there's no point in putting it in writing, and then both being bound by it. That philosophy has worked all these years so there is no reason why it should change now.'

Underlying everything has been Johnny's burning ambition, his utter commitment and dedication, his own tremendous inner strength. Although he possesses boundless talent he has still put in endless hours of hard work which have enabled him to get where he has. It began, after all, when as a kid of nine or ten he feel in love with singing and music.

'Motivation is the key word,' he says. 'Why does one do certain things? I just wanted to be. And to do what I wanted it would have to be real and honest, not a fake.

'You have to be positive in what you do. You have to go into things with enthusiasm. What you do must present a challenge. You say "yes" to something and you should keep to it. I may say I will tour Britain then even if nearer the time I am saying, "Why am I going?" I still go. I said I would.

'But you have to find time for yourself, to be alone, for otherwise show-business can be destructive and you can become neurotic. Golf means the time when I cannot have my voice, in fact, of course, to put it another way it's a situation where my voice doesn't matter.

'I've learned to say no for my sanity. I've learned to say no to many things because they distract from what I do. You need to let people know you're still alive from time to time and do it carefully.'

For Johnny knows full well he may receive an invitation not for himself, it's so that someone else or an organization can boost their own standing.

'You go to something. They greet you when you come. They've got you! After that? No one cares about you. OK it's part of the business but I'd rather not get too involved.'

His life is worth something – that's why.

FACTURAMA

Contents

SINGLES

This section lists all single releases in the US and UK and some from elsewhere. It gives the chart positions of those records which reached the relevant listing. All other 'special' single releases (including picture disc, flexi, twelve-inch and promotional) can be found listed.

Chart Hits – UK

Date first entered	Highest position	Weeks on chart	Song
5-23-58	27	5	'Teacher Teacher'
9-26-58	4	16	'A Certain Smile'
12-19-58	17	3	'Winter Wonderland'
8- 7-59	6	15	'Someone'
11-27-59	30	1	'The Best Of Everything'
1-29-60	12	13	'Misty'
3-24-60	38	9	'You Are Beautiful'
7-28-60	47	2	'Starbright'
10- 6-60	9	18	'My Love For You'
4- 4-63	49	1	'What Will My Mary Say'
1-25-75	10	12	'I'm Stone In Love With You'
11-13-76	1	12	'When A Child Is Born'
3-25-78	3	14	'Too Much Too Little Too Late'*
7-29-78	45	6	'You're All I Need To Get By'*
8-11-79	15	10	'Gone Gone Gone'

*with Deniece Williams, also same titles US.
US Charts: Top 100. UK Charts. Top 20, 50, 75 (as British chart expanded)

Total US hits: 43   *US: Top Twenty hits:* 9
      UK hits: 15   *UK: Top Ten hits:* 9.
British titles not charting in the US as A-sides: 'Winter Wonderland' (1968)
'Someone' (1959) 'When A Child Is Born' (1976) 'Gone Gone Gone' (1979).
Total Weeks On Chart: US: 434 UK: 137
It should be noted Johnny Mathis is an album orientated artiste.

UK single releases year by year

1957

'It's Not For Me To Say'/'Warm And Tender' Philips PB 692
'Wonderful Wonderful'/'When Sunny Gets Blue' Philips PB 713
'Chances Are'/'The 12th Of Never' Philips PB 749

1958

'Wild Is The Wind'/'No Love' Fontana H 130
'Teacher Teacher'/'Easy To Love' Fontana H 130
'A Certain Smile'/'Let It Rain' Fontana H 142
'Call Me'/'Stairway To The Sea' Fontana H 163
'Winter Wonderland'/'Sleigh Ride' Fontana H 165

'Let's Love'/'You'd Be So Nice To
Come Home To'   Fontana H 186

1959
'Someone'/'They Say It's Wonderful'
                       Fontana H 199
'The Best Of Everything'/'Cherie'
                       Fontana H 218
'Misty'/'The Story Of Our Love'
                       Fontana H 219
'It's Not For Me To Say'/'Warm and
Tender'   Fontana H 220

1960
'You Are Beautiful'/'Very Much In
Love'   Fontana H 234
'The Twelfth Of Never'/'Get Me To
The Church On Time'   Fontana H 248
'Starbright'/'All Is Well' Fontana H 254
'My Love For You'/'Oh That Feeling'
                       Fontana H 267
'Maria'/'Hey Love'   Fontana H 272

1961
'You Set My Heart To Music'/
'Jenny'   Fontana H 316
'Laurie My Love'/'Should I Wait'
                       Fontana H 328
'Love Look Away'/'When My Sugar
Walks Down The Street'
                       Fontana H 335
'My Kind Of Christmas'/'Christmas
Eve'   Fontana H 349

1962
'Sweet Thursday'/'One Look'
                       Fontana H 372
'Marianna'/'Unaccustomed As I Am'
                       CBS 110
'Gina'/'I Love Her That's Why' CBS 117
'Small World'/'Everythings Coming
Up Roses'   CBS 124
'What Will My Mary Say'/'Quiet
Girl'   CBS 135

1963
'No Man Can Stand Alone'/'Every
Step Of The Way'   CBS 152
'Wonderful, Wonderful'/'Wild Is The
Wind'   CBS 171

'Sooner Or Later'/'In Wisconsin'
                       CBS 168
'Too Young To Go Steady'/'How To
Handle A Woman'   CBS 209
'Your Teenage Dreams'/'Come
Back'   HMV 1217

1964
'A Great Night For Crying'/'Bye, Bye
Barbara'   HMV 1267
'The Fall Of Love'/'No More'
                       HMV 1294
'Taste Of Tears'/'White Roses From A
Blue Valentine'   HMV 1318
'Listen Lonely Girl'/'All I Wanted'
                       HMV 1365
'Mirage'/'The Sweetheart Tree'
                       HMV 1467

1965
'Danny Boy'/'This Is Love'   HMV 1491
'On A Clear Day You Can See For-
ever'/'Come Back To Me   HMV 1503

1966
'Moment To Moment'/'The Glass
Mountain'   HMV 1527
'The Impossible Dream'/'Hurry, It's
Lovely Up Here'   HMV 1550

1967
'Don't Talk To Me'/'Misty Roses'
                       CBS 2969
1968
'Venus'/   CBS
'You Make Me Think About You'/ CBS

1969
'Among The First To Know'/'Long
Winter Nights'   CBS 3236
'A Time For Us'/'The World I Threw
Away'   CBS 4455
'Midnight Cowboy'/'We'   CBS 4721

1970
'Odds And Ends'/'For All We Know'
                       CBS 4968
'The Last Time I Saw Her'/'Wherefore
And Why'   CBS 5127
'Evil's Way'/'Everybody's Talkin''
                       CBS 5283

1971
'Long Ago And Far Away'/'For All We Know' CBS 7459

1972
'If We Only Have Love'/'This Way Mary' CBS 7093
'Make It Easy On Yourself'/'Sometimes' CBS 8322

1973
'Soul And Inspiration'/'Don't Let Me Be Lonely Tonight' CBS 1423
'I'm Coming Home'/'Stop, Look And Listen' CBS 1732

1974
'Life Is A Song Worth Singing'/'I Just Wanted To Be Me' CBS 2026
'I'm Stone In Love With You'/'Sweet Child' CBS 2653

1975
'Feel Like Makin' Love'/'The Heart Of A Woman' CBS 3496
'Only You'/'The Things I Might Have Been' CBS 3673

1976
'Stardust'/'What I Did For Love' 'CBS 3913
'I'm Stone In Love With You'/'A Certain Smile' CBS 3958
'99 Miles From LA'/'The Greatest Gift' CBS 4280
'When A Child Is Born'/'Every Time You Touch Me (I Get High)' CBS 4599

1977
'Sweet Love Of Mine'/'I Don't Want To Say No' CBS 5026
'Loving You, Losing You'/'World Of Laughter' CBS 5146
'Sweet Surrender'/'99 Miles From LA' CBS 5698

1978
'Too Much, Too Little, Too Late'/'Emotion' CBS 6164
'You Light Up My Life'/'I Wrote A Symphony On My Guitar' CBS 6352

'You're All I Need To Get By'/'You're A Special Part Of My Life' CBS 6483
'Until You Come Back To Me'/'Just The Way You Are' CBS 6700

1979
'The Last Time I Felt Like This'/'As Time Goes By' CBS 7091
'Gone, Gone, Gone'/'Best Days Of My Life' CBS 7730
'No One But The One You Love'/'New York State Of Mind' CBS 7915

1980
'You Saved My Life'/'Love' CBS 8151
'Midnight Blue'/'Just The Way You Are' CBS 8253
'I'll Do It All For You'/'Lights Of Rio' CBS 8696
'Three Times À Lady'/'I Will Survive' CBS 8927

1981
'You Saved My Life'/'When I Need You' CBS 1602
'When A Child Is Born'/'The Lord's Prayer' CBS 1758

1982
'Friends In Love'/'When The Lovin' Goes Out Of The Livin'' CBS 2371
'Something's Goin' On'/'Memory' CBS 2605

UK Picture Sleeve Singles

'My Love For You'/'Oh That Feeling' UK Fontana H 267
'Your Teenage Dreams'/'Come Back' UK HMV POP 1217
Pressed in the UK for export only
'Maria'/'B' Side Julie Andrews Track UK CBS Special Products WB 725
'I'm Stone In Love With You'/'A Certain Smile' UK CBS 3958
(Hall Of Fame Series)
'Stardust'/'What I Did For Love' UK CBS 3913
'When A Child Is Born'/'Every Time You Touch Me (I Get High)' UK CBS 4599

'You Saved My Life'/'When I Need You' UK CBS A1602	'Friends In Love'/'When The Lovin' Goes Out Of The Livin'' UK CBS A2371
'When A Child Is Born'/'The Lord's Prayer' UK CBS A1758	'Somethin's Goin On'/'Memory' UK CBS A2605
(Duet with Glady's Knight & the Pips on both tracks)	

Single Cassettes

In 1983 CBS began issuing a series of singles in special cassette form. One of these releases was a four-track of Johnny's songs: 'I'm Stone In Love With You', 'Misty', 'A Certain Smile' and 'The Twelfth Of Never'.

Flexi Disc

'When A Child Is Born'/'Send In The Clowns'/'Do Me Wrong' 'But Do Me'. This was a gift enclosed with the magazine *Radio Guide,* December 1976. Johnny Mathis/Abba—released by *Readers Digest* to promote box-set.

Chart Hits – US (Singles)

Date first entered	Highest position	Weeks on chart	Song
1-30-57	17	39	'Wonderful, Wonderful'
4-24-57	5	34	'It's Not For Me To Say'
9- 7-57	5	28	'Chances Are'
10-26-57	51	17	'The Twelfth Of Never'
12- 7-57	37	18	'Wild Is The Wind'
12-14-57	48	10	'No Love (But Your Love)'
2- 1-58	43	13	'Come To Me'
4-12-58	42	14	'All The Time'
4-26-58	43	14	'Teacher, Teacher'
6-21-58	19	14	'A Certain Smile'
10- 5-58	21	15	'Call Me'
1-11-59	60	6	'You Are Beautiful'
1-11-59	44	9	'Let's Love'
3-29-59	35	13	'Someone'
6-21-59	20	15	'Small World'
10-11-59	12	17	'Misty'
10-18-59	93	2	'The Story Of Our Love'
11-22-59	62	5	'The Best Of Everything'
3- 6-60	25	11	'Starbright'
6- 5-60	78	4	'Maria'
9- 4-60	47	11	'My Love For You'
1- 1-61	64	3	'How To Handle A Woman'
10-29-61	83	1	'Wasn't The Summer Short'
12-17-61	88	3	'Maria'
3-17-62	99	2	'Sweet Thursday'
6-16-62	86	1	'Marianna'

Date first entered	Highest position	Weeks on chart	Song
9-22-62	6	12	'Gina'
1-26-63	9	12	'What Will My Mary Say'
5-25-63	30	7	'Every Step Of The Way'
9- 7-63	84	3	'Sooner Or Later'
12-14-63	90	4	'I'll Search My Heart'
10-12-63	68	7	'Your Teenage Dreams'
10-12-63	61	6	'Come Back'
2- 1-64	53	7	'Bye, Bye Barbara'
6-20-64	87	3	'Taste Of Tears'
10-24-64	62	8	'Listen Lonely Girl'
12-18-65	98	2	'On A Clear Day You Can See Forever'
7-26-69	96	3	'A Time For Us'
9-22-73	75	8	'I'm Coming Home'
12-29-73	54	11	'Life Is A Song Worth Singing'
4- 1-78	1	18	'Too Much, Too Little, Too Late'
7-29-78	47	8	'You're All I Need To Get By'
4-17-82	38	11	'Friends In Love'

US single releases

Columbia singles

'Wonderful! Wonderful!'/'When Sunny Gets Blue' 4-40784

'It's Not For Me To Say'/'Warm And Tender' 4-40851

'Chances Are'/'The Twelfth Of Never' 4-40993

'Wild Is The Wind'/'No One (But Your Love) 4-41060

'Come To Me'/'When I Am With You' 4-41082

'All The Time'/'Teacher, Teacher' 4-41152

'A Certain Smile'/'Let It Rain' 4-41193

'Call Me'/'Stairway To The Sea' 4-41253

'You Are Beautiful'/'Let's Love' 4-41304

'Someone'/'Very Much In Love' 4-41355

'Small World'/'You Are Everything To Me' 4-41410

'Misty'/'The Story Of Our Love' 4-41483

'The Best Of Everything'/'Cherie' 4-41491

'Starbright'/'All Is Well' 4-41583

'Maria'/'Hey Love' 4-41684

'My Love For You'/'Oh That Feeling' 4-41764

'How To Handle A Woman'/'While You're Young' 4-41866

'You Set My Heart To Music'/'Jenny' 4-41980

'Laurie, My Love'/'Should I Wait' 4-42048

'Wasn't The Summer Short'/'There You Are' 4-42156

'My Kind Of Christmas'/'Christmas Eve' 4-42238

'Sweet Thursday'/'One Look' 4-42261

'Marianna'/'Unaccustomed As I Am' 4-42420

'That's The Way It Is'/'I'll Never Be Lonely Again' 4-42509

'Gina'/'I Love Her That's Why' 4-42582

'What Will My Mary Say'/'Quiet Girl' 4-42666

'Every Step Of The Way'/'No Man Can Stand Alone' 4-42799

'In Wisconsin'/'Sooner Or Later' 4-42836

'I'll Search My Heart'/'All The Sad Young Men' 4-42916

'Don't Talk To Me'/'Misty Roses' 4-44266

'Among The First To Know'/'Long Winter Nights'   4-44357
'Venus'/'Don't Go Breakin' My Heart'   4-44517
'You Make Me Think About You'/'Night Dreams'   4-44637
'The 59th Street Bridge Song (Feelin' Groovy)'/'The End Of The World'   4-44728
'Whoever You Are, I Love You'/'I'll Never Fall In Love Again'   4-44837
'Love Theme From *Romeo And Juliet*'/'The World I Threw Away'   4-44915
'Midnight Cowboy'/'We'   4-45022
'Give Me Your Love For Christmas'/'Calypso Noel'   4-45035
'Give Me Your Love For Christmas'/'Calypso Noel'   4-45100
(Special item for National Tuberculosis)
'Odds And Ends'/'For All We Know'   4-45104
'Wherefore And Why'/'The Last Time I Saw Her'   4-45183
'Pieces Of Dreams'/'Darling Lili'   4-45223
'Evil Ways'/'Until It's Time For You To Go'   4-45263
'Sign Of The Dove'/'Christmas Is'   4-45281
'Ten Times Forever More'/'I Was There'   4-45323
'Evie'/'Think About Things'   4-45371
'Long Ago And Far Away'/'For All We Know'   4-45415
'If We Only Have Love'/'How Can You Mend A Broken Heart'   4-45470
'Sign Of The Dove'/'Christmas Is'   4-45513
'If We Only Have Love'/'This Way, Mary'   4-45559
'Make It Easy On Yourself'/'Sometimes'   4-45635
'Soul And Inspiration'/'Just Once In My Life I'   4-45729
'Take Good Care Of Her'/'Walking Tall'   4-45777
'Show And Tell'/'Happy'   4-45835
'I'm Coming Home'/'Stop Look And Listen To Your Heart'   4-45908

'Life Is A Song Worth Singing'/'I Just Wanted To Be Me'   4-45975
'Sweet Child'/'I'm Stone In Love With You'   4-46048
'Sail On White Moon'/'The Heart Of A Woman'   3-10080
'I'm Stone In Love With You'/'Foolish'   3-10112
'The Greatest Gift'/'You're As Right As Rain'   3-10175
'Stardust'/'What I Did For Love'   3-10250
'One Day In Your Life'/'Midnight Blue'   3-10291
'Yellow Roses On Her Gown'/'Every Time You Touch Me (I Get High)'   3-10350
'Do Me Wrong But Do Me'/'Send In The Clowns'   3-10404
'Turn The Lights Down'/'When A Child Is Born'   3-10447
'Loving You, Losing You'/'World Of Laughter'   3-10496
'Arianne'/'99 Miles From LA'   3-10574
'Hold Me, Thrill Me, Kiss Me'/'The Most Beautiful Girl'   3-10611
'When A Child Is Born'/'Every Time You Touch Me (I Get High)'   3-10640
'Too Much, Too Little, Too Late' (W/Deniece Williams)/'Emotion'   3-10693
'You're All I Need To Get By' (W/Deniece Williams)/'You're A Special Part Of My Life'   3-10772
'I Just Can't Get Over You' (W/Deniece Williams)/'That's What Friends Are For'   3-10826
'The Last Time I Felt Like This' (W/Olivor)/'As Time Goes By'   3-10902
'Begin The Beguine'/'Gone, Gone, Gone'   3-11001
'No One But The One You Love'/'To The Ends Of The Earth'   1-11091
'Christmas In The City Of The Angels'/'The Very First Christmas Day'   1-11158
'Different Kinda Different' (W/McWilliams) 'The Lights Of Rio'   1-11313
'Nothing Between Us But Love'/'Deep Purple'   18-02194

'The Lords Prayer' (W/Knight &
Pips)/'When A Child Is Born' 11-11409

(Columbia Hall Of Fame)
'It's Not For Me To Say'/'Chances
Are' 4-33001
'Maria'/'Misty' 4-33042
'Wonderful! Wonderful!'/'The Twelfth
Of Never' 4-33048
'A Certain Smile'/'Small World'
4-33056
'Venus'/'Gina' 4-33142
'Love Theme From *Romeo And
Juliet*'/'I'll Never Fall In Love Again'
4-33174
'What Will My Mary Say'/'Call Me'
4-33226
'Show And Tell'/'Soul And
Inspiration'/'Just Once In My Life'
4-33253
'I'm Coming Home'/'I'm Stone In Love
With You' 4-33264
'Too Much, Too Little, Too Late'/
'You're All I Need To Get By'
4-33360

Arista Single

'Friends In Love' AS 0673

Mercury singles

'Your Teenage Dreams'/'Come
Back' 72184
'Have Reindeer, Will Travel'/'The
Little Drummer Boy' 72217
'Bye Bye Barbara'/'Take the Time'/'A
Great Night For Crying' 72229
'The Fall Of Love'/'No More' 72263
'Taste Of Tears'/'White Roses From A
Blue Valentine' 72287
'Listen Lonely Girl'/'All I Wanted'
72339
'Take The Time'/'Dianacita' 72432
'The Sweetheart Tree'/'Mirage' 72464
'On A Clear Day You Can See
Forever'/'Come Back To Me' 72493
'Moment To Moment'/'The Glass
Mountain' 72539
'The Shadow Of Your Smile'/'The
Sweetheart Tree' 72568

'The Impossible Dream'/'So Nice'
72610
'Saturday Sunshine'/'Two Tickets
And A Candy Heart' 72653

**US Picture Sleeve Singles (Columbia
and Mercury)**

*Columbia Records Presents Johnny
Mathis: special combination pack
issued only to US disc jockeys*
'It's Not For Me To Say'/'Warm And
Tender' 4-40851
'Wonderful, Wonderful'/'When Sunny
Gets Blue' 4-40784
'Chances Are'/'The Twelfth Of Never'
4-40993
'Wild Is The Wind'/'No Love' 4-41060
'A Certain Smile'/'Let It Rain' 4-41193
'Call Me'/'Stairway To The Sea'
4-41253
'Misty'/'The Story Of Our Love'
4-41483
'The Best Of Everything'/'Cherie'
4-41491
'Starbright'/'All Is Well' 4-41583
'How To Handle A Woman'/'While
You're Young' 4-41866
'Starbright'/'While You're Young'
D43 (6726)
(Special enrolment record to
Columbia record club) *cardboard
record like picture disc*
'You Set My Heart To Music'/'Jenny'
4-41980
'Laurie My Love'/'Should I Wait'
4-42048
'Wasn't The Summer Short'/'There
You Are' 4-42156
'Christmas Eve'/'My Kind Of
Christmas' 4-42238
'Sweet Thursday'/'One Look' 4-42261
'Marianna'/'Unaccustomed As I Am'
4-42420
'That's The Way It Is'/'I'll Never Be
Lonely Again' 4-42509
'Gina'/'I Love Her That's Why' 4-42582
'What Will Mary Say'/'Quiet Girl'
4-42666
'Every Step Of The Way'/'No Man Can
Stand Alone' 4-42799

'Your Teenage Dreams'/'Come
Back'   72184
'The Little Drummer Boy'/'Have
Reindeer Will Travel'   72217
'Bye Bye Barbara'/'A Great Night For
Crying'   72229
'Listen Lonely Girl'/'All I Wanted'
                                     72339
'Take The Time'/'Dianacita'   72432
'Sweetheart Tree'/'Mirage'   72464
'Shadow Of Your Smile'/'The
Sweetheart Tree'   72568
(Special DJ issue)
'So Nice'/'The Impossible Dream'
                                     72610
'Two Tickets And A Candy
Heart'/'Saturday Sunshine'   72653
'Give Me Your Love For Christmas'/
'Calypso Noel'   4-45035
'Give Me Your Love For Christmas'/
'Calypso Noel'   4-45100
(Special item for National
Tuberculosis)
'When A Child Is Born'/'Every Time
You Touch Me (I Get High)'   3-10640
'Christmas Is'/'Sleigh Ride'   AE7 1148
(Special item for National
Tuberculosis)

Miscellaneous US Singles
Picture Disc:
'That's What Friends Are For'
                        Columbia JC 35435
Special Disc:
'Starbright'/'While You're Young'
(Special gift with enrolment to
Columbia Record Club, made of
cardboard with a picture of Johnny
stamped on the record, like a picture
disc.
Special Red vinyl (promotional issue)
'Gina'/'Gina'   Columbia 4-42582
'What Will Mary Say'/'What Will Mary
Say'   Columbia 4-42582
'I'll Search My Heart'/'I'll Search My
Heart'   Columbia 4-42916

Foreign Picture Sleeve Singles
(This includes most of the released
material.)

Australia
'When A Child Is Born'/'Every Time
You Touch Me (I Get High)' BA 222254

Belgium
'Life Is A Song Worth Singing'/'I Just
Wanted To Be Me'   CBS 2702

Brazil
'Granada'/'Tres Palabras'
                          ODEON 71 3120

France
'Love Story'/'My Sweet Lord'
                              CBS 7166
'When A Child Is Born'/'Every Time
You Touch Me (I Get High)'   CBS 4599
'Too Much, Too Little, Too
Late'/'Emotion'   CBS 6164
'Begin The Beguine'/'Gone, Gone,
Gone'   CBS 7418

Germany
'Every Step Of The Way'/'No Man Can
Stand Alone'   CBS CW281 207
'When A Child Is Born'/'Every Time
You Touch Me (I Get High)'   CBS 4599
'Too Much, Too Little, Too
Late'/'Emotion'   CBS 6164

Holland
'Someone'/'Very Much In Love'
                        Fontana 263067TF
'On The Sunny Side Of The
Street'/'You Do Something To Me'
                        Fontana 271148TF
'Misty'/'They Say It's Wonderful'
              CBS 1.352 (orange heading)
'Misty'/'They Say It's Wonderful'
              CBS 1.352 (green heading)
'What Will Mary Say'/'Quiet Girl'
                       CBS CA 281159
'Every Step Of The Way'/'No Man Can
Stand Alone'   CBS CA 281207
'I'll Search My Heart'/'All The Sad
Young Men'   CBS 1.383
'I'm Stone In Love With You'/'Sweet
Child'   CBS 2653
'When A Child Is Born'/'Every Time
You Touch Me (I Get High)'   CBS 4599

'Too Much, Too Little, Too Late'/'Emotion'   CBS 6164
'Too Much, Too Little, Too Late'/'Emotion'   CBS 6164
(re issue drawing cover)
'You're All I Need To Get By'/'You're A Special Part Of My Life'   CBS 6483
'Just The Way You Are'/'You're A Special Part Of My Life'   CBS 6679
'The Last Time I Felt Like This'/'As Time Goes By'   CBS 7091
'No One But The One You Love'/'New York State Of Mind'   CBS 7935
'Gone, Gone, Gone'/'Begin The Beguine'   CBS A 1582

Italy
'Gina'/'I Love Her That's Why'
     CBS BA 121004
'When A Child Is Born'/'Every Time You Touch Me (I Get High)'   CBS 4599
'Too Much, Too Little, Too Late'/'Emotion'   CBS 6164

Japan
'The Twelfth Of Never'/'B' side/Marty Robbins track   Columbia LL 100
'Maria'/'Tonight'   Columbia LL 321
'Too Much, Too Little, Too Late'/'Emotion'   CBS 06SP 234
'Friends In Love'/'When The Lovin' Goes Out Of The Livin''
     CBS 07SP 638
'Somethin's Goin' On'/'Lately'
     CBS 07SP 649

Portugal
'A Time For Us (Love Theme From *Romeo and Juliet*)'/'The World I Threw Away   CBS 4455
'Too Much, Too Little, Too Late'/'Emotion'   CBS 6164

Spain
'Midnight Cowboy'/'Raindrops Keep Fallin' On My Head'   CBS 4993
'Close To You' (sung in Spanish)/'Bridge Over Troubled Water' (sung in Spanish)   CBS 5328
'Love Story' (sung in Spanish)/'We've Only Just Begun'   CBS 7272

'If We Only Have Love'/'This Way Mary'   CBS 7993
'When A Child Is Born'/'Every Time You Touch Me (I Get High)'   CBS 4599
'Too Much, Too Little, Too Late' (sung in Spanish)/'How Deep Is Your Love'
     CBS 6522
'The Last Time I Felt Like This'/'As Time Goes By'   CBS 7091
'Begin The Beguine'/'Gone, Gone, Gone'   CBS 7418

Songs on singles that were never included on any US LPs

Columbia
'Among The First To Know'   4-44357
'Christmas Eve'   3-42238
'Christmas In The City Of The Angels'   1-11158
'Christmas Is'   4-45513
'Darling Lili'   4-45223
'Don't Talk To Me   4-44266
'Evie'   4-45371
'For All We Know'   4-45104
'I'   4-45729
'Laurie, My Love'   4-42048
'Long Winter Nights'   4-44357
'My Kind Of Christmas'   4-42238
'Night Dreams'   4-44637
'Sign Of The Dove'   4-45281
'Sometimes'   4-45635
'Take Good Care Of Her'   4-45777
'The Last Time I Saw Her'   4-45183
'The Very First Christmas'   1-11158
'Think About Things'   4-45371
'This Way, Mary'   4-45559
'Turn The Lights Down'   3-10447
'Walking Tall'   4-45777
'Wherefore And Why'   4-45183
'Whoever You Are, I Love You'
     4-44837
'The Lords Prayer' (with Gladys Knight and The Pips)   11-11409
'When A Child Is Born' (with Gladys Knight and The Pips)   11-11409

Mercury
'A Great Night For Crying'   72229
'All I Wanted'   72339
'Bye Bye Barbara'   72229

'Come Back'	72184
'Dianacita'	72432
'Listen Lonely Girl'	72339
'No More'	72263
'Take The Time'	72432
'Taste Of Tears'	72287
'The Fall Of Love'	72263
'The Glass Mountain'	72539
'Two Tickets And A Candy Heart'	
	72653
'White Roses From A Blue Valentine'	
	72287
'Your Teenage Dreams'	72184

CBS

'Gina'	AGS 20.043
'Historia De Amor'	7272
'Cerca De Ti'	5328
'Puente Sobre Aguas Turbulentas'	
	5328
'Aun No Es Tarde'	6522

Singles that were never included on LPs – US and UK

This includes UK and US record numbers. Brief notes on some of the records can be found at the end of this section.

'Evie'/'Think About Things'
　　　　USA Columbia 4-45371
Issued only in the USA
'This Way Mary'/'If We Only Have Love' (re-recorded version)
USA Columbia 4-45371; UK CBS 7993
'I'/'Soul And Inspiration'/'Just Once In My Life' (on an LP)
　　　　USA Columbia 4-45729
Issued only in the USA
'Sometimes'/'Make It Easy On Yourself' (on an LP)
　　　　USA Columbia; UK CBS 8322
'Walking Tall'/'Take Good Care of Her'　　　USA Columbia 4-45777
Issued only in the USA
'Turn The Lights Down'/'When A Child Is Born (on an LP)
　　　　USA Columbia 3-10447
Issued only in the USA
Christmas In The City Of Angels'/'The

Very First Christmas Day'
　　　　USA Columbia 1-11158
Issued only in the USA
'When A Child Is Born' (on an LP)/'The Lords Prayer' (Duet on both recordings with Gladys Knight & The Pips)　　　USA Columbia 11-11409;
　　　　UK CBS 1758
'Don't Talk To Me'/'Misty Roses' (on an LP)
USA Columbia 4-44266; UK CBS 2969
'Among The First To Know'/'Long Winter Nights'
USA Columbia 4-44357; UK CBS 3236
'Night Dreams'/'You Make Me Think About You' (on an LP)
　　　　USA Columbia 4-44637
Issued only in the USA
'Whoever You Are I Love You'/'I'll Never Fall In Love Again' (on an LP)
　　　　USA Columbia 4-44837
Issued only in the USA
'Midnight Cowboy' (re-recorded version)/'We' (on an LP)
USA Columbia 4-45022; UK CBS 4721
'For All We Know'/'Odds And Ends' (on an LP)
USA Columbia 4-45104; UK CBS 4968
'Wherefore And Why'/'The Last Time I Saw Her'
USA Columbia 4-45183; UK CBS 5127
'Darling Lili'/'Pieces Of Dreams' (on an LP)　　　USA Columbia 4-45223
Issued only in the USA
'Sign Of The Dove'/'Christmas Is'
　　　　USA Columbia 4-45281
and also Columbia 4-45513
Issued only in the USA
'My Kind Of Christmas'/'Christmas Eve'
USA Columbia 42238; UK Fontana
　　　　H 349
'Your Teenage Dreams'/'Come Back'
　　　　USA Mercury 72184;
　　　　UK HMV POP1217
'Bye Bye Barbara'/'A Great Night For Crying'　　　USA Mercury 72229;
　　　　UK HMV POP1267
'The Fall Of Love'/'No More'
　　　　USA Mercury 72263;
　　　　UK HMV POP1294

'Taste Of Tears'/'White Roses From A Blue Valentine'
USA Mercury 72287;
UK HMV POP1318
'Listen Lonely Girl'/'All I Wanted'
USA Mercury 72339;
UK HMV POP1365
'The Glass Mountain'/'Moment To Moment' (on an LP)
USA Mercury 72; UK HMV POP1527
'The Impossible Dream' (re-recorded version)/'Hurry It's Lovely Up Here' (on an LP)
UK HMV POP1550
Issued only in the UK
'Take The Time'/'Dianacita'
USA Mercury 72432
Issued only in the USA
'Two Tickets And A Candy Heart'/'Saturday Sunshine' (on an LP)
USA Mercury 72653
Issued only in the USA

Notes:
1 'Bye, Bye Barbara'. This *is* found on the US Box Set LP, 'The Complete Johnny Mathis Treasury' (P6 14628). The album was not issued through US record shops but was available from a mail order company.
2 'Elvie' *is* found on the Brazilian LP 'Os Grandes Sucessor – Johnny Mathis'. D6 412024.
3 'Take Good Care Of Her' *is* found on the USA, Box Set LP, 'The Complete Johnny Mathis Treasury' P6 14628. The set was available by mail order only.

Johnny Mathis Radio Transcription Singles
'The Woodsy Owl Radio Theatre'
(30-Second Announcement)
'Educational Opportunities At The USA Coast Guard Academy'
(Spot Announcement)
1969: 'Christmas Seals'
(Announcement and Records)
Columbia 4-45100

1977: 'Christmas Seals'
(Announcement and Records)
Columbia AE7-1148
1980: 'What's It All About?' (5-Minute Interview and Records)   MA 2812

Juke Box Records
'Johnny's Greatest Hits', 'Chances Are', 'The Twelfth Of Never', 'Wonderful Wonderful', 'It's Not For Me To Say', 'Come To Me', 'Wild Is The Wind'   Columbia CS 8634
'The Shadow Of Your Smile'
Mercury SR 664 C
'So Nice'   Mercury SR 665 C

Singles produced for Radio Stations
'Unaccustomed As I Am'/'Marianna'
Columbia 45 4-42420
'Evil Ways'   Columbia 45 4-45263
'If We Only Have Love'
Columbia 45 4-45559
'I'm Coming Home'
Columbia 45 4-45908
'Show And Tell' Columbia 45 4-45835
'I'm Stone In Love With You'
Columbia 45 3-10112
'I'm Stone In Love With You'/'Sweet Child'   Columbia 45 4-46048
'Yellow Roses On Her Gown'
Columbia 45 3-10350
'Arianne'   Columbia 45 3-10574
'Sign Of The Dove'
Columbia 45 4-45513
'Stardust'   Columbia 45 3-10250
'Don't Go Breakin' My Heart'/'Venus'
Columbia 45 4-44517

Single Releases 33⅓ RPM 7″ Disc
'Crazy In The Heart'/'Too Much Too Soon'   Columbia S731347
'I Won't Dance'/'Johnny One Note'
Columbia S731346
'Why Not'/'On A Cold And Rainy Day'
Columbia S731345
'Live It Up'/'Just Friends'
Columbia S731344
'Hey Look Me Over'/'Love'
Columbia S731348

English Imports EPs
'Let's Do It'   Fontana EP TFE 17355

English Imports 33⅓ Anthologies
'Command Performance'
 Ronco Teleproducts (UK) MSD 2005
Johnny Sings – 'Misty'
'Chestnut Mare'
  CBS Special Products WSR 960
Johnny Sings – 'Love Story'

English Imports 33⅓ LP
'J.M. Sings The Music Of Bert
Kaempfert CBS 31518
'Warm' Fontana TFL 5015
'Johnny's Greatest Hits'
  Fontana TFL 5083
'Swing Softly' (cover only)
  Fontana TFL 5039
'Open Fire, Two Guitars' (cover only)
  Fontana TFL 5050
'Merry Christmas' CBS 69217
'Love Songs' CBS 31538
'Tears And Laughter' CBS 10019

Brazilian imports
'Evie' CBS EP 56414

Johnny Mathis twelve-inch Singles
USA
'Begin The Beguine'/'Gone, Gone,
Gone' Columbia 23-11002

UK
'Gone, Gone, Gone'/'Best Days Of My
Life'/'I'm Stone In Love With
You'/'Loving You, Losing You'
  CBS 12-7730
Red/black vinyl

Holland
'Begin The Beguine'/'Gone, Gone,
Gone' CBS 12-7418
Gone, Gone, Gone'/'Begin The
Beguine' CBS 12-1582

EXTENDED PLAYS

This section gives a list of Johnny's
EPs as well as a note of any special
product in this form. See also
Anthologies.

US EPs

'JOHNNY MATHIS': B8871
'Autumn In Rome'/'Love, Your Spell Is
Everywhere'/'Cabin In The Sky'/'In
Other Words'

'JOHNNY MATHIS': B8872
'Caravan'/'Star Eyes'/'It Might As Well
Be Spring'/'Street Of Dreams'

'JOHNNY MATHIS': B8873
'Easy To Love'/'Prelude To A Kiss'/
'Babalu'/'Angel Eyes'

'WONDERFUL, WONDERFUL VOL1':
  B10281
'Will I Find My Love Today'/'Looking
At You'/'Let Me Love You'/'All
Through The Night'

'WONDERFUL, WONDERFUL VOL2':
  B10282
'It Could Happen To You'/'That Old
Black Magic'/'Too Close For
Comfort'/'In The Wee Small Hours Of
The Morning'

'WONDERFUL, WONDERFUL VOL3':
  B10283
'Year After Year'/'Early Autumn'/'You
Stepped Out Of A Dream'/'Day In, Day
Out'

'WARM': B10781
'Warm'/'A Handful Of Stars'/'My One
And Only Love'/'While We're Young'

'WARM VOL2': B10782
'By Myself'/'I've Grown Accustomed
To Her Face'/'Baby, Baby, Baby'/
'What'll I Do'

'WARM VOL3': B10783
'I'm Glad There Is You'/'The Lovely
Things You Do'/'There Goes My
Heart'/'Then I'll Be Tired Of You'

'GOODNIGHT, DEAR LORD': B11191
'Goodnight, Dear Lord'/'I Heard A
Forest Praying'/'Deep River'/'Swing
Low, Sweet Chariot'

'ELI ELI': B11192
'Eli Eli'/'Kol Nidre'/'Where Can I Go?'/'One God'

'AVE MARIA': B11193
'Ave Maria' (Bach-Gounod)/'The Rosary'/'May The Good Lord Bless And Keep You'/'Ave Maria' (Schubert)

'SWING SOFTLY': B11651
'To Be In Love'/'You'd Be So Nice To Come Home To'/'It's De-Lovely'/'I've Got The World On A String'

'SWING SOFTLY VOL2': B11652
'Sweet Lorraine'/'Can't Get Out Of This Wood'/'You Hit The Spot'/'Get Me To The Church On Time'

'SWING SOFTLY VOL3': B11653
'Love Walked In'/'Easy To Say'/'This Heart Of Mine'/'Like Someone In Love'

'MERRY CHRISTMAS': B11951
'Winter Wonderland'/'Blue Christmas'/'White Christmas'/'Sleigh Ride'

'MERRY CHRISTMAS VOL2': B11952
'The Christmas Song'/'I'll Be Home For Christmas'/'O Holy Night'/'Silver Bells'

'MERRY CHRISTMAS VOL3': B11953
'The First Noel'/'It Came Upon A Midnight Clear'/'What Child Is This'/'Silent Night, Holy Night'

'OPEN FIRE, TWO GUITARS': B12701
'Open Fire'/'Please Be Kind'/'Bye Bye Blackbird'/'Tenderly'

'OPEN FIRE, TWO GUITARS': B12702
'Embraceable You'/'My Funny Valentine'/'I'll Be Seeing You'/'I'm Just A Boy In Love'

'OPEN FIRE, TWO GUITARS': B12703
'I Concentrate On You'/'You'll Never Know'/'When I Fall In Love'/'In The Still Of The Night'

'HEAVENLY': B13511
'Heavenly'/'Misty'/'Hello Young Lovers'/'I'll Be Easy To Find'

'HEAVENLY VOL2': B13512
'Something I Dreamed Last Night'/'Moonlight Becomes You'/'They Say It's Wonderful'/'More Than You Know'

'HEAVENLY VOL3': B13513
'A Lovely Way To Spend An Evening'/'That's All'/'A Ride On A Rainbow'/'Stranger In Paradise'

'FAITHFULLY': B14221
'Secret Love'/'Where Are You?'/'Maria'/'Where Do You Think You're Going'

'FAITHFULLY VOL2': B14222
'Faithfully'/'One Starry Night'/'Nobody Knows'/'You Better Go Now'

'FAITHFULLY VOL3': B14223
'Tonight'/'Blue Gardenia'/'Follow Me'/'And This Is My Beloved'

'JOHNNY'S MOOD': B15261
'Goodnight My Love'/'There's No You'/'I'm So Lost'/'Once'

'JOHNNY'S MOOD': B15262
'Stay Warm'/'Corner To Corner'/'I'm In The Mood For Love'/'The Folks Who Live On The Hill'

'JOHNNY'S MOOD': B15263
'I'm Gonna Laugh You Out Of My Life'/'April In Paris'/'In Return'/'How High The Moon'

'SONGS FROM "LIZZIE"': B2129
'It's Not For Me To Say'/'Warm And Tender'/'Wonderful, Wonderful'/'Babalu'

'JOHNNY MATHIS SINGS':   B2143
'Come To Me'/'Wild Is The Wind'/'No
Love'/'When I Am With You'

'JOHNNY MATHIS':   B2537
'It's Not For Me To Say'/'Wonderful,
Wonderful'/'Chances Are'/'The
Twelfth Of Never'

'JOHNNY MATHIS':   B2616
'Call Me'/'A Certain Smile'/'All The
Time'/'When Sunny Gets Blue'

'JOHNNY MATHIS':   B2640
'Come To Me'/'Wild Is The
Wind'/'Someone'/'You Are Beautiful'

'RAPTURE':   78715
'Rapture'/'Here I'll Stay'/'Stars Fell On
Alabama'/'I Was Telling Her About
You'

'LOVE IS EVERYTHING':   SR 651 C
'Never Let Me Go'/'Dancing In The
Dark'/'An Affair To Remember'/
'People'/'This Is All I Ask'

'THE SHADOW OF YOUR SMILE':
                SR 664 C
'The Shadow Of Your Smile'/'(I Left
My Heart) In San Francisco'/'Quiet
Nights'/'A Taste Of Honey'/
'Yesterday'/'Michelle'

'LOVE IS BLUE':   7 9637
'I Say A Little Prayer'/'Love Is
Blue'/'Never My Love'/'Venus'/'Moon
River'/'Walk On By'

'JOHNNY'S GREATEST HIT'S': 7 8634
'Chances Are'/'The Twelfth Of
Never'/'Wonderful, Wonderful'/'It's
Not For Me To Say'/'Come To
Me'/'Wild Is The Wind'

'CLOSE TO YOU'   7 30210
'Come Saturday Morning'/'Yellow
Days'/'Why Can't I Touch You'/'Until
It's Time For You To Go'/'Everything Is
Beautiful'

'SO NICE':   Mercury SR 665C
'I Will Wait For You'/'Elusive
Butterfly'/'So Nice'/'What Now My
Love'/'What The World Needs
Now'/'Man Of La Mancha'

'Greatest Hits', 'Love is Everything',
'Shadow of Your Smile', 'So Nice',
'Love is Blue', 'Close To You' were
classed as Mini-Juke Box LPs and
marked on the record as 'special coin
operated items'.

UK and European EPs

France

'AVE MARIA':   CBS 5921EP
'Ave Maria'/'Ave Maria'/'The Rosary'

'THE FALL OF LOVE':
                Pathe Marconi EGF718
'The Fall Of Love'/'Bye Bye Barbara'/
'No More'/'A Great Night For Crying'

'''4 JOHNNY'S SUCCESS':
                Fontana 467082ME
'Misty'/'Call Me'/'Let's Love'/'Teacher,
Teacher'

'KOL NIDRE':   CBS 5917EP
'Kol Nidre'/'Deep River'/'Eli Eli'

'JOHNNY MATHIS':
                Fontana 462035ME
'It's Not For Me To Say'/'Warm And
Tender'/'Chances Are'/'Early Autumn'

'JOHNNY MATHIS':
                Fontana 467224ME
'Kol Nidre'/'Eli Eli'/'Ave Maria'/'Ave
Maria'

'JOHNNY MATHIS CINEMONDE':
                Fontana 462085ME
'A Certain Smile'/'Warm And
Tender'/'Wild Is The Wind'/'It's Not
For Me To Say'

'JOHNNY "TRIPLE OCTAVE"
MATHIS':
                Fontana 462041ME

'Angel Eyes'/'Caravan'/'Babalu'/
'Autumn In Rome'

'JOHNNY "TRIPLE OCTAVE"
MATHIS':   Phillips 429253BE
'Angel Eyes'/'Caravan'/'Babalu'/
'Autumn In Rome'

'TASTE OF TEARS':
          Pathe Marconi EGF821
'Taste Of Tears'/'White Roses From A
Blue Valentine'/'Listen Lonely
Girl'/'All I Wanted'

'JOHNNY MATHIS':
          Fontana 467016ME
'Warm'/'My One And Only Love'/
'When Sunny Gets Blue'/'What'll I Do'

Holland
'CALL ME':   Fontana 467002TE
'Call Me'/'Like Someone In
Love'/'You'd Be So Nice To Come
Home To'/'Loved Walked In'

'CHRISTMAS WITH JOHNNY
MATHIS':   Fontana 467038TE
'Winter Wonderland'/'The Christmas
Song'/'Silent Night, Holy Night'/'O
Holy Night'
'HELLO, YOUNG LOVERS':
          Fontana 467132TE
'They Say It's Wonderful'/'More Than
You Know'/'A Lovely Way To Spend
An Evening'/'Hello, Young Lovers'

'JOHNNY HITS AGAIN':
          Fontana 467033TE
'Someone'/'Very Much In Love'/'Let's
Love'/'To Be In Love'

'JOHNNY MATHIS':
          Fontana 462074TE
'A Certain Smile'/'Let It
Rain'/'Teacher, Teacher'/'I've Grown
Accustomed To Her Face'

'JOHNNY MATHIS':
          Fontana 467159TE
'Maria'/'You Better Go Now'/'Secret
Love'/'Blue Gardenia'

'JOHNNY MATHIS':
          Fontana 462026TE
'Wild Is The Wind'/'No Love'/'What'll I
Do'/'Come To Me'

'JOHNNY MATHIS': Philips 429329BE
'Wonderful, Wonderful'/'It's Not For
Me To Say'/'It Could Happen To
You'/'You Stepped Out Of A Dream'

'MEET JOHNNY MATHIS':
          Fontana 493200DE
'Come To Me'/'Wild Is The
Wind'/Interview With Johnny Mathis*
*(record not for sale item)

'MISTY':   Fontana 467097TE
'Misty'/'The Story Of Our Love'/'The
Best Of Everything'/'Cherie'

'MY LOVE FOR YOU':
          Fontana 467197TE
'My Love For You'/'O That
Feeling'/'You Do Something To Me'/'I
Wish I Were In Love Again'

'THE RHYTHMS OF BROADWAY':
          Fontana 467215TE
'Let's Do It'/'I Just Found Out About
Love'/'I Am In Love'/'I Could Have
Danced All Night'

Italy
'CALL ME':   Fontana 467002TE
'Call Me'/'Like Someone In
Love'/'You'd Be So Nice To Come
Home To'/'Love Walked In'

'JOHNNY MATHIS'
          Fontana 462075TE
'Warm And Tender'/'It's Not For Me
To Say'/'No Love'/'Chances Are'

'JOHNNY MATHIS':
          Fontana 462076TE
'Wild Is The Wind'/'That Old Black
Magic'/'The Twelfth Of
Never'/'Wonderful, Wonderful'

Spain
'FALL OF LOVE':   EMI 7EPL 14075
'Fall Of Love'/'No More'/'Bye, Bye,

Barbara'/'A Great Night For Crying'

'GINA':   CBS 20043AGS
'Gina' (sung in Spanish)/'Small
World'/'Maria'/'Tonight'

'JOHNNY MATHIS':
                Fontana 462074TE
'A Certain Smile'/'Let It
Rain'/'Teacher, Teacher'/'I've Grown
Accustomed To Her Face'

'JOHNNY MATHIS'
                Fontana 429329TE
'Wonderful, Wonderful'/'It's Not For
Me To Say'/'It Could Happen To
You'/'You Stepped Out Of A Dream'

'NUEVOS EXITOS DE JOHNNY
MATHIS':   CBS 20128AGS
'What Will My Mary Say'/'Sweet
Thursday'/'Every Step Of The
Way'/'No Man Can Stand Alone'

'THE SHADOW OF YOUR SMILE':
                EMI EPL14291
'The Shadow Of Your
Smile'/'Moment To Moment'/'Lovers
In New York'/'Sweetheart Tree'

UK
'A HANDFUL OF STARS':
                Fontana 46098TE
'Looking At You'/'A Handful Of
Stars'/'All Through The Night'/'Early
Autumn'

'AVE MARIA':   Fontana 462086TE
'Ave Maria' (Schubert)/'I Heard A
Forest Praying'/'The Rosary'/'Ave
Maria' (Bach-Gounod)

'CALL ME':   Fontana 467188TE
'Call Me'/'Blue Gardenia'/'My Love
For You'/'When Sunny Gets Blue'

'CHRISTMAS WITH JOHNNY
MATHIS':   Fontana 467038TE
'Winter Wonderland'/'The Christmas
Song'/'Silent Night, Holy Night'/'O
Holy Night'

'COME TO ME':   Fontana 462052TE
'I've Grown Accustomed To Her
Face'/'Wild Is The Wind'/'Teacher,
Teacher'/'Come To Me'

'ELI ELI':   Fontana 467146TE
'One God'/'Eli Eli'/'Kol Nidre'/'Where
Can I Go?'

'I'LL BE SEEING YOU':
                Fontana 467147TE
'My Funny Valentine'/'I'll Be Seeing
You'/'Bye Bye Blackbird'/'I
Concentrate On You'

'FOUR HITS!':   Fontana 467144TE
'The Best Of Everything'/'Very Much
In Love'/'You Are Beautiful'/'Misty'

'FOUR SHOW HITS':
                Fontana 467187TE
'Hello Young Lovers'/'Stranger In
Paradise'/'They Say It's Wonderful'/
'Tonight'

'IT'S DE-LOVELY': Fontana 467065TE
'You Hit The Spot'/'Can't Get Out Of
This Mood'/'Get Me To The Church
On Time'/'It's De-Lovely'

'IT'S LOVE':   Fontana 467189TE
'Hey Love'/'No Love'/'Let's Love'/'To
Be In Love'

'I AM IN LOVE':   Fontana 467235TE
'I Could Have Danced All Night'/'I Just
Found Out About Love'/'Love Eyes'/'I
Am In Love'

'JOHNNY MATHIS':
                Fontana 462019TE
'Will I Find My Love Today?'/'Too
Close For Comfort'/'You Stepped Out
Of A Dream'/'Day In Day Out'

'JOHNNY MATHIS': Philips 429359BE
'Wonderful, Wonderful'/'Chances
Are'/'When Sunny Gets Blue'/'It's Not
For Me To Say'

'LET ME LOVE YOU':
Fontana 462043TE
'It Could Happen To You'/'That Old Black Magic'/'Let Me Love You'/'In The Wee Small Hours Of The Morning'

'LET'S DO IT':   Fontana 467236TE
'A Cock-Eyed Optimist'/'Let's Do It'/'Let's Misbehave'/'Love Is A Gamble'

'LIKE SOMEONE IN LOVE':
Fontana 467149TE
I've Got The World On A String'/'Easy To Say'/'To Be In Love'/'Like Someone In Love'

'LIVE IT UP!' No. 1:   CBS 20001AGG
'Live It Up'/'On A Cold And Rainy Day'/'Love'/'Hey, Look Me Over'

'LIVE IT UP!' No. 2:   CBS 20006AGG
'Just Friends'/'Ace In The Hole'/'Why Not?'/'I Wont't Dance'

'LIVE IT UP' No.3:   CBS 20012AGG
'Johnny One Note'/'Too Much Too Soon'/'The Riviera'/'Crazy In The Heart'

'MATHIS ON BROADWAY':
CBS 20032AGG
'The Sound Of Music'/'Getting To Know You'/'Small World'/'Joey, Joey, Joey'

'MEET MR MATHIS':
Fontana 467050TE
'I've Grown Accustomed To Her Face'/'A Certain Smile'/'Someone'/'Chances Are'

'MOONLIGHT AND MATHIS':
Fontana 467186TE
'Moonlight Becomes You'/'A Lovely Way To Spend An Evening'/'More Than You Know'/'Heavenly'

'MY LOVE FOR YOU':
Fontana 467197TE

'My Love For You'/'O That Feeling'/'You Do Something To Me'/'I Wish I Were In Love Again'

'THE PARTY'S OVER':
Fontana 467261TE
'Guys And Dolls'/'The Party's Over'/'I'll Be Easy To Find'/'When My Sugar Waiks Down The Street'

'RAPTURE':   CBS 20028AGG
'Rapture'/'Love Me As Though There Were No Tomorrow'/'Moments Like This'/'Here I'll Stay'

'RING THE BELL':   Fontana 467260TE
'Ring The Bell'/'Stairway To The Stars'/'Sudden Love'/'The Best Is Yet To Come'

'SECRET LOVE':   Fontana 467237TE
'Secret Love'/'Follow Me'/'And This Is My Beloved'/'Faithfully'

'SO NICE':   Fontana
'You'd Be So Nice To Come Home To'/'Love Walked In'/'Sweet Lorraine'/'This Heart of Mine'

'SWING LOW':   Fontana 462097TE
'Star Eyes'/'Deep River'/'Love, You Spell Is Everywhere'/'Swing Low Sweet Chariot'

'TENDERLY':   Fontana 467145TE
'You'll Never Know'/'Tenderly'/'When I Fall In Love'/'In The Still Of The Night'

'THERE GOES MY HEART':
Fontana 462096TE
'There Goes My Heart'/'Street Of Dreams'/'I'm Glad There Is You'/'My One And Only Love'

'THE TWELFTH OF NEVER':
Fontana 462080TE
'The Twelfth Of Never'/'It Might As Well Be Spring'/'The Lovely Things You Do'/'I'm Glad There Is You'

'WHILE WE'RE YOUNG':
Fontana 462077TE
'While We're Young'/'Warm'/'What'll I
Do'/'Baby, Baby, Baby'

Miscellaneous EPs
These EPs were produced, under
licence, for promotional purposes.

Australia
'JOHNNY MATHIS':   Coronet KEP085
'My One And Only Love'/'Warm'/
'While We're Young'/'A Handful Of
Stars'

'MERRY CHRISTMAS':
Coronet KEP220
'White Christmas'/'Silent Night, Holy
Night'/'Winter Wonderland'/'The First
Noel'

'THE RHYTHMS OF BROADWAY
VOL1':
Coronet KEP252
'I Could Have Danced All Night'/'Love
Is A Gamble'/'Guys And Dolls'/'You
Do Something To Me'

'THE RHYTHMS OF BROADWAY
VOL2':
Coronet KEP253
'A Cockeyed Optimist'/'I Just Found
Out About Love'/'Let's Do It'/'Love
Eyes'

'JOHNNY MATHIS' GREATEST HITS':
CBS BG225092
'The Twelfth Of Never'/'Chances
Are'/'It's Not For Me To
Say'/'Wonderful, Wonderful'

'JOHNNY MATHIS':   Coronet KEP170
'All Through The Night'/'You Stepped
Out Of A Dream'/'In The Wee Small
Hours Of The Morning'/'I've Grown
Accustomed To Her Face'

'I'LL NEVER FALL IN LOVE AGAIN':
CBS BG 225229
'I'll Never Fall In Love Again'/
'Aquarius'/'Let The Sunshine

In'/'Didn't We'/'Yesterday When I Was
Young'

Brazil
'AQUARIUS':   CBS 56370
'Midnight Cowboy'/'Love Me
Tonight'/'Aquarius'/'Let The Sunshine
In'/'We'

'CLOSE TO YOU':   CBS 56395
'Song Of Joy'/'Evil Ways'/'The Long
And Winding Road'/'Wave'

'EVIE':   CBS 56414
'Evie'/'Think About Things'/'It's
Impossible'/'For The Good Times'

'JOHNNY MATHIS':   CBS 56354
'A Time For Us'/'The World I Threw
Away'/'I'll Never Fall In Love
Again'/'Whoever You Are I Love You'

'JOHNNY MATHIS':   CBS 56447
'Happy'/'Show And Tell'/'I'/'Soul And
Inspiration'/'Just Once In My LIfe'

'JOHNNY MATHIS':   CBS 56428
'This Way Mary'/'Life And Breath'/'I
Need You'/'If We Only Have Love'

'LOVE IS BLUE':   CBS 56323
'The Look Of Love'/'Here, There And
Everywhere'/'Never My Love'/'Love
Is Blue'

'LOVE STORY':   CBS 56405
'Love Story'/'I Was There'/'My Sweet
Lord'/'Ten Times Forever More'

'OS GRANDES SUCESSOS':
Columbia 56017
'A Certain Smile'/'It's Not For Me To
Say'/'Chances Are'/'Wild Is The Wind'

'RAINDROPS KEEP FALLIN' ON MY
HEAD':   CBS 56378
'Raindrops Keep Fallin' On My
Head'/'Odds And Ends'/'Everybody's
Talkin' '/'Watch What Hapens'

'SONG SUNG BLUE':   56441

'Song Sung Blue'/'Run To
Me'/'Goodbye To Love'/'Play Me'

'THOSE WERE THE DAYS': CBS 56343
'Those Were The Days'/'The End Of
The World'/'Light My Fire'/'Little
Green Apples'

'WHEREFORE AND WHY': CBS 56389
'The Last Time I Saw Her'/'Honey
Come Back'/'Wherefore And
Why'/'Bridge Over Troubled Water'

Hong Kong
'JOHNNY'S GREATEST HITS':
                         CBS CE4003
'Chances Are'/'Misty'/'September
Song'/'Wonderful, Wonderful'

'MERRY CHRISTMAS':   CBS CE4035
'The Christmas Song'/'Blue
Christmas'/'Winter Wonderland'/'I'll
Be Home For Christmas'

South Africa
'RELAX WITH JOHNNY MATHIS':
                        CBS EXP2071
'A Certain Smile'/'Stairway To The
Sea'/'Warm'/'Teacher, Teacher'

'MATHIS AT MIDNIGHT':
                        CBS EXP2082
'The Best Of Everything'/'It's
De-Lovely'/'Misty'/'The Story Of Our
Love'

Special EPs:
UK releases

'For You' Coronet Yogurt promotion:
'Up Up And Away'   WEP 1138
'Easy To Get On With' a Marigold
Flowers promotion: 'Chances
Are'   WEP 1130
'Hits From The Shows' for Ambrosia:
'The Sound Of Music'   WEP 1124
'Showtime' for Lion's Bakery:
'Tonight'/'How To Handle A
Woman'   WEP 1132

Non-UK releases
'Five Fomosos': 'It's Not For Me To
Say'   Phillips (Spain) 429 346BE
'The Big Four': 'It's Not For Me To
Say'   Phillips (Holland) 429 346BE
(same number as Spanish release but
one less track).
'The Big Four': 'Chances Are'
          Phillips (Holland) 430 500BE
'Johnny Mathis & Sarah Vaughan':
'Eli Eli' 'Col Nidre' France 467 134 ME
'Para Sempre': 'Ave Maria' (Bach-
Gounod-Schubert)
                        CBS (Brazil) 56050
'Sucessos De Cinema': 'Maria'
                        Brazil (CBS) 56081
'Exitos Para Bailar No. 1': 'Teacher,
Teacher'   Fontana (Spain) 464400TE
'The Godfather': 'Speak Softly Love'
          Maxi-Single CBS (UK) S7LP2
'Popular Favourites': 'Warm &
Tender'   Phillips (Italy) 429 416
'Hit Parade No. 1': 'Wild Is The Wind'
          (Europe) Fontana 462017TE

ANTHOLOGIES

Albums, singles, EPs, and
maxi-singles which feature one or
more tracks by Johnny amongst
material from other artists.
'Song Of The Seasons': 'An Open
Fire'
  Columbia Special Products CSM 421
'Great Songs Of Christmas': 'The
Christmas Song'
  Columbia Special Products CSS 388
'Music Of Spring': 'Spring Is Here'
                             CSP 263
'A Very Merry Christmas': 'O Holy
Night'   CSS 563
'A Very Merry Christmas': 'Silver
Bells'   CSS 788
'Hitmakers Vol II': 'Stella By
Starlight'   CSP 320
'Vocally Speaking': 'Walk On By'
                             CSS 1338
'The Headliners': 'Unaccustomed As I
Am'   Columbia Record Club CS 7
'Parade Of Show Stoppers': 'Maria'
  Columbia Special Products CSP 237

'Singer Presents': 'Taking A Chance
On Love'
  Columbia Special Products CSS 552
'Let Yourself Go': 'Warm And Willing'
  Columbia Special Products CSM 477
'The Spirit Of Chirstmas': 'Oh Holy
Night'
  Columbia Special Products CSS 853
'Parade Of Roses': 'Everything's
Coming Up Roses'
  Columbia Special Products CSS 615
'Easy Does It': 'Walk On By'
  Columbia Special Products CSS 873
'M'm! M'm! Good!': 'I Say A Little
Prayer'
  Columbia Special Products CSS 918
'Great Songs Of Christmas': 'A
Marshmello World'
  Columbia Special Products CSS 888
'Let The Sunshine In': 'Aquarius/Let
The Sunshine In'
Columbia House –
  A Columbia Musical Treasury DS 943
'Hit Songs From Broadway –
Hollywood Musicals': 'The
Impossible Dream (The Quest)'
        Harmony, Headliner Series,
            Columbia KH 31790
'Broadway & Hollywood Today':
'Guys And Dolls'
        Columbia Special Products
            2 Records CSS 1476/7
'Jonathan Livingston Seagull': 'Play
Me'   Harmony House KH 32709
'Winter Serenades': 'Sleigh Ride'
  Columbia Special Products RSC 0104
'A Very Merry Christmas': 'I'll Be
Home For Christmas'
  Columbia Special Products CSS 997
'A Summer Place': 'The Best Of
Everything'   Columbia CL 1421
'Hall Of Fame Hits': 'Chances Are'
            Columbia CL 1308
'Hits From The Movies': 'The Best Of
Everything'   Columbia CL 1421
'20 Greatest Hits Of The 60's': 'I Say A
Little Prayer'   Columbia GP 25

LPs

This section lists, track by track, the
LPs which have been released in the
US and Britain. It is followed by a
listing for non-US/UK material. In
each case a US and UK number is
given and where one is not found it
means the LP was not issued in that
country or the LP appears under a
different title. During the early years
of Johnny's career records were
available in both mono and stereo
and this accounts for the long list of
numbers which come with the first
releases.

  Under *Miscellaneous* can be found
LPs which were/are issued by record
clubs, record houses, mail order
companies etc.

  All records with prefix CL, C, JC,
PC, CS, MR, SR, KH, G, KC are US
releases. All others are British
Catalogue numbers

1956
'JOHNNY MATHIS', USA No CL 887
'Autumn In Rome'/'Easy To
Love'/'Street Of Dreams'/'Love, Your
Magic Spell Is Everywhere'/'Prelude
To A Kiss'/'Babalu'/'Caravan'/'In
Other Words'/'Star Eyes'/'It Might As
Well Be Spring'/'Cabin In The
Sky'/'Angel Eyes'

1957
'WONDERFUL, WONDERFUL', CL
1028, CS 9046; Fontana TFL 5003
'Will I Find My Love Today'/'Looking
At You'/'Let Me Love You'/'All
Through The Night'/'It Could Happen
To You'/'That Old Black Magic'/'Too
Close For Comfort'/'In The Wee Small
Hours Of The Morning'/'Year After
Year'/'Early Autumn'/'You Stepped
Out Of A Dream'/'Day In, Day Out'

'JOHNNY MATHIS' Fontana TFL 5011
'Wild Is The Wind'/'Easy To
Love'/'Street Of Dreams'/'Love, Your

Magic Spell Is Everywhere'/'Prelude To A Kiss'/'No Love'/'Come To Me'/'In Other Words'/'Star Eyes'/'It Might As Well Be Spring'/'When I Am With You'/'The Twelfth Of Never'

1958
'WARM', CL 1078, CS 8039; Fontana TFL 5015, Fontana STFL 510
'Warm'/'My One And Only Love'/'Baby Baby Baby'/'A Handful Of Stars'/'By Myself'/'I've Grown Accustomed To Her Face'/'Then I'll Be Tired Of You'/'I'm Glad There Is You'/'What'll I Do'/'The Lovely Things You Do'/'There Goes My Heart'/'While We're Young'

'GOODNIGHT DEAR LORD' (USA title)
'HEAVENLY' (UK title)
Fontana TFL 5023
'Good Night Dear Lord'/'Swing Low, Sweet Chariot'/'May The Good Lord Bless And Keep You'/'I Heard A Forest Praying'/'The Rosary'/'One God'/'Deep River'/'Where Can I Go?'/'Eli Eli'/'Kol Nidre'/'Ave Maria' (Schubert)/'Ave Maria' (Bach-Gounod)

'JOHNNY'S GREATEST HITS'
CL 1133, CS 8634
'Chances Are'/'All The Time'/'The Twelfth Of Never'/'When Sunny Gets Blue'/'When I Am With You'/ 'Wonderful, Wonderful'/'It's Not For Me To Say'/'Come To Me'/'Wild Is The Wind'/'Warm And Tender'/'No Love'/'I Look At You'

'JOHNNY'S GREATEST HITS
Fontana TFL 5058
'Chances Are'/'Teacher, Teacher'/'The Twelfth Of Never'/'When Sunny Gets Blue'/'When I Am With You'/ 'Wonderful, Wonderful'/'It's Not For Me To Say'/'Come To Me'/'Wild Is The Wind'/'Warm And Tender'/'No Love'/'I Look At You'

'SWING SOFTLY', CL 1165, CS 8023;

Fontana TFL 5039, Fontana STFL 500, CBS BPG 62062, CBS SBPG 62062
'You Hit The Spot'/'It's De Lovely'/'Get Me To The Church On Time'/'Like Someone In Love'/'You'd Be So Nice To Come Home To'/'Love Walked In'/'This Heart Of Mine'/'To Be In Love'/'Sweet Lorraine'/'Can't Get Out Of This Mood'/'I've Got The World On A String'/'Easy To Say'

'MERRY CHRISTMAS', CL 1195, CS 802; Fontana TFL 5031, CBS 62806
'Winter Wonderland'/'The Christmas Song'/'Sleigh Ride'/'Blue Christmas'/'I'll Be Home For Christmas'/'White Christmas'/'O Holy Night'/'What Child Is This?'/'The First Noel'/'Silver Bells'/'It Came Upon A Midnight Clear'/'Silent Night, Holy Night'

1959
'OPEN FIRE, TWO GUITARS', CL 1270, CS 8056; Fontana TFL 5050, Fontana STFL 515, CBS BPG 62063, CBS SBPG 62063
'An Open Fire'/'Bye Bye Blackbird'/'In The Still Of The Night'/'Embraceable You'/'I'll Be Seeing You'/'Tenderly'/ 'When I Fall In Love'/'I Concentrate On You'/'Please Be Kind'/'You'll Never Know'/'I'm Just A Boy In Love'/'My Funny Valentine'

'MORE JOHNNY'S GREATEST HITS', CL 1344, CS 8150; CBS 62774
'Small World'/'Someone'/'Very Much In Love'/'You Are Everything To Me'/'Let It Rain'/'The Flame Of Love'/'A Certain Smile'/'Call Me'/'You Are Beautiful'/'Teacher, Teacher'/ 'Stairway To The Sea'/'Let's Love'

'MORE JOHNNY'S GREATEST HITS'
Fontana TFL 5083
'A Certain Smile'/'Call Me'/'You Are Beautiful'/'This Heart Of Mine'/ 'Stairway To The Sea'/'Let's Love'/ 'The Best Of Everything'/'Someone'/ 'Very Much In Love'/'You Are

Everything To Me'/'Let It Rain'/'The Flame Of Love'

'MORE JOHNNY'S GREATEST HITS'
STFL 517
'A Certain Smile'/'Call Me'/'To Be In Love'/'Teacher, Teacher'/'Stairway To The Sea'/'Let's Love'/'Someone'/'Very Much In Love'/'You Are Everything To Me'/'Let It Rain'/'The Flame Of Love'/'This Heart Of Mine'

'HEAVENLY' (USA title)
'RIDE ON A RAINBOW' (UK title), CL 1351, CS 8152; Fontana TFL 5061, Fontana STFL 516, CBS BPG 62064, CBS SBPG 62064
'Heavenly'/'Hello, Young Lovers'/'A Lovely Way To Spend An Evening'/'A Ride On A Rainbow'/'More Than You Know'/'Something I Dreamed Last Night'/'Misty'/'Stranger In Paradise'/'Moonlight Becomes You'/'They Say It's Wonderful'/'I'll Be Easy To Find'/'That's All'

1960
'FAITHFULLY', CL 1422, CS 8219; Fontana TFL 5084, Fontana STFL 522, CBS BPG 62061, CBS SBPG 62067
'Faithfully'/'Tonight'/'Nobody Knows'/'One Starry Night'/'Follow Me'/'You Better Go Now'/'Secret Love'/'Maria'/'Where Do You Think You're Going'/'And This Is My Beloved'/'Where Are You?'/'Blue Gardenia'

'THE RHYTHMS AND BALLADS OF BROADWAY', C 2L17, C 25803
'Moanin' Low'/'Fun To Be Fooled'/'I Have Dreamed'/'On The Sunny Side Of The Street'/'My Romance'/ 'Dancing On The Ceiling'/'I Married An Angel'/'Isn't It A Pity'/'Spring Is Here'/'Don't Blame Me'/'Taking A Chance On Love'/'The Party's Over' 'Everything's Coming Up Roses'/'Guys And Dolls'/'I Wish I Were In Love Again'/'You Do

Something To Me'/'Let's Misbehave'/'I Could Have Danced All Night'/'A Cock-Eyed Optimist'/'I Just Found Out About Love'/'Let's Do It'/'I Am In Love'/'Love Eyes'/'Love Is A Gamble'

'THE BALLADS OF BROADWAY'
CL 1506
Moanin' Low'/'Fun To Be Fooled'/'I Have Dreamed'/'On The Sunny Side Of The Street'/'My Romance'/ 'Dancing On The Ceiling'/'I Married An Angel'/'Isn't It A Pity'/'Spring Is Here'/'Don't Blame Me'/'Taking A Chance On Love'/'The Party's Over'

'THE RHYTHMS OF BROADWAY'
CL 1507
'Everything's Coming Up Roses'/'Guys And Dolls'/'I Wish I Were In Love Again'/'You Do Something To Me'/'Let's Misbehave'/'I Could Have Danced All Night'/'A Cock-Eyed Optimist'/'I Just Found Out About Love'/'Let's Do It'/'I Am In Love'/'Love Eyes'/'Love Is A Gamble'

'THE RHYTHMS AND BALLADS OF BROADWAY'   Fontana Set 101
'Moanin' Low'/'Fun To Be Fooled'/'I Have Dreamed'/'On The Sunny Side Of The Street'/'My Romance'/ 'Dancing On The Ceiling'/'I Married An Angel'/'Isn't It A Pity'/'Spring Is Here'/'Don't Blame Me'/'Taking A Chance On Love'/'The Party's Over' 'Guys And Dolls'/'I Wish I Were In Love Again'/'You Do Something To Me'/'Let's Misbehave'/'I Could Have Danced All Night'/'A Cock-Eyed Optimist'/'I Just Found Out About Love'/'Let's Do It'/'I Am In Love'/'Love Eyes'/'Love Is A Gamble'

'JOHNNY'S MOOD', CL 1526, CS 8326; Fontana TFL 5117, Fontana STFL 545, CBS BPG 62072, CBS SBPG 62072
'I'm Gonna Laugh You Out Of My

Life'/'Stay Warm'/'There's No
You'/'How High The Moon'/'I'm So
Lost'/'Once'/'Goodnight My Love'/
'The Folks Who Live On The
Hill'/'April In Paris'/'Corner To
Corner'/'In Return'/'I'm In The Mood
For Love'

1961
'I'LL BUY YOU A STAR', CL 1623, CS
8423; Fontana TFL 5134, Fontana
STFL 557
'I'll Buy You A Star'/'Stairway To The
Stars'/'When My Sugar Walks Down
The Street'/'Magic Garden'/
'Smile'/'Oh How I Try'/'Ring The
Bell'/'Love Look Away'/'Sudden
Love'/'The Best Is Yet To
Come'/'Warm And Willing'/'My Heart
And I'

'PORTRAIT OF JOHNNY', CL 1644, CS
8444
'Starbright'/'While You're
Young'/'Should I Wait'/'All Is
Well'/'You Set My Heart To
Music'/'My Love For You'/'Oh That
Feeling'/'How To Handle A
Woman'/'Cherie'/'Hey
Love'/'Jenny'/'The Story Of Our Love'

'PORTRAIT OF JOHNNY', Fontana
TFL 5153, Fontana STFL 571, CBS
BPG 62077, CBS SBPG 62077
'Starbright'/'While You're Young'/
'Should I Wait'/'All Is Well'/'You
Set My Heart To Music'/'My Love For
You'/'Oh That Feeling'/'Laurie My
Love'/'Cherie'/'Hey Love'/'Jenny'/'The
Story Of Our Love'

1962
'LIVE IT UP!', CL 1711, CS 8511;
Fontana TFL 5177, CBS BPG 62105,
CBS SBPG 62105
'Live It Up'/'Just Friends'/'Ace In The
Hole'/'On A Cold And Rainy Day'/
'Why Not'/'I Won't Dance'/'Johnny
One Note'/'Too Much, Too Soon'/'The
Riviera'/'Crazy In The Heart'/'Hey,
Look Me Over'/'Love'

'RAPTURE', CL 1915, CS 8715; CBS
BPG 62106, CBS SBPG 62106
'Rapture'/'Love Me As Though There
Were No Tomorrow'/'Moments Like
This'/'You've Come Home'/'Here I'll
Stay'/'My Darling, My Darling'/'Stars
Fell On Alabama'/'I Was Telling Her
About You'/'Lament'/'The Love
Nest'/'Lost In Loveliness'/'Stella By
Starlight'

1963
'JOHNNY'S NEWEST HITS', CL 2016,
CS 8816; CBS BPG 62147, CBS SBPG
62147
'What Will My Mary Say'/
'Unaccustomed As I Am'/'Sweet
Thursday'/'There You Are'/'Wasn't
The Summer Short?'/'That's The Way
It Is'/'Gina'/'Marianna'/'I Love Her
That's Why'/'I'll Never Be Lonely
Again'/'One Look'/'Quiet Girl'

'JOHNNY', CL 2044, CS 8844; CBS
BPG 62172, CBS SBPG 62172
'Easy Does It'/'The Most Beautiful Girl
In The World'/'Miracles'/'When The
World Was Young'/'Never Never
Land'/'Poor Butterfly'/'Jump For
Joy'/'Joey, Joey, Joey'/'I Can't
Believe That You're In Love With
Me'/'I Love You'/'Weaver Of
Dreams'/'No Man Can Stand Alone'

'ROMANTICALLY', CBS BPG 62202,
CBS SBPG 62202
'Getting To Know You'/'Moonlight In
Vermont'/'Hi Lili, Hi-Lo'/'Friendly
Persuasion'/'Autumn In New York'/'In
Wisconsin'/'All That Is Missing'/'The
Sound Of Music'/'Theme from
Carnival'/'Too Young To Go Steady'/
'It's Only A Paper Moon'/'September
Song'

'I'LL SEARCH MY HEART', CL 2143,
CS 8943; CBS BPG 62270, CBS SBPG
62270
'Starbright'/'Every Step Of The Way'/
'Wherever You Are It's Spring'/'The
Joy Of Loving You'/'Each Time We

Kiss'/'A Clock Without Hands'/'I'll
Search My Heart'/'Sooner Or
Later'/'My Favourite Dream'/'The Best
Of Everything'/'What To Do About
Love'/'All The Sad Young Men'

'SOUNDS OF CHRISTMAS', Mercury
MG 20837, SR 60837; HMV CLP 1696,
CSD 1521
'The Sounds Of Christmas'/'Have
Yourself A Merry Little Christmas'/'A
Marshmallow World'/'God Rest Ye
Merry Gentlemen'/'Let It Snow, Let It
Snow, Let It Snow'/'The Little
Drummer Boy'/'Have Reindeer Will
Travel'/'The Secret Of Christmas'/
'Rudolph The Red Nose Reindeer'/
'The Carol Of The Bells'/'Christmas Is
A Feeling In Your Heart'/'Hallelujah
Chorus'

1964
'TENDER IS THE NIGHT', Mercury MG
20890, SR 60890; HMV CLP 1721, CSD
1535
'Tender Is The Night'/'Laura'/'No
Strings'/'I Can't Give You Anything
But Love Baby'/'April Love'/'Call Me
Irresponsible'/'A Dream Is A Wish
Your Heart Makes'/'A Ship Without A
Sail'/'Forget Me Not'/'Where Is
Love?'/'Somewhere'/'Tomorrow
Song'

'THE GREAT YEARS', C 2L34, C 2S834
'Fly Me To The Moon (In Other
Words)'/'Street Of Dreams'/
'Wonderful, Wonderful'/'It's Not For
Me To Say'/'Chances Are'/'The
Twelfth Of Never'/'A Certain
Smile'/'Deep River'/'Can't Get Out Of
This Mood'/'Misty'/'Small World'/
'When I Fall In Love'

'Maria'/'Tonight'/'How To Handle A
Woman'/'Stairway To The
Stars'/'Love Look Away'/'Sweet
Thursday'/'Stella By
Starlight'/'Unaccustomed As I
am'/'Gina'/'What Will Mary
Say'/'Every Step Of The

Way'/'September Song'
(This album consists of previously
released material)

'BALLADS OF BROADWAY', CL 2223,
CS 9023
'Moanin' Low'/'Fun To Be Fooled'/'I
Have Dreamed'/'On The Sunny Side
Of The Street'/'My Romance'/
'Dancing On The Ceiling'/'I Married
An Angel'/'Isn't It A Pity'/'Spring Is
Here'/'Don't Blame Me'/'Taking A
Chance On Love'/'The Party's Over'
(This album consists of previously
released material)

'RHYTHMS OF BROADWAY', CL 2224,
CS 9024
'Everything's Coming Up
Roses'/'Guys And Dolls'/'I Wish I
Were In Love Again'/'You Do
Something To Me'/'Let's Misbehave'/
'I Could Have Danced All Night'/'A
Cock-Eyed Optimist'/'I Just Found Out
About Love'/'Let's Do It'/'I Am In
Love'/'Love Eyes'/'Love Is A Gamble'
(This album consists of previously
released material)

'THE WONDERFUL WORLD OF
MAKE—BELIEVE', Mercury MG 20193,
SR 60913; HMV CLP 1755, CSD 1553
'Camelot'/'I'm Always Chasing
Rainbows'/'House Of Flowers'/
'Beyond The Sea'/'Sky Full Of
Rainbows'/'Sands Of Time'/
'Shangri-La'/'Alice in Wonderland'/
'Dream, Dream, Dream'/'The World
Of Make-Believe'/'When You Wish
Upon A Star'/'Beyond The Blue
Horizon'

'THIS IS LOVE', Mercury MG 20942,
SR 60942; HMV CLP 1859, CSD 1600
'Put On A Happy Face'/'Poinciana
(Song Of The Tree)'/'The Touch Of
Your Lips'/'Just Move Along,
Meadow Lark'/'Under A Blanket Of
Blue'/'Over The Weekend'/
'More'/'You Love Me'/'Limehouse
Blues'/'What Do You Feel In Your

Heart'/'The End Of A Love
Affair'/'Fantastic'

'OLÉ', Mercury MG 20988, SR 60988;
HMV CLP 1818, CSD 1578
'Granada'/'Without You'/'Generique/
Felicidade' (medley)/'Manha De
Carnaval'/'Samba De Orfeu'/'La
Montana'/'Babalu'/'Serenata'/
'Bachianas Brasilieras' – Part 1/
'Bachianas Brasilieras' – Part 2/
'Bachianas Brasilieras' – Part 3

1965
'LOVE IS EVERYTHING', Mercury MG
20991, SR 20991; HMV CLP 3522, CSD
3522
'Never Let Me Go'/'People'/'A
Thousand Blue Bubbles'/'Love Is
Everything'/'Young And Foolish'/'An
Affair To Remember'/'Come Ride The
Wind With Me'/'Go Away Little
Girl'/'Dancing In The Dark'/'Long Ago
(And Far Away)'/'This Is All I
Ask'/'One More Mountain'

'AWAY FROM HOME', HMV CLP 1926,
CSD 1638
'On A Wonderful Day Like
Today'/'Clopin Clopant'/'The Skye
Boat Song'/'If I Had You'/'Symphony'/
'Try A Little Tenderness'/'If Love Were
All'/'Danny Boy'/'The Very Thought
Of You'/'Autumn Leaves'/'I'll Close
My Eyes'/'This Is Love'/'Arrivederci
Roma'/'I'm In Love For The Very First
Time'

'THE SWEETHEART TREE', Mercury
MG 21041, SR 61041
'A Wonderful Day Like Today'/
'Arrivederci Roma'/'Clopin Clopant'/
'This Is Love'/'I'll Close My Eyes'/'The
Very Thought Of You'/'Danny Boy'/
'The Sweetheart Tree'/'Symphony'/
'The Skye Boat Song'/'Autumn
Leaves'/'Mirage'

'THE YOUNG AMERICANS
PRESENTED BY JOHNNY MATHIS',
Mercury MG 21023, SR 61023

'The Young Americans'/'What's New
At The Zoo'*/'Round And Round The
Romance Tree'/'Daniel Boone'/'I Love
To Hear A Banjo'/'Clap Yo'
Hands'*/'Chim Chim Cheree'*/
'Winter'/'Klondike'/'One Fine
Day'/'Hard Travelin''/'Swanee'
*Johnny Mathis tracks

'SONGS FOR THE YOUNG'*, Mercury
MG 21068, SR 61068
No track details/never released.

'WARM'   CBS REALM RM52064
'Warm'/'My One And Only
Love'/'Baby Baby Baby'/'A Handful Of
Stars'/'By Myself'/'I've Grown
Accustomed To Her Face'/'Then I'll Be
Tired Of You'/'I'm Glad There Is
You'/'What'll I Do'/'The Lovely Things
You Do'/'There Goes My Heart'/'While
We're Young'
(This album consists of previously
released material)

'JOHNNY'S GREATEST HITS'
                      CBS 62569
'Chances Are'/'All The Time'/'The
Twelfth Of Never'/'When Sunny Gets
Blue'/'When I Am With
You'/'Wonderful, Wonderful'/'It's Not
For Me To Say'/'Come To Me'/'Wild Is
The Wind'/'Warm And Tender'/'No
Love'/'I Look At You'
(This album consists of previously
released material)

1966
'THE SHADOW OF YOUR SMILE',
Mercury MG 21073, SR 61073
'Moment To Moment'/'The Shadow
Of Your Smile'/'Michelle'/
'Yesterday/'Something's Coming'/'A
Taste Of Honey'/'I'm In Love For The
Very First Time'/'Quiet Nights
(Corcovado)'/'(I Left My Heart) In San
Francisco'/'On A Clear Day You Can
See Forever'/'Melinda'/'Come Back
To Me'

'THE SHADOW OF YOUR SMILE',

HMV CLP 3556, CSD 3556
'Moment To Moment'/'The Shadow
Of Your Smile'/'Michelle'/
'Yesterday'/'Something's Coming'/'A
Taste Of Honey'/'Lovers In New
York'/'Quiet Night (Corcovado)'/'(I
Left My Heart) In San Francisco'/'On A
Clear Day You Can See Forever'/
'Melinda'/'Come Back To Me'

'MERRY CHRISTMAS'   CBS 62806
'Winter Wonderland'/'The Christmas
Song'/'Sleigh Ride'/'Blue Christmas'/
'I'll Be Home For Christmas'/'White
Christmas'/'O Holy Night'/'What Child
Is This?'/'The First Noel'/'Silver
Bells'/'It Came Upon A Midnight
Clear'/'Silent Night, Holy Night'
(This album consists of previously
released material)

'SO NICE', Mercury MG 21091, SR
61091
'The Impossible Dream'/'I Will Wait
For You'/'What The World Needs
Now Is Love'/'Hurry! It's Lovely Up
Here'/'Elusive Butterfly'/'So Nice
(Samba De Verao)'/'Dulcinea'/'What
Now My Love'/'Man Of La Mancha (I,
Don Quixote)'/'The Music That Makes
Me Dance'/'I Dream Of You'/'Baubles,
Bangles And Beads'

1967
JOHNNY MATHIS SINGS', Mercury
MG 21107, SR 61107
'Saturday Sunshine'/'Lovers In New
York'/'Eleanor Rigby'/'Sunny'/'Who
Can I Turn To'/'Strangers In The
Night'/'(There's) Always Something
There To Remind Me'/'Somewhere
My Love'/'Who Can Say'/'I Wish You
Love'/'The Second Time Around'/
'Wake The Town And Tell The People'

1968
'UP, UP AND AWAY', CL 2726, CS
9526; CBS 63104
'Up, Up And Away'/'The More I See
You'/'Where Are The Words'/'The
Morningside Of The Mountain'/'I

Won't Cry Anymore'/'Far Above
Cayuga's Waters'/'Misty Roses'/
'Drifting'/'At The Crossroads'/'I
Thought Of You Last Night'/'When I
Look In Your Eyes'

'LOVE IS BLUE', CS 9637; CBS 63301
'I Say A Little Prayer'/'By The Time I
Get To Phoenix'/'The Look Of Love'/
'Don't Go Breakin' My Heart'/'Here,
There And Everywhere'/'Never My
Love'/'Moon River'/'Walk On
By'/'Venus'/'Love Is Blue'

'WARM/OPEN FIRE, TWO GUITARS'
                                GP 2
'Warm'/'My One And Only Love'/
'Baby Baby Baby'/'A Handful Of
Stars'/'By Myself'/'I've Grown
Accustomed To Her Face'/'Then I'll Be
Tired of You'/'I'm Glad There Is
You'/'What'll I Do'/'The Lovely Things
You Do'/'There Goes My Heart'/'While
We're Young'

'An Open Fire'/'Bye Bye Blackbird'/'In
The Still Of The Night'/'Embraceable
You'/'I'll Be Seeing You'/'Tenderly'/
'When I Fall In Love'/'I Concentrate On
You'/'Please Be Kind'/'You'll Never
Know'/'I'm Just A Boy In Love'/'My
Funny Valentine'
'This album consists of previously
released material)

'THOSE WERE THE DAYS', CS 9705;
CBS 63427
'Those Were The Days'/'Little Green
Apples'/'The End Of The World'/'This
Guy's In Love With You'/'The 59th
Street Bridge Song (Feelin' Groovy)'/
'Light My Fire'/'Every Time I Dream Of
You'/'The World I Used To
Know'/'You Make Me Think About
You'/'Turn Around Look At Me'

1969
'JOHNNY MATHIS SINGS THE
MUSIC OF BERT KAEMPFERT'
                            CBS 63524
'Wonderland By Night'/'Spanish

Eyes'/'The Lady Smiles'/'Danke
Schon'/'The Times Will Change'/
'Remember When'/'Strangers In
The Night'/'Don't Stay'/'If There's A
Way'/'Lady'/'L-o-v-e'/'It Makes No
Difference'

'PEOPLE'   CS 9871
'Sunny'/'More'/'The Shadow Of Your
Smile'/'Elusive Butterfly'/'Autumn
Leaves'/'A Wonderful Day Like
Today'/'Laura'/'Quiet Nights'
(Corcovado)/'What The World Needs
Now Is Love'/'People'
(This album consists of previously
released material)

'THE IMPOSSIBLE DREAM', CS 9872;
CBS 63718
'I Will Wait For You'/'Strangers In The
Night'/'So Nice'/'The Very Thought Of
You'/'On A Clear Day You Can See
Forever'/'Moment To Moment'/
'Somewhere, My Love'/'Go Away
Little Girl'/'Eleanor Rigby'/'The
Impossible Dream'
(This album consists of previously
released material)

'LOVE THEME FROM *ROMEO AND
JULIET*'   CS 9909
'Love Theme From *Romeo And
Juliet*'/'Aquarius'/'Let The Sunshine
In'/'Without Her'/'I'll Never Fall In
Love Again'/'Live For Life'/'We'/
'Didn't We'/'Love Me Tonight'/'The
Windmills Of Your Mind'/'The World I
Threw Away'/'Yesterday When I Was
Young'

'GIVE ME YOUR LOVE FOR
CHRISTMAS'   CS 9923
'Jingle Bell Rock'/'Have Yourself A
Merry Little Christmas'/'My Favourite
Things'/'Give Me Your Love For
Christmas'/'Santa Claus Is Comin' To
Town'/'What Are You Doing New
Year's Eve'/'Do You Hear What I
Hear?'/'Calypso Noel'/'The Little
Drummer Boy'/'Christmas Eve'/'The
Lord's Prayer'

1970
'RAINDROPS KEEP FALLIN' ON MY
HEAD', CS 1005; CBS 64012
'Raindrops Keep Fallin' On My Head'/
'Honey Come Back'/'Watch What
Happens'/'Something'/'Alfie'/
'Midnight Cowboy'/'A Man And A
Woman'/'Odds And Ends'/'Jean'/
'Everybody's Talkin' '/'Bridge Over
Troubled Water'

'JOHNNY MATHIS', Harmony KH
30017; Hallmark CHM 684
'A Lovely Way To Spend An
Evening'/'I'm In The Mood For
Love'/'Don't Blame Me'/'Warm And
Willing'/'I Just Found Out About
Love'/'Love Me As Though There
Were No Tomorrow'/'Where Are
You?'/'Can't Get Out Of This
Mood'/'On The Sunny Side Of The
Street'/'Let's Misbehave'
(This album consists of previously
released material)

'CLOSE TO YOU' (USA title)
'THE LONG AND WINDING ROAD'
(UK title), C 30210; CBS 64176
'They Long To Be Close To You'/'Evil
Ways'/'Come Saturday Morning'/
'Yellow Days'/'Pieces Of Dreams'/
'Song Of Joy'/'Everything Is
Beautiful'/'The Long And Winding
Road'/'Why Can't I Touch You?'/
'Wave'/'Until It's Time For You
To Go'

1971
'JOHNNY MATHIS SINGS THE
MUSIC OF BACHARACH AND
KAEMPFERT', G 30350; CBS 66275
'Wonderland By Night'/'Spanish
Eyes'/'The Lady Smiles'/'Danke
Schon'/'The Times Will Change'/
'Remember When'/'Strangers In The
Night'/'Don't Stay'/'If There's A
Way'/'Lady'/'L-o-v-e'

'Walk On By'/'The Look Of Love'/'I Say
A Little Prayer'/'Heavenly'/'This Guy's
In Love With You'/'I'll Never Fall In

Love Again'/'Alfie'/'Odds And Ends'/
'Faithfully'/'Don't Go Breaking My
Heart'
(This album consists of previously
released material)

'LOVE STORY', C 30499; CBS 64334
'Love Story'/'Rose Garden'/'Ten
Times Forever More'/'It's
Impossible'/'I Was There'/'What Are
You Doing The Rest Of Your
Life'/'We've Only Just Begun'/
'Traces'/'For The Good Times'/'My
Sweet Lord'/'Loss Of Love'

'CHRISTMAS WITH JOHNNY
MATHIS', KH 30864; Hallmark SHM
765
'The Sounds Of Christmas'/'Have
Yourself A Merry Little Christmas'/'A
Marshmallow World'/'God Rest Ye
Merry Gentlemen'/'Let It Snow, Let It
Snow, Let It Snow'/'The Secret Of
Christmas'/'Rudolph The Red Nose
Reindeer'/'Carol Of The Bells'/
'Christmas Is A Feeling In Your
Heart'/'Hallelujah Chorus'
(This album consists of previously
released material)

'YOU'VE GOT A FRIEND (TODAY'S
GREAT HITS)', C 307040; CBS 64448
'You've Got A Friend'/'How Can You
Mend A Broken Heart'/'Help Me Make
It Through The Night'/'If You Could
Read My Mind'/'Never Can Say
Goodbye'/'It's Too Late'/'We Can
Work It Out'/'Long Ago And Far
Away'/'If'/'For All We Know'/'If We
Only Have Love'

'TENDERLY'   US KH 30917
'Bye Bye Blackbird'/'In The Still Of
The Night'/'Embraceable You'/'I'll Be
Seeing You'/'Tenderly'/'When I Fall In
Love'/'Please Be Kind'/'You'll Never
Know'/'I'm Just A Boy In Love'/'My
Funny Valentine'
(This album consists of previously
released material)

'JOHNNY MATHIS GREATEST HITS
VOL 3'   CBS 64651
'This Guy's In Love With You'/'A Man
And A Woman'/'I Say A Little
Prayer'/'Evil Ways'/'Raindrops Keep
Fallin' On My Head'/'Turn Around
Look At Me'/'Up, Up And Away'/'Love
Story'/'Moon River'/'Honey Come
Back'/'Love Theme From *Romeo And
Juliet*'/'Misty Roses'

1972
'JOHNNY MATHIS IN PERSON', KG
30979; CBS 67321
'In The Morning'/'They Long To Be
Close To You/We've Only Just Begun'
(medley)/'Dreamy/Misty' (medley)/
'Come Runnin''/'Love Story'/'April In
Paris'/'Day In, Day Out'

(Hits Medley) 'Twelfth Of Never'/'Wild
Is The Wind'/'When Sunny Gets
Blue'/'It's Not For Me To Say'/
'Chances Are'/'Love Theme from
Romeo And Juliet'/'Tonight'/
'Dulcinea'/'The Impossible
Dream'/'Wonderful, Wonderful'/'And
Her Mother Came Too'/'I Got
Love'/'Maria'/'If We Only Have Love'

'JOHNNY MATHIS SINGS OF LOVE'
                Hallmark SHM 749
'Everything's Come Up Roses'/'Guys
And Dolls'/'I Wish I Were In Love
Again'/'You Do Something To
Me'/'Let's Misbehave'/'I Could Have
Danced All Night'/'A Cock-Eyed
Optimist'/'I Just Found Out About
Love'/'Let's Do It'/'I Am In Love'/'Love
Eyes'/'Love Is A Gamble'
(This album consists of previously
released material)

'ALL–TIME GREATEST HITS'
                CBS 67253
'A Certain Smile'/'When Sunny Gets
Blue'/'Small World'/'Misty'/'Chances
Are'/'Venus'/'Maria'/'Misty Roses'/
'Gina'/'What Will My Mary Say'

'Love Story'/'If We Only Have

Love'/'My Funny Valentine'/'Come To Me'/'Love Theme From *Romeo And Juliet*'/'Wonderful, Wonderful'/'All The Time'/'The Twelfth Of Never'/'Wild Is The Wind'/'It's Not For Me To Say'
(This album consists of previously released material)

'THE FIRST TIME EVER (I SAW YOUR FACE)'   KC 31342
'The First Time Ever (I Saw Your Face)'/'Speak Softly Love'/'The Summer Knows'/'Brian's Song'/'Since I Fell For You'/'Without You'/'Betcha By Golly Wow'/'Life And Breath'/'I Need You'/'(Last Night) I Didn't Get To Sleep At All'/'Life Is What You Make It'

'SONG SUNG BLUE' (USA title)
'MAKE IT EASY ON YOURSELF' (UK title), KG 31626; CBS 65161
'Play Me'/'Alone Again (Naturally)'/ 'Where Is The Love'/'Goodbye To Love'/'Too Young'/'Make It Easy On Yourself'/'Lean On Me'/'How Can I Be Sure'/'Run To Me'/'Song Sung Blue'/'He Ain't Heavy, He's My Brother'

1973
'ME AND MRS JONES', CBS KC 32114; CBS 65443
'Me And Mrs Jones'/'Sweet Surrender'/'Summer Breeze'/'Corner Of The Sky'/'Happy'/'Soul And Inspiration/Just Once In My Life'/ 'Don't Let Me Be Lonely Tonight'/ 'If I Could Reach You'/'Remember'/ 'You're A Lady'/'I Was Born In Love With You'/'Summer Me, Winter Me'

'THIS GUY'S IN LOVE WITH YOU'
                    Harmony KH 31935
'Up, Up And Away'/'Tonight'/'Turn Around Look At Me'/'The 59th Street Bridge Song (Feelin' Groovy)'/'This Guy's In Love With You'/'Those Were The Days'/'You Better Go Now'/'Light My Fire'/'The More I See You'/'Little

Green Apples'
(This album consists of previously released material)

'KILLING ME SOFTLY (WITH HER SONG)', KC 32258; CBS 65672
'Killing Me Softly (With Her Song)'/ 'Aubrey'/'And I Love Her So'/'Break Up To Make Up'/'Arianne'/'Neither One Of Us (Wants To Be The First To Say Goodbye)'/'Wild Flower'/ 'You Are The Sunshine Of My Life'/ 'Sing'/'Good Morning Heartache'/ 'Show And Tell'

'I'M COMING HOME', KC 32435; CBS 65690
'I'm Coming Home'/'I'd Rather Be Here With You'/'Foolish'/'I'm Stone In Love With You'/'And I Think That's What I'll Do'/'Life Is A Song Worth Singing'/'A Baby's Born'/'Sweet Child'/'Stop Look Listen To Your Heart'/'I Just Wanted To Be Me'

1974
'WARM'   Embassy EMB 31045
'Warm'/'My One And Only Love'/'Baby, Baby, Baby'/'A Handful Of Stars'/'By Myself'/'I've Grown Accustomed To Her Face'/'Then I'll Be Tired Of You'/'I'm Glad There Is You'/ 'What'll I Do'/'The Lovely Things You Do'/'There Goes My Heart'/'While We're Young'
(This album consists of previously released material)

'WHAT'LL I DO'   C 32963
'Put On A Happy Face'/'Poinciana'/ 'The Touch Of Your Lips'/'Under A Blanket Of Blue'/'What'll I Do'/'More'/ 'Over The Weekend'/'Limehouse Blues'/'The End Of A Love Affair'
(This album consists of previously released material)

'THE HEART OF A WOMAN', KC 33251; CBS 80533
'Woman, Woman'/'Sail On White Moon'/'It's Gone'/'House For Sale'/

'Feel Like Makin' Love'/'Memories Don't Leave Like People Do'/'Strangers In Dark Corners'/'Wendy'/'The Heart Of A Woman'/'The Way We Planned It'

'PORTRAIT OF JOHNNY'
Hallmark SHM 806
'Starbright'/'While You're Young'/ 'Should I Wait'/'All Is Well'/'You Set My Heart To Music'/'My Love For You'/'Oh That Feeling'/'How To Handle A Woman'/ 'Cherie'/'Hey Love'/'Jenny'/'The Story Of Our Love'
(This album consists of previously released material)

'JOHNNY MATHIS SINGS THE GREAT SONGS'   CBS 88085
'Alfie'/'Little Green Apples'/'Alone Again (Naturally)'/'Rose Garden'/ 'Stranger In Paradise'/'Aquarius/Let The Sunshine In'/'Strangers In The Night'/'My Sweet Lord'/'Everything Is Beautiful'/'Somewhere My Love'/'Long Ago And Far Away'/'Those Were The Days'

'By The Time I Get To Phoenix'/ 'Eleanor Rigby'/'They Long To Be Close To You'/'I'll Never Fall In Love Again'/'The Very Thought Of You'/'Make It Easy On Yourself'/'Bridge Over Troubled Water'/'It's Impossible'/'Too Young'/'Go Away Little Girl'/'Moonlight Becomes You'/'Walk On By'

1975
'HEAVENLY'   Embassy EMB 31084
'Heavenly'/'Hello, Young Lovers'/'A Lovely Way To Spend An Evening'/'A Ride On A Rainbow'/'More Than You Know'/'Something I Dreamed Last Night'/'Misty'/'Stranger In Paradise'/ 'Moonlight Becomes You'/'They Say It's Wonderful'/'I'll Be Easy To Find'/'That's All'
(This album consists of previously released material)

'WHEN WILL I SEE YOU AGAIN', PC 33420; CBS 80738
'Mandy'/'Nice To Be Around'/'You're As Right As Rain'/'When Will I See You Again'/'Only You (And You Alone)'/'Let Me Be The One/I Won't Last A Day'/'The Way We Were'/ 'Laughter In The Rain'/'You And Me Against The World'/'The Things I Might Have Been'

'THIS GUY'S IN LOVE WITH YOU'
Hallmark SHM 872
'Up, Up And Away'/'Tonight'/'Turn Around Look At Me'/'The 59th Street Bridge Song (Feelin' Groovy)'/'This Guy's In Love With You'/'Those Were The Days'/'Maria'/'Light My Fire'/'The More I See You'/'Little Green Apples'
(This album consists of previously released material)

'FEELINGS', PC 33887; CBS 69180
'One Day In Your Life'/'Stardust'/ 'What I Did For Love'/'Midnight Blue'/'The Greatest Gift'/'99 Miles From LA'/'Hurry Mother Nature'/'Feelings'/'That's All She Wrote'/'Solitaire'

'JOHNNY MATHIS SINGS THE MUSIC OF BERT KAEMPFERT'
Embassy EMB 31209
'Wonderland By Night'/'Spanish Eyes'/'The Lady Smiles'/'Danke Schon'/'The Times Will Change'/ 'Remember When'/'Strangers In The Night'/'Don't Stay'/'If There's A Way'/'Lady'/'L-o-v-e'/'It Makes No Difference'
(This album consists of previously released material)

'HEAVENLY AND FAITHFULLY'
CG 33621
'Heavenly'/'Hello, Young Lovers'/'A Lovely Way To Spend An Evening'/'A Ride On A Rainbow'/'More Than You Know'/'Something I Dreamed Last Night'/'Misty'/'Stranger In Paradise'/ 'Moonlight Becomes You'/'They Say

It's Wonderful'/'I'll Be Easy To
Find'/'That's All'

'Faithfully'/'Tonight'/'Nobody Knows
(How Much I Love You)'/'One Starry
Night'/'Follow Me'/'You Better Go
Now'/'Secret Love'/'Maria'/'Where Do
You Think You're Going'/'And This Is
My Beloved'/'Where Are You?'/'Blue
Gardenia'
(This album consists of previously
released material)

'MERRY CHRISTMAS'   CBS 69217
'Winter Wonderland'/'The Christmas
Song'/'Jingle Bell Rock'/'Have
Yourself A Merry Little Christmas'/
'Sleigh Ride'/'Silver Bells'/'Rudolph
The Red-Nosed Reindeer'/'White
Christmas'/'The Little Drummer
Boy'/'O Holy Night'/'God Rest Ye
Merry Gentlemen'/'What Child Is
This?'/'The First Noel'/'Carol Of The
Bells'/'It Came Upon A Midnight
Clear'/'Silent Night, Holy Night'
(This album consists of previously
released material)

1976
'THE JOHNNY MATHIS COLLECTION'
                    Hallmark PDA 015
'Starbright'/'While You're Young'/
'Should I Wait'/'All Is Well'/'You
Set My Heart To Music'/'My Love
For You'/'Oh That Feeling'/'How To
Handle A Woman'/'Cherie'/'Hey
Love'/'Jenny'/'Story Of Our Love'

'Up, Up And Away'/'Tonight'/'Turn
Around Look At Me'/'The 59th Street
Bridge Song (Feelin' Groovy)'/'This
Guy's In Love With You'/'Those Were
The Days'/'Maria'/'Light My Fire'/'The
More I See You'/'Little Green Apples'
(This album consists of previously
released material)

'I ONLY HAVE EYES FOR YOU', PC
34117; CBS 81329
'I Write The Songs'/'Do Me Wrong But
Do Me'/'The Hungry Years'/'I Only

Have Eyes For You'/'Yellow Roses On
Her Gown'/'(Do You Know Where
You're Going To) Theme from
Mahogany'/'Ooh What We Do'/'Send
In The Clowns'/'Every Time You
Touch Me (I Get High)'/'When A Child
Is Born'

'JOHNNY MATHIS'   Encore EN 13089
'Autumn In Rome'/'Easy To Love'/
'Street Dreams'/'Love, Your Magic
Spell Is Everywhere'/'Prelude To A
Kiss'/'Babalu'/'Caravan'/'In Other
Words'/'Star Eyes'/'It Might As Well
Be Spring'/'Cabin In The Sky'/'Angel
Eyes'
(This album consists of previously
released material)

'LOVE SONGS'   Embassy EMB 31393
'Love Story'/'The Look Of Love'/
'Never My Love'/'Somewhere My
Love'/'Goodbye To Love'/'If We Only
Have Love'/'This Guy's In Love With
You'/'Love Is Blue'/'The Flame Of
Love'/'Let's Love'/'Love Me
Tonight'/'I'll Never Fall In Love Again'
(This album consists of previously
released material)

1977
GREATEST HITS VOLUME FOUR'
                              CBS 86022
'When A Child Is Born'/'I'm Coming
Home'/'99 Miles From LA'/'The First
Time Ever (I Saw Her Face)'/'Laughter
In The Rain'/'Feelings'/'I'm Stone In
Love With You'/'Stardust'/'When Will
I See You Again'/'Me And Mrs Jones'/
'Killing Me Softly With Her Song'/'If
We Only Have Love'
(This album consists of previously
released material)

'MATHIS IS', PC 34441; CBS 86023
'Lullaby Of Love'/'Loving You, Losing
You'/'I'll Make You Happy'/'Heaven
Must Have Made You Just For Me'/
'Hung Up In The Middle Of Love'/
'World Of Laughter'/'I Don't Want
To Say No'/'Sweet Love Of Mine'

'MISTY' Hallmark SHM 913
'What'll I Do'/'More Than You
Know'/'Strangers In The Night'/'Baby,
Baby, Baby'/'Danke Schon'/'Stranger
In Paradise'/'Misty'/'By Myself'/
'Spanish Eyes'/'There Goes My
Heart'/'L-o-v-e'/'That's All'
(This album consists of previously
released material)

'JOHNNY'S GREATEST HITS'
PC 34667
'Chances Are'/'All The Time'/'The
Twelfth Of Never'/'When Sunny Gets
Blue'/'When I Am With You'/
'Wonderful, Wonderful'/'It's Not For
Me To Say'/'Come To Me'/'Wild Is The
Wind'/'Warm And Tender'/'No Love
(But Your Love)'/'I Look At You'
(This album consists of previously
released material)

'THE MATHIS COLLECTION'
CBS 10003
'We've Only Just Begun'/
'Everybody's Talkin''/'I'm Stone In
Love With You'/'The Look Of Love'/
'The Way We Were'/'Didn't We'/'The
Windmills Of Your Mind'/'What I
Did For Love'/'Stardust'/'When A
Child Is Born'/'I'm Coming Home'/
'Love Is Blue'/'The Summer Knows
(Summer of '42)'/'Betcha By Golly
Wow'/'Love Story'/'If'/'Send In The
Clowns'/'Speak Softly Love'/'And I
Love You So'/'Feelings'

'A Certain Smile'/'Wonderful,
Wonderful'/'Someone'/'Winter
Wonderland'/'The Twelfth Of
Never'/'Misty'/'My Funny
Valentine'/'I've Grown Accustomed
To Her Face'/'Tonight'/'Maria'/'What
Are You Doing The Rest Of Your
Life'/'A Man And A Woman'/'Help Me
Make It Through The Night'/'Moon
River'/'Raindrops Keep Fallin' On My
Head'/'People'/'On A Clear Day You
Can See Forever'/'99 Miles From
LA'/'I'll Never Fall In Love Again'
(This album consists of previously
released material)

'THE JOHNNY MATHIS COLLECTION
VOL. 2' Hallmark PDA 032
'Everything's Coming Up
Roses'/'Guys And Dolls'/'I Wish I
Were In Love Again'/'You Do
Something To Me'/'Let's
Misbehave'/'I Could Have Danced All
Night'/'A Cock-Eyed Optimist'/'I Just
Found Out About Love'/'Let's Do It'/'I
am In Love'/'Love Eyes'/'Love Is A
Gamble'

'Bye Bye Blackbird'/'In The Still Of
The Night'/'Embraceable You'/'I'll Be
Seeing You'/'Tenderly'/'When I Fall In
Love'/'Please Be Kind'/'You'll Never
Know'/'I'm Just A Boy In Love/'My
Funny Valentine'
(This album consists of previously
released material)

'WARM' Embassy 31499
'Warm'/'My One And Only
Love'/'Baby, Baby, Baby'/'A Handful
of Stars'/'By Myself'/'I've Grown
Accustomed To Her Face'/'Then I'll Be
Tired Of You'/'I'm Glad There Is
You'/'What'll I Do'/'The Lovely Things
You Do'/'There Goes My Heart'/'While
We're Young'
(This album consists of previously
released material)

'HOLD ME, THRILL ME, KISS ME'
PC 34872
'Hold Me, Thrill Me, Kiss Me'/'We're
All Alone'/'All The Things You Are'/
'One'/'When I Need You'/'The Most
Beautiful Girl'/'Tomorrow'/
'Evergreen'/'I Always Knew I Had
It In Me'/'Don't Give Up On Us'

'SWEET SURRENDER' CBS 86036
'Hold Me, Thrill Me, Kiss Me'/'We're
All Alone'/'All The Things You
Are'/'One'/'When I Need You'/'Sweet
Surrender'/'The Most Beautiful
Girl'/'Tomorrow'/'Evergreen'/'I
Always Knew I Had It In Me'/'Don't
Give Up On Us'

1978
YOU LIGHT UP MY LIFE', JC 35259;
CBS 86055
'You Light Up My Life'/'Emotion'
(Duet with Deniece Williams)/'All I
Ever Need'/'Where Or When'/'If You
Believe'/'Too much, Too Little, Too
Late' (Duet with Deniece
Williams)/'How Deep Is Your
Love'/'Till Love Touches Your Life'/'I
Wrote A Symphony On My Guitar'/'It
Was Almost Like A Song'

'THAT'S WHAT FRIENDS ARE FOR'*,
JC 35435 (also picture disc); CBS
86068
'You're All I Need To Get By'/'Until
You Come Back To Me'/'You're A
Special Part Of My Life'/'Ready Or
Not'/'Me For You, You For
Me'/'Heaven Must Have Sent
You'/'Just The Way You Are'/'That's
What Friends Are For'/'I Just Can't
Get Over You'/'Touching Me With
Love'
*Duet with Deniece Williams on all
tracks

'JOHNNY MATHIS'
St Michael 2094/0102
'Honey Come Back'/'Something'/
'Until It's Time For You To Go'/'The
Long And Winding Road'/'We've Only
Just Begun'/'I'll Never Fall In Love
Again'/'Don't Go Breakin' My
Heart'/'The Way We Were'/'You've
Got A Friend'/'We Can Work It
Out'/'Song Sung Blue'/'He Ain't
Heavy, He's My Brother'/'Me And Mrs
Jones'/'Killing Me Softly With Her
Song'/'I'm Stone In Love With
You'/'Betcha By Golly Wow'
(This album consists of previously
released material)

'WHEN A CHILD IS BORN' CBS 83266
'When A Child Is Born'/'Winter
Wonderland'/'Jingle Bell Rock'/'Have
Yourself A Merry Little Christmas'/
'Sleigh Ride'/'Silver Bells'/'The
Christmas Song'/'White

Christmas'/'Little Drummer Boy'/'O
Holy Night'/'God Rest Ye Merry
Gentlemen'/'What Child Is This?'/'The
First Noel'/'Carol Of The Bells'/'It
Came Upon A Midnight Clear'/'Silent
Night, Holy Night'
(This album consists of previously
released material)

'CHRISTMAS ALBUM'
St Michael 2094/0501
'Winter Wonderland'/'The Christmas
Song'/'Sleigh Ride'/'Blue Christmas'/
'I'll Be Home For Christmas'/'White
Christmas'/'Silver Bells'/'Have
Yourself A Merry Little Christmas'/
'Carol Of The Bells'/'What Child Is
This?'/'The First Noel'/'Rudolph The
Red Nosed Reindeer'
(This album consists of previously
released material)

1979
'THE BEST DAYS OF MY LIFE', JC
35649; CBS 86080
'Would You Like To Spend The Night
With Me'/'As Time Goes By'/'The Best
Days Of My Life'/'Gone, Gone,
Gone'/'The Bottom Line'/'The Last
Time I Felt Like This' (Duet with Jane
Olivor)/'Begin The Beguine'/'How Can
I Make It On My Own'/'There You
Are'/'We're In Love'

'MATHIS MAGIC', JC 36216; CBS
86103
'No One But The One You Love'/
'Night And Day'/'Love'/'My Body
Keeps Changing My Mind'/'New York
State Of Mind'/'She Believes In
Me'/'That Old Black Magic'/'You
Saved My Life' (Duet with Stephanie
Lawrence)/'To The Ends Of The
Earth'/'Heart, Soul, Body And Mind'

1980
'TEARS AND LAUGHTER' CBS 10019
'Don't Give Up On Us'/'Goodbye To
Love'/'Gone, Gone, Gone'/'Midnight
Blue'/'Solitaire'/'The Hungry
Years'/'Alone Again (Naturally)'/'Too

Much, Too Little, Too Late' (Duet with Deniece Williams)/'Without You'/'It's Too Late'/'Laughter In The Rain'/'You Are The Sunshine Of My Life'/ 'Everything Is Beautiful'/'The Most Beautiful Girl'/'You Light Up My Life'/ 'Just The Way You Are' (Duet with Deniece Williams)/'And I Love You So'/'Song of Joy'/'Life Is A Song Worth Singing'/'Betcha By Golly Wow'
(This album consists of previously released material)

'DIFFERENT KINDA DIFFERENT'
JC 36505
'Different Kinda Different' (Duet with Paulette)/'With You I'm Born Again'/'I'll Do It All For You' (Duet with Paulette)/'Never Givin' Up On You'/'Deep Purple'/'I Will Survive'/ 'Paradise'/'The Lights Of Rio'/'Love Without Words'/'Temptation'

'ALL FOR YOU'   CBS 86115
'Different Kinda Different' (Duet with Paulette)/'With You I'm Born Again'/'I'll Do It All For You' (Duet with Paulette)/'Never Givin' Up On You'/'Deep Purple'/'Three Times A Lady'/'I Will Survive'/'Paradise'/'The Lights Of Rio'/'Love Without Words'/'Temptation'

'THE BEST OF JOHNNY MATHIS 1975–1980'   JC 36871
'Too Much, Too Little, Too Late' (Duet with Deniece Williams)/'What I Did For Love'/'You Light Up My Life'/'99 Miles From LA'/'When A Child Is Born'/'Just The Way You Are' (Duet with Deniece Williams)/'With You I'm Born Again'/'Gone, Gone, Gone'/'The Best Days Of My Life'/'The Last Time I Felt Like This' (Duet with Jane Olivor)
(This album consists of previously released material)

'99 MILES FROM LA' Hallmark SHM 3091; St Michael 2188/2010
'You Light Up My Life'/'Do You Know

Where You're Going To'/'Laughter In The Rain'/'Mandy'/'When I Need You'/'I'm Coming Home'/'99 Miles From LA'/'I Write The Songs'/ 'Evergreen'/'What I Did For Love'/ 'How Deep Is Your Love'/'Feelings' (This album consists of previously released material and was first issued through Marks and Spencer)

'EVERGREENS'   St Michael 2188/8000
'Misty'/'Starbright'/'I'm In The Mood For Love'/'That's All'/'Jenny'/'59th Street Bridge Song (Feelin' Groovy)'/'I'm Stone In Love With You'/'Love Me As Though There Were No Tomorrow'/'Maria'/'You've Got A Friend'/'You Set My Heart To Music'/'In The Still Of The Night'

'A Lovely Way To Spend An Evening'/'Up, Up And Away'/'Danke Schon'/'L-o-v-e'/'When I Fall In Love'/'Bye, Bye Blackbird'/'Strangers In The Night'/'More Than You Know'/ 'I Only Have Eyes For You'/'Turn Around Look At Me'/'Little Green Apples'/'Never Can Say Goodbye' (This album consists of previously released material)

'JOHNNY MATHIS SINGS CHRISTMAS SONGS'
St Michael 2188/2020
'Have Yourself A Merry Little Christmas'/'Sleigh Ride'/'Silver Bells'/'Blue Christmas'/'Winter Wonderland'/'White Christmas'/ 'Rudolph The Red Nosed Reindeer'/ 'Carol Of The Bells'/'What Child Is This?'/'The First Noel'/'I'll Be Home For Christmas'/'The Christmas Song' (This album consists of previously released material)

'NIGHT AND DAY'   CBS 31863
'Night And Day'/'Would You Like To Spend The Night With Me'/'Help Me Make It Through The Night'/'Midnight Blue'/'Stardust'/'(Last Night) I Didn't Get To Sleep At All'/'Midnight

Cowboy'/'Come Saturday Morning'/
'You Are The Sunshine Of My
Life'/'Yesterday When I Was Young'/
'Those Were The Days'/'Aquarius/Let
The Sunshine in'/'Yellow Days'/'One
Day In Your Life'/'Good Morning
Heartache'/'On A Clear Day You Can
See For Ever'
(This album consists of previously
released material)

1981
'THE FIRST 25 YEARS – THE SILVER
ANNIVERSARY ALBUM'   C2X 37440
'Misty'/'Begin The Beguine'/'Didn't
We'/'It Doesn't Have To Hurt Every
Time'*/'Wonderful, Wonderful'/'It's
Not For Me To Say'/'Stardust'/'Three
Times A Lady'/'The Way You Look
Tonight'*/'Deep Purple'

'Chances Are'/'All The Things You
Are'/'A Time For Us'/'Nothing
Between Us But Love'*/'There! I've
Said It Again'*/'Too Much, Too Little,
Too Late' (Duet with Deniece
Williams)/'As Time Goes By'/'When
Sunny Gets Blue'/'Ready Or Not'/'I'm
Coming Home'
*(This album contains previously
released material with these
exceptions)

'CELEBRATION'   CBS 10028
'You Saved My Life' (Duet with
Stephanie Lawrence)/'Wonderful,
Wonderful'/'It's Not For Me To
Say'/'Chances Are'/'When A Child Is
Born'* (Duet with Gladys Knight)/'Too
Much, Too Little, Too Late' (Duet with
Deniece Williams)/'The Last Time I
Felt Like This' (Duet with Jane
Olivor)/'Stop, Look And Listen To
Your Heart'/'With You I'm Born
Again'/'Three Times A Lady'/'She
Believes In Me'/'I Wiil Survive'/
'Evergreen'/'When I Need
You'/'Sweet Surrender'/'How Deep Is
Your Love'/'We're All
Alone'/'Misty'/'I'd Rather Be Here
With You'/'If It's Magic'*
*(This album contains previously

released material with these
exceptions)

1982
'FRIENDS IN LOVE'
                 FC 37748; CBS 85652
'Got You Where I Want You' (Duet
with Dionne Warwick)/'I Remember
You And Me'/'When The Lovin' Goes
Out Of The Lovin' '/'Somethin's Goin'
On'/'What Do You Do With The
Love'/'Friends In Love' (Duet with
Dionne Warwick)/'What's Forever
For'/'Warm'/'Memory'/'Lately'

Miscellaneous US LPs

'COLUMBIA RECORDS PRESENTS
JOHNNY MATHIS'
'Chances Are'/'All The Time'/'The
Twelfth Of Never'/'When Sunny Gets
Blue'/'When I Am With You'/
'Wonderful, Wonderful'/'It's Not For
Me To Say'/'Come To Me'/'Wild Is The
Wind'/'Warm And Tender'/'No
Love'/'I Look At You'

'Small World'/'Someone'/'Very Much
In Love'/'You Are Everything To
Me'/'Let It Rain'/'The Flame Of
Love'/'A Certain Smile'/'Call Me'/'You
Are Beautiful'/'Teacher, Teacher'/
'Stairway To The Sea'/'Let's Love'

'THE MAGIC OF JOHNNY MATHIS'
                              STS 2006
'Small World'/'Call Me Irresponsible'/
'The Shadow Of Your Smile'/'Long
Ago And Far Away'/'Moon
River'/'Moonlight Becomes
You'/'Don't Blame Me'/'It Could
Happen To You'/'On A Clear Day You
Can See Forever'/'Love Look Away'

'How To Handle A Woman'/'I'm In
The Mood For Love'/'Shangri-La'/
'Somewhere, My Love'/'You Stepped
Out Of A Dream'/'Stella By
Starlight'/'Hi-Lili Hi-Lo'/'That Old
Black Magic'/'Laura'/'An Affair To
Remember'

'I JUST FOUND OUT ABOUT LOVE'
DS 446, D 446
'A Lovely Way To Spend An Evening'/'I'm In The Mood For Love'/'I Just Found Out About Love'/'Can't Get Out Of This Mood'/'Don't Blame Me'/'Warm And Willing'/'When My Sugar Walks Down The Street'/'Love Me As Though There Were No Tomorrow'/'Where Are You?'/'Too Young To Go Steady'/'On The Sunny Side Of The Street'

'CHRISTMAS WITH JOHNNY MATHIS & RAY CONNIFF'   CSP C10905
'O Holy Night'/'It Came Upon A Midnight Clear'/'Greensleeves'/'The First Noel'/'Ave Maria'/'Silent Night, Holy Night'
Side 2 The Ray Conniff Singers

'THE WORLD'S GREAT LOVE SONGS'
DS 616
'Misty'/'Where Are You?'/'The Twelfth Of Never'/'Tenderly'/'Friendly Persuasion'/'Wonderful, Wonderful'/ 'Chances Are'/'Embraceable You'/'That Old Black Magic'/'Stella By Starlight'

'EMBRACEABLE YOU'   CMT 1P6031
'When The World Was Young'/'I Can't Believe That You're In Love With Me'/'The Story Of Our Love'/ 'Embraceable You'/'Hey, Look Me Over'/'My Funny Valentine'/'I'll Be Seeing You'/'When Sunny Gets Blue'/'Moments Like This'/'Moonlight In Vermont'

'THE EARLY YEARS'   CMT 2P6083
'Chances Are'/'It's Not For Me To Say'/'The Twelfth Of Never'/'Fly Me To The Moon'/'That's All'/'Tenderly'/ 'Maria'/'It's Only A Paper Moon'/'You'll Never Know'/'Hello Young Lovers'

'Misty'/'A Certain Smile'/'I've Grown Accustomed To Her Face'/'Small World'/'My Funny

Valentine'/'Wonderful, Wonderful'/ 'Stella By Starlight'/'That Old Black Magic'/'Faithfully'/'Embraceable You'

'JOHNNY TODAY'   CMT 1P6084
'Alfie'/'What The World Needs Now Is Love'/'Brian's Song'/'Traces'/'The First Time Ever'/'Up, Up And Away'/'Yesterday When I Was Young'/'Bridge Over Troubled Water'/'On A Clear Day You Can See Forever'/'Come Saturday Morning'

'CHRISTMAS WITH JOHNNY MATHIS & PERCY FAITH'   CSP P11805
'Sleigh Ride'/'What Child Is This?'/'Jingle Bell Rock'/'Silver Bells'/'Silent Night, Holy Night'
Side 2 Percy Faith

'WARM AND TENDER' CMT 2P6276/7
'Tenderly'/'My Funny Valentine'/'A Certain Smile'/'Come To Me'/'Warm And Tender'/'What Will My Mary Say'/'You'll Never Know'/'Street Of Dreams'/'Misty'/'A Lovely Way To Spend An Evening'

'Maria'/'Love, Look Away'/'Hello, Young Lovers'/'Day In, Day Out'/'It's Not For Me To Say'/'Call Me Irresponsible'/'It Could Happen To You'/'Gina'/'I've Grown Accustomed To Her Face'/'In The Wee Small Hours Of The Morning'

'Moonlight Becomes You'/'Stella By Starlight'/'It Might As Well Be Spring'/'Secret Love'/'That's All'/'Let Me Love You'/'Too Close For Comfort'/'When I Fall In Love'/'Bye, Bye Blackbird'/'My Darling, My Darling'/'The Twelfth Of Never'/'I'm Just A Boy In Love'/'Wonderful, Wonderful'/'When Sunny Gets Blue'/'Love, Your Spell Is Everywhere'/'Chances Are'/'Small World'/'Faithfully'/'Embraceable You'/'I'll Be Seeing You'

'THE HEART OF JOHNNY MATHIS'
P 14908
'Soul And Inspiration/Just Once In My Life'/'My Love For You'/'I Won't Last A Day Without You/Let Me Be The One'/'Bridge Over Troubled Water'/'Traces/'Spanish Eyes'/'Secret Love'/'Turn Around Look At Me'/'Fly Me To The Moon'

'WONDERFUL'   P16658
'The Look of Love'/'Heavenly'/'Chances Are'/'Wonderful Wonderful'/'The More I See You'/'It's Not For Me to Say'/'Up Up and Away'/'Spanish Eyes'/'Where Where Or When'/'The Twelfth of Never'

Johnny Mathis US Box-Set LPs

'THE JOHNNY MATHIS TREASURY'
6P6030
'Chances Are'/'Wonderful, Wonderful'/'It's Not For Me To Say'/'Small World'/'All The Time'/'Warm'/'That's All'/'Misty'/'Come To Me'/'Maria'

'Fly Me To The Moon'/'September Song'/'Tenderly'/'Getting To Know You'/'By Myself'/'The Twelfth Of Never'/'Heavenly'/'Secret Love'/'Warm And Tender'/'That Old Black Magic'

'Friendly Persuasion'/'While We're Young'/'Stella By Starlight'/'I've Grown Accustomed To Her Face'/ 'And This Is My Beloved'/'A Certain Smile'/'Quiet Girl'/'Faithfully'/ 'Gina'/'Too Close For Comfort'

'People'/'Alfie'/'The Look Of Love'/'Love Is Blue'/'For The Good Times'/'A Time For Us'/'Yesterday When I Was Young'/'Sunny'/'Love Story'/'This Guy's In Love With You'

'The Windmills Of Your Mind'/'Never My Love'/'Brian's Song'/'A Man And A Woman'/'Those Were The Days'/'Up, Up And Away'/'Autumn

Leaves'/'Come Saturday Morning'/'Go Away Little Girl'/'By The Time I Get To Phoenix'

'Raindrops Keep Fallin' On My Head'/'The First Time Ever'/'Everything Is Beautiful'/'The Shadow Of Your Smile'/'Somewhere, My Love'/'Turn Around Look At Me'/'Traces'/'Bridge Over Troubled Water'/'On A Clear Day You Can See Forever'/'Little Green Apples'

'HOLIDAY AT THE FIRESIDE'
'White Christmas'/'Winter Wonderland'/'Silver Bells'/'The Christmas Song'/'Silent Night, Holy Night'/'I'll Be Home For Christmas'/'Jingle Bell Rock'/'What Are You Doing New Year's Eve'/'Sleigh Ride'/'Have Yourself A Merry Little Christmas'
This LP was given free with the 'Johnny Mathis Treasury'

'ROMANTICALLY, JOHNNY MATHIS'
P3 I1837
3LP Box Set that consists of LPs
'WARM'   Columbia S8039
'OPEN FIRE, TWO GUITARS'
Columbia CS8056
'ROMANTICALLY'   Columbia CS8898

'SOMETHING VERY SPECIAL FROM MATHIS & CONNIFF'
CSP C4 10303
Side 1 Ray Conniff
'The Twelfth Of Never'/'Rose Garden'/'Tenderly'/'Sunny'/'Traces'
Side 1 Ray Conniff
'Jean'/'Didn't We'/'Misty'/'Spanish Eyes'/'We've Only Just Begun'
Side 1 Ray Conniff
'I'll Never Fall In Love Again'/'I Say A Little Prayer'/'Alfie'/'The Look Of Love'/'This Guy's In Love With You'
Side 1 Ray Conniff
'Fly Me To The Moon'/'You Stepped Out Of A Dream'/'By The Time I Get To Phoenix'/'The World I Used To Know'/'Until It's Time For You To Go'

'MAGIC MOMENTS WITH MATHIS &
CONNIFF'   CSP P5 13109
'You Are The Sunshine Of My Life'/
'The Way We Were'/'Everything Is
Beautiful'/'For The Good Times'/
'When Will I See You Again'
Side 2 Ray Conniff
'Love Story'/'Maria'/'Feelings'/'Love
Theme From *The Godfather*'/'The
First Time Ever'
Side 2 Ray Conniff
'The Impossible Dream'/'People'/
'Aquarius/Let The Sunshine In'/'What
I Did For Love'/'If We Only Have Love'
Side 2 Ray Conniff
'Light My Fire'/'My Sweet Lord'/'Feel
Like Makin' Love'/'Let Me Be The
One/I Won't Last A Day Without
You'/'Why Can't I Touch You'
Side 2 Ray Conniff
'Chances Are'/'When Sunny Gets
Blue'/'Wonderful, Wonderful'/'A
Certain Smile'/'It's Not For Me To Say'
Side 2 Ray Conniff

'THE COMPLETE JOHNNY MATHIS
TREASURY'   Candlelite P6 14628
'Chances Are'/'Up, Up And Away'/'All
The Time'/'Song Sung Blue'/'Take
Good Care Of Her'/'The Twelfth Of
Never'/'I Say A Little Prayer'/'The
Impossible Dream'/'Call Me'/'Make It
Easy On Yourself'

'A Certain Smile'/'You Are The
Sunshine Of My Life'/'Venus'/'And I
Love You So'/'Everything Is
Beautiful'/'Misty'/'Sunny'/'Feelings'/
'Hold Me, Thrill Me, Kiss Me'/'For The
Good Times'

'Wonderful, Wonderful'/'Mandy'/'I'll
Never Fall In Love Again'/'I Only Have
Eyes For You'/'Send In The
Clowns'/'It's Not For Me To
Say'/'Didn't We'/'Stardust'/'What Will
My Mary Say'/'The Way We Were'

'Small World'/'Killing Me Softly With
Her Song'/'Love Is Blue'/'Close To
You'/'On A Clear Day You Can See

Forever'/'Maria'/'The First Time
Ever'/'This Guy's In Love With
You'/'You've Got A Friend'/'Those
Were The Days'

'Wild Is The Wind'/'Never, My
Love'/'Until It's Time For You To
Go'/'The Most Beautiful Girl In The
World'/'A Time For Us'/'Gina'/'I Write
The Songs'/'Where Or When'/'Help
Me Make It Through The
Night'/'Yesterday When I Was Young'

'Bye' Bye' Barbara'/'We've Only Just
Begun'/'When I Fall In Love'/'Laughter
In The Rain'/'Since I Fell For
You'/'When Sunny Gets Blue'/'You
Light Up My Life'/'What I Did For
Love'/'It's Impossible'/'The Look Of
Love'/'Someone'

'JOHNNY'   CSP 414971
'Solitaire'/'Don't Let Me Be Lonely
Tonight'/'Neither One Of Us'/'When
Will I See You Again'/'Alone Again
(Naturally)'/'You Light Up My Life'/
'Laughter In The Rain'/'Sing'/
'Summer Breeze'/'Everytime You
Touch Me (I Get High)'

'I Write The Songs'/'When I Need
You'/'We're All Alone'/'Life Is A Song
Worth Singing'/'Stardust'/
'Evergreen'/'Raindrops Keep Fallin'
On My Head'/'Theme From
Mahogany'/'Tonight'/'Come Saturday
Morning'

'One'/'Send In The Clowns'/'Guy's
And Dolls'/'Let's Do It'/
'Tomorrow'/'I'm Coming Home'/'As
Long As We're Together'/'I'm Stone
In Love With You'/'The More I See
You'/'The Long And Winding Road'

'Me And Mrs Jones'/'Midnight Blue'/'I
Only Have Eyes For You'/'The Hungry
Years'/'He Ain't Heavy, He's My
Brother'/'Lean On Me'/'Warm And
Tender'/'Close To You'/'Do Me
Wrong, But Do Me'/'Goodnight My
Love'

UK Box-Sets

'THE BEST OF JOHNNY MATHIS'
CBS 66415
4-LP Box Set that consists of LPs'
'JOHNNY MATHIS SINGS THE
GREAT SONGS'   CBS 88085
'ALL–TIME GREATEST HITS'
CBS 67253

'JOHNNY MATHIS'   CBS 66355
3-LP Box Set that consists of LPs:
'GREATEST HITS VOL4'   CBS 86022
'YOU LIGHT UP MY LIFE'   CBS 86055
'THE BEST DAYS OF MY LIFE'
CBS 86080

'THE BEST OF JOHNNY MATHIS'
Reader's Digest
'It's Not For Me To Say'/'Wonderful,
Wonderful'/'I'll Never Fall In Love
Again'/'Song Sung Blue'/'Misty'/'Love
Story'/'By The Time I Get To
Phoenix'/'L-o-v-e'/'The Look Of
Love'/'Alone Again (Naturally)'/'How
Deep Is Your Love?'/'You're All I Need
To Get By'/'Someone'/'Moon
River'/'Aquarius/Let The Sunshine
In'/'Don't Go Breaking My Heart'

'The Twelfth Of Never'/'My Sweet
Lord'/'A Certain Smile'/'Love Is
Blue'/'I Say A Little Prayer'/'Killing Me
Softly With Her Song'/'For All We
Know'/'The Windmills Of Your
Mind'/'Small World'/'This Guy's In
Love With You'/'Something'/'My Love
For You'/'Gina'/'You Light Up My
Life'/'Spanish Eyes'/'Those Were The
Days'

'Everything Is Beautiful'/'Winter
Wonderland'/'A Man And A
Woman'/'End Of The World'/
'Strangers In The Night'/'Little Green
Apples'/'Teacher, Teacher'/'Close To
You'/'Chances Are'/'What Will My
Mary Say'/'Go Away Little Girl'/'Me
And Mrs Jones'/'Light My Fire'/'Help
Me Make It Through The Night'/'Here,
There And Everywhere'/'Speak Softly
Love'

'The Best Of Everything'/'Raindrops
Keep Fallin' On My Head'/'Walk On
By'/'You've Got A Friend'/
'Emotions'*/'Too Much, Too Little,
Too Late'*/'Send In The
Clowns'/'Gone, Gone, Gone'/'When A
Child Is Born'/'He Ain't Heavy, He's
My Brother'/'The Way We
Were'/'Bridge Over Troubled
Water'/'Didn't We'/'Honey Come
Back'/'I'm Stone In Love With
You'/'We've Only Just Begun'
*Duets with Deniece Williams

Miscellaneous UK LPs

'JOHNNY MATHIS'   Hallmark
(3 LPs)
'Tenderly'/'When I Fall In Love'/'I
Could Have Danced All Night'/'Bye
Bye Blackbird'/'In The Still Of The
Night'/'Embraceable You'/'I'll Be
Seeing You'/'Please Be Kind'/'You'll
Never Know'/'I'm Just A Boy In
Love'/'My Funny Valentine'/
'Everything Is Coming Up Roses'

'Let's Do It'/'I Am In Love'/'Guys And
Dolls'/'I Wish I Were In Love
Again'/'You Do Something To
Me'/'Let's Misbehave'/'A Cock-Eyed
Optimist'/'I Just Found Out About
Love'/'Love Eyes'/'Love Is A Gamble'

'Starbright'/'While You're
Young'/'Should I Wait'/'All Is
Well'/'You Set My Heart To
Music'/'My Love For You'/'Oh That
Feeling'/'How To Handle A
Woman'/'Cherie'/'Hey
Love'/'Jenny'/'The Story Of Our Love'
*Not in track order

'THE ULTIMATE JOHNNY MATHIS'
Open 1/LSP 14256 1982
'Chances Are'/'The Twelfth Of
Never'/'What Will Mary Say'/'Misty'/
'Wonderful, Wonderful'/'A Certain
Smile'/'You're All I Need To Get By'/
'Winter Wonderland'/'I'm Stone In
Love With You'/'When A Child Is Born

(Soleado)'/'Someone'/'The First Time Ever (I Saw Your Face)'/'Where Do I Begin (Love Story)'/'The Way We Were'/'Too Much, Too Little, Too Late'/'With You I'm Born Again'/'Tonight'/'How Deep Is Your Love'/'It's Too Late'/'Night And Day'/'Just The Way You Are'/'Begin The Beguine'/'Moon River'/'Three Times A Lady'/'Venus'/'Gone, Gone, Gone'

Other Miscellaneous LPs

Soundtracks
US
'WILD IS THE WIND'
                Columbia CL 1090
'A CERTAIN SMILE'
                Columbia CS 8068

US/UK
'THE BIGGEST BUNDLE OF THEM ALL': 'Most Of All There Is You'
                MS 8066

UK
'COMMAND PERFORMANCE': 'Misty' (Live Recording)
                Ronco MSD 2005

Germany
'NANA MOUSKOURIS EINE WELT VOLL MUSIK': 'Love Story' '(Duet with Nana Mouskouri)
                Phillips 9286611

Spain
'TODOS LOS EXITOS': 'Gina' (sung in Spanish)   CBS APS 60023

UK
'TED HEATH ANNIVERSARY ALBUM': Spoken tribute to Ted Heath
                Decca LK 4903

US/UK
'A PORTRAIT OF JOHNNY MATHIS'*
                Philips PHM 200167
'Misty'/'The Twelfth Of Never'/'It's Not For Me To Say'/'What Will My

Mary Say'/'When Sunny Gets Blue'/'Maria'/'Chances Are'/'A Certain Smile'/'Gina'/'Small World'/'Wonderful, Wonderful'/'Someone'
*Played by Robert Farnon and his Orchestra

Worldwide LPs
(excluding UK and US releases)

Australia
'A LOVELY WAY TO SPEND AN EVENING WITH JOHNNY MATHIS'
                MFP 2398013
'A Lovely Way To Spend An Evening'/'I'm In The Mood For Love'/Don't Blame Me'/'Warm And Willing'/'I Just Found Out About Love'/'Love Me As Though There Were No Tomorrow'/'Where Are You?'/'Can't Get Out Of This Mood'/'On The Sunny Side Of The Street'

'Bye Bye Blackbird'/'In The Still Of The Night'/'Embraceable You'/'I'll Be Seeing You'/'Tenderly'/'When I Fall In Love'/'You'll Never Know'/'I'm Just A Boy In Love'/'My Funny Valentine'

'THE BEST OF JOHNNY MATHIS'
                CBS CSP 008
'Wonderful, Wonderful'/'Sing'/'And I Love You So'/'Chances Are'/'I'll Never Fall In Love Again'/'Send In The Clowns'/'I'm Coming Home'/'Feelings'/'Aquarius'/'Let The Sunshine In'/'You Are The Sunshine Of My Life'/'Raindrops Keep Fallin' On My Head'/'The Twelfth Of Never'/'For All We Know'/'Song Sung Blue'/'How Can You Mend A Broken Heart?'/'Yesterday When I Was Young'/'A Certain Smile'/'A Wonderful Day Like Today'/'I Write The Songs'

'THE JOHNNY MATHIS COLLECTION'
                CBS CSP 062
'Evergreen'/'How Deep Is Your Love'/'Walk On By'/'Love Theme

From *The Godfather*'/'Love Story'/'Help Me Make It Through The Night'/'Danke Schoen'/'It's Impossible'/'Moon River'/'When A Child Is Born'/'You Light Up My Life'/'I Only Have Eyes For You'/'Don't Give Up On Us'/'I Say A Little Prayer'/'What I Did For Love'/'Summer Of 42'/'Laughter In The Rain'/'Stardust'/ 'We've Only Just Begun'/'The Way We Were'

'JOHNNY MATHIS SOUVENIR ALBUM'   CBS CSP 120
'Begin The Beguine'/'As Time Goes By'/'That Old Black Magic'/When I Need You'/'Evergreen'/'Gone, Gone, Gone'/'Just The Way You Are'*/'The Twelfth Of Never'/'Wonderful, Wonderful'/'Emotion'*/'Night And Day'/'Chances Are'/'Too Much, Too Little, Too Late'*/'My Funny Valentine'/'I'm Stone In Love With You'/'How Deep Is Your Love'/'We're All Alone'
*Duets with Deniece Williams

Brazil
'OS GRANDES SUCESSOS DE JOHNNY MATHIS'   LPCB 42039
'Chances Are'/'Teacher, Teacher'/'The Twelfth Of Never'/'When Sunny Gets Blue'/'When I Am With You'/ 'Wonderful, Wonderful'/'It's Not For Me To Say'/'Come To Me'/'Wild Is The Wind'/'Warm And Tender'/'No Love'/'I Look At You'

'MY LOVE FOR YOU'   CBS 37141
'Blue Gardenia'/'April In Paris'/'Maria'/ 'How High The Moon'/'Where Are You?'/'Corner To Corner'/'My Love For You'/'I'm In The Mood For Love'/ 'Secret Love'/'There's No You'/ 'Tonight'/'Goodnight My Love'

'SMILE'   CBS 37183
'Faithfully'/'Hey, Love'/'Starbright'/'I'll Buy You A Star'/'You Better Go Now'/ 'You Set My Heart To Music'/'Smile'/ 'All Is Well'/'Stairway To The Stars'/ 'Oh, That Feeling'/'Cherie'/'When My

Sugar Walks Down The Street'

'JOHNNY MATHIS'   CBS 37289
'Warm And Willing'/'You'll Never Know'/'Baby, Baby, Baby'/'In The Still Of The Night'/'The Lovely Things You Do'/'I'm Just A Boy In Love'/'My Funny Valentine'/'I've Grown Accustomed To Her Face'/'Tenderly'/ 'I'm Glad There Is You'/'Embraceable You'/'Caravan'

'OS GRANDES SUCESSOS DE JOHNNY MATHIS'   412024
'My Love For You'/'A Certain Smile'/'Maria'/'A Time For Us'/ 'Getting To Know You'/'Wild Is The Wind'/'Too Much, Too Little, Too Late'/'Evie'/'It's Not For Me To Say'/'Tonight'/'Gina'/'The Best Of Everything'/'Misty'/'Midnight Cowboy'

'GINA'   CBS 37253
'Gina'/'I Have Dreamed'/'I Married An Angel'/'Don't Blame Me'/'Taking A Chance On Love'/'The Party's Over'/'You Do Something To Me'/'I Could Have Danced All Night'/'On The Sunny Side Of The Street'/'My Romance'/'Spring Is Here'/'And This Is My Beloved'

'GRANDES INTERPRETACEOS'
            CBS 37425
'Misty'/'Stranger In Paradise'/'Warm'/ 'Heavenly'/'Wonderful, Wonderful'/ 'Chances Are'/'Gina'/'A Certain Smile'/'Faithfully'/'Wild Is The Wind'/'Starbright'/'It's Not For Me To Say'

'GRANDES INTERPRETACEOS VOL2'
            CBS 37465
'Taking A Chance On Love'/'Warm And Willing'/'I Look At You'/'Baby, Baby, Baby'/'They Say It's Wonderful'/'You Set My Heart To Music'/'Smile'/'The Party's Over'/ 'Wild Is The Wind'/'I Married An Angel'/'When I Am With You'/'Heavenly'

'ESPECIAL JOHNNY MATHIS'
CBS 138081
'Too Much, Too Little, Too Late'*/
'Aquarius/Let The Sunshine In'/'Rose
Garden'/'My Sweet Lord'/'It's
Impossible'/'A Time For Us'/'It's Not
For Me To Say'/'My Love For
You'/'Tonight'/'They Long To Be
Close To You'/'Up, Up And Away'/'I'll
Never Fall In Love Again'/'Love
Story'/'Love Is Blue'
*Duet with Deniece Williams

Canada

WONDERFUL, WONDERFUL
JOHNNY MATHIS'
Concept CSPS 1062
'Misty'/'Wonderful, Wonderful'/'The
First Time Ever'/'The Twelfth Of
Never'/'Tenderly'/'It's Not For Me To
Say'/'Brian's Song'/'Embraceable
You'/'Maria'/'Traces'/'Chances
Are'/'Hello Young Lovers'/'Alfie'/'I've
Grown Accustomed To Her
Face'/'Small World'/'A Certain
Smile'/'My Funny Valentine'/'Bridge
Over Troubled Water'/'Fly Me To The
Moon'/'Come Saturday Morning'

'JOHNNY MATHIS SUPER
SELECTION'
SL 4001
'They Long To Be Close To You'/'Evil
Ways'/'Come Saturday Morning'/
'Yellow Days'/'Pieces Of Dreams'/
'Song Of Joy'/'Everything Is Beautiful'/
'The Long And Winding Road'/'Why
Can't I Touch You?'/'Wave'/'Until It's
Time For You To Go'

'SINCERELY YOURS'
Kelo/Music NC 505
'The Twelfth Of Never'/'It's Not For
Me To Say'/'A Certain Smile'/'Life Is A
Song Worth Singing'/'Theme From
Mahogany'/'Chances Are'/'Gina'/
'What Will My Mary Say'/'Mandy'/'I'm
Coming Home'/'Too Much, Too Little,
Too Late'*/'Don't Give Up On Us'/
'You Light Up My Life'/'The Most
Beautiful Girl'/'Hold Me, Thrill Me,

Kiss Me'/'Everytime You Touch Me (I
Get High)'/'One Day In Your Life'/'Put
On A Happy Face'/'Misty'/'I Write The
Songs'
*Duet with Deniece Williams

France
'JOHNNY MATHIS'
Fontana 662011MR 10"
'Will I Find My Love Today'/'Chances
Are'/'Looking At You'/'Let Me Love
You'/'All Through The Night'/'It's Not
For Me To Say'/'Warm And Tender'/
'Too Close For Comfort'/'Early
Autumn'/ 'The Twelfth Of Never'

'SWING SOFTLY' Fontana 662041MR
'You'd Be So Nice To Come Home
To'/'Like Someone In Love'/'Love
Walked In'/'It's De-Lovely'/'Get Me To
The Church On Time'/'Sweet
Lorraine'/'Easy To Say'/'Can't Get Out
Of This Mood'/'To Be In Love'/'This
Heart Of Mine'

'JOHNNY MATHIS' GREATEST
HITS'
CBS 88087
'Love Story'/'Tonight'/'Sunny'/'I Will
Wait For You'/'Somewhere My
Love'/'The Windmills Of Your
Mind'/'They Long To Be Close To
You'/'Raindrops Keep Fallin' On My
Head'/'The Look Of Love'/'Bridge
Over Troubled Water'/'Song Sung
Blue'/'I'm Coming Home'

'Ave Maria' (Gounod)/'Kol Nidre'/'Eli
Eli'/'Deep River'/'The Rosary'/'Ave
Maria' (Schubert)/'Venus'/'Maria'/
'Misty'/'The Shadow Of Your Smile'/
'Strangers In The Night'/'A Man And
A Woman'

'JOHNNY MATHIS "A PARIS"'
CBS 81160
'Misty'/'Love Theme From *The
Godfather*'/'If We Only Have
Love'/'When Will I See You
Again'/'Live For Life'/'Theme From
Summer Of 42'/'Maria'/'When A Child
Is Born'/'In The Morning'/'I Got

Love'/'Sing'/'Killing Me Softly With
Her Song'/'Ave Maria'

'CHANTE NOEL'   CBS 81481
'Silent Night, Holy Night'/'The First
Noel'/'What Child Is This?'/'Rudolph
The Red-Nosed Reindeer'/'The
Christmas Song'/'White Christmas'/
'Ave Maria'/'The Little Drummer Boy'/
'Sleigh Ride'/'Winter Wonderland'/
'Silver Bells'/'O Holy Night'

'THE BEST OF JOHNNY MATHIS'
                         CBS 88293
'A Wonderful Day Like Today'/'Misty'/
'Laughter In The Rain'/'Only
You'/'Live For Life'/'99 Miles From
LA'/'Tonight'/'Maria'/'A Certain
Smile'/'On A Clear Day You Can See
Forever'/'The Way We Were'/'I'll
Never Fall In Love Again'/'Autumn
Leaves'/'More'/'Love Is Blue'/'Sing'

'I Will Wait For You'/'People'/'Moon
River'/'Song Sung Blue'/'My Funny
Valentine'/'A Man And A Woman'/
'Too Young'/'Ave Maria' (Gounod)/
'The Windmills Of Your Mind'/
'Eleanor Rigby'/'Feelings'/'What
The World Needs Now Is Love'/
'Solitaire'/'Everybody's Talkin''/
'When A Child Is Born'/'If We Only
Have Love'

'JOHNNY MATHIS VOL1'   VER 34117
'Bye Bye Blackbird'/'In The Still Of
The Night'/'Embraceable You'/'I'll Be
Seeing You'/'Tenderly'/'When I Fall In
Love'/'Please Be Kind'/'You'll Never
Know'/'I'm Just A Boy In Love'/'My
Funny Valentine'

'JOHNNY MATHIS VOL2'   VER 34155
'Wonderland By Night'/'Spanish
Eyes'/'The Lady Smiles'/'Danke
Schoen'/'The Times Will Change'/
'Remember When'/'Strangers In The
Night'/'Don't Stay'/'If There's A
Way'/'Lady'/'L-o-v-e'/'It Makes No
Difference'

**'JOHNNY MATHIS GREATEST HITS
VOL1'**   CBS 84636
'That Old Black Magic'/'New York
State Of Mind'/'Begin The Beguine'/
'Stardust'/'Night And Day'/'I Will
Survive'/'Deep Purple'/'My Sweet
Lord'/'Kol Nidre'/'How Deep Is Your
Love'/'What I Did For Love'/'Maria'

**'JOHNNY MATHIS GREATEST HITS
VOL2'**   CBS 85637
'L-o-v-e'/'We've Only Just Begun'/
'Danke Schoen'/'Wonderland By
Night'/'Eli Eli'/'Where Or When'/
'Misty'/'It Makes No Difference'/
'Strangers In The Night'/'Remember
When'/'Laura'/'Ave Maria' (Bach-
Gounod)/'Ave Maria' (Schubert)

'GRANDS SUCCES'   CBS LSP 13672
'Ave Maria' (Schubert)/'Live For
Life'/'Tonight'/'Song Sung
Blue'/'Maria'/'Raindrops Keep Fallin'
On My Head'/'Love Story'/'A Man And
A Woman'/'Misty'/'Kol Nidre'/'Eli
Eli'/'Ave Maria' (Bach-Gounod)

'JOHNNY MATHIS'   CBS CM 13
3-LP Box Set that consists of LPs
'JOHNNY MATHIS "A PARIS"'
                         CBS 81160
'MATHIS IS'   CBS 86023
'CHANTE NOEL'   CBS 81481

Germany
'EIN ABEND MIT JOHNNY MATHIS'
                         CBS S 62829
'Tonight'/'The Twelfth Of Never'/'Wild
Is The Wind'/'Starbright'/'Wonderful,
Wonderful'/'Hey Love'/'Secret
Love'/'The Story Of Our Love'/
'Chances Are'/'When Sunny Gets
Blue'/'I Look At You'/'No Man Can
Stand Alone'/'All The Time'/'Maria'

'JOHNNY MATHIS IN PARIS'
                         CBS 81624
'In The Morning'/'The Windmills Of
Your Mind'/'A Man And A Woman'/
'Sing'/'I Will Wait For You'/'When Will
I See You Again'/'Raindrops Keep

Fallin' On My Head'/'Killing Me Softly
With Her Song'/'Love Story'/'Maria'/'If
We Only Have Love'

Holland
'SOMETHING FOR EVERYONE'
S 52883 (KH 31935)
1972 CBS Inc (Green Coloured Label)
'Up, Up And Away'/'Tonight'/'Turn
Around Look At Me'/'The 59th Street
Bridge Song'/'This Guy's In Love With
You'/'Those Were The Days'/'You
Better Go Now'/'Light My Fire'/'The
More I See You'/'Little Green Apples'

'WONDERFUL'   Fontana 662005 TR
'Will I Find My Love Today'/'Looking
At You'/'Let Me Love You'/'That Old
Black Magic'/'Too Close For
Comfort'/'Year After Year'/'Early
Autumn'/'Day In, Day Out'

'LET THERE BE LOVE'
Arcade/ADE H 61
'Too Much, Too Little, Too
Late'*/'Speak Softly Love'/'Don't Give
Up On Us'/'Gone, Gone Gone'/'Alone
Again (Naturally)'/'You Are The
Sunshine Of My Life'/'Just The Way
You Are'*/'And I Love You
So'/'Without You'/'It's Too
Late'/'Feelings'/'Love Story'/'You
Light Up My Life'/'Love Is
Blue'/'Everybody's Talkin' '/'When I
Need You'/'Solitaire'/'You Are
Beautiful'/'I'm Stone In Love With
You'/'Send In The Clowns'
*Duets with Deniece Williams

'THE BALLADS OF BROADWAY'
Fontana 682081
'Moanin' Low'/'Fun To Be Fooled'/'I
Have Dreamed'/'On The Sunny Side
Of The Street'/'My Romance'/
'Dancing On The Ceiling'/'I Married
An Angel'/'Isn't It A Pity'/'Spring Is
Here'/'Don't Blame Me'/'Taking A
Chance On Love'/'The Party's Over'

'THE RHYTHMS OF BROADWAY'
Fontana 682082

'Guys And Dolls'/'I Wish I Were In
Love Again'/'You Do Something To
Me'/'Let's Misbehave'/'I Could Have
Danced All Night'/All Is Well'/'A
Cock-Eyed Optimist'/'I Just Found Out
About Love'/'Let's Do It'/'I Am In
Love'/'Love Eyes'/'Love Is A Gamble'

'THE SILVER ANNIVERSARY AND
THE FIRST 25 YEARS'   CBS 88534
All songs same as US release apart
from omission of 'Ready Or Not'.
Dutch LP has 'Gone, Gone, Gone'.

Italy
'JOHNNY MATHIS WONDERFUL'
Fontana 782045
'Wild Is The Wind'/'Wonderful,
Wonderful'/'What'll I Do'/'No Love'/
'You Stepped Out Of A Dream'/'Let It
Rain'/'Warm And Tender'/'A Certain
Smile'/'Too Close For Comfort'/
'Chances Are'/'It's Not For Me To Say'/
'That Old Black Magic'/'Year After Year'

Japan
'JOHNNY MATHIS'   CSJ 166
(red vinyl)
'April Love'/'No Strings'/'I Can't Give
You Anything But Love'/'Call Me
Irresponsible'/'Tender Is The
Night'/'Beyond The Blue Horizon'/
'House Of Flowers'/'Beyond The
Sea'/'Somewhere'/'Laura'/'Camelot'/
'I'm Always Chasing Rainbows'/
'Sands Of Time'/'Alice In Wonderland'

'JOHNNY MATHIS GOLD DISC'
CBS SOPN 48
'A Certain Smile'/'Small World'/
'Misty'/'Chances Are'/'Venus'/
'Maria'/'What Will My Mary
Say'/'Love Story'/'My Funny
Valentine'/'Gina'/'Wonderful,
Wonderful'/'The Twelfth Of
Never'/'Wild Is The Wind'/'It's Not For
Me To Say'

'MY NAME IS JOHNNY' CBS YS 594C
(green vinyl)
'My Funny Valentine'/'Misty'/

'Tenderly'/'Rapture'/'In The Still Of The Night'/ 'Stairway To The Sea'/'It's Not For Me To Say'/'Wonderful, Wonderful'/ 'Embraceable You'/'A Certain Smile'/'Bye Bye Blackbird'/'Chances Are'

South Africa
'SPECTACULAR JOHNNY MATHIS'
'A Time For Us'/'Aquarius/Let The Sunshine In'/'The Impossible Dream'/'Those Were The Days'/'Love Story'/'My Sweet Lord'/'Something'/ 'Raindrops Keep Fallin' On My Head'/'Elusive Butterfly'/'The End Of The World'/'Never My Love'/'Love Is Blue'/'How Can You Mend A Broken Heart'/'We Can Work It Out'/'Wonderland By Night'/'L-o-v-e'/'Walk On By'/'Rose Garden'

Spain
'JOHNNY MATHIS'   CAU 498
'Aquarius/Let The Sunshine In'/'We've Only Just Begun'/'My Sweet Lord'/'Song Of Joy'/'They Long To Be Close To You'/'Love Me Tonight'/'Yesterday When I Was Young'/'Rose Garden'/'Something'/ 'Love Story'/'A Time For Us'

Czechoslovakia
'JOHNNY MATHIS'
 CBS/Supraphon 1113 3007 2D (1981)
'A Certain Smile'/'When Sunny Gets Blue'/'Small World'/'Misty'/'Chances Are'/'Maria'/'If We Only Have Love'/ 'Love Story'/'Come To Me'/'Love Theme From *Romeo And Juliet*'/ 'Wonderful, Wonderful'/'All The Time'/ 'Wild Is The Wind'/'It's Not For Me To Say'

Radio Transcription LPs

1957
'STARS FOR DEFENCE'   58
'All Through The Night'/'In The Wee Small Hours Of The Morning'/'You Stepped Out Of A Dream'
('Live' Recordings)

1959
'GUEST STAR'   636
'Someone'/'Very Much In Love'
('Live' Recordings)

1960
'THE FRANCES LANGFORD SHOW'
          KY 2175/6
'Rockin' Chair' (With Bob Cummings, Frances Langford, Hermione Gingold, Three Stooges & Mary Costa)/ 'Skyliner' (Duet with Frances Langford & Chorus)/'Puttin' On The Ritz'/'That's Amore' ('Live' Programme)

'STARS FOR DEFENCE'   202
'Hey Love'/'Nobody Knows'/'Guys And Dolls'
('Live' Programme)

1961
'STARS FOR DEFENCE'   251
'Live It Up'/'My Love For You'/'Jenny'
('Live' Programme)

'CHRISTMAS SEALS'   M8 MR 9858
'Ring The Bell'/'Stairway To The Stars'/'Chances Are'/'The Party's Over'

1962
'EASTER SEALS'   CPM 12/2358
'Wasn't The Summer Short'

1963
'STARS FOR DEFENCE'   340
'The Most Beautiful Girl In The World'/'What Will My Mary Say'/'Jump For Joy'
('Live' Programme)

'TALKING ABOUT BLINDNESS'
Spot Announcement

'USA CANCER SOCIETY'   129225
'Love Nest'

'USA CANCER SOCIETY'   129033
Spot Announcement

'CHRISTMAS SEALS'   MG 79604
'Ring The Bell'/'When Sunny Gets

Blue'/'Smile'/'Chances Are'/'I Look At You'

1964
'GUARD SESSION' XP 1429/30
Preview of the LP 'ROMANTICALLY'

1966
'USA HEART FUND' GRC 9315
Spot Announcement

1967
'USA HEART FUND' GRC 10024
Spot Announcement

1969
'VOICES OF VISTA' 37100
2 Spot Announcements

'VOICES OF VISTA' 191
'Windmills Of Your Mind'/'A Time For Us'/'Aquarius/Let The Sunshine In'/'Didn't We'

'GUEST STAR' 36
'Give Me Your Love For Christmas'/'Calypso Noel'/'Have Yourself A Merry Little Christmas' ('Live' Programme)

'CHRISTMAS SEALS' MG 202205
Spot Announcement

1970
'USA HEART FUND' GRC 11845
'Do You Remember'

'MARCH OF DIMES' ER 3052
'I'll Never Fall In Love Again'

'CHRISTMAS SEALS' MG 202585
'Chances Are'/'Aquarius/Let The Sunshine In'/'Windmills Of Your Mind'/'Wonderful, Wonderful'/'It's Not For Me To Say'

1971
'GUEST STAR' 1/71
'I'm Just A Boy In Love'/'In The Still Of The Night'/'Tenderly'/'I Concentrate On You'

'USA HEART FUND' GRC 12199
Spot Announcement

'CHRISTMAS SEALS' MG 203040
'We've Only Just Begun'/'I Was There'

1972
'GUEST STAR' 17/72
'If You Really Love Me'/'In The Morning'/'If We Only Have Love'/'Over The Weekend' ('Live' Programme)

'CHRISTMAS SEALS' 203305
'Winter Wonderland'

'CHRISTMAS SEALS' 203307
'I Was There'

1973
'LOUIS BRAILLE FOUNDATION FOR BLIND MUSICIANS'
2 Spot Announcements

'ARMY RESERVE' 71715
'Where Is The Love'/'Me And Mrs Jones'/'Summer Breeze'

'CHRISTMAS SEALS' CO 5985
Spot Announcement

'CHRISTMAS SEALS' CO 5983
'Calypso Noel'

1974
'USA HEART ASSOCIATION'
 GS 1378
Spot Announcement

'CHRISTMAS SEALS' AS 8086
'I'll Be Home For Christmas'

'CHRISTMAS SEALS' AS 8087
'Every Step Of The Way'

'DEPARTMENT OF THE TREASURY'
 74/94
Carol Of The Bells'

1975
'DEPARTMENT OF THE TREASURY'
75/107
'Woman, Woman'/'The Heart Of A
Woman'

'USA HEART ASSOCIATION'
TS 1002
'Heart To Heart' (Jingle)
'ARMY RESERVE'
2 Spot Announcements
'ARMY RESERVE'
'Do You Hear What I Hear'
'SKITCH HENDERSON MEETS
JOHNNY MATHIS FOR THE DAY'
193 1994
'Stone In Love With You'/'Touch Of
Your Lips'/'More'/'What'll I
Do'/'Sweet Surrender'/'Feel Like
Makin' Love'/'Life Is a Song Worth
Singing'/'Song Sung Blue'/'The End
Of A Love Affair'/'Woman Woman'.
Plus interview material.

1977
'CHRISTMAS SEALS'   CO 9346
Spot Announcement

1978
'CHRISTMAS SEALS'   CO 9795
Spot Announcement

1979
'USA HEART ASSOCIATION'
AHA 1979
Spot Announcement

'CHRISTMAS SEALS'   CX 174
'Winter Wonderland'

1980
'SOCIAL SECURITY PRESENTS
MELLOW MOMENTS HOSTED BY
JOHNNY MATHIS'

Record 1
'I Look At You'/'Just The Way You
Are'/'The Best Days Of My Life'/'That
Old Black Magic'/'That's What Friends
Are For'/'Deep Purple'/'If You
Believe'/'Chances Are'/'The Last Time

I Felt Like This'/'Begin The
Beguine'/'No One But The One You
Love'/'Me For You, You For Me'/'The
Lights Of Rio'

Record 2
'You're A Special Part Of My
Life'/'Come To Me'/'Different Kinda
Different'/'Gone, Gone, Gone'/'I Just
Can't Get Over You'/'Night And
Day'/'Temptation'/ 'When A Child Is
Born'/'How Can I Make It On My
Own'/'With You I'm Born Again'/'The
Twelfth Of Never'

Record 3
'Mandy'/'Hello Young Lovers'/'And
This Is My Beloved'/'Tomorrow/One'/
'It's Only A Paper Moon'/'And I Think
That's What I'll Do'/'Show And Tell'/
'I Only Have Eyes For You'/'Play Me'/
'Speak Softly Love'/'Nice To Be
Around'/'They Say It's Wonderful'/
'Maria'

Record 4
'Goodbye To Love'/'Wildflower'/
'Send In The Clowns'/'Since I Fell For
You'/'Secret Love'/'A Ride On A
Rainbow'/'Heaven Must Have Sent
You'/'We're In Love'/'I Wrote A
Symphony On My Guitar'/'Never
Givin' Up On You'/'I Will
Survive'/'Love Without Words'/'Love'

'DICK CLARK MUSIC MACHINE No
57'
'It's Not For Me To Say'/Interview

1980
'USA DEPT OF HEALTH & SOCIAL
SECURITY'

Record No 1
2 Spot Announcements

Record No 2
2 Spot Announcements

Record No 3
2 Spot Announcements

Record No 4
2 Spot Announcements

Record No 5
2 Spot Announcements
'USO'
2 Spot Announcements

'JOHNNY MATHIS AT THE ROYAL
ALBERT HALL'   CN 3652/S
'Life Is A Song Worth Singing'/'Stone
In Love With You'/'And I Love You
So'/'Begin The Beguine'/'Chances
Are'/'Three Times A Lady'/'Alone
Again (Naturally)'

'Betcha By Golly Wow'/'Twelfth Of
Never'/'Over The Rainbow'/'Ease On
Down The Road'/'Still'/'99 Miles From
LA'/'With You I'm Born Again'/'I Will
Survive'

1981
'THE 1972 MARCH OF DIMES'
                              ER 7140B
Spot Announcement

**Songs On Miscellaneous Albums And
Soundtracks**

'THE YOUNG AMERICANS
PRESENTED BY JOHNNY MATHIS'
          Mercury MG 21023/SR 61023
'What's New At The Zoo'/'Clap Yo'
Hands'/'Chim Chim Cheree'

'JOHNNY MATHIS AWAY FROM
HOME'   EMI CLP 1926
'If I Had You'/'Try A Little
Tenderness'/'If Love Were All'/'I'm In
Love For The Very First Time'

'THE BIGGEST BUNDLE OF THEM
ALL' (Movie Soundtrack)
                      MGM SE 4446 ST
'Most Of All There's You'

'THE FRANCES LANGFORD SHOW'
(TV Soundtrack)
                  Chanford Records
'Puttin' On The Ritz'

'COMMAND PERFORMANCE' (Ed
Sullivan TV Soundtrack)
                      Ronco MSD 2005
'Misty'

'EINE WELT VOLK MUSIK'
                     Philips 8286 611
'Love Story' (W/Nana Mouskouri)

'JOHNNY MATHIS CELEBRATION'
                        CBS 10028
'If It's Magic'

A–Z OF SONG TITLES

This A–Z of song titles gives a
complete guide to all LP tracks issued
on UK and US LPs. The LPs on which
the songs are found are in italics.

Recorded Song Titles

A
'A Baby's Born' *I'm Coming Home* US
KC 32435; UK 65690 CBS, 1973

'Ace In The Hole' *Live It UP!* US CL
1711, CS 8511; UK TFL 5177 Fontana;
BPG 62105; SBPG 62105 CBS, 1962

'A Certain Smile' *The Great Years* US
C2L34; C2S834, 1964: *More Johnny's
Greatest Hits* STFL 517, 1959; *All
Time Greatest Hits* UK SHM 749
Hallmark, 1972; *More Johnny's
Greatest Hits* TFL 5083 Fontana, 1959;
More Johnny's Greatest Hits US CL
1344, CS 8150; UK 62774 CBS,
1959; *The Mathis Collection* UK
100030 CBS, 1977

'A Clock Without Hands' *I'll Search
My Heart* US CL 2143, CS 8943; UK
BPG 62270, SBPG 62270 CBS, 1963

'A Cock-Eyed Optimist' *Johnny
Mathis Sings Of Love* UK SHM 749
Hallmark, 1972; *The Johnny Mathis
Collection Vol 2* UK PDA 032
Hallmark, 1977; *The Rhythms Of*

Broadway US CL 1507, 1960; *The Rhythms & Ballads Of Broadway* US C2L17, C2S803; UK Set 101 Fontana, 1960; *Rhythms Of Broadway* US CL 2224, CS 9024, 1964

'A Dream Is A Wish A Heart Makes' *Tender Is The Night* US MG 20890, SR 60890 Mercury; UK CLP 1721, CSD 1535 HMV, 1964

'Alfie' *Johnny Mathis Sings The Great Songs* UK 88085 CBS, 1974; *Raindrops Keep Fallin' On My Head* US CS 1005; UK 64012 CBS, 1970; *Johnny Mathis Sings The Music Of Bacharach & Kaempfurt* US G30350; UK 66275 CBS, 1971

'A Handful Of Stars' *Warm* UK EMB 31045 Embassy, 1974; *Warm* UK 31499 Embassy, 1977; *Warm* US CL 1078, CS 8039; UK TFL 5015, STFL 510 Fontana, 1958; *Warm* UK RM 52064 CBS Realm, 1965; *Warm, Open Fire, 2 Guitars* US GP2, 1968

'Alice In Wonderland' *The Wonderful World Of Make Believe* US MG 20193, SR 60913; UK CLP 1755, CSD 1553 HMV, 1964

'All I Ever Need' *You Light Up My Life* US JC 35259; UK 86055 CBS, 1978

'All Is Well' *Portrait Of Johnny* US CL 1644, CS 8444; UK TFL 5153, STFL 571 Fontana, BPG 62077, SBPG 62077, 1961; *Portrait Of Johnny* UK SHM 806 Hallmark, 1974; *The Johnny Mathis Collection* UK PDA 015 Hallmark, 1976

'All That Is Missing' *Romantically* US CL 2098, CS 8898; UK BPG 62202, 5BPG 62202 CBS, 1963

'All The Sad Young Men' *I'll Search My Heart* US CL 2143, CS 8943; UK BPG 62270, 5BPG 62270 CBS, 1963

'All The Things You Are' *The First 25 Years, The Silver AA* US C2X 37440, 1981; *Hold Me, Thrill Me, Kiss Me* US PC 34872, 1977

'All The Time' *All Time Greatest Hits*

UK SHM 749 Hallmark, 1972; *Johnny's Greatest Hits* US PC 34667, 1977; *Johnny's Greatest Hits* UK 62569 CBS, 1965; *Johnny's Greatest Hits* US CL 1133, CS 8634, 1958

'All Through The Night' *Wonderful, Wonderful* US CL 1028, CS 9046; UK TFL 5003, 1957; US CL 1028, CS 9046; UK TFL 5003, 1957

'Alone Again (Naturally)' *Make It Easy On Yourself (UK)/Song Sung Blue (US)* US KG 31626; UK 65161 CBS, 1972; *Johnny Mathis Sings The Great Songs* UK 88085 CBS, 1974; *Tears And Laughter* UK 10019 CBS, 1980

'A Lovely Way To Spend An Evening' *Ride On A Rainbow (UK)/Heavenly (US)* US CL 1351, CS 8152; UK TFL 5061, STFL 516 Fontana, BPG 62064, SBPG 62064 CBS, 1959: *Heavenly* UK EMB 31084 Embassy, 1975; *Heavenly And Faithfully* US CG 33621, 1975; *Evergreens* UK 2188/8000 St Michael, 1980; *Johnny Mathis* US KH 30017 Harmony; UK CHM 684 Hallmark, 1970

'A Man And A Woman' *Raindrops Keep Fallin' On My Head* US CS 1005; UK 64012 CBS, 1970; *Johnny Mathis Greatest Hits Vol 3* UK 64651 CBS, 1971; *The Mathis Collection* UK 100030 CBS, 1977

'A Marshmallow World' *Sounds Of Christmas* US MG 20837 Mercury; UK CLP 1696, CSD 1521 HMV, 1963; *Christmas With Johnny Mathis* US KH 30864 Harmony; UK SHM 765 Hallmark, 1971

'An Affair To Remember' *Love Is Everything* US MG 20991, SR 20991 Mercury; UK CLP 3522, CSD 3522 HMV, 1965

'And Her Mother Came Too' *Johnny Mathis In Person* US KG 30979; UK 67231 CBS, 1972

'And I Love Her So' *Killing Me Softly (With Her Song)* US KC 32258; UK

65672 CBS, 1973; *The Mathis Collection* UK 100030 CBS, 1977; *Tears And Laughter* UK 10019 CBS, 1980

'And I Think That's What I'll Do' *I'm Coming Home* US KC 32435; UK 65690 CBS, 1973

'And This Is My Beloved' *Faithfully* US CL 1422, CS 8219; UK TFL 5084, STFL 522 Fontana, BP8 62061 SBP8 62067 CBS, 1960; *Heavenly And Faithfully* US CG 33621, 1975

'Angel Eyes' *Johnny Mathis* US CL 887, 1956; *Johnny Mathis* US EN 13089 Encore, 1976

'And Open Fire' *Open Fire, Two Guitars* US CL 1270, CS 8056; UK TFL 5050, STFL 515 Fontana, BPG 62063, SBPG 62063 CBS, 1959; *Warm, Open Fire, 2 Guitars* US GP2, 1968

'April In Paris' *Johnny's Mood* 1960; *Johnny Mathis In Person* US KG 30979; UK 67231 CBS, 1972

'April Love' *Tender Is The Night* US MG 20890, SR 60890 Mercury; UK CLP 1721, CSD 1535 HMV, 1964

'Aquarius/Let The Sunshine In' *Love Theme From 'Romeo & Juliet'* US CS 9909, 1969; *Johnny Mathis Sings The Great Songs* UK 88085 CBS, 1974; *Night And Day* UK 31863 CBS, 1980

'Arianne' *Killing Me Softly (With Her Song)* US KC 32258; UK 65672 CBS, 1973

'A Ride On A Rainbow' *Ride On A Rainbow (UK)/Heavenly (US)* US CL 1351, CS 8152; UK TFL 5061, STFL 516 Fontana, BPG 62064, SBPG 62064 CBS, 1959; *Heavenly* UK EMB 31084 Embassy, 1975; *Heavenly And Faithfully* US CG 33621, 1975

'Arrivederci Roma' *Away From Home (UK)/The Sweetheart Tree (US)* US MG 21041, SR 61041; Mercury UK CLP 1926, CSD 1638 HMV, 1965

'A Ship Without A Sail' *Tender Is The Night* US MG 20890, SR 60890 Mercury; UK CLP 1721, CSD 1535 HMV, 1964

'As Long As We're Together' *Mathis Is* US 34441; UK 86023 CBS, 1977

'As Time Goes By' *The Best Days Of My Life* US JC 35649; UK 86080 CBS, 1979; *The First 25 Years* US C2X 37440, 1981

'A Taste Of Honey' *The Shadow Of Your Smile* US MG 21073, SR 61073 Mercury; UK CLP 3556, CSD 3556 HMV, 1966

'A Thousand Blue Bubbles' *Love Is Everything* US MG 20991, SR 20991 Mercury; UK CLP 3522; CSD 3522 HMV, 1965

'A Time For Us' *The First 25 Years, The Silver AA* US C2X 37440, 1981

'At The Crossroads' *Up, Up And Away* US CL 2726, C 59526; UK 63104, 1968

'Aubrey' *Killing Me Softly (With Her Song)* US KC 32258; UK 65672 CBS, 1973

'Autumn In New York' *Romantically* US CL 2098, CS 8898; UK BPG 62202, SBPG 62202 CBS, 1963

'Autumn In Rome' *Johnny Mathis 1956* US CL 887, 1956; *Johnny Mathis* US EN 13089 Encore, 1976

'Autumn Leaves' *The Sweetheart Tree (US)/Away From Home (UK)* US MG 21041, SR 61041 Mercury; UK CLP 1926, CSD 1638 HMV, 1965; *People* US CS 9871, 1969

'Ave Maria' (Bach-Gounod) *Goodnight Dear Lord (US)/Heavenly (UK)* US CL 1119, CS 8012; UK TFL 5023 Fontana, 1958

'Ave Maria' (Schubert) *Goodnight Dear Lord (US)/Heavenly (UK)* US CL 1119, CS 8012; UK TFL 5023 Fontana, 1958

'A Wonderful Day Like Today' *People* US CS 9871, 1969

B

'Babalu' *Johnny Mathis* US CL 887, 1956; *Olé* US MG 20988, SR 60988 Mercury; UK CLP 1818, CSD 1578 HMV, 1964; *Johnny Mathis* US EN 13089 Encore, 1976

'Baby, Baby, Baby' *Warm* US CL 1078, CS 8039; UK TFL 5015, STFL 510 Fontana, 1958; *Warm* UK RM 52064 CBS Realm, 1965; *Warm, Open Fire, 2 Guitars* US GP2, 1968; *Warm* UK EMB 31045 Embassy, 1974; *Warm* UK 31499 Embassy, 1977; *Misty* UK SHM 913 Hallmark, 1977

'Bachianas Brasileiras Part 1, 2, 3' *Olé* US MG 20988, SR 60988 Mercury; UK CLP 1818, CSD 1578 HMV, 1964

'Baubles, Bangles And Beads' *So Nice* US MG 21091, SR 61091, 1966

'Begin The Beguine' *The Best Days Of My Life* US JC 35649; UK 86080 CBS, 1979; *The First 25 Years, The Silver AA* US C2X 37440, 1981

'Betcha By Golly Wow' *The First Time Ever I Saw Your Face* US KC 31342; UK 6490 CBS, 1972; *The Mathis Collection* UK 100030 CBS, 1977; *Johnny Mathis* UK 2094/0102 St Michael, 1978; *Tears And Laughter* UK 10019 CBS, 1980

'Beyond The Blue Horizon' *The Wonderful World Of Make Believe* US MG 20193, SR 60913 Mercury; UK CLP 1755, CSD 1553 HMV, 1964

'Beyond The Sea' *The Wonderful World Of Make Believe* US MG 20192, SR 60913 Mercury; UK CLP 1755, CSD 1553 HMV, 1964

'Blue Christmas' *Merry Christmas* US CL 1195, CS 8021; UK TFL 5031 Fontana, 62806 CBS, 1958; *Merry Christmas* UK 62806 CBS, 1966; *Christmas Album* UK 2094/0102 St Michael, 1978; *Johnny Mathis Sings Christmas Songs* UK 2188/2020 St Michael, 1980

'Blue Gardenia' *Faithfully* US CL 1422, CS 8219; UK TFL 5084, STFL 522 Fontana, BP 862061, SBP 862067 CBS, 1960; *Heavenly And Faithfully* US CG 33621, 1975

'Break Up To Make Up' *Killing Me Softly (With Her Song)* US KC 32258; UK 65672 CBS, 1973

'Brian's Song' *The First Time Ever I Saw Your Face* US KC 31342; UK 64930 CBS, 1972

'Bridge Over Troubled Water' *Raindrops Keep Fallin' On My Head* US CS 1005; UK 64012 CBS, 1970; *Johnny Mathis Sings The Great Songs* UK 88085 CBS, 1974

'Bye Bye Blackbird' *Open Fire, Two Guitars* US CL 1270, CS 8056, TFL 5050, STFL 515 Fontana, BPG 61063, SBPG 62063 CBS, 1959; *Warm/Open Fire Two Guitars* US GP2, 1968; *Tenderly* 1971; *The Johnny Mathis Collection Vol 2* UK PDA 032 Hallmark, 1977; *Evergreens* UK 2188/2020 St Michael, 1980

'By Myself' *Warm* US CL 1078, CS 8039; UK TFL 5015, STFL 510 Fontana, 1958; *Warm* UK RM 52064 CBS Realm, 1965; *Warm/Open Fire, Two Guitars* US GP 2, 1968; *Warm* UK EMB 31045 Embassy, 1974; *Misty* UK SHM 913 Hallmark, 1977; *Warm* UK 31499 Embassy, 1977

'By The Time I Get To Phoenix' *Love Is Blue* US CS 9637; UK 63301, 1968; *Johnny Mathis Sings The Great Songs* UK 88085 CBS, 1974

C

'Cabin In The Sky' *Johnny Mathis* US CL 887, 1956; *Johnny Mathis* US EN 13089 Encore, 1976

'Call Me' *More Johnny's Greatest Hits* UK TFL 5083 Fontana, 1959; *More Johnny's Greatest Hits* UK STFL 517, 1959; *More Johnny's Greatest Hits* US CL 1344, CS 8150; UK 62772 CBS, 1959

'Call Me Irresponsible' *Tender Is The Night* US MG 20890, SR 60890 Mercury; UK CLP 1721, CSD 1535 HMV, 1964

'Calypso Noel' *Give Me Your Love For Christmas* US C 59923, 1969

'Camelot' *The Wonderful World Of Make Believe* US MG. 20193, SR 60913 Mercury; UK CLP 1755, CSD 1553 HMV, 1964

'Can't Get Out Of This Mood' *Swing Softly* US CL 1165, CS 8023; UK TFL 5039, STFL 500 Fontana, BPG 62062, SBPG 62062 CBS, 1958; *The Great Years* US C2L34, C2S834, 1964; *Johnny Mathis* US KH 30017 Harmony; UK CHM 684 Hallmark, 1970

'Caravan' *Johnny Mathis* US CL 887, 1956; *Johnny Mathis* US EN 13089 Encore, 1976

'Carol Of The Bells' *Christmas With Johnny Mathis* US KH 30864 Harmony; UK SHM 765 Hallmark, 1971; *White Christmas* UK 69217, 1975; *Christmas Album* UK 2094/0501 St Michael, 1978; *When A Child Is Born* UK 83266 CBS, 1978; *Johnny Mathis Sings Christmas Songs* UK 2188/2020 St Michael, 1980

'Chances Are' *Johnny's Greatest Hits* US CL 1133, CS 8634, 1958; *Johnny's Greatest Hits* UK TFL 5058 Fontana, 1958; *The Great Years* US C2L34, C2S834, 1964; *Johnny's Greatest Hits* UK 62569 CBS, 1965; *All Time Greatest Hits* UK 67253 CBS, 1972; *Johnny Mathis In Person* US KG 30979; UK 67231 CBS, 1972; *Johnny's Greatest Hits* US PC 34667, 1977; *The First 25 Years, The Silver AA* US C2X 37440, 1981; *Celebration* UK 10028 CBS, 1981

'Cherie' *Portrait Of Johnny* US CL 1644, CS 8444, 1961; *Portrait Of Johnny* UK TFL 5153, STFL 571 Fontana, BPG 62077, SBPG 62077 CBS, 1961; *Portrait Of Johnny* UK

SHM 806 Hallmark, 1974; *The Johnny Mathis Collection* UK PDA 015 Hallmark, 1976

'Chim Chim Cheree' *The Young Americans Presented By Johnny Mathis* US MG 21023 Mercury, 1965

'Christmas Eve' *Give Me Your Love For Christmas* US C59923, 1969

'Christmas Is A Feeling In Your Heart' *Christmas With Johnny Mathis* US KH 30864 Harmony; UK SHM 765 Hallmark, 1971; *Sounds Of Christmas* US MG 20837, SR 60837 Mercury; UK CLP 1696, CSD 1521 HMV, 1963

'Clap Yo' Hands' *The Young Americans Presented By Johnny Mathis* US MG 21023, SR 61023 Mercury, 1965

'Clopin Clopant' *The Sweetheart Tree (US)/Away From Home (UK)* US MG 21041, SR 61041 Mercury; UK CLP 1926, CSD 1638 HMV, 1965

'Come Back To Me' *The Shadow Of Your Smile* US MG 21073, SR 61073 Mercury; UK CLP 3556, CSD 3556 HMV, 1965

'Come Ride The Wind With Me' *Love Is Everything* US MG 20991, SR 20991 Mercury; UK CLP 3522, CSD 3522 HMV, 1965

'Come Runnin'' *Johnny Mathis In Person* US KG 30979; UK 67231 CBS, 1972

'Come Saturday Morning' *Close To You (US)/The Long And Winding Road (UK)* US C30210; UK 64176 CBS, 1970; *Night And Day* UK 31863 CBS, 1980

'Come To Me' *Johnny's Greatest Hits* UK 62569 CBS, 1965; *Johnny Mathis* UK TFL 5011 Fontana, 1957; *Johnny's Greatest Hits* UK TFL 5058 Fontana, 1958; *Johnny's Greatest Hits* US CL 1133, CS 8634, 1958; *All Time Greatest Hits* UK 67253 CBS, 1972; *Johnny's Greatest Hits* US PC 34667, 1977

'Corner Of The Sky' *Me And Mrs Jones* UK 65443 CBS, 1973

'Corner To Corner' *Johnny's Mood* 1960

'Crazy In The Heart' *Live It UP!* US CL1711, CS 8511; UK TFL 5177 Fontana, BPG 62105, SBPG 62105 CBS, 1962

D

'Dancing In The Dark' *Love Is Everything* US MG 20991, SR 20991 Mercury; UK CLP 3522, CSD 3522 HMV, 1965

'Dancing On The Ceiling' *The Ballads Of Broadway* US CL 1506, 1960; *The Rhythm And Ballads Of Broadway* UK SET 101 Fontana, 1960; *Ballads Of Broadway* US CL 2223, CS 9023, 1964

'Daniel Boone' *The Young Americans Presented By Johnny Mathis* US MG 21023, SR 61023 Mercury, 1965

'Danke Schon' *Johnny Mathis Sings The Music Of Bert Kaempfert* UK 63524 CBS, 1969; *Johnny Mathis Sings The Music Of Bacharach & Kaempfert* US G 30350; UK 66275 CBS, 1971; *Johnny Mathis Sings The Music Of Bert Kaempfert* UK EMB 31209 Embassy, 1975; *Misty* UK SHM 913 Hallmark, 1977; *Evergreens* UK 2188/8000 St Michael, 1980

'Danny Boy' *The Sweetheart Tree (US)/Away From Home (UK)* US MG 21041, SR 61041 Mercury; UK CLP 1926, CSD 1638 HMV, 1965

'Day In Day Out' *Wonderful, Wonderful* US CL 1028, CS, 9046; UK TFL 5003 Fontana, 1957; *Johnny Mathis In Person* US KG 30979; UK 67231 CBS, 1972

'Deep Purple' *Different, Kinda Different* US JC 36505, 1980; *All For You* UK 86115 CBS, 1980

'Deep River' *Goodnight Dear Lord (US/Heavenly (UK)* US CL 1119, CS 8012; UK TFL 5023, 1958; *The Great Years* US CLL 34, C2S834, 1964

'Didn't We' *Love Theme From 'Romeo & Juliet'* US CS 9909, 1969; *The Mathis Collection* UK 100030 CBS, 1977; *The First 25 Years, The Silver AA* US C2X 37440, 1981

'Different Kinda Different' *All For You* UK 86115 CBS, 1980

'Do Me Wrong But Do Me' *I Only Have Eyes For You* US PC 34117; UK 81329 CBS, 1976

'Don't Blame Me' *The Rhythm & Ballads Of Broadway* UK SET 101, 1960; *Ballads Of Broadway* US CL 2223, CS 9023, 1964; *Johnny Mathis* US KH 30017 Harmony; UK CHM 684 Hallmark, 1970

'Don't Give Up On Us' *Hold Me, Thrill Me, Kiss Me* US PC 34872, 1977; *Sweet Surrender* UK 86036 CBS, 1977

'Don't Go Breaking My Heart' *Love Is Blue* US CS 9637; UK 63301, 1968; 'Don't Go Breaking My Heart' *Johnny Mathis Sings The Music Of Bacharach & Kaempfert* US G 30350; UK 66275 CBS, 1971; *Johnny Mathis* UK 2094/0102 St Michael, 1978

'Don't Let Me Be Lonely Tonight' *Me & Mrs Jones* UK 65443, 1973

'Don't Stay' *Johnny Mathis Sings The Music Of Bert Kaempfert* UK 63524 CBS, 1969; *'Johnny Mathis Sings The Music Of Bacharach & Kaempfert* US G30350; UK 66275 CBS, 1971; *Johnny Mathis Sings The Music Of Bert Kaempfert* UK EMB 31209 Embassy, 1975

'Do You Hear What I Hear' *Give Me Your Love For Christmas* US CS 9923, 1969

'Do You Know Where You're Going To' *I Only Have Eyes For You* US PC 34117; UK 81329 CBS, 1976 *99 Miles From LA* UK 2188/2010 St Michael, 1980

'Dream, Dream, Dream' *The Wonderful World Of Make Believe* US MG 20193, SR 60913 Mercury; UK CLP 1755, CSD 1553 HMV, 1964

'Dreamy'/'Misty' (Medley) *Johnny Mathis In Person* US KG 30979; UK 67231 CBS, 1972

'Drifting' *Up, Up And Away* US CL 2726, CS 9526; UK 63104, 1968

'Dulcinea' *So Nice* US MG 21091, SR 61091, 1966; *Johnny Mathis In Person* US KG 30979; UK 67231 CBS, 1972

E

'Each Time We Kiss' *I'll Search My Heart* US CL 2143, CS 8943; UK BPG 62270, SBPG 62270 CBS, 1963

'Early Autumn' *Wonderful, Wonderful* US CL 1028, CS 9046; UK TFL 5003, 1957

'Easy Does It' *Johnny* US CL 2044, CS 8844; UK BPG 62172, SBPG 62172 CBS, 1963

'Easy To Love' *Johnny Mathis* US CL 887, 1956; *Johnny Mathis* TFL 5011 Fontana, 1957; *Johnny Mathis* US EN 13089 Encore, 1976; *Swing Softly* US CL 1165, CS 8023; UK TFL 5039, STFL 500 Fontana, BPG 62061, SBPG 62062 CBS, 1958

'Eleanor Rigby' *Johnny Mathis Sings* US MG 21107, SR 61107, 1967; *The Impossible Dream* US CS 9872; UK 63718 CBS, 1969; *Johnny Mathis Sings The Great Songs* UK 88085 CBS, 1974

'Eli Eli' *Goodnight Dear Lord (US)/Heavenly (UK)* US CL 1119, CS 8012; UK TFL 5023 Fontana, 1958

'Elusive Butterfly' *So Nice* US MG 21091, SR 61107, 1968; *People* US CS 9871, 1969

'Embraceable You' *Open Fire, Two Guitars* US CL 1270, CS 8056; UK TFL 5050, STFL 515 Fontana, BPG 62063, SBPG 62063 CBS, 1959; *Warm/Open Fire, Two Guitars* US GP2, 1968; *Tenderly* 1971; *The Johnny Mathis Collection Vol 2* UK PDA 032 Hallmark, 1977

'Emotion' (with Deniece Williams) *You Light Up My Life* US JC 35259; UK 86055 CBS, 1978

'Evergreen' *Hold Me, Thrill Me, Kiss Me* US PC 34872, 1977; *Sweet Surrender* UK 86036 CBS, 1977; *99 Miles From LA* UK 2188/2010 St Michael, 1980; *Celebration* UK 10028 CBS, 1981

'Everybody's Talkin'' *Raindrops Keep Fallin' On My Head* US CS 1005; UK 64012 CBS, 1970; *The Mathis Collection* UK 10003 CBS, 1977

'Every Step Of The Way' *I'll Search My Heart* US CL 2143, CS 8943; UK BPG 62270, SBPG 62270 CBS, 1963; *The Great Years* US C2L34, C2S834, 1964

'Everything Is Beautiful' *Close To You (US)/The Long And Winding Road (UK)* US C30210; UK 64176 CBS, 1970; *Johnny Mathis Sings The Great Songs* UK 88085 CBS, 1974; *Tears And Laughter* UK 10019 CBS, 1980

'Everything's Coming Up Roses' *The Rhythms Of Broadway* US CL 1507, 1960; *Rhythms Of Broadway* US CL 2224, CS 9024, 1964; *Johnny Mathis Sings Of Love* UK SHM 749 Hallmark, 1972; *The Johnny Mathis Collection Vol 2* UK PDA 032 Hallmark, 1977

'Every Time I Dream Of You' *Those Were The Days* US CS 9705; UK 63427 CBS, 1968

'Every Time You Touch Me (I Get High)' *I Only Have Eyes For You* US PC 34117; UK 81329 CBS, 1976

'Evil Ways' *Close To You (US)/The Long And Winding Road (UK)* US C 30210; UK 64176, 1970; *Johnny Mathis Greatest Hits Vol 3* UK 64651 CBS, 1971

F

'Faithfully' *Faithfully* US CL 1422, CS 8219; UK TFL 5084, STFL 522 Fontana, BPG 62061, SBPG 62067 CBS, 1960; *Johnny Mathis Sings The Music Of Bacharach & Kaempfert* US G 30350; UK 66275 CBS, 1971; *Heavenly And Faithfully* US CG 33621, 1975

'Fantastic' *This Is Love* US MG 20942, SR 60942; UK CLP 1859, CSD 1600 HMV, 1964 'Feelings' *Greatest Hits Vol 4* UK 86022 CBS, 1977; *The Mathis Collection* UK 100030 CBS, 1977; *99 Miles From LA* UK 2188/2101 St Michael, 1980; *Feelings* US PC 33887; UK 69180 CBS, 1975

'Feel Like Makin' Love' *The Heart Of A Woman* US KC 33251; UK 80533 CBS, 1974

'Fly Me To The Moon (In Other Words)' *The Great Years* US C2L34, C2S834, 1964

'Follow Me' *Faithfully* US CL 1422, CS 8219; UK TFL 5084, STFL 522 Fontana, BPG 62061, SBP 662067 CBS, 1960; *Heavenly And Faithfully* US CG 33621, 1975

'Foolish' *I'm Coming Home* US KC 32435; UK 65690 CBS, 1973

'For All We Know' *You've Got A Friend (Today's G. Hits)* US C 30740; UK 64448 CBS, 1971

'Forget Me Not' *Tender Is The Night* US MG 20890, SR 60890 Mercury; UK CLP 1721, CSD 1535 HMV, 1964

'For The Good Times' *Love Story* US C 30499; UK 64334 CBS, 1971

'Friendly Persuasion' *Romantically* US CL 2098, CS 8898; UK BPG 62202, SBPG 62202 CBS, 1963

'Friends In Love' *Friends In Love* FC 37748; CBS 85652, 1982

'Fun To Be Fooled' *The Ballads Of Broadway* US CL 1506, 1960; 'Fun To Be Fooled' *The Rhythm & Ballads Of Broadway* US C2L17, C2S803; UK SET 101 Fontana, 1960; *Ballads Of Broadway* US CL 2223, CS 9023, 1964

G

'Generique'/Felicidade (Medley) *Olé* US MG 20988, SR 60988 Mercury; UK CLP 1818, CSD 1578 HMV, 1964

'Get Me To The Church On Time' *Swing Softly* US CL 1165, CS 8023; UK TFL 5039, STFL 500 Fontana, BPG 62062, SBPG 62062 CBS, 1958

'Getting To Know You' *Romantically* US CL 2098, CS 8898; UK BPG 62202, SBPG 62202 CBS, 1963

'Gina' *Johnny's Newest Hits* US CL 2016, CS 8816; UK BPG 62147, SBPG 62147 CBS, 1963; *The Great Years* US C2L34, C 2584, 1964; *All Time Greatest Hits* UK 67253 CBS, 1972

'Give Me Your Love For Christmas' *Give Me Your Love For Christmas* US CS 9923, 1969

'Go Away Little Girl' *Love Is Everything* US MG 20991, SR 20991 Mercury; UK CLP 3522, CSD 3522 HMV, 1965; *The Impossible Dream* US CS 9872; UK 63718 CBS, 1969; *Johnny Mathis Sings The Great Songs* UK 88085 CBS, 1974

'God Rest Ye Merry Gentlemen' *Sounds Of Christmas* US MG 20837, SR 60837 Mercury; UK CLP 1696, CSD 1521 HMV, 1963; *Christmas With Johnny Mathis* US KH 30864 Harmony; UK 5HM 765 Hallmark, 1971; *Merry Christmas* UK 69217 CBS, 1975; *When A Child Is Born* UK 83266 CBS, 1978

'Gone, Gone, Gone' *The Best Days Of My Life* US JC 35649; UK 86080 CBS, 1979; *Tears And Laughter* UK 10019 CBS, 1980; *The Best Of Johnny Mathis 1975–1980* US JC 36871, 1980

'Goodbye To Love' *Song Sung Blue (US)/Make It Easy On Yourself (UK)* US KG 31626; UK 65161 CBS, 1972;

Love Songs UK EMB 31393 Embassy, 1976; *Tears And Laughter* UK 10019 CBS, 1980

'Good Morning Heartache' *Killing Me Softly With Her Song* US KC 32258; UK 65672, 1973; *Night And Day* UK 31863 CBS, 1980

'Goodnight Dear Lord' *Goodnight Dear Lord (US)/Heavenly (UK)* US CL 119, CS 8012; UK TFL 5023 Fontana, 1958

'Goodnight My Love' *Johnny's Mood* CL 1526, CS 8326, 1960

'Got You Where I Want You' *Friends In Love* FC 37748; CBS 85652, 1982

'Granada' *Olé* US MG 20988, SR 60988 Mercury; UK CLP 1818, CSD 1578 HMV, 1964

'Guys And Dolls' *The Rhythms & Ballads Of Broadway* US C2L17, C 2803; UK SET 101 Fontana, 1960; *The Rhythms Of Broadway* US CL 1507, 1960; *Rhythms Of Broadway* US CL 2224, CS 9024, 1964; *Johnny Mathis Sings Of Love* UK SHM 749 Hallmark, 1972; *The Johnny Mathis Collection Vol 2* UK PDA 032 Hallmark, 1977

H

'Hallelujah Chorus' *Sounds Of Christmas* US MG 20837, SR 60837 Mercury; UK CLP 1696, CSD 1521 HMV, 1963; *Christmas With Johnny Mathis* US KH 30864 Harmony; UK SHM 765 Hallmark, 1971

'Happy' *Me And Mrs Jones* UK 65443 CBS, 1973

'Hard Travellin'' *The Young Americans Presented By Johnny Mathis* US MG 21023, SR 61023 Mercury, 1965

'Have Reindeer Will Travel' *Sounds Of Christmas* US MG 20837, SR 60837 Mercury; UK CLP 1696, CSD 1521 HMV, 1963

'Have Yourself A Merry Little

Christmas' *Sounds Of Christmas* US MG 20837, SR 60837 Mercury; UK CLP 1696, CSD 1521 HMV, 1963; *Give Me Your Love For Christmas* US CS 9923, 1969; *Christmas With Johnny Mathis* US KH 30864 Harmony; UK SHM 765 Hallmark, 1971; *Merry Christmas* UK 69217 CBS, 1975; *Christmas Album* UK 2094/0501 St Michael, 1978; *When A Child Is Born* UK 83266 CBS, 1978; *Johnny Mathis Sings Christmas Songs* UK 2188/2020 St Michael, 1980

'He Ain't Heavy, He's My Brother' *Song Sung Blue (US)/Make It Easy On Yourself (UK)* US KG 31626; UK 65161 CBS, 1972; *Johnny Mathis* UK 2094/0102 St Michael, 1978

'Heart, Soul, Body & Mind' *Mathis Magic* US 36216; UK 86103 CBS, 1979

'Heavenly' *Heavenly (US)/Ride On A Rainbow (UK)* US CL 1351, CS 8152; US TFL 5061, STFL 516 Fontana, BPG 62064, SBPG 62064 CBS, 1959; *Johnny Mathis Sings The Music Of Bacharach & Kaempfert* US G 30350; UK 66275 CBS, 1971; *Heavenly* UK EMB 31084, Embassy, 1975; *Heavenly And Faithfully* US CS 33621, 1975

'Heaven Must Have Made You Just For Me' *Mathis Is* US 34441; UK 86023 CBS, 1977

'Heaven Must Have Sent You' *That's What Friends Are For* US JC 35435; UK 86068 CBS, 1978

'Hello, Young Lovers' *Heavenly (US)/Ride On A Rainbow (UK)* US CL 1351, CS 8152; UK TFL 5061, STFL 516 Fontana, BPG 62064, SBPG 62064 CBS, 1959; *Heavenly* UK EMB 31084 Embassy, 1975; *Heavenly & Faithfully* US CG 33621, 1975

'Help Me Make It Through The Night' *The Mathis Collection* UK 10030 CBS, 1977; *Night And Day* UK 31863 CBS, 1980; *You've Got A Friend* US C 30740; UK 64448 CBS, 1971

'Here I'll Stay' *Rapture* US CL 1915, CS 8715; UK BPG 62106, SBPG 62106 CBS, 1962

'Here, There & Everywhere' *Love Is Blue* US CS 9637; UK 63301 CBS, 1968

'Hey, Look Me Over' *Live It UP!* US CL 1711, CS 8511; UK TFL 5177 Fontana, BPG 62105, SBPG 62105 CBS, 1962

'Hey Love' *Portrait Of Johnny* UK TFL 5153, STFL 571 Fontana, BPG 62077, SBPG 62077 CBS, 1961; *Portrait Of Johnny* US CL 1644, CS 8444; *Portrait Of Johnny* UK SHM 806 Hallmark, 1974; *The Johnny Mathis Collection* UK PDA 015 Hallmark, 1976

'Hi Lili, Hi-Lo' *Romantically* US CL 2098, CS 8898; UK BPG 62202, SBPG 62202 CBS, 1963

'Hold Me, Thrill Me, Kiss Me' *Hold Me, Thrill Me, Kiss Me* US PC 34872, 1977; *Sweet Surrender* UK 86036 CBS, 1977

'Honey Come Back' *Raindrops Keep Fallin' On My Head* US CS 1005; UK 64012 CBS, 1970; *Johnny Mathis Greatest Hits Vol 3* UK 64651 CBS, 1971; *Johnny Mathis* UK 2094/0102 St Michael, 1978

'House For Sale' *The Heart Of A Woman* US KC 33251; UK 80533 CBS, 1974

'House Of Flowers' *The Wonderful World Of Make Believe* US MG 20193, SR 60913 Mercury; UK CLP 1755, CSD 1553 HMV, 1964

'How Can I Be Sure' *Song Sung Blue (US)/Make It Easy On Yourself (UK)* US KG 31626; UK 65161 CBS, 1972

'How Can I Make It On My Own' *The Best Days Of My Life* US 35649; UK 86080 CBS, 1979

'How Can You Mend A Broken Heart' *You've Got A Friend* US C 30740; UK 64448 CBS, 1971

'How Deep Is Your Love' *You Light Up My Life* US JC 35259; UK 86055 CBS, 1978; *99 Miles From LA* UK 2188/2010 St Michael, 1980; *Celebration* UK 10028 CBS, 1981

'How High The Moon' *Johnny's Mood* CL 1526, CS 8326, 1960

'How To Handle A Woman' *The Great Years* US C2L34, C2S834, 1964; *Portrait Of Johnny* US CL 1644, CS 84444, 1961; *Portrait Of Johnny* UK SHM 806 Hallmark, 1974; *The Johnny Mathis Collection* UK PDA 015 Hallmark, 1976

'Hung Up In The Middle Of Love' *Mathis Is* US 34441; UK 86023 CBS, 1977

'Hurry! It's Lovely Up Here' *So Nice* US MG 21091, SR 61091; UK Rec Number?, 1966

'Hurry Mother Nature' *Feelings* US PC 33887; UK 69180 CBS, 1975

I

'I Always Knew I Had It In Me' *Hold Me, Thrill Me, Kiss Me* US PC 34872, 1977; *Sweet Surrender* UK 86036 CBS, 1977

'I Am In Love' *The Rhythms & Ballads Of Broadway* US C2L17, C 2803; UK SET 101 Fontana, 1960; *The Rhythms Of Broadway* US CL 1507, 1960; *Rhythms Of Broadway* US CL 2224, CS 9024, 1964; *Johnny Mathis Sings Of Love* UK SHM 749 Hallmark, 1972; *The Johnny Mathis Collection Vol 2* UK PDA 032 Hallmark, 1977

'I Can't Believe That You're In Love With Me' *Johnny* US CL 2044, CS 8844; UK BPG 62172, SBPG 62172 CBS, 1963

'I Can't Give You Anything But Love Baby' *Tender Is The Night* US MG 20890, SR 60890 Mercury; UK CLP 1721, CSD 1535 HMV, 1964

'I Concentrate On You' *Open Fire,*

Two Guitars US CL 1270, CS 8056; UK TFL 5050, STFL 515 Fontana, BPG 62063, SBPG 62063 CBS, 1959; *Warm, Open Fire, Two Guitars* US GP 2, 1968

'I Could Have Danced All Night' *The Rhythms Of Broadway* US CL 1507, 1960; *The Rhythms & Ballads Of Broadway* US C2L17, C2S803; UK SET 101 Fontana, 1960; *Rhythms Of Broadway* US CL 2224, CS 9024, 1964; *Johnny Mathis Sings Of Love* UK SHM 749 Hallmark, 1972; *The Johnny Mathis Collection Vol 2* UK PDA 032 Hallmark, 1977

'I Don't Want To Say No' *Mathis Is* US 34441; UK 86023 CBS, 1977

'I'd Rather Be Here With You' *I'm Coming Home* US KC 32435; UK 65690 CBS, 1973; *Celebration* UK 10028 CBS, 1981

'I Dream Of You' *Album Title* US MC 21091, SR 61091, 1966

'If' *The Mathis Collection* UK 10003 CBS, 1977; *You've Got A Friend (Today's Greatest Hits)* US C 30740; UK 64448 CBS, 1971

'If I Could Reach You' *Me & Mrs Jones* UK 65443 CBS, 1973

'If I Had You' *Away From Home* UK CLP 1926, CSD 1638 HMV, 1965

'If It's Magic' *Celebration* UK 10028 CBS, 1981

'If Love Were All' *Away From Home* UK CLP 1926, CSD 1638 HMV, 1965

'If There's A Way' *Johnny Mathis Sings The Music Of Bert Kaempfert* UK 63524 CBS, 1969; *Johnny Mathis Sings The Music Of Bacharach & Kaempfert* US G 30350; UK 66275 CBS, 19??; *Johnny Mathis Sings Bert Kaempfert* UK EMB 31209 Embassy, 1975

'If We Only Have Love' *Greatest Hits Vol 4* UK 86022 CBS, 1977; *You've Got A Friend* US C 30740; UK 64448

CBS, 1971; *All Time Greatest Hits* UK 67253, 1972; *Johnny Mathis In Person* US KG 30979; UK 67253 CBS, 1972; *Love Songs* UK EMB 31393 Embassy, 1976

'If You Believe' *You Light Up My Life* US JC 35259; UK 86055 CBS, 1978

'If You Could Read My Mind' *You've Got A Friend* US C 30740; UK 64448 CBS, 1971

'I Got Love' *Johnny Mathis In Person* US KG 30979; UK 67231 CBS, 1972

'I Have Dreamed' *Ballads Of Broadway* US CL 2223, CS 9023, 1964; *The Rhythms & Ballads Of Broadway* US C2L17, C 2803; UK SER 101 Fontana, 1960; *The Ballads Of Broadway* US CL 1506, 1960

'I Heard A Forest Praying' *Goodnight Dear Lord (US)/Heavenly (UK)* US CL 1119, CS. 8012: UK TFL 5023 Fontana, 1958

'I Just Can't Get Over You' *That's What Friends Are For* US 35435; UK 86068 CBS, 1978

'I Just Found Out About Love' *The Rhythms Of Broadway* US CL 1507, 1960; *The Rhythms & Ballads Of Broadway* US C2L17, C 2803; UK SET 101 Fontana, 1960; *Rhythms Of Broadway* US CL 2224, CS 9024, 1964; *Johnny Mathis* US KH 30017 Harmony; UK CHM 684 Hallmark, 1970; *Johnny Mathis Sings Of Love* UK SHM 749 Hallmark, 1972; *The Johnny Mathis Collection Vol 2* UK PDA 032 Hallmark, 1977

'I Just Wanted To Be Me' *I'm Coming Home* US KC 32435; UK 65690 CBS, 1973

'(I Left My Heart) In San Francisco' *The Shadow Of Your Smile* US MG 21073, SR 6107 Mercury; UK CLP 3556, CSD 3556 HMV, 1966

'I'll Be Easy To Find' *Heavenly (US)/Ride On A Rainbow (UK)* US CL

1351, CS 8152; UK TFL 5061, STFL 516 Fontana, BPG 62064, SBPG 62064 CBS, 1959; *Heavenly* UK EMB 31084 Embassy, 1975; *Heavenly And Faithfully* US C 83362, 1975

'I'll Be Home For Christmas' *Merry Christmas* US CL 1195, CS 8021; UK TFL 5031 Fontana, 6L806 CBS, 1958; *Merry Christmas* UK 62806 CBS, 1966; *Christmas Album* UK 2094/0501 St Michael, 1978; *Johnny Mathis Sings Christmas Songs* UK 2188/2020 St Michael, 1980

'I'll Be Seeing You' *Open Fire, Two Guitars* US CL 1270, CS 8056; UK TFL 5050, STFL 515 Fontana, BPG 62063, SBPG 62063 CBS, 1959; *Warm/Open Fire, Two Guitars* US GP 2, 1968; *Tenderly* KH 30917, 1971; *The Johnny Mathis Collection Vol 2* UK PDA 032 Hallmark, 1977

'I'll Buy You A Star' *I'll Buy You A Star* US CL 1623, CS 8423; UK TFL 5134, STFL 557 Fontana, 1961

'I'll Close My Eyes' *The Sweetheart Tree (US)/Away From Home (UK)* US MG 21041, SR 61041; UK CLP 1926, CSD 1638 HMV, 1965

'I'll Do It All For You' *Different Kinda Different* US JC 36505, 1980; *All For You* UK 86115 CBS, 1980

'I'll Make You Happy' *Mathis Is* US 34441; UK 86023 CBS, 1977

'I'll Never Be Lonely Again' *Johnny's Newest Hits* US CL 2016, CS 8816; UK BPG 62147, SBPG 62147 CBS, 1963

'I'll Never Fall In Love Again' *Love Theme From 'Romeo & Juliet'* US CS 9909, 1969; *Again Johnny Mathis Sings The Great Songs* UK 88085 CBS, 1974; *Again Johnny Mathis Sings The Music Of Bacharach & Kaempfert* US G 30350; UK 66275 CBS, 19??; *Love Songs* UK EMB 31393 Embassy, 1976; *The Mathis Collection* UK 10003 CBS, 1977;

Johnny Mathis UK 2094/0102 St Michael, 1978

'I'll Search My Heart' *I'll Search My Heart* US CL 2143, CS 8943; UK BPG 62270, SBPG 62270 CBS, 1963

'I Look At You' *Johnny's Greatest Hits* UK TFL 5058 Fontana, 1958; *Johnny's Greatest Hits* US CL 1133, CS 8634, 1958; *Johnny's Greatest Hits* UK 62569 CBS, 1965; *Johnny's Greatest Hits* US PC 3466, 1977

'I Love Her That's Why' *Johnny's Newest Hits* US CL 2016, CS 8816; UK BPG 62147 SBPG 62147 CBS, 1963

'I Love To Hear A Banjo' *The Young Americans Presented By Johnny Mathis* US MG 21023, SR 61023 Mercury, 1965

'I Love You' *Johnny* US CL 2044, CS 8844; UK BPG 62172, SBPG 62172 CBS, 1963

'I'm Always Chasing Rainbows' *The Wonderful World Of Make Believe* US MG 20193, SR 60913 Mercury; UK CLP 1755, CSD 1553 HMV, 1964

'I Married An Angel' *The Ballads Of Broadway* US CL 1506, 1960; *The Rhythms & Ballads Of Broadway* US C2L17, C2S803; UK SET 101 Fontana, 1960; *Ballads Of Broadway* US CL 2223, CS 9023, 1960

'I'm Coming Home' *I'm Coming Home* US KC 32435; UK 65690 CBS, 1973; *The Mathis Collection* UK 10003 CBS, 1977; *Greatest Hits Vol 4* UK 86022 CBS, 1977; *99 Miles From LA* UK 2188/2010 St Michael, 1980; *The First 25 Years, The Silver AA* US C2X 37440, 1981

'I'm Glad There Is You' *Warm* US CL 1078, CS 8039; UK TFL 5015, STFL 510 Fontana, 1958; *Warm* UK RM 52064 CBS Realm, 1965; *Warm/Open Fire, Two Guitars* US GP 2; 1968; *Warm* UK EMB 31045 Embasssy, 1974; *Warm* UK 31499 Embassy, 1977

'I'm Gonna Laugh You Out Of My Life' *Johnny's Mood* CL 1526, CS 8326, 1960

'I'm In Love For The Very First Time' *The Shadow Of Your Smile (US)/Away From Home (UK)* US MG 21073, SR 61073 Mercury; UK CLP 1926, CSD 1638 HMV, 1965

'I'm In The Mood For Love' *Johnny's Mood* CL 1526, CS 8326, 1960; *Johnny Mathis* US KH 30017 Harmony; UK CHM 684 Hallmark, 1970; *Evergreens* UK 2188/8000 St Michael, 1980

'I'm Just A Boy In Love' *Open Fire, Two Guitars* US CL 1270, CS 8056; UK TFL 5050, STFL 515 Fontana, BPG 62063, SBPG 62063 CBS, 1959; *Warm/Open Fire, Two Guitars* US GP 2, 1968; *Tenderly*, 1971; *The Johnny Mathis Collection Vol 2* UK PDA 032, 1977

'I'm So Lost' *Johnny's Mood* CL 1526, CS 8326, 1960

'I'm Stone In Love With You' *I'm Coming Home* US KC 32435; UK 65690 CBS, 1973; *The Mathis Collection* UK 10003 CBS, 1977; *Greatest Hits Vol 4* UK 86022 CBS, 1977; *Johnny Mathis* UK 2094/1002 St Michael, 1978; *Evergreens* UK 2188/8000 St Michael, 1980

'I Need You' *The First Time Ever I Saw Your Face* US KC 31342; UK 64930 CBS, 1972

'In Other Words' *Johnny Mathis* TFL 5011 Fontana, 1957; *Johnny Mathis* US CL 887, 1956; *Johnny Mathis* US EN 13089 Encore, 1976

'In Return' *Johnny's Mood* CL 1526, CS 8326, 1960

'In The Morning' *Johnny Mathis In Person* US KG 30979; UK 67231 CBS, 1972

'In The Still Of The Night' *Open Fire, Two Guitars* US CL 1270; CS 8056; UK TFL 5050, STFL 515 Fontana, BPG 62063, SBPG 62063 CBS, 1959; *Warm/Open Fire, Two Guitars* US GP 2, 1968; *Tenderly* KH 30917, 1971; *The Johnny Mathis Collection Vol 2* UK PDA 032 Hallmark, 1977; *Evergreens* UK 2188/8000 St Michael, 1980

'In The Wee Small Hours Of The Morning' *Wonderful, Wonderful* US CL 1028, CS 9046; UK TFL 5003 Fontana, 1957

'In Wisconsin' *Romantically* US CL 2098, CS 8898; UK BPG 62202, SBPG 62202 CBS, 1963

'I Only Have Eyes For You' *I Only Have Eyes For You* US PC 34117; UK 81329 CBS, 1976; *Evergreens* UK 2188/8000 St Michael, 1980

'I Remember You And Me' *Friends In Love* FC 37748; CBS 85652, 1982

'I Say A Little Prayer' *Love Is Blue* US CS 9637; UK 63301 CBS, 1968; *Johnny Mathis Greatest Hits Vol 3* UK 64651, 1971; *Johnny Mathis Sings The Music Of Bacharach & Kaempfert* US G 30350; UK 66275 CBS, 19??

'Isn't It A Pity' *The Rhythms & Ballads Of Broadway* US C2L17, C2S803; UK SET 101 Fontana, 1960; *The Ballads Of Broadway* US CL 1506; *Ballads Of Broadway* US CL 2223, CS 9023, 1964

'It Came Upon A Midnight Clear' *Merry Christmas* US CL 1195, CS 8021; UK TFL 5031 Fontana, 62806 CBS, 1958; *Merry Christmas* UK 62806 CBS, 1966; *Merry Christmas* UK 69217, 1975; *When A Child Is Born* UK 83266 CBS, 1978

'It Could Happen To You' *Wonderful, Wonderful* US CL 1028, CS 9046; UK TFL 5003 Fontana, 1957

'It Doesn't Have To Hurt Every Time' *The First 25 Years, The Silver AA* US C2X 37440, 1981

'I Thought Of You Last Night' *Up, Up And Away* US CL 2726; UK 63104, 1968

'It Makes No Difference' *Johnny Mathis Sings The Music Of Bert Kaempfert* UK 63524 CBS, 1969; *Johnny Mathis Sings Bert Kaempfert* UK EMB 31209 Embassy, 1975

'It Might As Well Be Spring' *Johnny Mathis* US CL 887, 1956; *Johnny Mathis* UK TFL 5011 Fontana, 1957; *Johnny Mathis* US EN 13089 Encore, 1976

'It's De Lovely' *Swing Softly* US CL 1165, CS 8023; UK TFL 5039, STFL 500 Fontana; BPG 62062, SBPG 62062 CBS, 1958

'It's Gone' *The Heart Of A Woman* US KC 33251; UK 80533 CBS, 1974

'It's Impossible' *Love Story* US 30499; UK 64334 CBS 1971; *Johnny Mathis Sings The Great Songs* UK 88085 CBS, 1974

'It's Not For Me To Say' *Johnny's Greatest Hits* US CL 1133, CS 8634, 1958; *Johnny's Greatest Hits* UK TFL 5058 Fontana, 1958; *The Great Years* US C2L34, C2S834, 1964; *Johnny's Greatest Hits* UK 62569 CBS, 1965; *All Time Greatest Hits* UK 67253 CBS, 1972; *Johnny Mathis In Person* US KG 30979; UK 67231 CBS, 1972; *Johnny's Greatest Hits* US PC 34667, 1977; *'The First 25 Years, The Silver AA* US C2X 37440, 1981; *Celebration* UK 10028 CBS, 1981

'It's Only A Paper Moon' *Romantically* US CL 2098, CS 8898; UK BPG 62202, SBPG 62202 CBS, 1963

'It's Too Late' *You've Got A Friend* US C 30740; UK 64448 CBS, 1971; *Laughter And Tears* UK 10019 CBS, 1980

'It Was Almost Like A Song' *You Light Up My Life* US JC 35259; UK 86055 CBS, 1978

'I've Got The World On A String' *Swing Softly* US CL 1165, CS 8023; UK TFL 5039, STFL 500 Fontana, BPG 62062, SBPG 62062 CBS, 1958

'I've Grown Accustomed To Her Face' *Warm* US CL 1078, CS 8039; UK TFL 5015, STFL 510 Fontana, 1958; *Warm* UK RM 52064 CBS Realm, 1965; *Warm/Open Fire, Two Guitars* US GP 2, 1968; *Warm* UK EMB 31045 Embassy, 1974; *Warm* UK 31499 Embassy, 1977; *The Mathis Collection* UK 10003 CBS, 1977

'I Was Born In Love With You/Summer Me, Winter Me' *Me And Mrs Jones* UK 65443 CBS, 1973

'I Was Telling Her About You' *Rapture* US CL 1915, CS 8715; UK BPG 62106, SBPG 62106 CBS, 1962

'I Was There' *Love Story* US 30499; UK 64334 CBS, 1971

'I Will Survive' *Different Kinda Different* US JC 36505, 1980; *All For You* UK 86115 CBS, 1980; *Celebration* UK 10028 CBS, 1981

'I Will Wait For You' *'So Nice'* MG 21091, SR 61091, 1966; *The Impossible Dream* US CS 9872; UK 63718 CBS, 1969

'I Wish I Were In Love Again' *The Rhythms Of Broadway* US CL 1507, 1960; *Rhythms & Ballads Of Broadway* US C2L17, C2S803; UK SET 101 Fontana, 1960; *Rhythms Of Broadway* US CL 2224, CS 9024, 1964; *Johnny Mathis Sings Of Love* UK SHM 749 Hallmark, 1972; *The Johnny Mathis Collection Vol 2* UK PDA 032 Hallmark, 1977

'I Wish You Love' *Johnny Mathis Sings* US MG 21107, SR 61107, 1966

'I Won't Cry Anymore' *Up, Up And Away* US C 59526, 19??

'I Won't Dance' *Live It Up!* US CL 1711, CS 8511; UK TFL 5177 Fontana, BPG 62105, SBPG 62105 CBS, 1962

'I Write The Songs' *I Only Have Eyes For You* US PC 34117; UK 81329 CBS, 1976; *99 Miles From LA* UK 2188/2010 St Michael, 1980

'I Wrote A Symphony On My Guitar' *You Light Up My Life* US JC 35259; UK 86055 CBS, 1978

J

'Jean' *Raindrops Keep Fallin' On My Head* US CS 1005; UK 64012 CBS, 1970

'Jenny' *Portrait Of Johnny* UK TFL 5153, DTFL 571 Fontana, BPG 62077, SBPG 62077 CBS, 1961; *Portrait Of Johnny* US CL 1644, CS 8444, 1961; *Portrait Of Johnny* UK SHM 806 Hallmark, 1974; *The Johnny Mathis Collection* UK PDA 015 Hallmark, 1976; *Evergreens* UK 2188/8000 St Michael, 1980

'Jingle Bell Rock' *Give Me Your Love For Christmas* US CS 9923, 1969; *When A Child Is Born* UK 83266 CBS, 1978; *Merry Christmas* UK 69217, 1975

'Joey, Joey, Joey' *Johnny* US CL 2044, CS 8844; UK BPG 62172, SBPG 62172 CBS, 1963

'Johnny One Note' *Live It Up!* US CL 1711, CS 8511; UK TFL 5177 Fontana, BPG 62105, SBPG 62105 CBS, 1962

'Jump For Joy' *Johnny* US CL 2044, CS 8844; UK BPG 62172, SBPG 62172 CBS, 1963

'Just Friends' *Live It Up!* US CL 1711, CS 8511; UK TFL 5177 Fontana, BPG 62105, SBPG 62105 CBS, 1962

'Just Move Along, Meadow Lark' *This Is Love* US MG 20942, SR 60942 Mercury; UK CLP 1859, CSD 1600 HMV, 1964

'Just The Way You Are' *That's What Friends Are For* US JC 35435; UK 86068 CBS, 1978; *Tears And Laughter* UK 10018 CBS, 1980; *The Best Of*

Johnny Mathis 1975–1980 US JC 36871, 1980

K

'Killing Me Softly With Her Song' *Killing Me Softly With Her Song* US KC 32258; UK 65672 CBS, 1973; *Greatest Hits Vol 4* UK 860022 CBS, 1977; *Johnny Mathis* UK 2094/0102 St Michael, 1978

'Klondike' *The Young Americans Presented By Johnny Mathis* US MG 21023, SR 61023 Mercury, 1965

'Kol Nidre' *Goodnight Dear Lord (US)/Heavenly (UK)* US CL 1119, CS 8012; UK TFL 5023 Fontana, 1958

L

'La Montana' *Olé* US MG 20988, SR 60988 Mercury; UK CLP 1818, CSD 1578 HMV, 1964

'Lady' *Johnny Mathis Sings The Music Of Bert Kaempfert* UK 63524 CBS, 1969; *Johnny Mathis Sings The Music Of Bacharach & Kaempfert* US G30350; UK 66275 CBS, 1971; *Johnny Mathis Sings The Music Of Bert Kaempfert* UK EMB 31209 Embassy, 1975

'Lament' *Rapture* US CL 1915, CS 8715; UK BPG 62106, SBPG 62106 CBS, 1962

'(Last Night) I Didn't Get To Sleep At All' *The First Time Ever I Saw Your Face* US KC 31342; UK 64930 CBS, 1972; *Night And Day* UK 31863 CBS, 1980

'Lately' *Friends In Love* FC 37748; CBS 85652, 1982

'Laughter In The Rain' *When Will I See You Again* US PC 33420; UK 80738 CBS, 1975; *Greatest Hits Vol 4* UK 86022 CBS, 1977; *99 Miles From LA* UK 2188/2010 St Michael, 1980; *Tears And Laughter* UK 10019 CBS, 1980

'Laura' *Tender Is The Night* US MG

20890, SR 60890 Mercury; UK CLP 1721, CSD 1535 HMV, 1964; *People* US CS 9871, 1969

'Laurie My Love' *Portrait Of Johnny* UK TFL 5153, STFL 571 Fontana, BPG 62077, SBPG 62077 CBS, 1961

'Lean On Me' *Song Sung Blue (US)/Make It Easy On Yourself (UK)* US KG 31626; UK 65161 CBS, 1972

'Let It Rain' *More Johnny's Greatest Hits* UK STFL 517, 1959; *More Johnny's Greatest Hits* US CL 1344, CS 8150; UK 62774 CBS, 1959; *More Johnny's Greatest Hits* UK TFL 5083 Fontana, 1959

'Let It Snow, Let It Snow, Let It Snow' *Sounds Of Christmas* US MG 20837, SR 60837 Mercury; UK CLP 1696, CSD 1521 HMV, 1963; *Christmas With Johnny Mathis* US KH 30864 Harmony; UK SHM 765 Hallmark, 1971

'Let Me Be The One/I Won't Last A Day' *When Will I See You Again* US PC 33420; UK 80738 CBS, 1975

'Let Me Love You' *Wonderful, Wonderful* US CL 1028, CS 9046; UK TFL 5003 Fontana, 1957

'Let's Do It' *The Rhythms & Ballads Of Broadway* US C2L17, C2S803; UK SET 101 Fontana, 1960; *The Rhythms Of Broadway* US CL 1507, 1960; *Rhythms Of Broadway* US CL 2224, CS 9024, 1964; *Johnny Mathis Sings Of Love* UK SHM 749 Hallmark, 1972; *The Johnny Mathis Collection Vol 2* UK PDA 032 Hallmark, 1977; *More Johnny's Greatest Hits* UK STFL 517 Fontana, 1959; *More Johnny's Greatest Hits* UK TFL 5083 Fontana, 1959; *More Johnny's Greatest Hits* US CL 1344, CS 8150; UK 62774 CBS, 1959; *Love Songs* UK EMB 31393 Embassy, 1976

'Let's Misbehave' *The Rhythms & Ballads Of Broadway* UK SET 101 Fontana, 1960; *The Rhythms Of*

Broadway US CL 1507, 1960; *Rhythms Of Broadway* US CL 2224, CS 9024, 1964; *Johnny Mathis* US KH 30017 Harmony; UK CHM 684 Hallmark, 1970; *Johnny Mathis Sings Of Love* UK SHM 749 Hallmark, 1972; *The Johnny Mathis Collection Vol 2* UK PDA 032 Hallmark, 1977

'Life And Breath' *The First Time Ever I Saw Your Face* US KC 31342; UK 64930 CBS, 1972

'Life Is A Song Worth Singing' *I'm Coming Home* US KC 32435; UK 65690 CBS, 1973; *Tears And Laughter* UK 10019 CBS, 1980

'Life Is What You Make It' *The First Time Ever I Saw Your Face* US KC 31342; UK 64930 CBS, 1972

'Light My Fire' *Those Were The Days* US CS 9705; UK 63427 CBS, 1968; *This Guy's In Love With You* US KH 31935 Harmony, 1973; *This Guy's In Love With You* UK SHM 872 Hallmark, 1975; *The Johnny Mathis Collection* UK PDA 015 Hallmark, 1976

'Like Someone In Love' *Swing Softly* US CL 1164, CS 8023; UK TFL 5039, STFL 500 Fontana, BPG 62062, SBPG 62062 CBS, 1958

'Limehouse Blues' *This Is Love* US MG 20942, SR 60942 Mercury; UK CLP 1859, CSD 1600 HMV, 1964; *What'll I Do* US C 32963, 1974

'Little Drummer Boy' *When A Child Is Born* UK 83266 CBS, 1978

'Little Green Apples' *Those Were The Days* US CS 9705; UK 63427 CBS, 1968; *This Guy's In Love With You* US KH 31935 Harmony, 1973; *Johnny Mathis Sings The Great Songs* UK 88085 CBS, 1974; *This Guy's In Love With You* UK SHM 872 Hallmark, 1975; *The Johnny Mathis Collection* UK PDA 015 Hallmark, 1976; *Evergreens* UK 2188/8000 St Michael, 1980

'Live For Life' *Love Theme From 'Romeo & Juliet'* US CS 9909, 1969

'Live It Up' *Live It UP!* US CL 1711, CS 8511; UK TFL 5177 Fontana, BPG 62105, SBPG 62105 CBS, 1962

'Long Ago (And Far Away)' *Love Is Everything* US MG 20991, SR 20991 Mercury; UK CLP, 3522, CSD 3522 HMV, 1965; *You've Got A Friend* US C30740; UK 64448 CBS, 1971; *Johnny Mathis Sings The Great Songs* UK 88085 CBS, 1974

'Looking At You' *Wonderful, Wonderful* US CL 11028, CS 9046; UK TFL 5003 Fontana, 1957

'Loss Of Love' *Love Story* US C 30499; UK 64334 CBS, 1971

'Lost In Loveliness' *Rapture* US CL 1915, CS 8715; UK BPG 62106, SBPG 62106 CBS, 1962

'L-O-V-E' *Live It UP!* US CL 1171, CS 8511; UK TFL 5177 Fontana, BPG 62105, SBPG 62105 CBS, 1962; *Johnny Mathis Sings The Music Of Bert Kaempfert* UK 63524 CBS, 1969; *Johnny Mathis Sings The Music Of Bacharach & Kaempfert* US G30350; UK 66275 CBS, 1971: *Johnny Mathis Sings The Music Of Bert Kaempfert* UK EMB 31209 Embassy, 1975; *Misty* UK SHM 913 Hallmark, 1977; *Mathis Magic* US JC 36216; UK 86103 CBS, 1979; *Evergreens* UK 2188/8000 St Michael, 1980

'Love Eyes' *The Rhythm & Ballads Of Broadway* US C2L17, C2S803; UK SET 101 Fontana, 1966; *The Rhythms Of Broadway* US CL 1507, 1966; *Rhythms Of Broadway* US CL 2224, CS 9024, 1964; *Johnny Mathis Sings Of Love* UK SHM 749 Hallmark, 1972; *The Johnny Mathis Collection Vol 2* UK PDA 032 Hallmark, 1977

'Love Is A Gamble' *The Rhythms & Ballads Of Broadway* US C2L17, C2S803; UK SET 101 Fontana, 1960; *The Rhythms Of Broadway* US CL

1507, 1960; *Rhythms Of Broadway* US CL 2224, CS 9024, 1964; *Johnny Mathis Sings Of Love* UK SHM 749 Hallmark, 1972; *The Johnny Mathis Collection Vol 2* UK PDA 032 Hallmark, 1977

'Love Is Blue' *Love Is Blue* US CS 9637; UK 63301 CBS, 1968; *Love Songs* UK EMB 31393 Embassy, 1976; *The Mathis Collection* UK 100030 CBS, 1977

'Love Is Everything' *Love Is Everything* US MG 20991, SR 20991 Mercury; UK CLP 3522, CSD 3522 HMV, 1965

'Love Look Away' *I'll Buy You A Star* US CL 1623, CS 8423; UK TFL 5134, STFL 557 Fontana, 1961; *The Great Years* US C2L34, C2S834, 1964

'Love Me As Though There Were No Tomorrow' *Rapture* US CL 1915, CS 8715; UK BPG 62106, SBPG 62106 CBS, 1962; *Johnny Mathis* US KH 30017 Harmony; UK CHM 684 Hallmark, 1970; *Evergreens* UK 2188/8000 St Michael, 1980

'Love Me Tonight' *Love Theme From 'Romeo & Juliet'* US CS 9909, 1969; *Love Songs* UK EMB 31393 Embassy, 1976

'Lovers In New York' *The Shadow Of Your Smile* UK CLP 3556, CSD 3556 HMV, 1966; *Johnny Mathis Sings* US MG 21107, SR 61107, 1967

'Love Story' *Johnny Mathis Greatest Hits Vol 3* UK 64651 CBS, 1971; *Love Story* US C 30499; UK 64334 CBS, 1971; *Johnny Mathis In Person* US KG 30979; UK 67231 CBS, 1972; *All-Time Greatest Hits* UK 67253 CBS, 1972; *Love Songs* UK EMB 31393 Embassy, 1976; *The Mathis Collection* UK 100030 CBS, 1977

'Love Theme (From *Romeo & Juliet*)' *Love Theme From 'Romeo & Juliet'* US CS 9909, 1969; *Johnny Mathis Greatest Hits Vol 3* UK 64651 CBS,

1971; *Johnny Mathis In Person* US KG 30979; UK 67231 CBS, 1972; *All-Time Greatest Hits* UK 67253 CBS, 1972

'Love Walked In' *Swing Softly* US CL 1165, CS 8023; UK TFL 5039, STFL 500 Fontana, BPG 62062, SBPG 62062 CBS, 1958

'Love Without Words' *Different Kinda Different* US JC 36505, 1980; *All For You* UK 86115 CBS, 1980

'Love, Your Magic Spell Is Everywhere' *Johnny Mathis* US CL 887, 1956; *Johnny Mathis* UK TFL 5011 Fontana, 1957; *Johnny Mathis* US EN 13089 Encore, 1976

'Loving You, Losing You' *Mathis Is* US 34441; UK 86023 CBS, 1977

'Lullaby Of Love' *Mathis Is* US 34441; UK 86023 CBS, 1977

M

'Magic Garden' *I'll Buy You A Star* US CL 1623, CS 8423; UK TFL 5134, STFL 557 Fontana, 1961

'Make It Easy On Yourself' *Song Sung Blue (US)/'Make It Easy On Yourself (UK)* US KG 31626; UK 651 CBS, 1972; *Johnny Mathis Sings The Great Songs* UK 88055 CBS, 1974

'Mandy' *When Will I See You Again* US PC 33420; UK 80738, 1975; *99 Miles From LA* UK 2188/2010 St Michael, 1980

'Manha De Carnival' *Olé* US MG 20988, SR 60988 Mercury; UK CLP 1818, CSD 1578 HMV, 1964

'Man Of La Mancha' *So Nice* US MG 21091, SR 61091, 1966

'Maria' *Faithfully* US CL 1422, CS 8219; UK TFL 5084, STFL 522 Fontana, BPG 62061, SBPG 62061 CBS, 1960; *The Great Years* US C2L34, C2S834, 1964; *All-Time Greatest Hits* UK 67253 CBS, 1972; *Johnny Mathis In Person* US KG

30979; UK 67231 CBS, 1972; *This Guy's In Love With You* UK SHM 8726 Hallmark, 1975; *Heavenly And Faithfully* US CG 33621, 1975; *The Johnny Mathis Collection* UK PDA 015 Hallmark, 1976; *The Mathis Collection* UK 100030 CBS, 1977; *Evergreens* UK 2188/8000 St Michael, 1980

'Marianna' *Johnny's Newest Hits* US CL 2016, CS 8816; UK BPG 62147, SBPG 62147 CBS, 1963

'May The Good Lord Bless You And Keep You' *Goodnight Dear Lord (US)/Heavenly (UK)* US CL 1119, CS 8012; UK TFL 5023 Fontana, 1958

'Me And Mrs Jones' *Me And Mrs Jones* UK 65443 CBS, 1973; *Greatest Hits Vol 4* UK 86022 CBS, 1977; *Johnny Mathis* UK 2094/0102 St Michael, 1978

'Me For You, You For Me' *That's What Friends Are For* US JC 34535; UK 86068 CBS, 1978

'Melinda' *The Shadow Of Your Smile* US MG 21073, SR 61073 Mercury; UK CLP 3556, CSD 3556 HMV, 1966

'Memories Don't Leave Like People' *The Heart Of A Woman* US KC 33251; UK 80533 CBS, 1974

'Memory' *Friends In Love* FC 37748; CBS 85652, 1982

'Michelle' *The Shadow Of Your Smile* US MG 21073, SR 61073 Mercury; UK CLP 3556, CSD 3556 HMV, 1966

'Midnight Blue' *Tears And Laughter* UK 10019 CBS, 1980; *Night And Day* UK 31863 CBS, 1980

'Midnight Cowboy' *Raindrops Keep Fallin' On My Head* US CS 1005; UK 64012 CBS, 1970; *Night And Day* UK 31863 CBS, 1980

'Midnight Rider' *Feelings* US PC 33887; UK 69180 CBS, 1975

'Miracles' *Johnny* US CL 2044, CS

8844; UK BPG 62172, SBPG 62172 CBS, 1963

'Mirage' *The Sweetheart Tree* US MG 21041; SR 61041 Mercury, 1965

'Misty' *Heavenly (US)/Ride On A Rainbow (UK)* US CL 1351, CS 8152; UK TFL 5061, STFL 516 Fontana, BPG 62064, SBPG 62064 CBS, 1959; *The Great Years* US C2L34, C2S834, 1964; *All-Time Greatest Hits* UK 67253 CBS, 1972; *Heavenly* UK EMB 31084 Embassy, 1974; *Heavenly And Faithfully* US CG 33621, 1975; *Misty* UK SHM 913 Hallmark, 1977; *The Mathis Collection* UK 100030 CBS, 1977; *Evergreens* UK 2188/8000 St Michael, 1980; *The First 25 Years, The Silver AA* US C2X 37440, 1981; *Celebration* UK 10028 CBS, 1981

'Misty Roses' *Up, Up And Away* US CL 2726, CS 9526; UK 63104, 1968; *Johnny Mathis Greatest Hits Vol 3* UK 64651 CBS, 1971; *All-Time Greatest Hits* UK 67253 CBS, 1972

'Moanin' Low' *The Rhythms & Ballads Of Broadway* US C2L17, C2S803; UK SER 101 Fontana, 1960; *The Ballads Of Broadway* US CL 1506; *Ballads Of Broadway* US CL 2223, CS 9023, 1964

'Moments Like This' *Rapture* US CL 1915, CS 8715; UK BPG 62106 SBPG 62106 CBS, 1962

'Moment To Moment' *The Shadow Of Your Smile* US MG 21073, SR 61073 Mercury; UK CLP 3556, CSD 3556 HMV, 1966; *The Impossible Dream* US CS 9872; UK 63718 CBS, 1969

'Moonlight Becomes You' *Heavenly (US)/Ride On A Rainbow (UK)* US CL 1351, CS 8152; UK TFL 5061, STFL 516 Fontana, BPG 62064, SBPG, 62064 CBS, 1959; *Heavenly* UK EMB 31084 Embassy, 1974; *Johnny Mathis Sings The Great Songs* UK 88055 CBS, 1974; *Heavenly And Faithfully* US CG 33621, 1975

'Moonlight In Vermont' *Romantically* US CL 2098, CS 8898; UK BPG 62202, SBPG 62202 CBS, 1963

'Moon River' *Love Is Blue* US CS 9637; UK 63301, 1968; *Johnny Mathis Greatest Hits Vol 3* UK 64651, 1971; *The Mathis Collection* UK 100030 CBS, 1977

'More' *This Is Love* US MG 20942, SR 60942 Mercury; UK CLP 1859, CSD 1600 HMV, 1964; *People* US CS 9871, 1969; *What'll I Do* US C 32963, 1974

'More Than You Know' *Heavenly (US)/Ride On A Rainbow (UK)* US CL 1351, CS 8152; UK TFL 5061, STFL 5061 Fontana, BPG 62064, SBPG 62064 CBS, 1959; *Heavenly* UK EMB 31084 Embassy, 1974; *Heavenly And Faithfully* US CG 33621; *Misty* UK SHM 913 Hallmark, 1977; *Evergreens* UK 2188/8000 St Michael, 1980

'My Body Keeps Changing My Mind' *Mathis Magic* US JC 36216; UK 86103 CBS, 1979

'My Darling, My Darling' *Rapture* US CL 1915, CS 8715; UK BPG 62106, SBPG 62106 CBS, 1962

'My Favourite Dream' *I'll Search My Heart* US CL 2143, CS 8943; UK BPG 62270, SBPG 62270 HMV, 1963

'My Favourite Things' *Give Me Your Love For Christmas* US CS 9923, 1969

'My Funny Valentine' *Open Fire, Two Guitars* US CL 1270, CS 8056; UK TFL 5050, STFL 515 Fontana, BPG 62063, SBPG 62063 CBS, 1959; *Warm/Open Fire, Two Guitars* US GP 2, 1968; *Tenderly* KH 30917, 1971; *All-Time Greatest Hits* UK 67253 CBS, 1972; *The Johnny Mathis Collection Vol 2* UK PDA 032 Hallmark, 1977; *The Mathis Collection* UK 100030 CBS, 1977

'My Heart And I' *I'll Buy You A Star* US CL 1623, CS 8423; UK TFL 5134, STFL 557 Fontana, 1961

'My Love For You' *Portrait Of Johnny* US CL 1644, CS, 8444, 1961; *Portrait Of Johnny* UK TFL 5153, STFL 571 Fontana, BPG 62077, SBPG 62077 CBS, 1961; *Portrait Of Johnny* UK SHM 806 Hallmark, 1974; *The Johnny Mathis Collection* UK PDA 015 Hallmark, 1976

'My One And Only Love' *Warm* US CL 1078, CS 8039; UK TFL 5015, STFL 510 Fontana, 1958; *Warm* UK RM 52064 CBS Realm, 1965; *Warm/Open Fire, Two Guitars* US GP 2, 1968; *Warm* UK EMB 31045 Embassy, 1974; *Warm* UK 31499 Embassy, 1977

'My Romance' *The Rhythms & Ballads Of Broadway* US C2L17, C2S803; UK SET 101 Fontana, 1960; *The Ballads Of Broadway* US CL 1506, 1960; *Ballads Of Broadway* US CL 2223, CS 9023, 1964

'My Sweet Lord' *Love Story* US C 30499; UK 64334 CBS, 1971; *Johnny Mathis Sings The Great Songs* UK 88055 CBS, 1974

N

'Neither One Of Us' *Killing Me Softly With Her Song* US KC 32258; UK 65672 CBS, 1973

'Never Can Say Goodbye' *You've Got A Friend* US C 30740; UK 64448 CBS, 1971; *Evergreens* UL 2188/8000 St Michael, 1980

'Never Givin' Up On You' *Different Kinda Different* US JC 36505, 1980; *All For You* UK 86115 CBS, 1980

'Never Let Me Go' *Love Is Everything* US MG 20991, SR 20991 Mercury; UK CLP 3522, CSD 3522 HMV, 1965

'Never My Love' *Love Is Blue* US CS 9637; UK 63301, 1968; *Love Songs* UK EMB 31398 Embassy, 1976

'Never Never Land' *Johnny* US CL 2044, CS 8844; UK BPG 62172, SBPG 62172 CBS, 1963

'New York State Of Mind' *Mathis Magic* US JC 36216; UK 86103 CBS, 1979

'Nice To Be Around' *When Will I See You Again* US PC 33420; UK 80738 CBS, 1975

'Night And Day' *Mathis Magic* US JC 36216; UK 86103 CBS, 1979; *Night And Day* UK 31865 CBS, 1980

'99 Miles From LA *Feelings* US PC 33887; UK 69180 CBS, 1975; *The Mathis Collection* UK 100030 CBS, 1977; *Greatest Hits Vol 4* UK 86022 CBS, 1977; *99 Miles From LA,* UK 2188/2010 St Michael, 1980; *The Best Of Johnny Mathis 1975–80* US JC 3687, 1980

'Nobody Knows' *Faithfully* US CL 1422, CS 8219; UK TFL 5084, STFL 522 Fontana, BPG 62061, SBPG 62061 CBS, 1960; *Heavenly And Faithfully* US CG 33621

'No Love' *Johnny Mathis* UK TFL 5011 Fontana, 1957; *Johnny's Greatest Hits* UK TFL 5058 Fontana, 1958; *Johnny's Greatest Hits* US CL 1133, CS 8634, 1958; *Johnny's Greatest Hits* UK 62569 CBS, 1965

'No Love (But Your Love)' *Johnny's Greatest Hits* US PC 34667, 1977

'No Man Can Stand Alone' *Johnny* US CL 2044, CS 8844; UK BPG 62172, SBPG 62172 CBS, 1963

'No One But The One You Love' *Mathis Magic* US JC 36216; UK 86103 CBS, 1979

'No Strings' *Tender Is The Night* US MG 20890, SR 60890 Mercury; UK CLP 1721, CSD 1535 HMV, 1964

'Nothing Between Us But Love' *The First 25 Years, The Silver AA* US C2X 37440, 1981

O

'Odds And Ends' *Raindrops Keep Fallin' On My Head* US CS 1005; UK

64012 CBS, 1970; *Johnny Mathis Sings The Music Of Bacharach & Kaempfert* US G 30350; UK 66275 CBS, 1971

'O Holy Night' *Merry Christmas* US CL 1195, CS 8021; UK TFL 5031 Fontana, 62806 CBS, 1958; *Merry Christmas* UK 62806 CBS, 1966; *Merry Christmas* UK 69217, 1975; *When A Child Is Born* UK 83266 CBS, 1978

'Oh How I Try' *I'll Buy You A Star* US CL 1623, CS 8423; UK TFL 5134, STFL 557 Fontana, 1961

'Oh That Feeling' *Portrait Of Johnny* UK TFL 5153, STFL 571 Fontana, BPG 62077, SBPG 62077 CBS, 1961; *Portrait Of Johnny* UK CL 1644, CS 8444, 1961; *Portrait Of Johnny* UK SHM 806 Hallmark, 1974; *The Johnny Mathis Collection* UK PDA 015 Hallmark, 1976

'On A Clear Day You Can See Forever' *The Shadow Of Your Smile* US MG 21073, SR 61073 Mercury; UK CLP 3556, CSD 3556 HMV, 1966; *The Impossible Dream* US CS 9872; UK 63718 CBS, 1969; *The Mathis Collection* UK 100030 CBS, 1977; *Night And Day* UK 31863 CBS, 1980

'On A Cold And Rainy Day' *Live It UP!* US CL 1711, CS 8511; UK TFL 5177 Fontana, BPG 62105, SBPG 62105 CBS, 1962

'On A Wonderful Day Like Today' *'The Sweetheart Tree (US)/Away From Home (UK)* US MG 21041, SR 61041 Mercury; UK CLP 1926, CSD 1638 HMV 1965

'Once' *Johnny's Mood* CL 1526, CS 8326, 1960

'One' *Hold Me, Thrill Me, Kiss Me* US PC 34872, 1977; *Sweet Surrender* UK 86036 CBS, 1977

'One Day In Your Life' *Feelings* US PC 33887; UK 69180 CBS, 1975; *Night And Day* UK 31863 CBS, 1980

'One Fine Day' *The Young Americans Presented By Johnny Mathis* US MG 21023, SR 61023 Mercury, 1965

'One God' *Goodnight Dear Lord (US)/Heavenly (UK)* US CL 1119, CS 8012; UK TFL 5023 Fontana, 1958

'One Look' *Johnny's Newest Hits* US CL 2016, CS 8846; UK BPG 62147, SBPG 62147 CBS, 1963

'One More Mountain' *Love Is Everything* US MG 20991, SR 20991 Mercury; UK CLP 3522, CSD 3522 HMV, 1965

'One Starry Night' *Faithfully* US CL 1422, CS 8219; UK TFL 5084, STFL 522 Fontana, BPG 62061, SBPG 62061 CBS, 1960; *Heavenly And Faithfully* US CG 33621, 1975

'Only You' *When Will I See You Again* US PC 33420; UK 80738 CBS, 1975

'On The Sunny Side Of The Street' *The Rhythms & Ballads Of Broadway* US C2L17, C2S803; UK SET 101 Fontana, 1960; *The Ballads Of Broadway* US CL 1506, 1960; *Ballads Of Broadway* US CL 2223, CS 9023, 1964; *Johnny Mathis* US KH 30017 Harmony; UK CHM 684 Hallmark, 1970

'Ooh What We Do' *I Only Have Eyes For You* US PC 34117; UK 81329 CBS, 1976

'Over The Weekend' *This Is Love* US MG 20942; SR 60942 Mercury; UK CLP 1859, CSD 1600 HMV, 1964; *What'll I Do* US C32963, 1974

P

'Paradise' *Different Kinda Different* US JC 36505, 1980; *All For You* UK 86115 CBS, 1980

'People' *Love Is Everything* US MG 20991, SR 20991 Mercury; UK CLP 3522, CSD 3522 HMV, 1965; *People* US CS 9871, 1969; *The Mathis Collection* UK 100030 CBS, 1977

'Pieces Of Dreams' *Close To You (US)/The Long And Winding Road (UK)* US C 30210; UK 64176 CBS. 1970

'Play Me' *Song Sung Blue (UK)/Make It Easy On Yourself (UK)* US KG 31616; UK 65161 CBS, 1972

'Please Be Kind' *Open Fire, Two Guitars* US CL 1270, CS 8056; UK TFL 5050, STFL 515 Fontana, BPG 62063, SBPG 62063, 1959; *Warm/Open Fire, Two Guitars* US GP 2, 1968; *Tenderly* KH 30917, 1971; *The Johnny Mathis Collection Vol 2* UK PDA 032 Hallmark, 1977

'Poinciana' (Song Of The Tree) *This Is Love* US MG 20942, SR 60942 Mercury; UK CLP 1859, CSD 1600 HMV, 1964; *What'll I Do* US C 32963, 1974

'Poor Butterfly' *Johnny* US CL 2044, CS 8844; UK BPG 62172; SBPG 62172 CBS, 1963

'Prelude To A Kiss' *Johnny Mathis* US CL 887, 1956; *Johnny Mathis* UK TFL 5011 Fontana, 1957; *Johnny Mathis* US EN 13089 Encore, 1976

'Put On A Happy Face' *This Is Love* US MG 20942, SR 60942 Mercury; UK CLP 1859; CSD 1600 HMV, 1964; *What'll I Do* US C 32963 1974

Q

'Quiet Girl' *Johnny's Newest Hits* US CL 2016, CS 8816; UK BPG 62147, SBPG 62147 CBS, 1963

'Quiet Nights (Corcovado)' *The Shadow Of Your Smile* US MG 21073, SR 61073; UK CLP 3556, CSD 3556 HMV, 1966; *People* US CS 9871, 1969

R

'Raindrops Keep Fallin' On My Head' *Raindrops Keep Fallin' On My Head* US CS 1005; UK 64012 CBS, 1970; *Johnny Mathis Greatest Hits Vol 3* UK 64651, 1971; *The Mathis Collection* UK 100030 CBS, 1977

'Rapture' *Rapture* US CL 1915, CS 8715; UK BPG 62106, SBPG 62106 CBS, 1962

'Ready Or Not' *That's What Friends Are For* US JC 25435; UK 86068 CBS, 1978; *The First 25 Years, The Silver AA* US C2X 37440; 1981

'Remember' *Me And Mrs Jones* UK 65443 CBS, 1973

'Remember When' *Johnny Mathis Sings The Music Of Bert Kaempfert* UK 63524 CBS, 1969; *Johnny Mathis Sings The Music Of Bacharach & Kaempfert* US G 30350; UK 66275 CBS, 1971; *Johnny Mathis Remembers Bert Kaempfert* UK EMB 31209 Embassy, 1975

'Ring The Bell' *I'll Buy You A Star* US CL 1623, CS 8423; UK TFL 5134, STFL 557 Fontana, 1961

'Rose Garden' *Love Story* US C 30499; UK 64334 CBS, 1971; *Johnny Mathis Sings The Great Songs* UK 88085 CBS, 1974

'Round And Round The Romance Tree' *The Young Americans Presented By Johnny Mathis* US MG 21023, SR 61023 Mercury, 1965

'Rudolph The Red Nosed Reindeer' *Sounds Of Christmas* US MG 20837, SR 60837; UK CLP 1696, CSD 1521 HMV, 1963; *Christmas With Johnny Mathis* US KH 30864 Harmony; UK SHM 765 Hallmark, 1971; *Merry Christmas* UK 69217 CBS, 1975; *Christmas Album* UK 2094/0501 St Michael, 1978; *Johnny Mathis Sings Christmas Songs* UK 2188/2020 St Michael, 1980

'Run To Me' *Song Sung Blue (US)/Make It Easy On Yourself (UK)* US KG 31626; UK 65161 CBS, 1972

S

'Sail On White Moon' *The Heart Of A Woman* US KC 33251; UK 80533 CBS, 1974

'Samba De Orfeu *Olé* US MG 20988, SR 60988 Mercury; UK CLP 1818, CSD 1578 HMV, 1964

'Sands Of Time' *The Wonderful World Of Make Believe* US MG 20193, SR 60913 Mercury; UK CLP 1755, CSD 1553 HMV, 1964

'Santa Claus Is Comin' To Town' *Give Me Your Love For Christmas* US CS 9923, 1969

'Saturday Sunshine' *Johnny Mathis Sings* US MG 21107, SR 61107, 1966

'Secret Love' *Faithfully* US CL 1422, CS 8219; UK TFL 5084, STFL 522 Fontana, BPG 62061, SBPG 62061 CBS, 1960; *Heavenly And Faithfully* US CG 33621, 1975

'Send In The Clowns' *I Only Have Eyes For You* US PC 34117; UK 81329 CBS, 1976; *The Mathis Collection* UK 100030 CBS, 1977

'September Song' *Romantically* US CL 2098, CS 8898; UK BPG 62202, SBPG 62202 CBS, 1963; *The Great Years* US C2L34, C2S834, 1964

'Serenata' *Olé* US MG 20988, SR 60988 Mercury; UK CLP 1818, CSD 1578 HMV, 1964

'Shrangri-La' *The Wonderful World Of Make Believe* US MG 20193; SR 60913 Mercury; UK CLP 1755, CSD 1553 HMV, 1964

'She Believes In Me' *Mathis Magic* US JC 36216; UK 86103 CBS, 1979; *Celebration* UK 10028 CBS, 1981

'Should I Wait' *Portrait Of Johnny* UK TFL 5153, STFL 571 Fontana; BPG 62077, SBPG 62077 CBS, 1961; *Portrait Of Johnny* US CL 1644, CS 8444, 1961; *Portrait Of Johnny* UK SHM 806 Hallmark, 1974; *The Johnny Mathis Collection* UK PDA 015 Hallmark, 1976

'Show And Tell' *Killing Me Softly With Her Song* US KC 32258; UK 65672 CBS, 1973

'Silent Night, Holy Night' *Merry Christmas* US CL 1195, CS 8021; UK TFL 5031 Fontana, 62806 CBS, 1958; *Merry Christmas* UK 62806 CBS, 1966; *Merry Christmas* UK 69217 CBS, 1975; *When A Child Is Born* UK 83266 CBS, 1978

'Silver Bells' *Merry Christmas* US CL 1195, CS 8021; UK TFL 5031 Fontana, 62806 CBS, 1958; *Merry Christmas* UK 62806 CBS, 1966; *Merry Christmas* UK 69217 CBS, 1975; *When A Child Is Born* UK 83266 CBS, 1978; *Christmas Album* UK 2094/0501 St Michael, 1978; *Johnny Mathis Sings Christmas Songs* UK 2188/2020 St Michael, 1980

'Since I Fell For You' *The First Time Ever I Saw Your Face* US KC 31342; UK 64930 CBS, 1972

'Sing' *Killing Me Softly With Her Song* US KC 32258; UK 65672 CBS, 1973

'Sky Full Of Rainbows' *The Wonderful World Of Make Believe* US MG 20193, SR 60913 Mercury; UK CLP 1755, CSD 1553 HMV, 1964

'Sleigh Ride' *Merry Christmas* US CL 1195, CS 8021; UK TFL 5031 Fontana, 62806 CBS, 1958; *Merry Christmas* UK 62806 CBS, 1966; *Merry Christmas* UK 69217 CBS, 1975; *Christmas Album* UK 2094/0501 St Michael, 1978; *When A Child Is Born* UK 83266 CBS, 1978; *Johnny Mathis Sings Christmas Songs* UK 2188/2020 St Michael, 1980

'Small World' *More Johnny's Greatest Hits* US CL 1344, CS 8150; UK 62774 CBS, 1959; *The Great Years* US C2L34, C2834, 1964; *All-Time Greatest Hits* UK 67253 CBS, 1972

'Smile' *I'll Buy You A Star* US CL 1623, CS 8423; UK TFL 5134, STFL 557 Fontana, 1961

'Solitaire' *Feelings* US PC 33887; UK 69180 CBS, 1975; *Tears And Laughter* UK 10019 CBS, 1980

'Someone' *More Johnny's Greatest Hits* UK STFL 517 Fontana, 1959; *More Johnny's Greatest Hits* TFL 5083 Fontana, 1959; *More Johnny's Greatest Hits* US CL 1344, CS 8150; UK 62774 CBS, 1959; *The Mathis Collection* UK 100030 CBS, 1977

'Something' *Raindrops Keep Fallin' On My Head* US C 1005; UK 64012 CBS, 1970; *Johnny Mathis* UK 2094/0102 St Michael, 1978

'Something I Dreamed Last Night' *Heavenly (US)/Ride On A Rainbow (UK)* US CL 1351, CS 8152; UK TFL 5061, STFL 516 Fontana, BPG 62064, SBPG 62064 CBS, 1959; *Heavenly And Faithfully* US CG 33621, 1975; *Heavenly* UK EMB 31084 Embassy, 1975

'Something's Coming' *The Shadow Of Your Smile* US MG 21073, SR 61073 Mercury; UK CLP 3556, CSD 3556 HMV, 1966

'Somethin's Goin' On' *Friends In Love* FC 37748; CBS 85652, 1982

'Somewhere' *Tender Is The Night* US MG 20890, SR 60890 Mercury; UK CLP 1721, CSD 1535 HMV, 1964

'Somewhere My Love' *The Impossible Dream* US CS 9872; UK 63718 CBS, 1969; *Johnny Mathis Sings The Great Songs* UK 88085 CBS, 1974; *Love Songs* UK EMB 31393 Embassy, 1976

'Song Of Joy' *Close To You (US)/The Long And Winding Road (UK)* US C 30210; UK 64176 CBS, 1970; *Tears And Laughter* UK 100019 CBS, 1980

'Song Sung Blue' *Song Sung Blue (US)/Make It Easy On Yourself (UK)* US KG 31626; UK 65161, 1972; *Johnny Mathis* UK 2094/0102 St Michael, 1978

'So Nice' *So Nice* US MG 21091, SR 61091, 1966; *The Impossible Dream* US CS 9872; UK 63718 CBS, 1969

'Sooner Or Later' *I'll Search My Heart* US CL 2143, CS 8943; UK BPG 62270, SBPG 62270 CBS, 1963

'Soul And Inspiration'/'Just Once In My Life' *Me And Mrs Jones* UK 65443 CBS, 1973

'Spanish Eyes' *Johnny Mathis Sings The Music Of Bert Kaempfert'* UK 63524 CBS, 1969; *Johnny Mathis Sings The Music Of Bacharach & Kaempfert* US G 30350; UK 66275 CBS, 1971; *Johnny Mathis Sings The Music Of Bert Kaempfert* UK EMB 31209 Embassy, 1975; *Misty* UK SHM 913 Hallmark, 1977

'Speak Softly Love' *The Mathis Collection* UK 100030 CBS, 1977; *The First Time Ever I Saw Your Face* US KC 31342; UK 64930 CBS, 1972

'Spring Is Here' *The Ballads Of Broadway* US CL 1506, 1960; *The Rhythms & Ballads Of Broadway* US C2L17, C2S883; UK SET 101 Fontana, 1960; *Ballads Of Broadway* US CL 2223, CS 9023, 1964

'Stairway To The Sea' *More Johnny's Greatest Hits* US CL 1344, CS 8150; UK 62774 CBS, 1959; *More Johnny's Greatest Hits* UK TFL 5083 Fontana, 1959; *More Johnny's Greatest Hits* UK STFL 517, 1959

'Stairway To The Stars' *I'll Buy You A Star* US CL 1623, CS 8423; UK TFL 5134, STFL 557 Fontana, 1961; *The Great Years* US C2L34, C2S834, 1964

'Starbright' *Portrait Of Johnny* UK TFL 5153, STFL 571 Fontana; BPG 62077, SBPG 62077 CBS, 1961; *Portrait Of Johnny* US CL 1644, CS 8444, 1961; *I'll Search My Heart* US CL 2143, CS 8943; UK BPG 62270, SBPG 62270 CBS, 1963; *Portrait Of Johnny* UK SHM 806 Hallmark, 1974; *The Johnny Mathis Collection* UK PDA 015 Hallmark, 1976; *Evergreens* UK 2188/8000 St Michael, 1980

'Stardust' *Feelings* US PC 33887; UK

69180 CBS, 1975; *The Mathis Collection* UK 100030 CBS, 1977; *Greatest Hits Vol 4* UK 86022 CBS, 1977; *Night And Day* UK 31863 CBS, 1980; *The First 25 Years, The Silver AA* US C2X 37440, 1981

'Star Eyes' *Johnny Mathis* US CL 887, 1956; *Johnny Mathis* UK TFL 5011 Fontana, 1957; *Johnny Mathis* US EN 13089 Encore, 1976

'Stars Fell On Alabama *Rapture* US CL 1915, CS 8715; UK BPG 62106, SBPG 62106 CBS, 1962

'Stay Warm' *Johnny's Mood* CL 1526, CS 8326, 1960

'Stella By Starlight' *Rapture* US CL 1915, CS 8715; UK BPG 62106, SBPG 62106 CBS, 1962; *The Great Years* US C2L34, C2S834, 1964

'Stop, Look, Listen To Your Heart' *I'm Coming Home* US KC 32435; UK 65690 CBS, 1973; *Celebration* UK 10028 CBS, 1981

'Story Of Our Love' *The Johnny Mathis Collection* UK PDA 015 Hallmark, 1976

'Stranger In Paradise' *Heavenly (US)/Ride On A Rainbow (UK)* US CL 1351, CS 8152; UK TFL 5061, STFL 516 Fontana, BPG 62064, SBPG 62064 CBS, 1959; *Johnny Mathis Sings The Great Songs* UK, 88085 CBS, 1974; *Heavenly* UK EMB 31084 Embassy, 1975; *Heavenly And Faithfully* US CG 33621, 1975; *Misty* UK SHM 913 Hallmark, 1977; 'Strangers In Dark Corners' *The Heart Of A Woman* US KC 33251; UK 80533 CBS, 1974

'Strangers In The Night' *Johnny Mathis Sings* US MG 21107, SR 61107, 1966; *Johnny Mathis Sings The Music Of Bert Kaempfert* UK 63524 CBS, 1969; *The Impossible Dream* US CS 9872; UK 63718 CBS, 1969; *Johnny Mathis Sings The Music Of Bacharach & Kaempfert* US G 30350; UK 66275 CBS, 1971;

Johnny Mathis Sings The Great Songs UK 88085 CBS, 1974; *The Music Of Bert Kaempfert* UK EMB 31209 Embassy, 1975; *Misty* UK SHM 913 Hallmark, 1977; *Evergreens* UK 2188/8000 St Michael, 1980

'Street Of Dreams' *Johnny Mathis* US CL 887, 1956; *Johnny Mathis* UK TFL 5011 Fontana, 1957; *The Great Years* US C2L34, C2S834, 1964; *Johnny Mathis* US EN 13089 Encore, 1976

'Sudden Love' *I'll Buy You A Star* US CL 1623, CS 8423; UK TFL 5134, STFL 577 Fontana, 1961

'Summer Breeze' *Me And Mrs Jones* UK 65443 CBS, 1973

'Sunny' *Johnny Mathis Sings* US MG 21107, SR 61107, 1966; *People* US CS 9871, 1969

'Swanee' *The Young Americans Presented By Johnny Mathis* US MG 21023, SR 61023 Mercury, 1965

'Sweet Child' *I'm Coming Home* US KC 32435; UK 65690 CBS, 1973

'Sweet Lorraine' *Swing Softly* US CL 1165, CS 8023; UK TFL 5039, STFL 500 Fontana, BPG 62062, SBPG 62062 CBS, 1958

'Sweet Love Of Mine' *Mathis Is* US 34441; UK 86023 CBS, 1977

'Sweet Surrender' *Me And Mrs Jones* UK 65443 CBS, 1973; *Sweet Surrender* UK 86036 CBS, 1977; *Celebration* UK 10028 CBS, 1981

'Sweet Thursday' *Johnny's Newest Hits* US CL 2016, CS 8816; UK BPG 62147, SBPG 62147 CBS, 1963; *The Great Years* US C2L34, C2S834, 1964

'Swing Low, Sweet Chariot' *Goodnight Dear Lord (US)/Heavenly (UK)* US CL 119, CS 8012; UK TFL 5023 Fontana, 1958

'Symphony' *The Sweetheart Tree (US)/Away From Home (UK)* US MG 21041, SR 61041 Mercury; UK CLP 1926, CSD 1638 HMV, 1965

T

'Taking A Chance On Love' *The Rhythms & Ballads Of Broadway* US C2L17, C2S 803; UK SER 101 Fontana, 1960; *The Ballads Of Broadway* US CL 1506, 1960; *The Ballads Of Broadway* US CL 2223, CS 9023, 1964

'Teacher, Teacher' *Johnny's Greatest Hits* UK TFL 5058 Fontana, 1958; *More Johnny's Greatest Hits* UK STFL 517, 1959; *More Johnny's Greatest Hits* US CL 1344, CS 8150; UK 62774 CBS, 1959

'Temptation' *Different Kinda Different* US JC 36505, 1980; *All For You* UK 86115 CBS, 1980

'Tender Is The Night' *Tender Is The Night* US MG 20890, SR 60890 Mercury; UK CLP 1721, CSD, 1535 HMV, 1964

'Tenderly' *Open Fire, Two Guitars* US CL 1270, CS 8056; UK TFL 5050, STFL 515 Fontana, BPG 62063, SBPG 62063 CBS, 1959; *Warm/Open Fire, Two Guitars* US GP 2, 1968; *Tenderly* KH 30917, 1971; *The Johnny Mathis Collection Vol 2* UK PDA 032 Hallmark, 1977

'Ten Times Forever More' *Love Story* US C 30499; UK 64334 CBS, 1971

'That Old Black Magic' *Wonderful, Wonderful* US CL 1028, CS 9046; UK TFL 5003 Fontana, 1957; *Mathis Magic* US JC 36216; UK 86103 CBS, 1979

'That's All' *Heavenly (US)/Ride On A Rainbow (UK)* US CL 1351, CS 8151; UK TFL 5061, STFL 516, BPG 62064, SBPG 62064 CBS, 1959; *Heavenly* UK EMB 31084 Embassy, 1975; *Heavenly And Faithfully* US CG 33621, 1975; *Misty* UK SHM 913 Hallmark, 1977; *Evergreens* UK 2188/8000 St Michael, 1980

'That's All She Wrote' *Feelings* US PC 33887; UK 69180 CBS, 1975

'That's The Way It Is' *Johnny's Newest Hits* US CL 2016, CS 8816; UK BPG 62147, SBPG 62147 CBS, 1963

'That's What Friends Are For' *That's What Friends Are For* US 35435; UK 86068 CBS, 1978

'The Best Days Of My Life' *The Best Days Of My Life* US JC 35649; UK 86080 CBS, 1979; *The Best Of Johnny Mathis 1975-1980* US JC 36871, 1980

'The Best Is Yet To Come' *I'll Buy You A Star* US CL 1623, CS 8423; UK TFL 5134, STFL 557 Fontana, 1961

'The Best Of Everything' *More Johnny's Greatest Hits* UK TFL 5083 Fontana, 1959; *I'll Search My Heart* US CL 2143, CS 8943; UK BPG 62270, SBPG 62270 CBS, 1963

'The Bottom Line' *The Best Days Of My Life* US JC 35649; UK 86080 CBS, 1979

'The Carol Of The Bells' *Sounds Of Christmas* US MG 20837, SR 60837 Mercury; UK CLP 1696, CSD 1521 HMV, 1963

'The Christmas Song' *Merry Christmas* US CL 1195, CS 8021; UK TFL 5031 Fontana, 62806 CBS, 1958; *Merry Christmas* UK 62806 CBS, 1966; *Merry Christmas* UK 69217, 1975; *When A Child Is Born* UK 83266 CBS, 1978; *Christmas Album* UK 2094/0501 St Michael, 1978; *Johnny Mathis Sings Christmas Songs* UK 2188/2020 St Michael, 1980

'The End Of A Love Affair' *This Is Love* US MG 20942, SR 60942 Mercury; UK CLP 1859, CSD 1600 HMV, 1964; *What'll I Do* US C 32963, 1974

'The End Of The World' *Those Were The Days* US CS 9705; UK 63427, 1968

'The 59th St Bridge Song (Feelin' Groovy)' *Those Were The Days* US CS 9705; UK 63457, 1968; *This Guy's In Love With You* US KH 31935

Harmony, 1973; *This Guy's In Love With You* UK SHM 872 Hallmark, 1975; *The Johnny Mathis Collection* UK PDA 015 Hallmark, 1976; *Evergreens* UK 2188/8000 St Michael, 1980

'The First Noel' *Merry Christmas* US CL 1195, CS 8021; UK TFL 5031 Fontana, 62806 CBS, 1958; *Merry Christmas* UK 62806 CBS, 1966; *Merry Christmas* UK 69217 CBS, 1975; *Christmas Album* UK 2094/0501 St Michael, 1978; *When A Child Is Born* UK 83266 CBS, 1978; *Johnny Mathis Sings Christmas Songs* UK 2188/2020 St Michael, 1980

'The First Time Ever I Saw Your Face' *The First Time Ever I Saw Your Face* US KC 31342; UK 64930 CBS, 1972; *Greatest Hits Vol 4* UK 86022 CBS, 1977

'The Flame Of Love' *More Johnny's Greatest Hits* UK TFL 5083 Fontana, 1959; *More Johnny's Greatest Hits* US CL 1344, CS 8150; UK 62774 CBS, 1959; *More Johnny's Greatest Hits* UK STFL 517, 1959; *Love Songs* UK EMB 31393 Embassy, 1976

'The Folks Who Live On The Hill' *Johnny's Mood* CL 1526, CS 8326, 1960

'The Greatest Gift' *Feelings* US PC 33887; UK 69180 CBS, 1975

'The Heart Of A Woman' *The Heart Of A Woman* US KC 33251; UK 80533 CBS, 1974

'The Hungry Years' *I Only Have Eyes For You* US PC 34117; UK 81329 CBS, 1976; *Tears And Laughter* UK 100019 CBS, 1980

'The Impossible Dream' *So Nice* US MG 21091, SR 61091, 1966; *The Impossible Dream* US CS 9872; UK 63718 CBS, 1969; *Johnny Mathis In Person* US KG 30979; UK 67231 CBS, 1972

'The Joy Of Loving You' *I'll Search My Heart* US CL 2143, CS 8943; UK BPG 62270, SBPG 62270 CBS, 1963

'The Lady Smiles' *Johnny Mathis Sings The Music Of Bert Kaempfert* UK 63524 CBS, 1969; *Johnny Mathis Sings The Music Of Bacharach & Kaempfert* US G 30350; UK 66275 CBS, 1971; *Johnny Mathis Sings The Music Of Bert Kaempfert* UK EMB 31209 Embassy, 1975

'The Last Time I Felt Like This' *The Best Days Of My Life* US JC 35649; UK 86080 CBS, 1979; *The Best Of Johnny Mathis 1975-1980* US JC 36871, 1980; *Celebration* UK 10028 CBS, 1981

'The Lights Of Rio' *Different Kinda Different* US JC 36505, 1980; *All For You* UK 86115 CBS, 1980

'The Little Drummer Boy' *Sounds Of Christmas* US MG 20837, SR 60837 Mercury; UK CLP 1696, CSD 1521 HMV, 1963; *Give Me Your Love For Christmas* US CS 9923, 1969; *Merry Christmas* UK 69217, 1975

'The Look Of Love' *Johnny Mathis Sings The Music Of Bacharach & Kaempfert* US G 30350; UK 66275 CBS, 1971; *Love Is Blue* US CS 9637; UK 63301, 1968; *Love Songs* UK EMB 31393 Embassy, 1976; *The Mathis Collection* UK 100030 CBS, 1977

'The Long And Winding Road' *Close To You (US)/The Long And Winding Road (UK)* US C 30210; UK 64176 CBS, 1970; *Johnny Mathis* UK 2094/0102 St Michael, 1978

'The Lord's Prayer' *Give Me Your Love For Christmas* US CS 9923, 1969

'The Lovely Things You Are' *Warm* UK RM 52064 CBS Realm, 1965; *Warm* US CL 1078, CS 8039; UK TFL 5015 STFL 510 Fontana, 1958; *Warm/Open Fire, Two Guitars* US GP 2, 1968; *Warm* UK EMB 31045

Embassy, 1974; *Warm* UK 31499 Embassy, 1977

'The Love Nest' *Rapture* US CL 1915, CS 8715; UK BPG 62106, SBPG 62106 CBS, 1962

'The More I See You' *Up, Up And Away* US CL 12726, CS 9526; UK 63104 CBS, 1968; *This Guy's In Love With You* US KH 31935 Harmony, 1973; *This Guy's In Love With You'* UK SHM 872 Hallmark, 1975; *The Johnny Mathis Collection* UK PDA 015 Hallmark, 1976

'The Morningside Of the Mountain' *Up, Up And Away* US CL 12726, CS 9526; UK 63104 CBS, 1968

'The Most Beautiful Girl In The World' *Johnny* US CL 2044, CS 8844; UK BPG 62172, SBPG 62172 CBS, 1963; *Sweet Surrender* UK 86036 CBS, 1977; *Hold Me, Thrill Me, Kiss Me* US PC 34872, 1977; *Tears And Laughter* UK 10019 CBS, 1980

'The Music Makes Me Dance' *So Nice* US MG 21091, SR 61091, 1966

'The Party's Over' *The Ballads Of Broadway* US CL 1506, 1964; *The Rhythms & Ballads Of Broadway* US C2L17, C2S803; UK SET 101 Fontana, 1964; *Ballads Of Broadway* US CL 2223, CS 9023, 1964; *The Mathis Collection* UK 100030 CBS, 1977

'The Riviera' *Live It UP!* US CL 1711, CS 8511; UK TFL 5177 Fontana, BPG 62105, SBPG 62105 CBS, 1962

'The Rosary' *Goodnight Dear Lord (US)/Heavenly (UK)* US CL 1119, CS 8012; UK TFL 5023 Fontana, 1958

'The Second Time Around' *Johnny Mathis Sings* US MG 21107, SR 611081 1967

'The Secret Of Christmas' *Sounds Of Christmas* US MG 20837, SR 60837 Mercury; UK CLP 1696, CSD 1521 HMV, 1963; *Christmas With Johnny Mathis* US KH 30864 Harmony; UK SHM 765 Hallmark, 1971

'The Shadow Of Your Smile' *The Shadow Of Your Smile* US MG 21073, SR 61073 Mercury; UK CLP 3556, CSD 3556 HMV, 1966; *People* US CS 9871, 1969

'The Skye Boat Song' *The Sweetheart Tree (US)/Away From Home (UK)* US MG 21041, SR 61041 Mercury; UK CLP 1926, CSD 1638 HMV, 1965

'The Sounds Of Christmas' *The Sounds Of Christmas* US MG 20837, SR 60837 Mercury; UK CLP 1696, CSD 1521 HMV, 1963; *Christmas With Johnny Mathis* US KH 30864 Harmony; UK SHM 765 Hallmark, 1971

'The Sound Of Music' *Romantically* US CL 2098, CS 8898; UK BPG 62202, SBPG 62202 CBS, 1963

'The Story Of Our Love' *Portrait Of Johnny* UK TFL 5153, STFL 571 Fontana, BPG 62077, SBPG 62077 CBS, 1961; *Portrait Of Johnny* US CL 1644, CS 8444, 1961; *Portrait Of Johnny* UK SHM 806 Hallmark, 1974

'The Summer Knows' *The First Time Ever I Saw Your Face* US KC 31342; UK 64930 CBS, 1972; *The Mathis Collection* UK 100030 CBS, 1977

'The Sweetheart Tree' *The Sweetheart Tree* US MG 21041, SR 61041 Mercury, 1965

'The Things I Might Have Been' *When Will I See You Again* US PC 33420; UK 80738 CBS, 1975

'The Times Will Change' *Johnny Mathis Sings The Music Of Bert Kaempfert'* UK 63524 CBS, 1969; *Johnny Mathis Sings The Music Of Bacharach & Kaempfert'* US G 30350; UK 66275 CBS, 1971; *Johnny Mathis Sings The Music Of Bert Kaempfert* UK EMB 31209 Embassy, 1975

'The Touch Of Your Lips' *This Is Love* US MG 20942, SR 60942 Mercury; UK CLP 1859, CSD 1600 HMV, 1964; *What'll I Do* US C 32963, 1974

'The Twelfth Of Never' *Johnny Mathis* UK TFL 5011 Fontana, 1957; *Johnny's Greatest Hits* UK TFL 5058 Fontana, 1958; *Johnny's Greatest Hits* US CL 1133, CS 8634, 1958; *The Great Years* US C2L34, C2S834, 1964; *Johnny's Greatest Hits* UK 62569 CBS, 1965; *Johnny's Greatest Hits* US PC 34667, 1977; *The Mathis Collection* UK 100030 CBS, 1977; *All-Time Greatest Hits* UK 67253 CBS, 1972; *Johnny Mathis In Person* US KG 30979; UK 67231 CBS, 1972

'The Very Thought Of You' *The Sweetheart Tree (US)/Away From Home (UK)* US MG 21041, SR 61041 Mercury; UK CLP 1926, CSD 1638 HMV, 1965; *The Impossible Dream* US CS 9872; UK 63718 CBS, 1969; *Johnny Mathis Sings The Great Songs* UK 88085 CBS, 1974

'The Way We Planned It' *The Heart Of A Woman* US KC 33251; UK 80533 CBS, 1974

'The Way We Were' *When Will I See You Again* US PC 33420; UK 80738 CBS, 1975; *The Mathis Collection* UK 100030 CBS, 1977; *Johnny Mathis* UK 2094/0102 St Michael, 1978

'The Way You Look Tonight' *The First 25 Years, The Silver AA* US C2X 37440, 1981

'The Windmills Of Your Mind' *Love Theme From 'Romeo & Juliet'* US CS 9909, 1969; *The Mathis Collection* UK 100030 CBS, 1977

'The World I Threw Away' *Love Theme From 'Romeo & Juliet'* US CS 9909, 1969

'The World I Used To Know' *Those Were The Days* US CS 9705; UK 63427 CBS, 1968

'The World Of Make Believe' *The World Of Make Believe* US MG 20193, SR 60913 Mercury; UK CLP 1755, CSD 1553 HMV, 1964

'The Young Americans' *The Young Americans Presented By Johnny Mathis* US MG 21023, SR 61023 Mercury, 1965

'Theme From Carnival' *Romantically* US CL 2098, CS 8898; UK BPG 62202, SBPG 62202 CBS, 1963

'Then I'll Be Tired Of You' *Warm* US CL 1078, CS 8039; UK TFL 5015, STFL 510 Fontana, 1958; *Warm* UK RM 52064 CBS Realm, 1965; *Warm/Open Fire, Two Guitars* US GP 2, 1968; *Warm* UK EMB 31045 Embassy, 1974; *Warm* UK 31499 Embassy, 1977

'There Goes My Heart' *Warm* US CL 1078, CS 8039; UK TFL 5015, STFL 510 Fontana, 1958; *Warm* UK RM 52064 CBS Realm, 1965; *Warm/Open Fire, Two Guitars* US GP 2, 1968; *Warm* UK EMB 31045 Embassy, 1974; *Misty* UK SHM 913 Hallmark, 1977; *Warm* UK 31499 Embassy, 1977

'There! I've Said It Again' *The First 25 Years, The Silver AA* US C2X 37440, 1981

'There's Always Something There To Remind Me' *Johnny Mathis Sings* US MG 21107, SR 61107

'There's No You' *Johnny's Mood* CL 1526, CS 8326, 1960

'There You Are' *Johnny's Newest Hits* US CL 2016, CS 8816; UK BPG 62147, SBPG 62147 CBS, 1963; *The Best Days Of My Life* US JC 35649; UK 86080 CBS, 1979

'They'll Say It's Wonderful' *Heavenly And Faithfully* US CG 33621, 1975

'They Long To Be Close To You' *Close To You (US)/The Long And Winding Road (UK)* US C 30210; UK 64176 CBS, 1970

'They Long To Be Close To You'/'We've Only Just Begun' (Medley) *Johnny Mathis In Person* US KG 30979; UK 67231 CBS, 1972

'They Long To Be Close To You' *Johnny Mathis Sings The Great Songs* UK 88085 CBS, 1974

'They Say It's Wonderful' *Heavenly (US)/Ride On A Rainbow (UK)* US CL 1351, CS 8152; UK TFL 5061, STFL 516 Fontana, BPG 62064, SBPG 62064 CBS, 1959

'This Guy's In Love With You' *Those Were The Days* US CS 9705; UK 63427 CBS, 1968; *Johnny Mathis Sings The Music Of Bacharach & Kaempfert* US G 30350; UK 66275 CBS, 1971; *The Greatest Hits Vol 3* UK 64651 CBS, 1971; *This Guy's In Love With You* US KH 31935 Harmony, 1973; *This Guy's In Love With You* UK SHM 872 Hallmark, 1975; *The Johnny Mathis Collection* UK PDA 015 Hallmark, 1976; *Love Songs* UK EMB 31393 Embassy, 1976

'This Heart Of Mine' *Swing Softly* US CL 1165, CS 8023; UK TFL 5039, STFL 500 Fontana, BPG 62062, SBPG 62062 CBS, 1958; *More Johnny's Greatest Hits* UK STFL 517 Fontana, 1959; *More Johnny's Greatest Hits* UK TFL 5083 Fontana, 1959

'This Is All I Ask' *Love Is Everything* US MG 20991, SR 20991 Mercury; UK CLP 3522, CSD 3522 HMV, 1965

'This Is Love' *The Sweetheart Tree (US)/Away From Home (UK)* US MG 21041, SR 61041 Mercury; UK CLP 1926, CSD 1638 HMV, 1965

'Those Were The Days' *Those Were The Days* US CS 9705; UK 63427 CBS, 1968; *This Guy's In Love With You* US KH 31935 Harmony, 1973; *Johnny Mathis Sings The Great Songs* UK 88085 CBS, 1974; *This Guy's In Love With You* UK SHM 872 Hallmark, 1975; *The Johnny Mathis Collection* UK PDA 015 Hallmark, 1976; *Night And Day* UK 31863 CBS, 1980

'Three Times A Lady' *Celebration* UK 10028 CBS, 1981; *All For You* UK

86115 CBS, 1980; *The First 25 Years, The Silver AA* US C2X 37440, 1981

'Till Love Touches Your Life' *You Light Up My Life* US JC 35259; UK 86055 CBS, 1978

'To Be In Love' *Swing Softly* US CL 1165, CS 8023; UK TFL 5039, STFL 500 Fontana, BPG 62062, SBPG 62062 CBS, 1958; *More Johnny's Greatest Hits* UK STFL 517 Fontana, 1959

'Tomorrow' *Hold Me, Thrill Me, Kiss Me* US PC 34872, 1977; *Sweet Surrender* UK 86036 CBS, 1977

'Tomorrow Song' *Tender Is The Night* US MG 20890, SR 60890 Mercury; UK CLP 1721, CSD 1535 HMV, 1964

'Tonight' *Faithfully* US CL 1422, CS 8219; UK TFL 5084, STFL 522 Fontana, BPG 62061, SBPG 62061 CBS, 1960; *The Great Years* US C2S 834, 1964; *Johnny Mathis In Person* US KG 30979; UK 67231 CBS, 1972; *This Guy's In Love With You* US KH 31935 Harmony, 1973; *This Guy's In Love With You* UK SHM 872 Hallmark, 1975; *Heavenly And Faithfully* US CG 33621, 1975; *The Johnny Mathis Collection* UK PDA 015 Hallmark 1976; *The Mathis Collection* UK 100030 CBS, 1977

'Too Close For Comfort' *Wonderful, Wonderful* US CL 1028, CS 9046; UK TFL 5003 Fontana, 1957

'Too Much, Too Little, Too Late' *You Light Up My Life* US JC 35259; UK 86055 CBS, 1978; *Tears And Laughter* UK 10019 CBS, 1980; *The Best Of Johnny Mathis 1975-1980* US JC 36871, 1980; *The First 25 Years, The Silver AA* US C2X 37440, 1981; *Celebration* UK 10028 CBS, 1981

'Too Much, Too Soon' *Live It UP!* US CL 1711, CS 8511; UK TFL 5177 Fontana, BPG 62105, SBPG 62105 CBS, 1962

'Too Young' *Song Sung Blue (US)/Make It Easy On Yourself (UK)*

US KG 31626; UK 65161 CBS, 1972; *Johnny Mathis Sings The Great Songs* UK 88085 CBS, 1974

'Too Young Too Go Steady' *Romantically* US CL 2098, CS 8898; UK BPG 62202, SBPG 62202 CBS, 1963

'To The Ends Of The Earth' *Mathis Magic* US JC 36216; UK 86103 CBS, 1979

'Touching Me With Love' *That's What Friends Are For* US 35435; UK 86068 CBS, 1978

'Traces' *Love Story* US C 30499; UK 64334 CBS, 1971

'Try A Little Tenderness' *Away From Home* UK CLP 1926, CSD 1638 HMV, 1965

'Turn Around, Look At Me' *Those Were The Days* US CS 9705; UK 63427 CBS, 1968; *Johnny Mathis Greatest Hits Vol 3* UK 64651 CBS, 1971; *This Guy's In Love With You* US KH 31935 Harmony, 1973; *This Guy's In Love With You* UK SHM 872 Hallmark, 1975; *The Johnny Mathis Collection* UK PDA 015 Hallmark 1976; *Evergreens* UK 2188/8000 St Michael, 1980

U

'Unaccustomed As I Am' *Johnny's Newest Hits* US CL 2016, CS 8816; UK BPG 62147, SBPG 62147 CBS, 1963; *The Great Years* US C2L834, 1964

'Under A Blanket Of Blue' *This Is Love* US MG 20942, SR 60942 Mercury; UK CLP 1859, CSD 1600 HMV, 1964; *What'll I Do* US C 32663, 1974

'Until It's Time For You To Go' *Close To You (US)/The Long And Winding Road (UK)* US C 30210; UK 64176 CBS, 1970; *Johnny Mathis* UK 2094/0102 St Michael, 1978

'Until You Come Back To Me' *That's*

What Friends Are For US JC 35435; UK 86068 CBS, 1978

'Up, Up And Away' *Up, Up And Away* US CL 2726, CS 9526; UK 63104 CBS, 1968; *Johnny Mathis Greatest Hits Vol 3* UK 64651 CBS, 1971; *This Guy's In Love With You* US KH 31935 Harmony, 1975; *This Guy's In Love With You* UK SHM 872 Hallmark, 1975; *The Johnny Mathis Collection* UK PDA 015 Hallmark, 1976; *Evergreens* UK 2188/8000 St Michael, 1980

V

'Venus' *Love Is Blue* US CS 9637; UK 63301 CBS, 1968; *All-Time Greatest Hits* UK 67253 CBS 1972

'Very Much In Love' *More Johnny's Greatest Hits* UK TFL 5083 Fontana, 1959; *More Johnny's Greatest Hits* UK STFL 517 Fontana, 1959; *More Johnny's Greatest Hits* US CL 1344, CS 8150; UK 62774 CBS, 1959

W

'Wake The Town And Tell The People' *Johnny Mathis Sings* US MG 21107, SR 61107, 1967

'Walk On By' *Love Is Blue* US CS 9637; UK 63301 CBS, 1968; *Johnny Mathis Sings The Music Of Bacharach & Kaempfert* US G 30350; UK 66275 CBS, 1971; *Johnny Mathis Sings The Great Songs* UK 88085 CBS, 1974

'Warm' *Warm* US CL 1078, CS 8039; UK TFL 5015, STFL 510 Fontana, 1958; *Warm* UK RM 52064 CBS Realm, 1965; *Warm/Open Fire, Two Guitars* US GP 2, 1968; *Warm* UK EMB 31045 Embassy, 1974; *Warm* UK 31499 Embassy, 1977; *Friends In Love* FC 37748; CBS 85652, 1982

'Warm And Tender' *Johnny's Greatest Hits* UK TFL 5058 Fontana, 1958; *Johnny's Greatest Hits* US CL 1133, CS 8634, 1958; *Johnny's*

Greatest Hits UK 62569 CBS, 1965; *Johnny's Greatest Hits* US PC 34677, 1977

'Warm And Willing' *I'll Buy You A Star* US CL 1623, CS 8423; UK TFL 5134, STFL 577 Fontana, 1961; *Johnny Mathis* US KH 30017 Harmony; UK CHM 684 Hallmark, 1970

'Wasn't The Summer Short' *Johnny's Newest Hits* US CL 2016, CS 8816; UK BPG 62147, SBPG 62147 CBS, 1963

'Watch What Happens' *Raindrops Keep Fallin' On My Head* US CS 1005; UK 64012 CBS, 1970

'Wave' *Close To You (US)/The Long And Winding Road (UK)* US C 30210; UK 64176 CBS, 1970

'We' *Love Theme From 'Romeo & Juliet'* US CS 9909, 1969

'Weaver Of Dreams' *Johnny* US CL 2044; CS 8844; UK BPG 62172, SBPG 62172 CBS, 1963

'We Can Work It Out' *You've Got A Friend* US C 30740; UK 64448 CBS, 1971; *Johnny Mathis* UK 2094/0102 St Michael, 1978

'Wendy' *The Heart Of A Woman* US KC 33251; UK 80533 CBS, 1974

'We're All Alone' *Hold Me, Thrill Me, Kiss Me* US PC 34872, 1977; *Sweet Surrender* UK 86036 CBS, 1977; *Celebration* UK 10028 CBS, 1981

'We're In Love' *The Best Days Of My Life* US JC 35649; UK 86080 CBS, 1979

'We've Only Just Begun' *Love Story* US C 30499; UK 64334 CBS, 1971; *The Mathis Collection* UK 100030 CBS, 1977; *Johnny Mathis* UK 2094/0102 St Michael, 1978

'What Are You Doing New Year's Eve?' *Give Me Your Love For Christmas* US CS 9923, 1969

'What Are You Doing The Rest Of Your Life' *Love Story* US C 30499; UK 64334 CBS, 1971; *The Mathis Collection* UK 10003 CBS, 1977

'What Child Is This' *Merry Christmas* US CL 1195, CS 8021; UK TFL 5031 Fontana, 62806 CBS, 1958; *Merry Christmas* UK 62806 CBS, 1966; *Merry Christmas* UK 69217 CBS, 1975; *When A Child Is Born* UK 83266 CBS, 1978; *Christmas Album* UK 2094/0501 St Michael, 1978; *Johnny Mathis Sings Christmas Songs* UK 2188/2020 St Michael, 1980

'What Do You Do With The Love' *Celebration* UK 10028 CBS, 1981

'What Do You Feel In Your Heart' *This Is Love* US MG 20942, SR 60942 Mercury; UK CLP 1859, CSD 1600 HMV, 1964

'What I Did For Love' *Feelings* US PC 33887; UK 69180 CBS, 1975; *The Mathis Collection* UK 10003 CBS, 1977; *99 Miles From LA* UK 2188/2010 St Michael, 1980; *The Best Of Johnny Mathis 1975-1980* US JC 36871, 1980

'What'll I Do' *Warm* US CL 1078, CS 8039; UK TFL 5015, STFL 510 Fontana, 1958; *Warm* UK RM 52064 CBS Realm, 1965; *Warm/Open Fire, Two Guitars* US GP 2, 1968; *Warm* UK EMB 31045 Embassy, 1974; *What'll I Do* US C 32963, 1973; *Warm* UK 31499 Embassy, 1977; *Misty* UK SHM 913 Hallmark, 1977

'What Now My Love' *So Nice* US MG 21091, SR 61091, 1966

'What's Forever For' *Friends In Love* FC 37748; CBS 85652, 1982

'What's New At The Zoo' *The Young Americans Presented By Johnny Mathis* US MG 21023, SR 61023 Mercury, 1965

'What The World Needs Now Is Love' *So Nice* US MG 21091, SR 61091, 1966; *People* US CS 9871, 1969

'What To Do About Love' *I'll Search My Heart* US CL 2143, CS 8943; UK BPG 62270, SBPG 62270 CBS, 1963

'What Will My Mary Say' *Johnny's Newest Hits* US CL 2016; CS 8816; UK BPG 62147, SBPG 62147 CBS, 1963; *The Great Years* US C2L34, C2S834, 1964; *All-Time Greatest Hits* UK 67253 CBS, 1972

'When A Child Is Born' *I Only Have Eyes For You* US PC 34117; UK 81329 CBS, 1976; *Greatest Hits Vol 4* UK 86022 CBS, 1977; *The Mathis Collection* UK 10003 CBS, 1977; *When A Child Is Born* UK 83266 CBS, 1978; *The Best Of Johnny Mathis 1975-1980* US JC 36871, 1980; *Celebration* UK 10028 CBS, 1981

'When I Am With You' *Johnny Mathis* UK TFL 5011 Fontana, 1957; *Johnny's Greatest Hits* UK TFL 5058 Fontana, 1958; *Johnny's Greatest Hits* US CL 1133, CS 8634, 1958; *Johnny's Greatest Hits* UK 62569 CBS, 1965; *Johnny's Greatest Hits* US PC 34667, 1977

'When I Fall In Love' *Open Fire, Two Guitars* US CL 1270, CS 8056; UK TFL 5050, STFL 515 Fontana, BPG 62063, SBPG 62063 CBS, 1959; *The Great Years* US C2L34, C2S834, 1964; *Warm/Open Fire, Two Guitars* US GP 2, 1968; *Tenderly* KH 30917, 1971, *The Johnny Mathis Collection Vol 2* UK PDA 032 Hallmark, 1977; *Evergreens* UK 2188/8000 St Michael, 1980

'When I Look Into Your Eyes' *Up, Up And Away* US CL 2726, CS 9526; UK 63104 CBS, 1968

'When I Need You' *Hold Me, Thrill Me, Kiss Me* US PC 34872, 1977; *Sweet Surrender* UK 86036 CBS, 1977; *99 Miles From LA* UK 2188/2010 St Michael, 1980; *Celebration* UK 10028 CBS, 1981

'When My Sugar Walks Down The Street' *I'll Buy You A Star* US CL 1623, CS 8423; UK TFL 5134, STFL 557 Fontana, 1961

'When Sunny Gets Blue' *Johnny's Greatest Hits* UK TFL 5058 Fontana, 1958; *Johnny's Greatest Hits* US CL 1133, CS 8634, 1958; *Johnny's Greatest Hits* UK 62569 CBS, 1965; *Johnny Mathis In Person* US KG 30979; UK 67231 CBS, 1972; *All-Time Greatest Hits* UK 67253 CBS, 1972; *Johnny's Greatest Hits* US PC 34667, 1977; *The First 25 Years, The Silver AA* C2X 37440, 1981

'When The Lovin' Goes Out Of The Livin'' *Friends In Love* FC 37748; CBS 85652, 1982

'When The World Was Young' *Johnny* US CL 2044, CS 8844; UK BPG 62172, SBPG 62172 CBS, 1963

'When Will I See You Again' *When Will I See You Again* US PC 33420; UK 80738 CBS, 1975; *Greatest Hits Vol 4* UK 86022 CBS, 1977

'When You Wish Upon A Star' *The Wonderful World Of Make Believe* US MG 20193, SR 60913 Mercury; UK CLP 1755, CSD 1553 HMV, 1964

'Where Are The Words' *Up, Up And Away* US CL 2726, CS 9526; UK 63104 CBS, 1968

'Where Are You?' *Faithfully* US CL 1422, CS 8219; UK TFL 5084, STFL 522; BPG 62061, SBPG 62061 CBS, 1960; *Johnny Mathis* US KH 30017 Harmony; UK CHM 684 Hallmark, 1970

'Where Are You Going' *Heavenly And Faithfully* CG 33621, 1975

'Where Can I Go?' *Goodnight Dear Lord (US)/Heavenly (UK)* US CL 1119, CS 8012; UK TFL 5023 Fontana, 1958

'Where Do You Think You're Going' *Faithfully* US CL 1422, CS 8219; UK TFL 5084, STFL 522; BPG 62061; SBPG 62061, 1960; *Heavenly And Faithfully* US CG 33621, 1975

'Where Is Love?' *Tender Is The Night* US MG 20890, SR 60890 Mercury; UK CLP 1721, CSD 1535 HMV, 1964

'Where Is The Love' *Song Sung Blue (US)/Make It Easy On Yourself (UK)* US KG 31626; UK 65161 CBS, 1972

'Where Or When' *You Light Up My Life* US JC 35259; UK 86055 CBS 1978

'Wherever You Are It's Spring' *I'll Search My Heart* US CL 2143, CS 8943; UK BPG 62270, SBPG 62270 CBS, 1963

'While We're Young' *Warm* US CL 1078, CS 8039; UK TFL 5015, STFL 510 Fontana, 1958; *Warm* UK RM 52064 CBS Realm, 1965; *Warm/Open Fire, Two Guitars* US GP 2, 1968; *Warm* UK EMB 31045 Embassy, 1974; *Warm* UK 31499 Embassy, 1977; *Portrait Of Johnny* US CL 1644, CS 8444, 1961; *Portrait Of Johnny* UK TFL 5153, STFL 571 Fontana, BPG 62077, SBPG 62077 CBS, 1961; *Portrait Of Johnny* UK SHM 806 Hallmark, 1974; *The Johnny Mathis Collection* UK PDA 015 Hallmark, 1976

'White Christmas' *Merry Christmas* US CL 1195, CS 8021; UK TFL 5031 Fontana, 62806 CBS, 1958; *Merry Christmas* UK 62806 CBS, 1966; *Merry Christmas* UK 69217 CBS, 1975; *Christmas Album* UK 2094/0501 St Michael, 1978; *When A Child Is Born* UK 83266 CBS, 1978; *Johnny Mathis Sings Christmas Songs* UK 2188/2020 St Michael, 1980

'What Can I Say' *Johnny Mathis Sings* US MG 21107, SR 61107, 1967

'Who Can I Turn To' *Johnny Mathis Sings* US MG 2KK07, SR 61107, 1967

'Why Can't I Touch You?' *Close To You (US)/The Long And Winding Road (UK)* US C30210; UK 64176 CBS, 1970

'Why Not' *Live It UP!* US CL 1711, CS 8511; UK TFL 5177 Fontana, BPG 62105, SBPG 62105 CBS, 1962

'Wild Flower' *Killing Me Softly With His Song* US KC 32258; UK 65672 CBS, 1973

'Wild Is The Wind' *Johnny Mathis* UK TFL 5011 Fontana, 1957; *Johnny's Greatest Hits* UK TFL 5058 Fontana, 1958; *Johnny's Greatest Hits* US CL 1133, CS 8634, 1958; *Johnny's Greatest Hits* UK 62569 CBS, 1965; *All-Time Greatest Hits* UK 67253 CBS, 1972; *Johnny Mathis In Person* US KG 30979; UK 67231 CBS, 1972; *Johnny's Greatest Hits* US PC 34667, 1977

'Will I Find My Love Today' *Wonderful, Wonderful* US CL 1028, CS 9046; UK TFL 5003 Fontana, 1957

'Winter' *The Young Americans Presented By Johnny Mathis* US MG 21023, SR 61023 Mercury, 1965

'Winter Wonderland' *Merry Christmas* US CL 1195, CS 8021; UK TFL 5031 Fontana, 62806 CBS, 1958; *Merry Christmas* UK 62806 CBS, 1966; *Merry Christmas* UK 69217 CBS, 1975; *The Mathis Collection* UK 10003 CBS, 1977; *Christmas Album* UK 2094/0501 St Michael, 1978; *When A Child Is Born* UK 83266 CBS, 1978; *Johnny Mathis Sings Christmas Songs* UK 2188/2020 St Michael, 1980

'Without Her' *Love Theme From 'Romeo & Juliet'* US CS 9909, 1969

'Without You' *Olé* US MG 20988, SR 60988 Mercury; UK CLP 1818, CSD 1578 HMV, 1964; *The First Time Ever I Saw Your Face* US KC 31342; UK 64930 CBS, 1972; *Tears And Laughter* UK 10010 CBS, 1980

'With You I'm Born Again' *The Best Of Johnny Mathis 1975-1980* US JC 36871, 1980; *Different Kinda Different* US JC 36505, 1980; *All For You* UK 86115 CBS, 1980; *Celebration* UK 10028 CBS, 1981

'Woman, Woman' *The Heart Of A Woman* US KC 33251; UK 80533 CBS, 1974

'Wonderful, Wonderful' *Johnny's Greatest Hits* UK TFL 5058 Fontana, 1958; *Johnny's Greatest Hits* USCL 1133, CS 8634, 1958; *The Great Years* US C2L34, C2S834, 1964; *Johnny's Greatest Hits* UK 62569 CBS, 1965; *All-Time Greatest Hits* UK 67253 CBS, 1972; *Johnny Mathis In Person* US KG 30979; UK 67231 CBS, 1972; *The Mathis Collection* UK 10003 CBS, 1977; *Johnny's Greatest Hits* US PC 34667, 1977; *Celebration* UK 10028 CBS, 1981

'Wonderland By Night' *Johnny Mathis Sings The Music Of Bert Kaempfert* UK 63524, 1969; *Johnny Mathis Sings The Music Of Bert Kaempfert* UK EMB 31209 Embassy, 1975

'World Of Laughter' *Mathis Is* US 34441; UK 86023 CBS, 1977

'Would You Like To Spend The Night With Me' *The Best Days Of My Life* UK JC 35649; UK 86080 CBS, 1979; *Night And Day* UK 31863 CBS, 1980

Y

'Year By Year' *Wonderful, Wonderful* US CL 1028, CS 9046; UK TFL 5003 Fontana, 1957

'Yellow Roses On Her Gown' *I Only Have Eyes For You* US PC 34117; UK 81329 CBS, 1976

'Yellow Days' *Close To You (US)/The Long And Winding Road (UK)* US C 30210; UK 64176 CBS, 1970; *Night And Day* UK 31863 CBS, 1980

'Yesterday' *The Shadow Of Your Smile* US MG 21073; SR 61073 Mercury; UK CLP 3556, CSD 3556 HMV, 1966

'Yesterday When I Was Young' *Love Theme From 'Romeo & Juliet'* US CS 9909, 1969; *Night And Day* UK 31863 CBS, 1980

'You And Me Against The Rain' *When*

Will I See You Again US PC 33420; UK 80738 CBS, 1975

'You Are Beautiful' *More Johnny's Greatest Hits* US CL 1344, CS 8150; UK 62774 CBS, 1959; *More Johnny's Greatest Hits* UK TFL 5083 Fontana, 1959

'You Are Everything' *More Johnny's Greatest Hits* US CL 1344, CS 8150; UK 62774 CBS, 1959; *More Johnny's Greatest Hits* UK STFL 517 Fontana, 1959; *More Johnny's Greatest Hits* UK TFL 5083 Fontana, 1959

'You Are The Sunshine Of My Life' *Killing Me Softly With Her Song* US KC 32258; UK 65672 CBS, 1973; *Night And Day* UK 31863 CBS, 1980; *Tears And Laughter* UK 10019 CBS, 1980

'You Better Go Now' *Faithfully* US CL 1422, CS 8219; UK TFL 5084 Fontana, BPG 62061, SBPG 62061 CBS, 1960; *This Guy's In Love With You* US KH 31935 Harmony, 1973; *Heavenly And Faithfully* US CG 33621, 1975

'You'd Be So Nice To Come Home To' *Swing Softly* US CL 1165, CS 8023; UK TFL 5039, STFL 500, BPG 62062, SBPG 62062 CBS, 1958

'You Do Something To Me' *The Rhythms Of Broadway* US CL 1507, 1960; *The Rhythms & Ballads Of Broadway* US C2L17, C 2803; UK SER 101 Fontana, 1964; *Rhythms Of Broadway* US C 12224, CS 9024, 1964; *Johnny Mathis Sings Of Love* UK SHM 749 Hallmark, 1972; *The Johnny Mathis Collection Vol 2* UK PDA 032 Hallmark, 1977

'You Hit The Spot' *Swing Softly* US CL 1165, CS 8023; UK TFL 5039, STFL 500 Fontana; BPG 62062, SBPG 62062 CBS, 1958

'You Light Up My Life' *You Light Up My Life* US JC 35259, UK 86055, 1978; *Tears And Laughter* UK 10019 CBS, 1980; *The Best Of Johnny Mathis 1975-1980* US JC 36871, 1980; *99*

Miles From LA UK 2188/2010 St Michael, 1980

'You'll Never Know' *Open Fire, Two Guitars* US CL 1270, CS 8056; UK TFL 5050, STFL 515 Fontana, BPG 62063, SBPG 62063 CBS, 1959; *Warm/Open Fire, Two Guitars* US GP 2, 1968; *Tenderly* KH 30917, 1971; *The Johnny Mathis Collection Vol 2* UK PDA 032 Hallmark, 1977

'You Love Me' *This Is Love* US MG 20842, SR 60942 Mercury; UK CLP 1859, CSD 1600 HMV, 1964

'You Make Me Think About Me' *Those Were The Days* US CS 9705; UK 63427 CBS, 1968

'Young And Foolish' *Love Is Everything* US MG 20991, SR 20991 Mercury; UK CLP 3522, CSD 3522 HMV, 1965

'You're A Lady' *Me And Mrs Jones* UK 65443 CBS, 1973

'You're All I Need To Get By' *That's What Friends Are For* US JC 35259; UK 86068 CBS, 1978

'You're A Special Part Of My Life' *That's What Friends Are For'* US JC 35259; UK 86068 CBS, 1978

'You're As Right As Rain' *When Will I See You Again* US PC 33420; UK 80738, 1975

'You Saved My Life' *Mathis Magic* US JC 36216; UK 86103 CBS, 1979; *Celebration* UK 10028 CBS, 1981

'You Set My Heart To Music' *Portrait Of Johnny* UK TFL 5153, STFL 571 Fontana, BPG 62077, SBPG 62077 CBS, 1961; *Portrait Of Johnny* US CL 1644, CS 8444, 1961; *Portrait Of Johnny* UK SHM 806 Hallmark, 1974; *The Johnny Mathis Collection* UK PDA 015 Hallmark, 1976; *Evergreens* UK 2188/8000 St Michael, 1980

'You Stepped Out Of A Dream' *Wonderful, Wonderful* US CL 1028, CS 9046; UK TFL 5003 Fontana, 1957

'You've Come Home' *Rapture* US CL 1915, CS 8715; UK BPG 62106, SBPG 62106 CBS, 1962

'You've Got A Friend' *You've Got A Friend (Today's Greatest Hits)* US C 30740; UK 64448 CBS, 1971; *Johnny Mathis* UK 2094/0102 St Michael, 1978; *Evergreens* UK 2188/8000 St Michael, 1980

MOTION PICTURES

Films Johnny appeared in:

1957
LIZZIE (MGM):
'It's Not For Me To Say', 'Warm And Tender'

1958
A CERTAIN SMILE (20th Century-Fox):
'A Certain Smile'

Films that used Johnny's voice over the credits, or otherwise:

1957
WILD IS THE WIND (Paramount):
'Wild Is The Wind'

1959
THE BEST OF EVERYTHING (20th Century-Fox):
'The Best Of Everything'

1967
THE BIGGEST BUNDLE OF THEM ALL (MGM):
'Most Of All There's You'

1973
WALKING TALL:
'Walking Tall'

1977
CLOSE ENCOUNTERS OF THE THIRD KIND:
'Chances Are'

1978
SAME TIME NEXT YEAR:
'The Last Time I Felt Like This'

Johnny sang at these Academy
Awards:

Awards for 1957, held in 1958:
'Wild Is The Wind'. From WILD IS THE
WIND

Awards for 1961, held in 1962:
'Love Theme From El Cid' (aka 'The
Falcon And The Dove'). From EL CID

Awards for 1971, held in 1972:

'Life Is What You Make It'. From
KOTCH

Awards for 1978, held in 1979:
'The Last Time I Felt Like This'. From
SAME TIME NEXT YEAR

TELEVISION SPECIALS

USA

1975
The Mathis Session

1975
Johnny Mathis In Concert (With The
Edmonton Symphony Orchestra)

1975
Johnny Mathis In The Canadian
Rockies

1977
The Johnny Mathis Christmas Special

UK

December 1962
Johnny Mathis

May 1965
Presenting Johnny Mathis

October 1967
Johnny Mathis Starring In
International Cabaret

October 1974
The Johnny Mathis Show

July 1975
Johnny Mathis In Concert

May 1977
Johnny Mathis

October 1978
The Mathis Collection

October 1981
The Mathis Magic

UK VISITS

July/August 1961
The first tour.
TV Debut – *Personal Appearance*
(Granada).

Nov/December 1962
The second tour.
TV Special – *Johnny Mathis* (BBC).

May 1965
Recorded album 'Away From Home'
with producer Norman Newell.
TV Special – *Presenting Johnny
Mathis* (BBC).

July/August 1966
Talk Of The Town Cabaret.
Prince Of Wales Theatre.
TV Show – *Something Special* (BBC).
(All performances with Our Young
Generation).

October 1967
Talk Of The Town Cabaret.
TV Show – *International Cabaret*
(BBC).
(Johnny performed on the last
voyage of the Queen Mary –
departing from Southampton on

October 31, arriving at Long Beach, California 39 days later).

November 1968
Tour.

Feb/March 1971
Tour.

Aug/September 1972
Tour.

Aug/September 1973
Tour.

Sept/October 1974
Tour.
TV Concert – *Johnny Mathis Show* (BBC 2) – (from Apollo Centre, Glasgow).
TV Golf Tournament – Tournberry, Scotland.

March 1975
TV – *Top Of The Pops* ('Stone In Love'). Lulu Show.

July 1975
TV – *In Concert, Musical Time Machine, International Pop Prom.*

March/April
Tour.

Oct/November 1976
TV – *Top Of The Pops* ('When A Child Is Born').
(Johnny travelled to Germany to record a TV concert there).

April/May 1977
Tour.
TV Special – *Johnny Mathis* (BBC).

April 9, 1978
Supernight – London Palladium.

Sept/October 1978
Tour.
TV Spectacular – *The Mathis Collection* (BBC).

August 1979
TV - *Top Of The Pops* ('Gone, Gone, Gone').

April/May 1980
Tour.

Sept/October 1981
Tour.
TV 3-Part Special – *The Mathis Magic* (BBC).

April/May 1983
Tour.

This list does not include television, radio and press interviews which Johnny gave on his various trips nor a complete guide to his general television appearances.

PEOPLE, PLACES AND EVENTS

An A to Z of some people, places and facts in Johnny's career.

A

A Certain Smile: 20th Century-Fox film. It opened in New York, July 31st, 1958. The premiere benefited the Nephrosis Foundation of New York. Johnny sang the theme song. It was this film theme which established him as a potential major artist in Britain.
Alabama; Birmingham, USA: Johnny appeared at the Civic Theatre, August 5th, 1963, in the first integrated show 'A Salute To Freedom 1963'.
Alda, Alan: He was the star of the movie *Same Time Next Year*. The soundtrack featured Johnny and Jane Olivor singing the title theme.
Avakian, George: CBS record executive who saw Johnny at the 440 Club. He signed him to Columbia-CBS records.

B

Baker, Jo: President of the British fan club, The Mathis Connection, which brings together and supplies relevant information to fans of Johnny.

Barber, Audrey: Co-ordinator for Johnny's British tours from mid-seventies.

Barnett, James: Past musical director-arranger of Johnny's.

Baverstock, Jack: A&R head at Fontana during Johnny's release on the label. Fontana was issued by Philips.

Bell, Thom: Famous black American producer-writer who – among others – was the man behind many successful acts like The Stylistics, Ronnie Dyson, Harold Melvin and the Bluenotes, The O'Jays, and The Delfonics. His first production with Johnny was 'I'm Coming Home' and this gave Johnny's career in the mid-seventies a new lease of life with a major push into the general black music market.

Beverly Hilton Hotel: This was the location of the twenty-fifth Anniversary Dinner.

Birmingham, UK: The British Johnny Mathis Connection gave a sum of money which provided a bed for a child in the kidney unit.

Black Hawk: This was the nightclub which the Nogas ran and where Helen, who became Johnny's manager, first heard him sing.

Blau, Ed: Johnny's attorney and legal adviser.

Derek, Block: A successful British promoter, he is responsible for Johnny's British tours.

Bolougne, Johnny: He was a fellow athlete with Johnny at State College, San Francisco, and he obtained musical work for Johnny at a local area club.

Bullard, Joan: She was publicist to Johnny in the seventies.

Burnier, Jeannine: A popular American comedienne who has supported Johnny in concert for the last ten years in America.

C

Carroll, Diahann: Johnny guested on her TV mini-series and she has been a guest on his TV specials. Johnny sang at her husband's funeral.

Carson, Johnny: He is a long-lasting and popular American-TV celebrity with the famous *Tonight* show on which Johnny has often guested.

Chartwell Agency: The Agency has handled Johnny's US touring arrangements for a considerable time.

Clark, Dick: American DJ and TV Presenter. Johnny often appeared on his show, which was aimed at the US teenager. On one *American Grandstand* Johnny told him he had contemplated being an English teacher.

Cole, Nat 'King': The late revered American jazz pianist and singer was much admired by Johnny. Johnny guested on daughter Natalie's TV special.

Columbia: The US record company giant which signed Johnny and has issued his material since 1956 save for a brief period in the sixties. Columbia trades in Britain under CBS.

Copacabana: A famous New York club – Johnny cancelled his engagement at the venue in February, 1962 owing to a back injury.

Cowan, Ralph: An American artist who has painted Johnny on many occasions. Many of his works can be seen at Johnny's business offices or on some album covers.

Cox, Connie: She was the lady who gave Johnny his early vocal lessons.

D

Dale, Fred: He is with the Chartwell Agency, which organised Johnny's

US touring activities.

Davidson, John: A singer and TV personality, Davidson was guest on Johnny's 1975 TV special – *The Mathis Session.* John appeared on his chat show early in 1981.

Dee, Ann: She was a musical talent scout who heard Johnny in a San Francisco dockside bar singing 'My Blue Heaven'. She told him she might be able to offer him a singing engagement and suggested he might ring her at the 440 Club the following day. He did.

Dilbeck, Mike: He was Columbia's West Coast VP of Artists and Repertoire at the time of Johnny's work with Deniece Williams.

Dorothy Chandler Pavillion: It is part of the L.A. Music Centre. Johnny was the first pop singer to perform there and did so for five evenings.

Douglas, Mike: American chat-show host on whose show John has often appeared. Douglas had a co-host who stayed with him for a week's run. Johnny often undertook this function. Mike and Johnny are firm friends and, through Douglas, John has become an avid golfer.

E

Eckstine, Billy: A famous US singer who knew Johnny's dad and the young John. Johnny has called him a 'second father'.

Edmonds, Noel: A British radio and television personality who interviewed John for *The Mathis Magic* TV presentation (BBC). On his programme, May 10, 1982 (British date), Johnny told him: 'I'm nervous, I'm insecure, I'm shy and not at all comfortable singing in front of people.'

EMI: This major British record company issued Johnny's records during a period in the sixties when the artist was released by Mercury in the States.

F

Farber, Morton H: John's attorney at the time of his controversial BBC TV *Juke Box Jury* programme in 1962. It was Farber who issued a statement in an effort to quell a rising crescendo of indignation from the British press and elsewhere.

440 Club: This was the club in which Columbia record executive George Avakian heard Johnny sing, prior to signing him for Columbia.

Francis Langford Show: One of the many American-TV shows on which Johnny has made appearances but noted here because Johnny in 1960 danced a routine 'Putting On The Ritz'.

G

Ganduglia, Jimmy: Johnny's present Musical Director. His association with the artist began in 1978.

Gary Cheses Entertainment Inc: The group has been associated with Johnny's musical presentations over the years in the States.

Gentleman's Quarterly: In April, 1980, Johnny posed for the magazine as a male model of Jean-Paul Germain's clothing.

Gillespie, Dizzy: A famed US jazz trumpeter who knew Johnny's father and encouraged the young Mathis in his singing and musical listening.

Glasser, Martha: Erroll Garner's manager who heard Johnny sing some songs at the end of Garner's set at the Blackhawk Club, 1956 and who, as Garner, became a firm friend of John.

Global Records: This company was formed by Johnny in the early sixties.

Gold, Jack: Gold was head of Columbia A&R and as a producer was involved, among others, with the major hit single 'Too Much, Too Little, Too Late'.

Griffin, Merv: American, TV compere

and chat-show host on whose show Johnny has often guested. In 1980 he sang with Paulette McWilliams on the Griffin show.

H

Haughn, Ray: Long-standing respected General Manager, Rojon and to Johnny since 1964 with an association going back to 1959.

Heath, Ted: Revered British dance and jazz band leader, now sadly deceased. His band provided backing for Johnny's first two British tours. It was due partially to the standard and renown of his band that Helen Noga, Johnny's manager, decided Johnny 'would' have decent musical accompaniment if he toured Britain.

Heineke, Skip: John's popular American publicist.

Hit Parade: A British teen pop magazine, an off-shoot of the *New Musical Express* in the late fifties and early sixties, which featured Johnny many times and awakened British pop fans to a new American star.

Hollywood Hills: The location of John's house which was once built for Howard Hughes. It was purchased for $170,000.

Holsten, Rick: Johnny's lighting man who first worked with him in December, 1972. He is a keen sportsman and a dedicated Mormon.

Hope, Bob: Hope is a revered comedian-actor born in Britain, but living in America who has sponsored Pro-Am Golf tournaments in which Johnny has participated.

J

J Is For Johnny: Title-slogan utilised by Fontana (UK) when launching label for Johnny in 1960.

Jefferies, Fran: She performed with Johnny at the small North Beach Club, San Francisco in his pre-Columbia days.

L

La Ronde: The famous club is located at Miami Beach, Florida and the headline for one of Johnny's appearances was JM IS SENSATIONAL IN OPENER AT LA RONDE ROOM.

Lawrence, Stephanie: She sang with Johnny on 'You Saved My Life'. She stars in Evita, London.

Legrand, Michel: French composer whose songs Johnny has recorded and featured on show medley. John has shared the stage with him on many tours.

Lewis, Ramsey: One of the more famous musicians who has supported Johnny on his singing engagements.

Lewis, Vic: British band-leader, turned promotor and who is now retired. Lewis is a keen sportsman and says he introduced John to golf while they were holidaying in Grenada. He promoted Johnny's tours through the sixties and early seventies in Britain

Littlewood, Yvonne: She is a BBC-TV producer with many 'name' shows under her belt. Yvonne has been responsible for most of Johnny's British TV specials, with the first in 1962.

Louw, Maria: The lady was the Queen of Soweto at the time of John's multi-racial shows in South Africa.

M

Mancini, Henry: A famous composer whose songs John has recorded and who has shared the stage with John at many concerts.

Marsha: She has been Johnny's house-keeper for many years; the tenth anniversary was 1982.

Mathis, Clement and Mildred: Johnny's parents.

Mercedes: The make of car which is favoured by Johnny. During the years he has had a variety of car colours and models.

Mercer, Mabel: A songwriter Johnny met in New York during his early career days and who taught him to sing many songs including 'Over The Weekend'.

Meriwether, Lee: A high-school buddy of Johnny's who is associated with the American TV show, *Barnaby Jones* and was co-hostess for the KTLA, L.A. TV filming of the Hollywood Parade, 1979, in which Johnny participated.

McKane, Fletcher: Fletcher was a Scotsman by birth and was Johnny's maternal grandfather.

McWilliams, Paulette (married name): A singer who recorded with Johnny in 1980, made television appearances with him and sang on the album 'Different Kinda Different'.

N

NAACP and Southern Christian Leadership Conference: Johnny gave them a minimum of $20,000 from programmes in Chicago and New York, in 1963.

Niemela, Maria: Maria is director and news letter editor for the Johnny Mathis International Fan Club. She has been a fan of Johnny's music since 1957 and is extremely knowledgeable on the star's musical history.

Noga, Beverly: Beverly, daughter of Helen and John Noga, was in her teens when Johnny lived with her parents.

Noga, Helen: The lady who discovered John in 1955 and became his manager. She was previously a night-club owner. John and Helen parted in 1964.

Noga, John: John is the husband of Helen and was often listed as Johnny's co-manager with Helen.

O

O'Keefe Centre: The centre is situated in Toronto and when Johnny performed there on June 7, 1982 he had a special party of 120 British fans in the audience. They had flown out from Britain. He crooned for them 'Wonderful, Wonderful'.

Olympics: Johnny stood a chance at appearing at the World's premiere sporting event in 1956 but chose a singing career instead. He attended the games as a special guest in 1972 (Munich).

R

Radio Luxembourg: In the 1960s Radio Luxembourg broadcast the Johnny Mathis Show on Tuesdays, 8 to 8.15 pm.

Regency Artists: They have represented Johnny since 1974, the year in which the Agency was established.

Riddle, Nelson: Many believe the two albums Riddle produced for Johnny rank as the best in the long Mathis record catalogue.

Robbins, Kirk: He is Johnny's sound man.

Rogers Gil: He qualifies as the longest serving musical member of Johnny's band. His real name is Gilbert John Reigers.

Rogosin, Roy: He is a past musical director of John's.

Rojon Company: This company was set-up to deal with Johnny's business affairs.

Russell, Billy: He held the State College, San Francisco high-jump record until Johnny topped his 6 feet 5 inches by half-an-inch.

S

Sam: The only non-human involved with Johnny's career. Sam is the computer at Rojon.

Shaw, George Bernard: Johnny once said the famous English literary figure was his favourite author.

Shore, Dinah: A famous US TV personality on whose shows John has appeared many times. He has played in her golf tournaments and on one occasion she devoted her show to him.

Sibley, Maxine: She is Johnny's executive secretary and has been so since 1969. Maxine is Johnny's tour manager when he tours the United States.

T

Tonight Show: Johnny Carson's US TV-chat show and it is estimated John has made over 45 appearances on the programme. The Carson programme became the first regular running US-chat show on British television during 1982.

V

Vance, David: Johnny's present photographer.

W

Warwick, Dionne: A famous US lady singer who has sung on record with John and on whose show he made an impromptu appearance on June 12, 1982 at the Ontario Place Forum. He did so for 'Friends And Lovers', a single release from Arista. During 1982 Dionne had another popularity peak.

Whitburn, Joel: Whitburn is a US music historian. His research reveals Johnny as second only to Frank Sinatra as the most successful record seller in the US. Whitburn points out that 'Johnny's Greatest Hits' charted in the Billboard listings for 9½ years or 480 weeks.

Wild Duck: This is one of Johnny's favourite recipes which he has featured on television.

Williams, Deniece: A successful US singer who teamed up with Johnny for the massive worldwide smash hit single 'Too Much, Too Little, Too Late' and the album 'That's What Friends Are For'.

MUSIC PEOPLE

Some of the people who have been listed as musical arrangers for records and concert charts.

Al Capps, Allyn Ferguson, Bert Kaempfert, Bob Mersey, Bob Prince, D'Arneill Pershing, Don Costa, Ernie Freeman, David Rhodes, Frank Comstock, Gene Page, Jack Elliott, Jack Feierman, James Barnett, H. B. Barnum, Jack Faith, Nelson Riddle, Morty Stevens, Percy Faith, Paul Reiser, Perry Botkin Jnr, Pete King, Ralph Burns, Ted Macero, Thom Bell, Tony Osbourne, Victor Vanacore, Alyn Ainsworth, Manny Albam.

Conductors And Musicians

25/7/66–1/10/66
Conductor: Dick Bellis; *Road Manager*: Don Riber; *Stage Manager*: Pete Perricone; *Sound Mixer*: Perry Phillips; *Dresser*: 'Burt' Ballard; *Singers/Dancers*: Ron Dexter, Barbara Dentino, Judy Lawrence, Taylor Pero, Bob Trevis, Mary Lou Volk.

2/10/67–29/10/67
Conductor: Dick Bellis; *Drummer*: John Beal; *Stage Manager*: Owen 'Mike' McGiveney; *Dresser*: Jonathan Myers; *Road Manager*: Ray E. Haughn.

30/10/67–5/11/67
Last voyage of 'Queen Mary'. Same group as above except that Stage Manager McGiveney was not on board.

1 & 2/11/68
Conductor: Allyn Ferguson; *Stage Manager*: Jerry Grollnek; *Dresser*: Jonathan Myers; *Road Manager*: Ray E. Haughn.

29 & 30/1/69
Conductor: Jack Feierman; *Stage Manager & Dresser*: Ralph Mathis (Brother); *Road Manager*: Ray E. Haughn.

21/2/71–3/3/71
Conductor: Roy Rogosin; *Stage Manager*: Owen 'Mike' McGiveney; *Public Relations*: Miss Joan Bullard; *Dresser*: Les Fink; *Road Manager*: Ray E. Haughn.

20/8/72–27/8/72
Conductor: Roy Rogosin; *Stage Manager*: Owen 'Mike' McGiveney; *Dresser*: Frank Sears; *Road Manager*: Ray E. Haughn.

19/8/73–16/9/73
Conductor: Roy Rogosin; *Piano*: Mike Lucas; *Drums*: Harry Blazer; *Bass*: Abraham Laboriel; *Guitar & Vocals*: Gil Reigers; *Dresser*: Frank Sears; *Road Manager*: Ray E. Haughn.

15/9/74–17/10/74
Conductor: James Barnett; *Piano*: James Barnett; *Drums*: Michael Stribling; *Bass*: Randy Barber; *Guitar & Vocals*: Gil Reigers; *Dresser*: Frank Sears; *Sound Mixer*: Kirk Robbins; *Road Manager*: Ray E. Haughn.

8/7/75–20/7/75
Conductor & Piano: James Barnett; *Drums*: Michael Stribling; *Bass*: Randy Barber; *Guitar & Vocals*: Gil Reigers; *Stage Manager*: Rick Holsten; *Sound Mixer*: Kirk Robbins; *Dresser*: Alan Jon; *Road Manager*: Ray E. Haughn.

9/3/76–8/4/76
Conductor & Piano: James Barnett; *Drums*: Jim Ganduglia; *Bass*: Randy Barber; *Guitar & Vocals*: Gil Reigers; *Stage Manager*: Rick Holsten; *Sound Mixer*: Kirk Robbins; *Dresser*: Don Gleason; *Road Manager*: Ray E. Haughn.

27/4/77–25/5/77
Conductor & Piano: James Barnett; *Drums*: Jim Ganduglia; *Bass*: Randy Barber; *Guitar & Vocals*: Gil Reigers; *Stage Manager*: Rick Holsten; *Sound Mixer*: Kirk Robbins; *Dresser*: Randy Saline; *Road Manager*: Ray E. Haughn.

5/4/78–9/4/78
Conductor & Piano: James Barnett; *Drums*: Randy Barber; *Guitar & Vocals*: Gil Reigers; *Stage Manager*: Rick Holsten; *Sound Mixer*: Kirk Robbins; *Dresser*: Wayne Saline; *Road Manager*: Ray E. Haughn.

23/9/78–25/10/78
Conductor: Frank Zottoli (Concerts), Jim Ganduglia (Royal Albert Hall TV); *Piano*: Frank Zottoli; *Drums*: Doug Thorngren; *Bass*: Randy Barber; *Stage Manager*: Rick Holsten; *Sound Mixer*: Kirk Robbins; *Dresser*: Wayne Saline; *Road Manager*: Ray E. Haughn.

7/12/79–14/12/79
(Promotions and Television only)
Dresser: Wayne Saline; *Road Manager*: Ray E. Haughn.

27/4/80–21/5/80
Conductor: Jim Ganduglia; *Piano*: Lance Dixon; *Drums*: Doug Thorngren; *Bass*: Randy Barber; *Guitar & Vocals*: Gil Reigers; *Stage Manager*: Rick Holsten; *Sound Mixer*: Kirk Robbins; *Dresser*: Wayne Saline; *Road Manager*: Ray E. Haughn.

5/9/81–7/10/81
Conductor: Jim Ganduglia; *Piano*: Larry Steelman; *Bass*: Michael Bach; *Guitar & Vocals*: Gil Reigers; *Stage Manager*: Rick Holsten; *Sound Mixer*: Kirk Robbins; *Dresser*: Wendell 'Kalani' Sarceda; *Road Manager*: Ray E. Haughn.